GOBI   6|2019   30—

D1481877

Lineberger Memorial Library
LTSS, Lenoir-Rhyne University
4201 North Main Street
Columbia, SC 29203

LOEB CLASSICAL LIBRARY

FOUNDED BY JAMES LOEB 1911

EDITED BY

JEFFREY HENDERSON

MENANDER RHETOR

[DIONYSIUS OF HALICARNASSUS]

ARS RHETORICA

LCL 539

MENANDER RHETOR

[DIONYSIUS OF HALICARNASSUS]

ARS RHETORICA

EDITED AND TRANSLATED BY

WILLIAM H. RACE

HARVARD UNIVERSITY PRESS
CAMBRIDGE, MASSACHUSETTS
LONDON, ENGLAND
2019

Lineberger Memorial Library
LTSS, Lenoir-Rhyne University
4201 North Main Street
Columbia, SC 29203

PA 4248 .M13 A26 2019

2019 1007

llahearn

Copyright © 2019 by the President and Fellows
of Harvard College
All rights reserved

LOEB CLASSICAL LIBRARY® is a registered trademark
of the President and Fellows of Harvard College

Library of Congress Control Number 2018957391
CIP data available from the Library of Congress

ISBN 978-0-674-99722-6

Composed in ZephGreek and ZephText by
Technologies 'N Typography, Merrimac, Massachusetts.
Printed on acid-free paper and bound by
Maple Press, York, Pennsylvania

CONTENTS

For Donald Russell

PREFACE

This volume contains three third-century AD rhetorical treatises that provide instructions on how to compose occasional speeches. These writings form the bulk of epideictic theory and practice from antiquity.[1] Two treatises are attributed to one Menander Rhetor of Laodicea, the other (incorrectly) to the early first-century AD historian and literary critic Dionysius of Halicarnassus, but which is actually much later. Its author is usually designated as Pseudo-Dionysius of Halicarnassus and abbreviated in this volume by [DH].

These treatises derive from the schools of rhetoric that flourished in the Roman Empire from the second through fourth centuries AD in the Greek East. They provide a window into the literary culture and social concerns of these Greeks under Roman rule, in both public and private life, and were of considerable influence on later pagan and Christian literature.[2]

[1] Some epideictic topics such as encomium are briefly treated in the progymnasmata. Burgess provides an excellent overview of epideictic rhetoric and its influence on Greek literature.

[2] Kennedy 2003, 295, sums up the importance of late rhetoric for our understanding of both Christian and pagan writings: "The numerous later Greek rhetorical treatises, dry reading as they may seem, sometimes even poorly written, have considerable

PREFACE

I wish to thank Donald Russell for his generous scrutiny of Treatise I and Andrew Miller and Cecil Wooten for corrections and improvements of the entire work more numerous than I can count or acknowledge. Gratitude is also owed to the TLG for generously providing the basic Greek texts.

---

significance for the intellectual history of the early centuries of the Christian era. They are a major source for our understanding of education, its materials, goals, and values, as experienced by most important thinkers of the times, pagan and Christian; the training they describe directly influenced the form and style of composition of much of the writing that has survived; they are evidence for cultural change and for the perception of Greek language and literature of the classical period more than five hundred years later; and they provide linguists and philologists with useful concepts and terminology to describe the workings of texts, pagan and Christian, ancient and modern."

MENANDER RHETOR

INTRODUCTION

Menander Rhetor's two treatises of instructions for composing epideictic speeches contain many errors and problems in the Greek text. Thanks, however, to the efforts of a series of editors and scholars, the text presented here makes sense in most places.

The first editor, a young German named Arnold Hermann Ludwig Heeren (1760–1842), published *Menandri Rhetoris Commentarius de Encomiis* in 1785. It consisted of a text of Treatise I based on the Aldine edition (1508) but with extensive emendations and critical notes. Later, in a biographical letter, he told of his encounter with Menander:

> In reading through the Rhetors of Aldus, however, for my collection of [lyric] fragments, I had stumbled upon a dissertation *de Encomiis* by Menander, a Greek rhetor, which as yet the hand of no critic had disturbed; indeed the work itself had been improperly confounded with that of another rhetor named Alexander. Some happy corrections of the very corrupted text led me to entertain the notion of giving an edition of this work. I bent myself therefore to the task; every new emendation spurred

me onwards, and thus was consumed nearly the whole of the year 1784. The next question was, where I should find a publisher? I went with my manuscript to the since deceased Dieterich, who now, for the first time in his life, heard the name of Menander the rhetor. "Young man," said he, when I had explained to him the object of my visit, "no one will ever read this." As however I asked for no pay, and as we were already on friendly terms, he undertook my work and "Menander Rhetor de Encomiis, ex recensione," etc. 1785, was placed before the public. It was the first critical labour of a young classic, done without any help from manuscripts, consequently very incomplete. Nevertheless it was something; and the good Menander might bless his kind fortune that had sent him such a sospitator; seeing that his pretensions to one were but very small.[1]

The subsequent editions of Walz (1836), Spengel (1856), Bursian (1882), and Russell-Wilson (1981) made many improvements, the latter of greatest importance, since it combined the skills of an outstanding textual critic (Nigel Wilson) with the broad knowledge of rhetoric by a foremost scholar of ancient literary criticism (Donald Russell). Their edition, which includes the first complete translation of Menander into a modern language,[2] contains a full

[1] Talboys, xvii–xviii.
[2] Soffel (1974) had previously translated 2.8, 2.10, and 2.15 into German.

apparatus criticus and extensive notes. It serves as the basis of the present text. My debt to this edition is obvious on every page.

The pagination and lineation of modern texts have traditionally been based on the 1856 edition of Spengel. These references (e.g., 371.26) are very difficult to follow and locate. I have therefore divided the overall text into numbered genres and divided the genres into the sections laid out in Bursian's edition. Thus, 1.5.4 refers to Treatise I, "Philosophical Hymns," section 4.

THE AUTHOR

The title in the main Manuscript (P) is ΜΕΝΑΝΔΡΟΥ ΡΗΤΟΡΟΣ [ΓΕΝΕΘΛΙΩΝ] ΔΙΑΙΡΕΣΙΣ ΤΩΝ ΕΠΙ-ΔΕΙΚΤΙΚΩΝ, "Menander Rhetor's [of Genethliōn] Analysis of Epideictic Speeches." Various emendations have tried to make sense of the bracketed genitive plural. A corrector of P suggested (supra lineam) ἢ Γενεθλίου "Or of Genethlius," who was a rhetor from Petra in the second half of the third century AD.[3] H. Valesius (1740), followed by Heeren and Walz, proposed πρὸς Γενέθλιον "[addressed] to Genethlius." RW obelize ΓΕΝΕΘΛΙΩΝ, while acknowledging that the attribution to Genethlius appears to have had "some early authority."

The entry in the Suda for Menander reads: Μένανδρος Λαοδικεὺς τῆς παρὰ τῷ Λύκῳ τῷ ποταμῷ, σοφιστής· ἔγραψεν ὑπομνήματα εἰς τὴν Ἑρμογένους τέχνην καὶ Μινουκιανοῦ προγυμνάσματα καὶ ἄλλα ("Menander of

---

[3] Nitsche (1883, 3) argued that Genethlius was the author of Treatise I.

Laodicea on the Lycus River, a sophist. He wrote commentaries on Hermogenes' *Technē* and Minucianus' *Progymnasmata* and others."). The Suda entry says nothing of Menander's epideictic treatise(s), nor does it mention Menander's commentaries on the speeches of Demosthenes (perhaps to be included in "and others"), to which there are numerous references in the Demosthenic scholia.[4]

The city of Laodicea suits the situation in Treatise II. Located in southwestern Asia Minor, it was a prosperous city in the third century AD that featured a stadium, baths, temples, colonnades, a gymnasium, aqueduct, and theaters—prominent structures mentioned in M.'s instructions for praising cities (2.2.16, 33; 2.13.22). It is located about two hundred miles south of Alexandria Troas, the city at the center of M.'s examples at 2.2.37, 2.12.2–3, 2.13.10–12, and 2.16.24.[5]

DATE OF THE TREATISES

There are compelling indications that the two treatises date from the late third century AD. Treatise I cites Roman cities settled along the Danube with Carpi (a defeated Dacian people) to prevent barbarian incursions

---

[4] For a full discussion of Menander's scholarship on Demosthenes, see Heath. Demosthenes figures rarely in the two treatises. Two famous passages from *De Corona* are briefly quoted (without attribution) at 1.9.3, while Demosthenes is mentioned only once by name in passing, as a lawgiver at 2.9.5.

[5] Laodicea was also the city of Marcus Antonius Polemon, a second-century AD sophist mentioned in 2.2.33.

into Roman territory (1.15.26). According to *Scriptores Historiae Augustae* (*Aurelian* 30) the Carpi were defeated under Aurelian around 272 AD and again, according to Ammianus Marcellinus (28.1.5), under Diocletian and Galerius in 294. Since these brief notices concern defeat rather than resettlement, the former date may serve as a *terminus post quem*, while the later date reflects the more likely time of composition, especially in the case of Treatise II, for although it generally varies between using the singular emperor (βασιλεύς) or generalized plural (with or without a definite article), at 2.2.4, 13, 18 and 2.9.2–3 the plurals must refer to jointly ruling emperors.[6]

All this admittedly scant evidence points to the reign of Diocletian (285–312) as the probable period of composition, and nothing in the treatises directly contradicts it. Furthermore, all external references to M.'s treatises are by much later rhetoricians, for example, Johannes Doxapatres, *Homiliae in Aphthonium* (Walz 2.415 and 449–50); Anonymous, Περὶ τῶν τεσσαρῶν μερῶν τοῦ τελείου λόγου (Walz 3.572); and Nicolaus, *Progymnasmata* (Felten 49.13–23).[7]

---

[6] At 2.2.35 the claim is made that "the Blemmyes, and tribes of the Erembi were acknowledged to be under our rule, since they were clearly our subordinates in the final days in the alliances and levies." This has generally been taken to refer to settlements of the Blemmyes by Diocletian on the Nile in 298, but RW (xxxix and 292–93) persuasively argue that in its context (instructions for composing a "Trojan oration") it probably refers to Trojan allies in the last days of the Trojan War.

[7] See the testimonia in RW, xxxiv–xxxvi, and Heath, 124–27. Of importance is a papyrus (P. Berol. 21849) of the fifth or sixth century that mentions Menander's *Technē*; cf. RW, xxxiv–xxxv.

THE CONDITION OF
THE TWO TREATISES

Treatise I

There are clear indications that Treatise I originally consisted of three books following the introductory section 1.1. Book 1 comprised the treatment of hymns (1.2–9), as is made clear at 1.9.6: τὸ μὲν δὴ περὶ τῶν εἰς τοὺς θεοὺς βιβλίον τέλος εἴληφεν ἡμῖν ("This marks the end of our book on hymns to the gods"). The second book comprised praise of countries and cities for their location, natural resources, and origins (1.10–15). Anomalous are the extremely short sections separated in the manuscripts on praising harbors (1.12), gulfs (1.13), and acropoleis (1.14). The third book is announced at 1.15.28: τρίτον τοίνυν ἡμῖν βιβλίον γραφέσθω τόδε περὶ ἐπιτηδεύσεων καὶ πράξεων ("Our third book, accordingly, will deal with activities and deeds"). There are some lacunae (e.g., 1.3.1, 1.6.8, 1.9.5) and references to missing material (e.g., 1.16.25). Furthermore, the outline given in the Introduction (1.1.2) is not entirely carried out, nor is there coverage of animals or inanimate things as promised in 1.1.4. The treatise also ends abruptly with a list of festivals.

Treatise II

The traditional order of the genres of speeches adopted by Walz, Spengel, and RW is preserved in this edition. There are, however, problems. First, manuscripts P and p present the speeches in very different orders. In addition, the consolation speech (2.8.1) refers to the monody (2.15)

as already having been discussed, and there are other discrepancies in cross-references. Attempts by Bursian and Nitsche to reorder the speeches have not proved convincing.[8] A further problem is that all manuscripts divide the Royal Oration into an additional part at §17, marked "Deeds," as if it were a separate speech. The present edition disregards that division, preserving sixteen distinctly different types of speeches.

THE RELATIONSHIP OF THE TWO TREATISES

The differences in style, vocabulary, detail, and presentation are sufficient to raise the strong possibility of separate authors. For example, Treatise I uses the term $\kappa\epsilon\phi\acute{\alpha}\lambda\alpha\iota o\nu$ to mean a general rhetorical topic like pleasure or utility (see on 1.1.4), whereas in Treatise II it consistently refers to sections of a speech containing related topics. Treatise I uses the rare term $\dot{\epsilon}\pi\iota\tau\eta\delta\epsilon\acute{\nu}\sigma\epsilon\iota\varsigma$ (1.16.1) for activities, whereas Treatise II uses the much more common term $\dot{\epsilon}\pi\iota\tau\eta\delta\epsilon\acute{\nu}\mu\alpha\tau\alpha$.[9] Treatise I refers to widespread geographical places and appears to favor no particular location. Treatise II is centered in Alexandria Troas and Athens.

Treatise II provides much more in the way of exemplary phrasing and differs from Treatise I in its introductions of this material. The two treatises also cite different authors. For example, Plato is cited and quoted frequently

---

[8] For a full discussion, see RW, xliv–xlvi, especially the table at xlv.

[9] For a list of more differences, see RW, xxxvii–xxxviii, and Heath, 127–31.

in Treatise I but is mentioned only once in passing in Treatise II. Homer, on the other hand, is much more prominent in Treatise II. The one possible cross-reference at 1.3.5, where M. refers to "my cletic hymn to Apollo," cannot refer to the extensive Sminthian Oration in Treatise II (2.16). These differences could arguably reflect the different subject matter of each treatise or their differing lengths (Treatise II is twice as long and much more diverse), or could represent compositions at different stages of a single author's career. There is thus no scholarly consensus on whether both works are M.'s or, assuming separate authors, who the other author would be. For convenience, I treat Menander as the author of both treatises.

THE RHETORICAL AND
CULTURAL CONTEXT

Menander's treatises at the end of the third century come at a juncture of the long development of Greek rhetorical theory and epideictic prose.[10] Although important examples of some genres of occasional prose were composed in the fifth and fourth centuries BC by Thucydides, Xenophon, Plato, and especially Isocrates,[11] it was with the flowering of rhetorical prose during the so-called Second Sophistic in the second half of the second century AD that more forms were developed as standard repertoire and became exemplary. Authors such as Dio Chrysostom and especially Aelius Aristides (both cited frequently in both

---

[10] RW, xi–xxxiv provide an excellent overview of epideictic theory and practice and M.'s place in it.

[11] Menander cites all these writers.

treatises) composed many occasional orations that served as models for theorists and practitioners.[12] Although little actual epideictic prose of the third century has survived, rhetorical treatises continued to be composed.[13]

In the fourth century, following Menander, epideictic prose became even more prominent with such authors as Libanius, Themistius, Himerius, Julian, and Choricius, whose extensive works exemplify many of the prescriptions and topics advised by Menander.[14] Although direct influence is unlikely, or at any rate impossible to trace, Menander's treatises foreshadowed many genres, topics, and general attitudes in the centuries that followed.[15]

Menander also draws heavily on the long Greek poetic tradition.[16] For example, for each of the eight types of hymn in Treatise I (1.2–9), he mentions poetic examples (e.g., Homer, Hesiod, Sappho, Alcaeus, Anacreon, Parmenides, Empedocles, and Bacchylides) and is careful to draw distinctions between the treatments permitted in poetry and those required in prose (1.3.3–5, etc.). The royal oration shows close affinities with Pindar's epinicia and shares striking similarities with Theocritus' *Idylls* 17

[12] For a survey of the writers and orators of the Second Sophistic, see Bowersock.

[13] For a thorough survey, see "The Third Century: Fruition" in Heath, 52–89.

[14] For a survey of these authors, see Kennedy 1983, 133–67. For specific examples, see Burgess, 241–44.

[15] Cf. Kennedy 1983, *passim*.

[16] As Burgess, 166–180 *et passim* points out, most of these occasional genres had poetic predecessors. See especially Cairns.

in praise of Ptolemy II.[17] In many ways, Menander's treatises provide a sketch of Greek epideictic poetry and prose from Homer to his time. A striking omission, however, is Attic drama, which is represented by only two citations: Sophocles, Fr. 740 (1.9.4) and Euripides, Fr. 449 (2.8.3).

Although Greek cities in the third century were securely under Roman rule, the culture of the speeches remains distinctly Hellenic. Even though the addresses and petitions to emperors and governors presume the dominance of Roman rule, there are only scattered indications of Roman cultural influence. Treatise I mentions Romans ten times: four times concerning cities they have founded (1.15.8, 22–23, 26) or granted freedom to (1.16.26); two brief mentions of their mixed constitution (1.16.2) and of hosting festivals (1.16.30). In addition, at 1.16.28 gladiatorial shows (μονομαχίαις, ἐν ἀγῶνι . . . ἐνοπλίῳ) are mentioned along with athletic and musical contests. There is, however, one acknowledged area of Roman dominance: its laws. Three times (1.16.5, 18, 22) the author insists that Roman rule precludes praising cities for their laws because "in these times, however, the topic of laws is irrelevant, for we govern our cities according to the universal laws of the Romans" (1.16.18, ἀλλὰ τὸ τῶν νόμων ἐν τοῖς νῦν χρόνοις ἄχρηστον· κατὰ γὰρ τοὺς κοινοὺς τῶν Ῥωμαίων νόμους πολιτευόμεθα).

Treatise II, even though twice as long, exhibits much less Roman cultural influence. There are only five very

[17] For a detailed comparison of M.'s royal oration and Theoc. *Id.* 17, see Cairns, 100–112. M.'s "Sminthian Oration" is especially replete with topics drawn from poetic hymns.

brief references to Roman examples, all but one (2.2.5) paired with Greek ones: Romulus with Cyrus (2.1.13), unnamed Roman emperors with famous Greeks (2.1.18), an unnamed Roman famed for justice with Aristides and Phocion (2.9.6), and Athens and Rome (2.13.13).

In Menander's world of the late third century, as reflected in both treatises, poleis remain the dominant centers of Greek culture, as evidenced by the space devoted to the praise of cities (1.11, 2.2.33) and a rhetor's serving as their ambassador (2.12.3–4) or spokesman (2.13.14–16). Many of the recommendations of cities sound familiar as attractions even today: a storied history (1.15.2–22, 1.16.12–14, 2.2.35–37, 2.13.10–11, 20), a good location (1.11.7–17), a mild climate (1.11.4–6, 2.9.13), beautiful buildings (2.3.24, 2.4.8, 2.9.13, 2.13.22, 2.14.3, 2.16.28–30), works of art (2.14.3), pleasant accommodations (2.2.33, 2.13.22), law-abiding citizens (2.2.24, 2.13.12), hospitable people (2.14.4), artistic activities (1.16.6–8), special attractions (2.3.24–26, 2.13.22), and last, but not least, lavish festivals (1.16.15–16, 29–32; 2.13.1–6, 2.16.26), athletic competitions (2.13.4, 22; 2.14.4), schools (2.3.15, 2.4.8, 2.13.12), and contests of oratory (2.3.15).

In Treatise II Athens remains the center of Greek culture and advanced rhetorical education. In the invitation speech, the speaker claims, "We send off our best men and receive them back from Athens with their excellence perfected" (2.13.12). In the leave-taking speech, the student is envisioned as going off to study in Athens, which is called "a workshop of oratory and of the Muses" (2.14.7) and "a veritable Pieria and Helicon" (2.14.8), with the words, "I shall obtain my share of oratory and philosophy.

I shall learn for your sakes and for the sake of the city we share, and when I feel fully able to benefit the town that gave me birth, then I shall again long for my city and my family" (2.14.10). Egyptian Alexandria, on the other hand, is mentioned merely in passing at 1.16.6 as "even to this day" proud "of its literary scholarship, geometry, and philosophy."

THE ADDRESSEE AND
THE IMPLIED AUDIENCE

The addressee is a second-person singular σέ/σοί, who appears to be a budding orator, one who may be called upon to deliver occasional speeches as part of his civic career. These speeches can be religious hymns to gods; civic orations, such as those praising cities or emperors, speeches welcoming governors, dedicating crowns, inviting dignitaries, bidding farewell, petitioning high officials; and private speeches, such as funeral speeches expressing lamentation and consolation, and speeches for birthdays, marriages, and weddings.

At 2.2.34, he addresses "my dearest companion" (ὦ γλυκύτατε τῶν ἑταίρων), the only such direct address in either treatise, as one potentially called upon to deliver a "Trojan oration," evidently at Alexandria Troas. At 2.14.10 his pupil is envisioned as receiving advanced training in rhetoric at Athens and returning to Alexandria Troas to benefit his city. At 2.4.12 the speaker predicts that his departing friend will usefully serve emperors and become the head of a school. In the birthday speech at 2.7.4, the speaker predicts that the boy "will attain the heights of

13

education and virtue, lavish benefits on cities, arrange games, and sponsor festivals," while in the monody at 2.15.3, the speaker claims that the deceased man would have become "a future leader, statesman, and organizer of games." The ideal student—and the audience who would appreciate his words—would speak up for the city's interests to the Roman authorities and be a defender of its Greek culture.

MANUSCRIPTS

The principal manuscripts that serve as the basis of modern editions are:

P Parisinus graecus 1741 mid. 10th c. both treatises, some omissions
p Parisinus graecus 1874 12th c. second treatise only

Additional manuscripts cited in the apparatus criticus are:

M Laur. 56.1, second half of the 12th c.
m Laur. 81.8, second quarter of the 14th c.
W Vaticanus graecus 306, ca. 1300
Z Parisinus graecus 2423, late 13th c.

P is a very important manuscript that contains Aristotle's *Poetics* and *Rhetoric*, Demetrius' *On Style*, and other rhetorical treatises, including the *Ars Rhetorica* of Pseudo-Dionysius of Halicarnassus. Manuscript p, representing a separate branch, contains only Treatise II and supplies a number of textual improvements. The very thorough and accurate apparatus of RW should be consulted for all fine points.

In this edition, I have relied on the texts of Bursian and RW. To simplify my text, I have not always indicated numerous minor corrections of the following sort:

insertions of ἄν (e.g., 1.5.6, 1.6.2, 1.6.6), when they do not affect the meaning.

corrections and insertions made by Heeren or Finckh and adopted by the majority of subsequent editors, like παρὰ at 1.6.8, ἐν ᾧ at 1.7.1, δὲ at 1.7.3, and γὰρ at 1.9.5.

corrections by Bursian adopted by RW (e.g., πρὸ at 1.8.5).

repetitions deleted by Heeren and all editors, such as [ἐν ᾧ τὸ γενεαλογικὸν μόνον φέρεται] at 1.7.1, the intrusive [ὑμνεῖ] at 1.9.4, [κατείληφεν] deleted by Bursian and RW at 1.11.9, and [αὕτη κατείληφεν] at 1.11.10.

supplements such as ⟨ἣ μεγάλαι καὶ ἐπιφανεῖς⟩ at 1.11.12, introduced by Heeren and adopted by Walz, Spengel, etc.; καὶ at 1.11.17; and ὡς (bis) at 1.15.23, 24.

glosses such as [ποταμὸς δὲ Θετταλίας ὁ Ἐνιπεύς] at 2.5.11, recognized by Spengel, Bursian, and RW; and [πότερον] at 2.16.4, recognized by Finckh, Bursian, RW.

In addition, I have sometimes included in the textual notes not only the original source of an emendation but also the successive editors who have adopted it, thereby indicating the extent of editorial consensus.

EDITIONS AND COLLECTIONS
OF EMENDATIONS

Aldus Manutius. 1508. *Rhetores Graeci*. Vol. 1, 594–641, *editio princeps*. Venice: Aldus.

Valesius, H. 1740. *Emendationum, Liber I*. Amsterdam: Salomon Schout.

Heeren, A. H. L. 1785. *Menandri Rhetoris Commentarius de Encomiis*. Göttingen: Dieterich.

Jacobs, F. 1828. "Variae Lectiones IV–VI." *Allgemeine Schulzeitung*. Vol. 5: 2.80–81.

Finckh, C. E. 1836. *De Libellis Menandro Rhetori vulto adscriptis ad editorem epistola critica*. In C. Walz, 1836, 737–78.

Walz, C. 1836 [repr., 1968. Osnabrück: Zeller]. *Rhetores Graeci*. Vol. 9, 127–330. Stuttgart and Tübingen: J. G. Cottae.

Spengel, L. 1856. *Rhetores Graeci*. Vol. 3. Leipzig: Teubner.

Bursian, C. 1882. *Der Rhetor Menandros und seine Schriften*. München: F. Straub.

Nitsche, W. 1883. *Der Rhetor Menandros und die Scholien zu Demosthenes*. Berlin: R. Gaertner.

Kroll, W. 1911. "Randbemerkungen XIX." *RhM* 66: 169–74.

Soffel, J. 1974. *Die Regeln Menanders für die Leichenrede: in ihrer Tradition dargestellt, herausgegeben, übersetzt und kommentiert*. Meisenheim am Glan: Anton Hain.

Russell, D. A., and N. Wilson. 1981. *Menander Rhetor*. Oxford: Oxford University Press.

Romero Cruz, F. 1989. *Menandro, sobre los géneros epidícticos: introducción, traducción y notas*. Salamanca: Ediciones Universidad de Salamanca.

Muñoz, F-G. Hernández. 1997. "Einige Bemerkungen Über Zwei Handschriften des Rhetors Menandros." *Hermes* 125: 123–29.

———. 2013. "The *Logos Basilikos* Text of Menander Rhetor." *RHT* n.s. 8: 371–85.

REFERENCES

Bowersock, G. W. 1969. *Greek Sophists in the Roman Empire*. Oxford: Oxford University Press.

Burgess, T. C. 1902. *Epideictic Literature*. PhD diss., University of Chicago.

Cairns, F. 1972. *Generic Composition in Greek and Roman Poetry*. Edinburgh: Edinburgh University Press.

Heath, M. *Menander: A Rhetor in Context*. 2004. Oxford: Oxford University Press.

Kennedy, G. A. 1983. *Greek Rhetoric under Christian Emperors*. Princeton: Princeton University Press.

———. 2003. "Some Recent Controversies in the Study of Later Greek Rhetoric." *AJP* 124: 295–301.

Talboys, D. A. 1838. "A Biographical Sketch of Professor Heeren Written by Himself in a Letter to a Friend." In *Historical Researches into the Politics, Intercourse, and Trade of the Carthaginians, Ethiopians, and Egyptians by A. H. L. Heeren, Translated from the German*, 1:xvii–xviii. 2nd ed. Oxford.

CONTENTS

Following are the contents of the two treatises in this edition with references to Spengel's pagination and lineation. Spengel pages are indicated in the margin of the Greek text.

18

Treatise II

ΜΕΝΑΝΔΡΟΥ ΡΗΤΟΡΟΣ
[ΓΕΝΕΘΛΙΩΝ][1] ΔΙΑΙΡΕΣΙΣ ΤΩΝ
ΕΠΙΔΕΙΚΤΙΚΩΝ

1. Τῆς ῥητορικῆς ἁπάσης τριχῶς διαιρουμένης ὡς μέ-
ρεσιν ἢ εἴδεσιν, ἢ ὅπως δεῖ καλεῖν, εἰς τοὺς λόγους
τοὺς ἐν δικαστηρίοις ὑπὲρ κοινῶν ἢ ἰδίων, καὶ οὓς ἐν
ἐκκλησίαις ἢ ἐν βουλαῖς διατίθενται, καὶ εἰς τρίτους
τοὺς ἐπιδεικτικούς, οὓς δὴ ἐγκωμιαστικοὺς ἢ ψεκτι-
κοὺς καλοῦσιν, ἀπολογεῖσθαι συμβαίνει ⟨ἡμῖν⟩[2] ὑπὲρ
τούτων τῶν τὴν τρίτην τάξιν εἰληφότων διδάσκουσιν
†ὀρθῶς†.[3] μὴ τοίνυν περὶ ῥητορικῆς προσδόκα ὅλης
ἀκροᾶσθαι ἐξ ἀρχῆς, κἂν ἄνωθεν ὑπὲρ παντὸς μέρους
διεξιέναι σοι ἐν βραχυτάτῳ προαιρήσωμαι. σκεψώμεθα τοίνυν τὴν μέθοδον, εἰ καθ᾽ ὁδὸν χωρήσει.
2. Τῶν δὴ ἐπιδεικτικῶν τὸ μὲν ψόγος, τὸ δὲ ἔπαινος·

[1] γενεθλίων PMW: ἢ Γενεθλίου P corr.s.l.: πρὸς Γενέθλιον
coni. Valesius: obel. RW
[2] suppl. Bursian: τοῖς RW
[3] obel. RW: ὀρθῶς MW: ὡρμῆσθαι P

MENANDER RHETOR[1]
AN ANALYSIS OF EPIDEICTIC SPEECHES

[BOOK 1]

1.1. [INTRODUCTION]

1. Rhetoric as a whole is divided into three branches (*merē*) or kinds (*eidē*) (or whatever they should be called):[2] speeches in law courts concerning public or private matters; those delivered in assemblies or councils; and thirdly, epideictic speeches which are called encomiastic or vituperative. It thus falls to us, who teach about those which fill the third division, to defend our practice. Therefore, do not expect to hear about the entire field of rhetoric from the beginning, even though I chose above to give you a very brief survey of every branch. So, let us see if our procedure will proceed on track.[3]

2. Epideictic speeches, then, have two aspects: blame

---

[1] For a discussion of the name perhaps embedded in ΓΕΝΕΘΛΙΩΝ, see the Introduction. The titles in brackets are not in the manuscripts, but are included here for convenience.

[2] This threefold division of rhetoric goes back at least to Aristotle, *Rh.* 1.3.1–3, where he calls the branches both *eidē* and *genē*.

[3] M. plays on μέθοδον (procedure) and καθ' ὁδόν (on track).

21

ἃς γὰρ ἐπιδείξεις λόγων πολιτικῶν οἱ σοφισταὶ κα-
λούμενοι ποιοῦνται, μελέτην ἀγώνων εἶναί φαμεν, οὐκ
ἐπίδειξιν. τὸ μὲν τοίνυν τοῦ ψόγου μέρος ἄτμητον.
ἔπαινος δέ τις γίνεται, ὁτὲ μὲν εἰς ⟨θεούς, ὁτὲ δὲ εἰς
τὰ θνητά· καὶ ὅτε μὲν εἰς⟩[4] θεούς, ὕμνους καλοῦμεν,
καὶ τούτους αὖ διαιροῦμεν κατὰ θεὸν ἕκαστον· τοὺς
μὲν γὰρ εἰς Ἀπόλλωνα παιᾶνας καὶ ὑπορχήματα ὀνο-
μάζομεν, τοὺς δὲ εἰς Διόνυσον διθυράμβους καὶ ἰο-
βάκχους, καὶ ὅσα τοιαῦτα [εἴρηται Διονύσου],[5] τοὺς
δὲ εἰς Ἀφροδίτην ἐρωτικούς, τοὺς δὲ τῶν ἄλλων θεῶν
ἢ τῷ ὅλῳ[6] γένει ὕμνους καλοῦμεν ἢ μερικώτερον[7]
⟨οἷον⟩[8] πρὸς Δία. ὅπως δὲ χρὴ μετιέναι τούτων τῶν
εἰδῶν ἕκαστον, καὶ εἰ ἁρμόττει ὅλως τοῖς καταλογάδην συγγράφουσιν, ἢ πόσα μὲν ἁρμόττει, πόσα δ᾽ οὔ,
ἢ πόσαι μέθοδοι καθ᾽ ἕκαστον, ἢ τίνες οἱ τρόποι,
ἐπειδὰν τὸ ὅλον διελώμεθα, τηνικαῦτα καθ᾽ ἕκαστα
ἐργασόμεθα.

3. Τῶν δ᾽ αὖ περὶ θνητῶν οἱ μὲν περὶ πόλεις γίνονται ἔπαινοι, οἱ δὲ περὶ ζῴων. τὸ μὲν δὴ περὶ τὰς πόλεις καὶ χώρας ἄτμητον, διὸ τὰς διαφορὰς ἐν ταῖς
τεχνικαῖς μεθόδοις ἐπιδειξόμεθα. οἱ δὲ περὶ ζῴων οἱ
μὲν περὶ λογικόν, ἄνθρωπον, οἱ δὲ περὶ ἀλόγων γίνονται ἔπαινοι. καὶ τὸν μὲν περὶ τὸν ἄνθρωπον μεθῶμεν,
τῶν δ᾽ αὖ περὶ τὰ ἄλογα οἱ μὲν περὶ χερσαῖα, οἱ δὲ

332

---

4 suppl. Heeren, Bursian, RW   5 secl. RW

6 Jacobs (cf. τὸ ὅλον infra): λόγῳ codd.: secl. RW: τῷ λόγῳ
τοῦ γένους Walz, Spengel   7 RW: γενικώτερον P: ἰδικώτε-
ρον Heeren   8 suppl. RW

1.1. [INTRODUCTION]

and praise. For we consider the demonstrations (*epideixeis*) of public speeches composed by men called sophists to be an exercise (*meletē*) for real cases, not an actual epideictic speech (*epideixis*).[4] The branch of blame has no subdivisions; praise of any sort, however, is sometimes directed to gods, sometimes to mortal subjects. When to gods, we speak of hymns, and in turn divide them according to each god. We call hymns to Apollo *paeans* and *hyporchemata*, those to Dionysus *dithyrambs* and *iobacchi*, and the like, and those to Aphrodite *erotic*. Those to other gods we designate either by the general term "hymns" or, more specifically, as "To Zeus." Once we have divided up the entire genre, we shall then treat individual types in detail, to see how one should handle each of the kinds, whether they are in general suitable for prose writers, or only some but not others, and how many procedures are involved in each case, and which types.[5]

3. Praise of mortal subjects deals either with cities or with living beings. Since that which concerns cities and countries has no subdivisions, we shall show their differences in our treatment of technical procedures.[6] Praise of living beings concerns either a rational being, that is, a human, or animals. Let us put aside for now praise of human beings. Praise of animals includes those on land and

---

[4] Such exercises—μελέται in Greek, *declamationes* in Latin— are based on fictitious deliberative and judicial cases.

[5] This outline is not followed in the ensuing discussions.

[6] These differences are covered extensively in 1.10–16.

περὶ ἔνυδρα ἔπαινοι γίνονται. καὶ τὸ μὲν περὶ τῶν
ἐνύδρων πάλιν ἀποτιθέμεθα, τῶν δ' αὖ ἄλλων ἐν γῇ
μέρος διττόν, ἢ πτηνὸν ἢ πεζόν. ἐφ' ἅπασι δὲ τούτοις
ἐξῆς⁹ μέτιμεν ἀπὸ τῶν ἐμψύχων ἐπὶ τὰ ἄψυχα.

4. Αἱ μὲν οὖν διαιρέσεις τοῦ ἐπιδεικτικοῦ μέρους
παντὸς πᾶσαι αὗται, οὐκ ἀγνοῶ δ' ὅτι ἐπιτηδευμάτων
καὶ τεχνῶν ἤδη τινὲς ἐγκώμια γεγράφασιν, ἀλλ' ἀφ'
οὗπερ ἡμῖν ὁ λόγος γίνεται περὶ τὸν ἄνθρωπον, πάντα
ταῦτα περιέξει,¹⁰ ὥστε λελήθασιν αὐτοὺς οἱ συγγρά-
φοντες μέρος τι τοῦ παντὸς ἐγκωμίου ὡς ὅλον ἐγκώμιον συνθέντες. οὐ μὴν οὐδ' ἐκεῖνο ἀγνοῶ, ὅτι καὶ τῶν
ἁλῶν καὶ τῶν τοιούτων ἤδη τινὲς τῶν πάλαι σοφιστῶν ἐπαίνους συνεγράψαντο, ἀλλ' ἀφ' οὗπερ ἡμῖν
ἀπὸ τῶν ἐμψύχων ἐπὶ τὰ ἄψυχα μεταβέβηκεν ἡ διαίρεσις, ἤδη περιείληφεν καὶ τοῦτο τὸ μέρος. ὅπως δὲ
τούτων ἕκαστον τμητέον, καὶ ὅπη τὰ αὐτὰ κεφάλαια
πᾶσιν ὕπεστιν, καὶ ὅπη ἑκάστῳ ἁρμόττει χρήσασθαι,
ἐφεξῆς [καὶ δὴ]¹¹ δείκνυμεν.

⁹ ἀνθέων καὶ φυτῶν post ἐξῆς secl. Spengel, RW
¹⁰ coni. RW: δείξειν P: δείξει codd.
¹¹ secl. Spengel, RW

those in water. The subject of water creatures, we once again set aside; those on land, however, are of two kinds, winged or on foot. After all these, we shall proceed from living creatures to inanimate things.

4. These then are all the divisions of the entire epideictic branch. I am not unaware, however, that some have in fact written encomia of activities and skills, but when our discussion turns to humans, it will include all these,[7] with the result that those writers have unwittingly composed a part of an entire encomium as if it were a whole encomium. Nor am I unaware of the fact that some of the ancient sophists have written praises of salt and such,[8] but once our analysis has turned from living to inanimate things, then it will have included that category as well.[9] We next show how each of these categories should be divided up; in what way the same general topics (*kephalaia*)[10] belong to all of them; and how each one is appropriately used.

---

[7] See 1.16 on the activities (ἐπιτηδεύματα/ἐπιτηδεύσεις) and skills (τέχναι) of cities.

[8] For salt, cf. Pl. *Symp.* 177b, and Isoc. *Helen* 12.

[9] There is no subsequent treatment of animals or inanimate things, another indication that portions of this treatise have been lost.

[10] In Treatise I, *kephalaia* (literally, "headings") refer to general topics for argumentation, such as pleasure and utility mentioned in 1.10.3. In Treatise II, *kephalaia* refer to sections of a speech containing related rhetorical topics.

1.2. ΠΕΡΙ ΤΩΝ ΥΜΝΩΝ ΤΩΝ ΕΙΣ
ΤΟΥΣ ΘΕΟΥΣ

333   1. Πρῶτον μὲν οὖν, ὥσπερ ἐξ ἀρχῆς διειλόμεθα, περὶ τῶν ὕμνων ἐπισκεψώμεθα τῶν εἰς θεούς. αὐτῶν γὰρ δὴ τῶν ὕμνων οἱ μὲν κλητικοί, οἱ δὲ ἀποπεμπτικοί, καὶ οἱ μὲν φυσικοί, οἱ δὲ μυθικοί, καὶ οἱ μὲν γενεαλογικοί, οἱ δὲ πεπλασμένοι, καὶ οἱ μὲν εὐκτικοί, οἱ δὲ ἀπευκτικοί, οἱ δὲ μικτοὶ ἢ δύο τούτων ἢ τριῶν ἢ πάντων ὁμοῦ.

  2. Κλητικοὶ μὲν οὖν ὁποῖοί εἰσιν οἱ πολλοὶ τῶν τε παρὰ τῇ Σαπφοῖ ἢ Ἀνακρέοντι ἢ τοῖς ἄλλοις μελικοῖς, κλῆσιν ἔχοντες πολλῶν θεῶν. ἀποπεμπτικοὶ δὲ ὁποῖοι καὶ παρὰ τῷ Βακχυλίδῃ ἔνιοι εὕρηνται, ἀποπομπὴν ὡς ἀποδημίας τινὸς γινομένης ἔχοντες. φυσικοὶ δὲ οἵους οἱ περὶ Παρμενίδην καὶ Ἐμπεδοκλέα ἐποίησαν, τίς ἡ τοῦ Ἀπόλλωνος φύσις, τίς ἡ τοῦ Διός, παρατιθέμενοι. καὶ οἱ πολλοὶ τῶν Ὀρφέως τούτου τοῦ τρόπου.

  3. Μυθικοὶ δὲ οἱ τοὺς μύθους ἔχοντες, κατ᾽ ἀλλη-

---

[1] At 1.1.2.

[2] For example, Sappho, Frr. 1 and 2; Anacreon, Fr. 357; Pind. *Pyth.* 11.1–11.

[3] There are no extant examples in Bacchylides, although Snell

1.2. HYMNS TO GODS

1. First of all, as in our initial outline,[1] let us examine hymns to gods. Some of these hymns are summonses (*klētikoi*), others dismissals (*apopemptikoi*); some are philosophical (*physikoi*), others mythical (*mythikoi*); some are genealogical (*genealogikoi*), others fictive (*peplasmenoi*); some are precatory (*euktikoi*), others deprecatory (*apeuktikoi*); and some are mixtures of two, three, or all of them together.

2. Now cletic hymns are the kind most frequently found in Sappho, Anacreon, and other lyric poets, containing as they do invocations of many gods.[2] Hymns of dismissal are found occasionally in Bacchylides, containing a sendoff (*apopompē*) at the departure of some god.[3] Philosophical are the kind composed by Parmenides and Empedocles, explaining the nature of Apollo or Zeus. Most of the hymns of Orpheus are of this type.[4]

3. Mythical hymns are those that contain stories

improbably claims that mere scraps on a papyrus of Fr. 1A (ὀρνυ[| Λοξία[ ) might come from an apopemptic hymn. A well-known Latin example is Horace, *Odes* 4.1, which sends away Venus to a younger man's more receptive house.

[4] As RW point out ad loc., the extant Orphic Hymns are not philosophical: "the reference is a more general one to the mass of 'Orphic' literature, esp. ἱεροὶ λόγοι."

γορίαν προϊόντες ψιλήν, οἷον Ἀπόλλων ἀνῳκοδόμησε τεῖχος, ἢ ἐθήτευσεν Ἀδμήτῳ ὁ Ἀπόλλων ἢ τὰ τοιαῦτα. γενεαλογικοὶ δὲ οἱ ταῖς τῶν ποιητῶν θεογονίαις ἀκολουθοῦντες, ὅταν Λητοῦς μὲν τὸν Ἀπόλλωνα, Μνημοσύνης δὲ τὰς Μούσας καλῶμεν.

4. Πεπλασμένοι δὲ ὅταν αὐτοὶ σωματοποιῶμεν καὶ θεὸν καὶ γονὰς θεῶν ἢ δαιμόνων, ὥσπερ Σιμωνίδης Αὔριον δαίμονα κέκληκε, καὶ ἕτεροι Ὄκνον, καὶ ἕτεροι ἕτερόν τινα. εὐκτικοὶ δὲ οἱ ψιλὴν εὐχὴν ἔχοντες ἄνευ τῶν ἄλλων μερῶν ὧν εἴπομεν, καὶ ἀπευκτικοὶ οἱ τὰ ἐναντία ἀπευχόμενοι ψιλῶς. καὶ παρὰ τούτους τοὺς τρόπους οὐκ ἂν ὕμνοι γίγνοιντο εἰς θεούς.

5. Τῷ δὲ μυθικῷ γένει καὶ γενεαλογικῷ τὰ πολλὰ εἰώθασι χρῆσθαι ἅπαντες γενέσεις διεξιόντες, καὶ ὅσων ἀγαθῶν ἀνθρώποις αἴτιοι κατέστησαν, ἀπὸ μύθων λαμβάνοντες. ἔστι δὲ τοῦτο ὡς ἐγώ φημι καὶ ζητῆσαι ἄξιον, πότερον ἑνὶ τούτων ἀεὶ χρηστέον ἢ πᾶσιν ἔξεστιν, ἢ τοῖς μὲν ποιηταῖς ἐξεῖναι χρὴ νομίζειν, τοῖς δὲ συγγραφεῦσιν ἢ λογοποιοῖς ⟨οὔ⟩.[1] τοῦ ⟨δὲ⟩[2] μηκέτι ἐξεῖναι ἕνα καὶ ἁπλοῦν ⟨τιθέμεθα⟩[3] ὅρον, ὅτι πλείονα τὴν ἐξουσίαν τὴν περὶ ταῦτα ποιήσει μὲν

334

---

[1] suppl. Heeren, Bursian   [2] addidi   [3] suppl. Bursian

---

5 In simple allegory, as RW explain ad loc., "the narrative has a hidden meaning, but no explanation of it is given . . . Similar is Quintilian's *tota allegoria*, opposed to the *mixta allegoria* in which the application is made explicit (8.6.47–8); but M.'s expression is noteworthy, and seems to imply that all μῦθοι concerning gods have an allegorical meaning."

(*mythoi*) and proceed by simple allegory,[5] recounting, for example, how Apollo built the wall,[6] or how Apollo became Admetus' servant,[7] and so forth. Genealogical hymns are those that follow the theogonies of the poets, as when we call Apollo the son of Leto or the Muses the daughters of Mnemosyne.

4. Hymns are fictive when we ourselves personify a god or the offspring of gods or divinities, as when Simonides calls Tomorrow (Aurion) a divinity, others deify Hesitation (Ocnus),[8] and so on. Precatory hymns contain a simple prayer without the other forms that we have named, while deprecatory ones simply pray that something untoward may be averted.[9] Besides these, no other types of hymns to gods are possible.

5. All authors normally employ both the mythical and genealogical types when they give details of births and derive from myths the benefits to mankind that the gods have made possible. In my estimation it is worth considering whether we should always use a single kind of hymn or if we can use them all; again, whether we should think that poets are allowed to use them, but that writers of prose and historians must not. As for the extent of their license,[10] we posit one simple rule: that the portion it de-

---

[6] That is, the wall of Troy; cf. Hom. *Il*. 7.452–53; Pind. *Ol*. 8.31–36.   [7] Cf. Bacchyl. 3.76–84; Eur. *Alc*.

[8] Although no textual versions are extant, an allegorical painting by Polygnotus depicted Ocnus in Hades weaving a rope that is being consumed by a donkey. Paus. 10.29.2 interprets the scene as a parable of an industrious husband's work being consumed by a spendthrift wife.   [9] In 1.9.1, Agamemnon's prayer to Zeus at Hom. *Il*. 2.412–13 is given as an example.

[10] That is, to employ hymns.

⟨παρέχει⟩⁴ ἡ περὶ τὸ θεῖον μερίς, ἀφορμὴ ⟨δὲ⟩⁴ πλεί-
στη ὑπόκειται τῇ συγγραφῇ ἡ περὶ τὸν ἄνθρωπον.

6. Χρηστέον γε μὴν καὶ τῷ συγγραφεῖ καὶ τῷ
λογογράφῳ καὶ τούτων ἑκάστῳ εἴδει καὶ ὁμοῦ πᾶσιν,
ὅπη καὶ Πλάτωνα περὶ τὴν γραφὴν ἄκρον καὶ ἄριστον εἶναι πεπιστεύκαμεν, ὁρῶμεν δὲ σχεδὸν τοῦτον
πᾶσι τοῖς εἴδεσι κεχρημένον, ἄλλῳ ἄλλοτε, ἀλλὰ καὶ
ἐν ἑνὶ βιβλίῳ τοῖς πλείστοις αὐτῶν, ἐν τῷ Συμποσίῳ.
7. ἃ μὲν γὰρ ὁ Φαῖδρος περὶ τοῦ Ἔρωτος ⟨λέγει⟩,⁵
γενεαλογικοῦ τύπου ἂν εἴη, ἃ δὲ Ἀριστοφάνης κομ-
ψεύεται διὰ μύθου, τοῦ μυθολογικοῦ, ἃ δὲ Ἀγάθων,
ὡσαύτως τοῦ μυθικοῦ, ἃ δ' αὖ Σωκράτης, αὐτὸ τοῦτο
κατὰ πλάσιν (πλάττει γὰρ Πόρους καὶ Πενίας), ἐγγυτάτω τοῦ φυσιολογικοῦ. 8. καὶ μὴν ἐν οἷς μὲν καλεῖ
τὰς Μούσας ἐν τῷ Φαίδρῳ, τὸν κλητικὸν τύπον δεί-
κνυσιν, ἐν οἷς δ' αὖ εὔχεται τῷ Πανί, τὸν εὐκτικόν.
καὶ ζητῶν ἂν εὕροις πανταχοῦ κεχρημένον, εἰ δὲ μὴ
πρὸς κόρον μηδ' ἐπ' ἀκριβείας, λογιστέον ὡς ἐξ ἐλάττονος ἐξουσίας μέτεστι τῇ συγγραφῇ. πῶς δὲ ἕκαστον τούτων τῶν εἰδῶν μετιτέον τε καὶ μέχρι τίνος
προσακτέον, καὶ τίς ἑρμηνεία πρέπουσα, ἑξῆς λέγειν
πειράσομαι.

⁴ παρέχει . . . δὲ suppl. Walz, RW
⁵ suppl. Heeren, RW: γενεαλογεῖ suppl. Spengel, Bursian

---

11 At 178a–80b Phaedrus cites Hesiod and Parmenides in lo-
cating the birth of Eros after the dissolution of Chaos.
12 At 189c–93d Aristophanes depicts Eros reuniting our once-

votes to gods gives poetry greater allowance for these topics, whereas the chief subject matter for prose concerns human beings.

6. Nevertheless, the prose writer and the orator must employ each of these types, both individually and all together, inasmuch as we see Plato, whom we consider to be the foremost and best writer of prose, employing almost all these types, one here, another there, but the majority of them in one book, the *Symposium*. 7. For what Phaedrus says about Eros would be of the genealogical type;[11] Aristophanes' clever inventions told through a story are of the mythological type,[12] as is Agathon's speech.[13] Socrates, on the other hand, does the same thing through fiction, inventing the gods Plenty (Poros) and Poverty (Penia)[14] in a manner very close to the philosophical type. 8. Furthermore, when he calls upon the Muses in the *Phaedrus*,[15] he illustrates the cletic type, and when he prays to Pan,[16] the precatory kind. If you make a survey, you will find him using them everywhere. If indeed he does not use them to excess nor with too much exactitude, we must take into account that prose provides less allowance for them. I shall next attempt to explain how each of these types should be handled, to what extent they should be used, and what style is appropriate.

whole selves that were severed by Zeus to weaken the human race.

[13] At 194e–97e Agathon describes all the blessings Eros brings to gods and mortals.   [14] 203b–4a.

[15] 237a: "Come, then, O Muses . . . join me in this speech."

[16] 279bc: "O dear Pan and all you other gods in this place, grant that I may become beautiful within."

1.3. ΠΕΡΙ ΤΩΝ ΚΛΗΤΙΚΩΝ

1. . . . μέτρον μέντοι τῶν κλητικῶν ὕμνων ἐν μὲν ποιήσει ἐπιμηκέστερον. ἀναμιμνήσκειν[1] γὰρ πολλῶν τόπων ἐκείνοις ἔξεστιν, ὡς παρὰ τῇ Σαπφοῖ καὶ τῷ
Ἀλκμᾶνι πολλαχοῦ εὑρίσκομεν. ὁ μὲν[2] γὰρ Ἄρτεμιν
ἐκ μυρίων ὀρέων, μυρίων δὲ πόλεων, ἔτι δὲ ποταμῶν
ἀνακαλεῖ, ἡ δὲ Ἀφροδίτην ⟨ἐκ⟩[3] Κύπρου, Κνίδου, Συ-
ρίας, πολλαχόθεν ἀλλαχόθεν ἀνακαλεῖ. 2. οὐ μόνον
335 γε, ἀλλὰ καὶ τοὺς τόπους αὐτοὺς ἔξεστι διαγράφειν,
οἷον εἰ ἀπὸ ποταμῶν καλοῖεν,[4] ὕδωρ ἢ ὄχθας καὶ τοὺς
ὑποπεφυκότας λειμῶνας καὶ χοροὺς ἐπὶ τοῖς ποταμοῖς
γινομένους καὶ τὰ τοιαῦτα προσαναγράφουσι. καὶ εἰ
ἀπὸ ἱερῶν, ὡσαύτως, ὥστε ἀνάγκη μακροὺς αὐτῶν
γίγνεσθαι τοὺς κλητικοὺς ὕμνους.

3. Τοῖς δὲ συγγραφεῦσι βραχυτέραν τὴν περὶ
ταῦτα διατριβὴν ἀναγκαῖον γίνεσθαι· οὔτε γὰρ ἐκ
πολλῶν τόπων καὶ χωρίων ἀνακαλέσουσιν, οὔτε ἐφ'
ἑκάστου μετὰ διαγραφῆς, ἀλλ' ὥσπερ Πλάτων,
ὅσπερ[5] ἐξηγούμενος τῷ εἴδει κέχρηται, "ἄγετε δὴ
Μοῦσαι λίγειαι, εἴτε δι' ᾠδῆς εἶδος εἴτε διὰ γένος
μουσικὸν τὸ Λιγύων ταύτην ἔσχετε τὴν ἐπωνυμίαν."

[1] Nitsche, RW: ἅμα μὲν P
[2] ὁ μὲν . . . ἡ δὲ Nitsche, RW: τὴν μὲν . . . τὴν δὲ P
[3] suppl. Finckh, RW   [4] Finckh: καλοίη P

1.3. CLETIC HYMNS

1. . . . [1] cletic hymns (*klētikoi*) are longer in poetry, because poets have license to mention many places, as we often find in Sappho and Alcman. The latter summons Artemis from myriad mountains, cities, and rivers as well, while the former summons Aphrodite from Cyprus, Cnidus, Syria, and many other places. 2. Not only that, but they have license to describe the places themselves. For example, if they summon the god from rivers, they add descriptions of the water, the banks, the meadows growing beside them, the choruses formed alongside the rivers, and the like. The same is true if they summon the god from sacred places, with the result that poets' cletic hymns are necessarily long.

3. But for prose writers the time spent on these topics is necessarily shorter, for they will not issue summonses from many places and locales, nor provide a description in each case, but will do as Plato does, who acts as a guide when employing this type with: "Come then, high-voiced Muses, whether you came by that epithet (*ligeiai*) from the nature of your song or from the musical race of the Ligyans."[2]

---

[1] The opening section is lost.
[2] *Phdr.* 237a, alluded to in 1.2.8.

---

5 ὥσπερ Πλάτων, ὅσπερ Heeren, Walz, Bursian: ὅπερ Πλάτων ὥσπερ codd.: ὁ μὲν Πλάτων ὥσπερ RW

4. Ὁ δὲ Ὅμηρος ἐν κλητικῷ κέχρηται τῷ εἴδει μετὰ τῆς ἰσοσυλλαβίας, ἐν οἷς ὁ Χρύσης εὔχεται τῆς Ἰλιάδος ἐν τοῖς πρώτοις,

> ὃς Χρύσην ἀμφιβέβηκας
> Κίλλαν τε ζαθέην, Τενέδοιό τε ἶφι ἀνάσσεις.

ἐν οὖν τόδε γίνωσκε, ὡς ποιητῇ μὲν ἐξουσία πλείων, τῷ δὲ συγγραφεῖ ἐλάττων. ἑρμηνεία δὲ πρέπουσα εἴη ἂν[6] τοῖς κλητικοῖς, ἥ τε δι' ὥρας προϊοῦσα καὶ κόσμου, διόπερ τὰς διατριβὰς προσλαμβάνουσιν οἱ ποιηταί. σχήματα δὲ τὰ ἀνακλητικὰ ἁρμόττοντα.

5. Οὐ χεῖρον δ' ἴσως καὶ τὴν μέθοδον, ᾗ κεχρήμεθα ἡμεῖς ἐν τῷ κλητικῷ τοῦ Ἀπόλλωνος ὕμνῳ, †βιβλίῳ πως θέσθαι†,[7] ὥσπερ ἂν ἡ ὥρα ἐνείη πλείων,[8] ἅμα τε μήτε ὑπερβαίνοιμεν τὸ μέτρον τὸ τῷ συγγραφεῖ πρέπον, μήτε ἡ περὶ τὴν κατασκευὴν ἁβρότης ὑπερφθέγγοιτο τὴν συγγραφήν· αὐτοῖς γὰρ τοῖς ποιηταῖς τὸ πλεῖον προστεθείκαμεν, καλοῦσιν ἐκ τῶν καὶ τῶν τό-

---

[6] εἴη ἂν Heeren, Bursian: οἴα καὶ P: obel. RW
[7] obel. RW: τούτῳ τῷ βιβλίῳ προσθέσθαι tent. Bursian, alii alia
[8] πλείω P: corr. Walz

---

[3] Evidently the type of invocation involving many places.
[4] Perhaps this refers to the fact that the three locations are rendered with roughly the same number of syllables.
[5] 1.37–38.

4. Homer uses this type[3] in a summons with equal syllables[4] in the lines where Chryses prays at the beginning of the *Iliad*:[5]

> "You who protect Chryse
> and holy Cilla and rule mightily over Tenedos."

Keep in mind this one thing: the poet has greater latitude, the prose writer less. The appropriate style for cletic hymns is one that proceeds with beauty (*hōra*) and embellishment (*kosmos*), which is why poets include these extended passages. The appropriate figures are those of invocations.[6]

5. Perhaps it is not a bad idea to include in this book(?)[7] the procedure that I myself employed in my cletic hymn to Apollo,[8] so as to increase the beauty (*hōra*), while at the same time not exceeding the proper length for a prose writer, nor allowing the delicacy (*habrotēs*) of the exposition to overwhelm the prose.[9] To the poets themselves I have granted greater scope, as they make summonses

[6] These presumably include apostrophes and imperatives.

[7] The text is corrupt and no emendation has proved satisfactory. I have translated Bursian's conjecture.

[8] No such hymn is extant. The hymn to Sminthian Apollo at the end of the second treatise is too extensive to be relevant here. Furthermore, it is doubtful that this author composed the second treatise.

[9] In this very corrupt passage, M. seems to claim that his hymn's style contains beauty in its descriptions of places, but is of moderate length, and that its delicacy (a reprise of *kosmos*, "embellishment," above) does not overwhelm (or "drown out") the prose.

πων,[9] ἐγὼ δὲ οὐκ ἂν καλέσαιμι. καὶ πολλὰ ἂν εὕροις
πεποικιλμένα τῇ μεθόδῳ.

6. Γίνωσκε δὲ τόδε τὸ θεώρημα οὐκ ἄχρηστον, ὅτι
336 εἰ μὲν εὐχὴ ἐπακολουθεῖ τῇ κλήσει, ἔτι ἐλάττων ἡ
διατριβὴ καὶ τοῖς ποιηταῖς καὶ τοῖς συγγραφεῦσιν· εἰ
δὲ αὐτὸ τοῦτο εἴη ψιλὴ κλῆσις, πλείων ἐστί, καὶ ζητῶν ἂν εὕροις παρὰ τοῖς ποιηταῖς τὴν συνήθειαν ταύτην πεφυλαγμένην.

[9] ἐκ τῶν καὶ τῶν τόπων Jacobs, Walz: ἐκ τῶνδε τῶν τόπων
codd.: ἐκ πολλῶν τόπων Heeren: †τῶνδε† obel. RW

from various places. But for my part, I would not summon (so extensively?).[10] You will find that there are many variations with this procedure.

6. Keep in mind this useful rule, that if a prayer follows the summons, the time spent on it is even less, whether for poets or prose writers. If, however, the hymn consists of a summons alone, the time spent on it is longer. You will find that this practice is maintained by the poets.

[10] RW propose that "I would not summon" is a quotation from the hymn. I have added "so extensively."

1.4. ΠΕΡΙ ΑΠΟΠΕΜΠΤΙΚΩΝ

1. Οἱ τοίνυν ἀποπεμπτικοί εἰσιν, ὡς καὶ τοὔνομα δηλοῖ, τοῖς κλητικοῖς ὑπεναντίοι, ἐλάχιστον δὲ τὸ τοιοῦτον εἶδος, καὶ παρὰ τοῖς ποιηταῖς μόνον εὑρίσκεται. ἐπιλέγονται δὲ ἀποδημίαις θεῶν νομιζομέναις ἢ γινομέναις, οἷον Ἀπόλλωνος ἀποδημίαι τινὲς ὀνομάζονται παρὰ Δηλίοις καὶ Μιλησίοις, καὶ Ἀρτέμιδος παρὰ Ἀργείοις. εἰσὶ τοίνυν καὶ τῷ Βακχυλίδῃ ὕμνοι ἀποπεμπτικοί.

2. Ἀφορμὴ δ᾽ ὑποβέβληται τοῖς τοιούτοις ὕμνοις ἡ χώρα ἣν καταλείπει, καὶ πόλεις καὶ ἔθνη, καὶ πρὸς ἣν ἄπεισι πόλιν ὁμοίως ἢ χώραν, καὶ διαγραφαὶ τόπων, καὶ ὅσα τοιαῦτα. γινέσθω δὲ δι᾽ ἡδονῆς προϊὼν ὁ λόγος· δεῖ γὰρ μετὰ ἀνειμένης τινὸς ἁρμονίας καὶ εὐμενεστέρας προπέμπεσθαι. διατριβὴν δὲ ἐνδέχεται πλείονα, οὐχ ὥσπερ οἱ κλητικοὶ ἐλάττονα. 3. ἐν μὲν γὰρ τοῖς ὅτι τάχιστα ἡμῖν συνεῖναι τοὺς θεοὺς βουλόμεθα, ἐν δὲ τοῖς ὅτι βραδύτατα ἀπαλλάττεσθαι. ἀνάγκη δὲ εἶναι καὶ εὐχὴν ἐπὶ ἐπανόδῳ καὶ ἐπιδημίᾳ δευτέρᾳ. ταῦτά σοι [καὶ]¹ περὶ ἀποπεμπτικῶν² ὕμνων εἰρήσθω.

¹ secl. Spengel, RW
² Finckh, RW: προπεμπτικῶν P

38

1.4. SENDOFF HYMNS

1. Sendoff hymns (*apopemptikoi*), as the name makes clear, are the opposite of cletic hymns. This genre is the rarest, and is only found in poets. They are delivered on the occasion of gods' departures abroad, imagined or actual, as for example, the so-called departures of Apollo at Delos and Miletus, and of Artemis at Argos.[1] There are also sendoff hymns in Bacchylides.[2]

2. The source material underlying such hymns is the land that the god is leaving, including its cities and nations, and likewise the city or land to which he will be going, with descriptions of these places, and the like. The speech should proceed in a pleasant manner, for sendoffs require a somewhat relaxed and rather genial tone. It admits greater expansion, not less as in cletic hymns. 3. For in the latter we want the gods to join us as soon as possible, whereas in the former we want to delay their departure as long as we can. There must also be a prayer for their return and a second visit. Let that suffice for sendoff hymns.

[1] Apollo travels to and from his cultic sites in Lycia, Delphi, Delos, and Miletus (Branchidae). Nothing is known of Artemis' departures from Argos.

[2] Mentioned also in 1.2.2 (see the note).

1.5. ΠΕΡΙ ΤΩΝ ΦΥΣΙΚΩΝ

1. Περὶ τοίνυν τῶν φυσικῶν ἐφεξῆς ἂν εἴη, ὥσπερ προεθέμεθα, λέγειν. πρῶτον τοίνυν τόδε περὶ αὐτῶν ῥητέον, ὅτι ἐλάχιστα μὲν τοῖς ἀφελεστέροις¹ τὸ εἶδος ἁρμόττει, μάλιστα δὲ τοῖς ἐμψυχοτέροις² καὶ μεγαλονουστέροις, ἔπειτα ὅτι ποιηταῖς μᾶλλον ἢ συγγραφεῦσιν ἢ λογογράφοις ἢ πολιτικοῖς ἁρμόττουσιν. 2. εἰσὶ δὲ τοιοῦτοι, ὅταν Ἀπόλλωνος ὕμνον λέγοντες ἥλιον αὐτὸν εἶναι φάσκωμεν, καὶ περὶ τοῦ ἡλίου τῆς φύσεως διαλεγώμεθα, καὶ περὶ Ἥρας ὅτι ἀήρ, καὶ Ζεὺς τὸ θερμόν· οἱ γὰρ τοιοῦτοι ὕμνοι φυσιολογικοί. καὶ χρῶνται δὲ τῷ τοιούτῳ τρόπῳ Παρμενίδης τε καὶ Ἐμπεδοκλῆς ἀκριβῶς, κέχρηται δὲ καὶ ὁ Πλάτων· ἐν τῷ Φαίδρῳ γὰρ φυσιολογῶν ὅτι πάθος ἐστὶ τῆς ψυχῆς ὁ Ἔρως, ἀναπτεροποιεῖ αὐτόν.

3. Αὐτῶν δὲ τῶν φυσικῶν οἱ μὲν ἐξηγητικοί, οἱ δὲ ἐν βραχεῖ προαγόμενοι· πλεῖστον γὰρ διαφέρει, ὡς εἰδότα ἀναμιμνήσκειν συμμέτρως, ἢ ὅλως ἀγνοοῦντα διδάσκειν. Παρμενίδης μὲν γὰρ καὶ Ἐμπεδοκλῆς ἐξηγοῦνται, Πλάτων δὲ ἐν βραχυτάτοις ἀναμιμνήσκει.³ ἔτι δὲ οἱ μὲν κατ᾽ αἰνίγματα, οἱ δὲ ἐκ τοῦ φανεροῦ

---

¹ Walz, RW: ἀσφαλεστέροις P   ² Ernesti: ψυχροτέροις P
³ ἀναμιμνήσκει Bursian: ἀνυμνεῖ P

1.5. PHILOSOPHICAL HYMNS

1. Next, according to our outline, comes a discussion of philosophical hymns (*physikoi*). The first thing that needs to be said about them is that this genre is least appropriate for simpler writers, but most fitting for those with more animated and elevated natures. Secondly, they suit poets rather than prose writers, historians, or speech writers. 2. Examples occur when, in a hymn to Apollo, we say that he is the sun and discuss the nature[1] of the sun, and that Hera is air, and that Zeus is heat—such are examples of philosophical hymns. Parmenides and Empedocles employ this type in the strict sense, but Plato uses it too, for in the *Phaedrus*, while explaining the nature of Eros as a sensation in the soul, he gives him wings.[2]

3. Some philosophical hymns offer explanations, others merely make brief statements. For there is a great difference between succinctly reminding one already knowledgeable and instructing one who is completely ignorant. Parmenides and Empedocles offer explanations, whereas Plato provides very brief reminders. Furthermore, some hymns make their case in riddles, others straightforwardly.

---

[1] *Physis* (nature), which gives its name to the genre, informed by the speculations of natural philosophers.

[2] For example, 252bc, where Plato quotes two spurious verses of Homer, "Mortals call him winged Eros, / but the immortals call him Pteros (Winged), because he must grow wings."

προάγονται· κατ' αἰνίγματα μέν, ὁποῖοί εἰσιν οἱ Πυθαγόρειοι φερόμενοι, ἐκ τοῦ φανεροῦ δὲ ὁποίους μικρῷ πρόσθεν ἐφάσκομεν.

4. Ὥσπερ δὲ καὶ αὐτῶν τῶν φυσιολογικῶν διαφορὰς ἐδείκνυμεν ταύτας οὔσας, οὕτω καὶ τῆς συμμετρίας διαφορὰς ὁριούμεθα. οἱ γὰρ κατ' αἰνίγματα προϊόντες βραχύτητα ἀπαιτοῦσιν, ἔτι δὲ οἱ καὶ μὴ διδασκαλικοὶ ἄλλως κεφαλαιωδέστεροι. οἱ δὲ ἕτεροι πλείστην καὶ μεγίστην διατριβὴν ἐνδέχονται.

5. Ὁ γοῦν Πλάτων ὕμνον τοῦ Παντὸς τὸν Τίμαιον καλεῖ ἐν τῷ Κριτίᾳ, καὶ οἱ φυσικώτεροι ποιηταί, ὧν ἐπεμνήσθημεν, πραγματείας ὅλας κατέθεντο. εὐχῆς δὲ οὐδέν τι πάνυ χρὴ ἐπὶ τούτων. ἐπιτηρεῖν δὲ χρὴ καὶ μὴ εἰς τὸν πολὺν ὄχλον καὶ δῆμον ἐκφέρειν τοὺς τοιούτους ὕμνους· ἀπιθανώτεροι γὰρ καὶ καταγελαστικώτεροι τοῖς πολλοῖς φαίνονται. 6. ἑρμηνεία δὲ καὶ πρὸς τὸν διθύραμβον ἀνελθεῖν μικρὸν διαφέρει· οὐ γάρ ἐστιν ὑπὲρ ὧν σεμνοτέρων ἂν ἄνθρωπος φθέγξαιτο.

Riddling hymns are of the sort that circulate as Pythagorean;[3] straightforward hymns are of the sort we mentioned just above.[4]

4. Just as we showed how philosophical hymns themselves differed in kind, so shall we define their differences in length. Riddling hymns require brevity; hymns that are not otherwise didactic proceed more summarily; the rest permit the longest and greatest expansions.

5. For instance, Plato in the *Critias* calls the *Timaeus* a "Hymn of Everything,"[5] and the more philosophical poets whom we have mentioned[6] have composed entire treatises. There is no need at all for a prayer in these hymns. But one must be careful and not present such hymns as these to the general public, since most people see them as unpersuasive and rather ridiculous. 6. The style approaches that of a dithyramb, for there are no grander subjects for a human being to give voice to.

[3] No such example is extant.

[4] That is, those by Parmenides, Empedocles, and Plato.

[5] In fact, he does not say that, although, as RW point out, the appellation is apt.

[6] Parmenides and Empedocles.

1.6. ΠΕΡΙ ΜΥΘΙΚΩΝ

338   1. Ἑξῆς ἂν εἴη περὶ τῶν μυθικῶν εἰπεῖν, οὓς ἔνιοι μὲν τοὺς αὐτοὺς εἶναι νομίζουσι τοῖς γενεαλογικοῖς, ἔνιοι δὲ οὐχ οὕτως [εἶναι νομίζουσι τοῖς γενεαλογικοῖς].[1] οἱ μέν γε νομίζοντες οὐδὲν διαφέρειν καὶ τὰς γενεαλογίας μύθους εἶναί φασιν, οἷον εἰ βούλει, ὅσα γε Ἀκουσίλεως καὶ Ἡσίοδος καὶ Ὀρφεὺς ἐν ταῖς θεογονίαις εἰρήκασιν· εἰσὶ μὲν γὰρ γενεαλογικαὶ αἵδε, οὐδὲν δὲ ἧττον μυθικαί. 2. τάδε δὲ αὖ φασιν οἱ διαφέρειν νομίζοντες, ὅτι καὶ χωρὶς τῶν γενεαλογικῶν εἴησαν ἄν τινες μυθικοὶ ὕμνοι, οἷον ὅτι Διόνυσος Ἰκαρίῳ ἐπεξενώθη, ἢ ὅτι ἐν Ζωστῆρι τὴν ζώνην ἐλύσατο ἡ Λητώ, ἢ ὅτι ἡ Δημήτηρ παρὰ Κελεῷ ἐπεξενώθη, ἢ ὅσα ἕτερα τοιαῦτα. ταῦτα γὰρ [καὶ][2] γενεαλογίαν μὲν οὐδεμίαν εἴληφε, μυθικὴν δέ τινα ἄλλην ἱστορίαν.

3. Ἃ μέντοι ἀμφότεροι λέγοντες τὰ σφῶν αὐτῶν ἑκάτεροι νικᾶν ἀξιοῦσι, σχεδὸν ἀκήκοας, ἐμοὶ δὲ δοκεῖ κάλλιον ἐν ὅρῳ εἶναι ἀκριβῶς διελέσθαι. πάσας μὲν γὰρ γενεαλογίας καὶ πάντας ὕμνους τοὺς διὰ γενεαλογικῶν διὰ μυθικῶν περιστάσεων προάγεσθαι νομίζω, οὐ μὴν πάντας γε τοὺς μυθικοὺς διὰ γενεα-

[1] secl. RW
[2] secl. Bursian, RW

44

1.6. MYTHICAL HYMNS

1. Next comes a discussion of mythical hymns (*mythikoi*), which some consider to be the same as genealogical hymns, whereas others do not. Those who think that there is no difference say that genealogies *are* myths. Examples might include what Acusilaus,[1] Hesiod, and Orpheus recount in their theogonies, for while these are genealogical, they are no less mythical. 2. On the other hand, those who consider them different say that certain mythical hymns can exist without being genealogical, as for example Dionysus being hosted by Icarius,[2] Leto loosening her girdle at Zoster,[3] Demeter being hosted by Celeus,[4] and other narratives of this nature. These contain no genealogy, but rather a different type of mythical narrative.

3. You have now heard, more or less, what each side claims as conclusive for its position, but when it comes to definitions, I believe it preferable to make accurate distinctions. I think that all genealogies and all hymns containing genealogies employ mythical elements, but that not all mythical hymns employ genealogies. Consequently,

[1] A prose writer of Argos (end of 6th c. BC), who relied heavily on Hesiod's *Theogony*.
[2] Icarius of Athens received the gift of wine from Dionysus.
[3] In Attica; cf. Paus. 1.31.1.
[4] *Hymn Hom. Dem.* 91–304.

λογίας, ὥστε τὸ μὲν τῶν μυθικῶν ὕμνων μέρος γενικώτερον ἂν εἴη, τὸ δὲ τῶν γενεαλογικῶν εἰδικώτερον.

4. Ταῦτά σοι περὶ διαφορᾶς εἴρηται, ὑπὲρ δὲ τῶν
μυθικῶν χωρὶς ἀποτεμόμενον χρὴ λέγειν. φημὶ δὴ τὸ
πρῶτον μὲν μηδαμῶς μετέχειν αὐτοὺς φυσιολογίας,
λέγω φανερᾶς· εἰ γάρ τις ἐγκεκρυμμένη καθ᾿ ὑπόνοιαν, ὥς γε πολλὰ ἔχει τῶν θείων, οὐδὲν τοῦτό γε
διαφέρει. ἔπειτα εἶναι τῷ ποιητῇ μᾶλλον προσφόρους·
ἡ γὰρ ἐξουσία καὶ τοῦ κατὰ σχολὴν λέγειν καὶ τοῦ
περιστέλλειν τοῖς ποιητικοῖς κόσμοις καὶ ταῖς κατασκευαῖς οὔτε κόρον οὔτε ἀηδίαν παρίστησι· καίτοι
οὐκ ἀγνοῶ ὡς αὐτῶν[3] ἔνιοι τῶν ποιητῶν προσφέρουσι
339 τὰς ἀκαίρους διατριβάς· συγγραφεῦσι δὲ ἢ λογοποιοῖς ἐλαχίστη ἐξουσία.

5. Γυμνοὶ δὲ οἱ μῦθοι τιθέμενοι σφόδρα λυποῦσι
καὶ ἐνοχλοῦσι τὰς ἀκοάς. δεῖ τοίνυν ὅτι βραχυτάτοις
ἀπαλλάττεσθαι. παραμυθίας οὖν προσακτέον καὶ
πρὸς συντομίαν καὶ πρὸς ἡδονήν, πρῶτον μὲν μὴ ἀπ᾿
εὐθείας πάντα εἰσάγειν, ἀλλὰ τὰ μὲν παραλείπειν λέγοντα, τὰ δὲ συγχωρεῖν, τὰ δὲ κατὰ συμπλοκὴν εἰσάγειν, τὰ δὲ προσποιεῖσθαι ἐξηγεῖσθαι, τὰ δὲ μὴ
πιστεύειν μηδὲ ἀπιστεῖν. καὶ ὅλως οὐκ ἀπορήσεις
μεθόδων, ἕν γε τοῦτο θεώρημα σώζων, ὡς διατριβὴ
ἀπρόσφορος.

6. Ἡ δὲ ἑρμηνεία, ὅπερ καὶ περὶ τῆς διατριβῆς
ἔφαμεν, ἐπὶ ἐλάττονος ἐξουσίας γινέσθω, σώζουσα

---

[3] ὡς αὐτῶν RW: ὡσαύτως P

the category of mythical hymns should be considered more general, that of genealogical hymns more specific.

4. Enough has been said about their differences. We must now discuss mythical hymns as a separate category. First, I insist that they must never include philosophical material—openly, that is, for it does not matter if some of it is concealed by allegory, as is often the case with divine matters. Secondly, mythical hymns are more appropriate for a poet, because he has license to speak at length and to deck out his subject with poetic embellishments and elaborations without producing satiety or displeasure—although I am not unaware that some poets themselves produce excessively long treatments. Prose writers or orators, however, have the least such license.

5. Myths presented as bare narratives are very painful and annoying for listeners. Therefore they must be dealt with as briefly as possible. You must then provide relief with a view to brevity and charm, first of all by not including everything straightforwardly, but by omitting some points while allowing others, introducing some by means of interweaving,[5] others by pretending to offer explanations, and still others by neither confirming nor denying them. In general, you will not lack for effective procedures, if you preserve this one rule: lengthy treatment is inappropriate.

6. What we just said about length applies as well to style: it must be allowed less license. It should preserve

---

[5] That is, inserting them in other genres as shown by the forthcoming examples from Isocrates, Thucydides, and Plato.

μὲν τὸν ἐπιδεικτικὸν κόσμον, πολὺ δὲ τοῦ διθυράμβου
ἀποβεβηκυῖα. γίγνοιτο δ' ἂν τοιαύτη, εἰ τῷ Ἰσοκράτους θεωρήματι χρησόμεθα, καὶ τὸ κάλλος καὶ τὴν
σεμνότητα μὴ ἀπὸ τῶν ὀνομάτων μᾶλλον ἢ τῆς ἀρ-
χαιότητος ἢ τοῦ μεγέθους θηρώμεθα, ἀλλ' ἀπὸ τῆς
ἁρμονίας καὶ τῶν σχημάτων, 7. ἐπεὶ αὐτό γε τοῦτο, ὃ
πάντες θρυλοῦσι, "Δήμητρος γὰρ ἀφικομένης εἰς τὴν
χώραν ἡμῶν" καὶ τὰ ἑξῆς, τίς οὐκ οἶδεν, ὅτι τοῖς μὲν
ὀνόμασιν ἐγγὺς τοῦ πολιτικοῦ καθήκει, τῇ δὲ συνθέ-
σει καὶ τῇ ἁρμονίᾳ καὶ τῷ σχήματι †ὀλίγα καὶ λείπει
ἔνια†[4] σεμνότερα εἶναι δοκεῖ; καὶ τὸ "Τηρεῖ δὲ τῷ Πρό-
κνην τὴν Πανδίονος" καὶ τὰ ἑξῆς τοῦ αὐτοῦ τύπου, εἰ
καὶ περὶ ἀνθρωπίνων εἴρηται. 8. καὶ παρὰ Πλάτωνι,
"φήμη τις καὶ λόγος διαρρεῖ, ὡς ἄρα ὁ θεὸς οὗτος
ὑπὸ μητρυιᾶς οὔσης τῆς Ἥρας ἐκινήθη," καὶ πολλὰ
παραδείγματα παρὰ τῷ Πλάτωνι, ὥστε εἰ σώζοις
τὸ θεώρημα, φυλακτήριον ἔσται πρὸς ἀρετὴν λόγου.
ὅλως δὲ περὶ τῶν μυθικῶν τούτων ὕμνων, περί τε ἔν-
νοιαν καὶ ἑρμηνείαν, ἐκεῖνο ἰστέον, ὅτι τῷ ἀξιώματι
κατ' ἄμφω τὸ μυθικὸν [λεῖπον].[5]

4 obel. RW
5 secl. RW

---

6 Contrast 1.5.6, where the dithyrambic style is recommended
for elevated philosophical hymns. Here the emphasis is on the
dithyramb's magniloquence.

7 Isoc., *Paneg.* 28.

epideictic adornment, but keep far from the style of a
dithyramb.[6] It will be such if we adopt the rule of Isocrates and seek beauty and dignity not through the use of
archaic or grandiose words, but through harmonious ar-
rangement and figures of style. 7. As for that famous passage everyone repeats, "For when Demeter came to our
land, etc.,"[7] who does not know that it consists of words
close to ordinary public speech, but gives the impression
of being rather more dignified because of its composition,
harmony, and figures?[8] There is also, "to the Tereus who
[seized] Procne, Pandion's daughter, etc.,"[9] although it
speaks of human affairs. 8. So too in Plato: "There is a
rumor and story current that this god was in fact mad-
dened by his stepmother Hera."[10] Indeed, there are many
examples in Plato. All in all, if you follow our rule,[11] it will
ensure the success of your speech. In general, keep in
mind that with regard to both the content and style of
these mythical hymns, the mythical element, in terms of
dignity, is. . . .[12]

[8] The bracketed words ὀλίγα καὶ λείπει ἔνια (a few things are
lacking) indicate a lacuna, as does λεῖπον at the end of §8.

[9] Thuc. 2.29.3. The context reads: "This Teres [with whom the
Athenians were allying] is no relation to the Tereus who seized
Procne, Pandion's daughter, from Athens."

[10] *Leg.* 2.672b. The god is Dionysus.

[11] That is, as exemplified by Isocrates in §6.

[12] This sentence is much in doubt. RW bracket λεῖπον (lacking), as an indication that the rest of the section is missing, and
comment: "The sense is presumably that μυθικοὶ ὕμνοι are in
both respects (content and style) on a lower level than φυσικοὶ
ὕμνοι." Cf. 1.5.6 for the elevated style of philosophical hymns.

1.7. ΠΕΡΙ ΓΕΝΕΑΛΟΓΙΚΩΝ

340   1. Περὶ δὲ τῶν γενεαλογικῶν ἐν μὲν ἤδη τοσοῦτον
εἴρηται, ὡς τοὺς αὐτοὺς ᾠήθησαν ἔνιοι τοῖς μυθικοῖς,
ἐν ᾧ καὶ τὴν διαφορὰν προσετίθεμεν· ἕτερον δὲ τοσοῦτον εἰρήσεται, ὡς σπανίως ἔστιν ὕμνον εὑρεῖν θεῶν,
ἐν ᾧ τὸ γενεαλογικὸν μόνον φέρεται, πλὴν εἴ τις ὑπο-
λαμβάνοι τὰς θεογονίας ὕμνους εἶναι τῶν θεῶν, ὡς
τὰ πολλὰ δὲ ἢ τοῖς μυθικοῖς παρεμπλέκονται ἢ ἄλλοις γε τῶν ὕμνων εἴδεσιν ἢ ἑνὶ ἢ καὶ πλείοσι. γραώ-
δες γὰρ καὶ δεινῶς μειρακιῶδες, ὕμνον Διὸς προελό-
μενον πραγματείαν, μόνον ⟨γονὰς⟩[1] ἐκλέξασθαι.[2]

  2. Ἀλλ' ἐπεὶ εὕρηται καὶ τοῦτο τὸ εἶδος τῶν ὕμνων
παρὰ τοῖς ἀρχαίοις, καὶ ἤδη τινὲς καὶ Διονύσου γονὰς ὕμνησαν, καὶ Ἀπόλλωνος ἕτεροι, καὶ Ἀλκαῖος
Ἡφαίστου καὶ πάλιν Ἑρμοῦ, καὶ τοῦτ' ἀποτετμήμεθα
τὸ μέρος. χρὴ τοίνυν, εἰ μὲν παρεμπεπλεγμένον εἴη
τοῖς ἄλλοις εἴδεσιν, εἰδέναι, ὅτι καὶ μῆκος προσίεται,
εἰ δὲ καθ' αὑτὸ εἴη τὸ μέρος, ὅτι βραχείας δεῖται δια-

1 suppl. Walz, RW
2 corr. Spengel: ἐκδέξασθαι codd.

1.7. GENEALOGICAL HYMNS

1. One point has already been made about genealogical hymns (*genealogikoi*), that some have considered them the same as mythical hymns; we there posited a distinction between them.[1] A second point needs to be made, that one can rarely find a hymn to the gods in which the genealogical element alone exists. For unless one considers theogonies to be hymns to the gods, genealogies are usually embedded in mythical hymns or in one or more of the other hymnic genres. It would be inane and utterly puerile[2] to propose a hymn to Zeus for treatment and then select only his birth.

2. But since this genre of hymn is found in archaic poets, and in fact some have sung of Dionysus' birth,[3] others of Apollo's,[4] and Alcaeus of Hephaestus' birth and again of Hermes',[5] we have differentiated this type as well. It is necessary, then, to understand that if it is embedded in other genres, it allows for lengthy treatment, but if it

---

[1] At 1.6.1–3 it was established that mythical hymns were more general, genealogical ones more specific.

[2] Literally, "like a garrulous old woman and an adolescent."

[3] Cf. Hes. *Theog.* 940–42 and *Hymn Hom. Dion.* 1–9.

[4] The most extensive example is *Hymn Hom. Ap.* 115–32.

[5] Nothing is known of Alcaeus' hymn to Hephaestus, but the opening stanza of his hymn to Hermes (Fr. 308 PLF) is preserved, in which he tells of Hermes' birth parents, Maia and Zeus.

51

τριβῆς· ἔτι δὲ ὡς ποιητῇ μὲν καθ᾽ αὑτὸ μόνον τὸ εἶδος χρήσιμον, συγγραφεῖ δὲ οὐδέποτε. ὁ μὲν γὰρ καὶ Χάριτας μαιουμένας καὶ Ὥρας ὑποδεχομένας καὶ τὰ τοιαῦτα πραγματεύεται, ὁ δ᾽ ἐπάναγκες ὅτι βραχύτατα ἐρεῖ.

3. Ἀρετὴ δ᾽ ἑρμηνείας ἐν τοῖς τοιούτοις καθαρότης καὶ τὸ ἀπροσκορές· γένοιτο δ᾽ ἂν ἐν ποιήσει ἐκ συμμετρίας τῶν περιφράσεων, ἐν δὲ τῇ συγγραφῇ ἐκ τῆς ποικιλίας τῶν κώλων. παρέσχετο δὲ τὴν μὲν ἐν ποιήσει ἀρετὴν Ἡσίοδος, καὶ γνοίη τις ἂν μᾶλλον, εἰ τοῖς Ὀρφέως παραθείη· τὴν δὲ ἐν τῇ συγγραφῇ πολλαχοῦ μὲν Πλάτων, πολλαχοῦ δὲ καὶ Ἡρόδοτος ἐν τοῖς Αἰγυπτιακοῖς.

exists by itself, it requires no more than a brief development. Furthermore, this genre by itself is useful only for a poet, never for a prose writer. For a poet can depict the Graces as midwives and the Hours as nurses, and the like, but a prose writer must necessarily be as brief as possible.

3. The stylistic virtue in such compositions is clarity (*katharotēs*) and avoidance of tedium. In poetry this can be achieved by the moderate use of periphrases, in prose by variety in clauses. Hesiod exhibits this virtue in poetry, as one can recognize all the more by comparing him with the Orphic poems.[6] Plato often exhibits this virtue in prose, as does Herodotus in his treatment of Egypt.[7]

---

[6] Only fragments remain of the theogonic poems attributed to the legendary Orpheus. The so-called Orphic Hymns contain little genealogical material.

[7] Herodotus, Book 2.

1.8. ΠΕΡΙ ΠΕΠΛΑΣΜΕΝΩΝ

1. Περὶ δὲ τῶν πεπλασμένων ταῦτα ἰστέον, πρῶτον
341 μὲν ὅτι οὐκ ἂν γένοιντο περὶ τοὺς περιφανεῖς τῶν
θεῶν ῥᾳδίως, καὶ ὧν αἱ γενέσεις καὶ δυνάμεις πρόδη-
λοι, ἀλλὰ περὶ τοὺς ἀφανεστέρους ὡς τὰ πολλὰ θεοὺς
καὶ δαίμονας, οἷον καὶ περὶ τὸν Ἔρωτα ὁ Πλάτων
ποτὲ μὲν ὡς πρὸ γῆς ἐγένετο, ποτὲ δὲ ὡς Ἀφροδίτης
ἐστὶ παῖς, πάλιν δὲ πεπλασμένος ὕστερον Πόρου καὶ
Πενίας, καὶ πάλιν [ὁ Παυσανίας],[1] ὅτι τῇ τέχνῃ τῇ
ἰατρικῇ ἐφέστηκεν ἡ δύναμις τοῦ Ἔρωτος, καὶ [Ἀρι-
στοφάνης][2] ὅτι συνάγει τὰ ἡμίτομα τῶν σωμάτων,
τούτους τοὺς ὕμνους ποικίλως σφόδρα πλάσας, τοὺς
μὲν περὶ φύσιν, τοὺς δὲ περὶ δύναμιν, τοὺς δὲ περὶ
γένος. 2. ἥκει καὶ αὕτη ἡ ἐξουσία παρὰ τῶν ποιητῶν
τοῖς συγγραφεῦσιν· Ἄρεως μὲν γὰρ θεράποντας Δεῖ-
μον καὶ Φόβον ἀναπλάττουσι, τοῦ δὲ Φόβου τὴν Φυ-
γὴν φίλην, καὶ τοῦ Θανάτου τὸν Ὕπνον ἀδελφόν· ἤδη

---

[1] secl. Nitsche, RW   [2] secl. Nitsche, RW

---

[1] Plato, *Symp.* 178b, where Phaedrus quotes from Hes.
Theog. 116–20. M. referred to the *Symposium* for some of these
examples at 1.2.7.

[2] *Phdr.* 242d, Socrates speaking.

[3] *Symp.* 203b, Socrates speaking.

δὲ καὶ ἡμεῖς τὸν Λόγον Διὸς ἀδελφὸν ἀνεπλάσαμεν, ὡς ἐν ἠθικῇ συνόψει.[3]

3. Ἃ τοίνυν χρὴ ἐν τοῖς πεπλασμένοις τῶν ὕμνων διορᾶν, ἔχοιτο ἂν λέγειν. φυλακτέον γὰρ πρῶτον μὲν μὴ ἀπηρτημένως ἀλλὰ συνεχῶς πλάττειν, εἴη δ' ἂν τὸ τοιοῦτο σωζόμενον, εἰ ἀπ' αὐτῶν <τῶν πραγμάτων>[4] λαμβάνοιτο ἡ πλάσις, καὶ μὴ ἀνακεχωρηκυῖα εἴη. ἔπειτα μὴ ἀηδῶς, ἀλλὰ στωμύλως καὶ γλαφυρῶς ἀναπλάττειν, οἷον Μούσας Μνημοσύνης παῖδας, ἢ ὅσα τοιαῦτα. 4. ἔνιαι γὰρ καὶ[5] ἀκοῦσαι ἀηδεῖς, οἷον ὅτι ἐκ τῆς κεφαλῆς τοῦ Διὸς ἀνέδραμεν ἡ Ἀθηνᾶ. μὴ γὰρ τοῦτο, εἰ καθ' ὑπόνοιαν εἴρηται καὶ πρὸς ἄλλο τι, ἔχει ὀρθῶς, ἄλλοτε δ'[6] ἀηδῶς πέπλασται. ἔπειτα δὲ πίστεις λαμβάνειν ἀπὸ τῶν ἀληθῶν, ἐν οἷς ἂν ψευδώμεθα, ὡς καὶ ἡμεῖς πεποιήκαμεν, πολλάκις δὲ καὶ ὁ Ὅμηρος.

5. Ἔτι δὲ καὶ τοὺς πεπλασμένους ὕμνους ἑαυτοῖς εἶναι συμφώνους, καὶ μὴ ἐναντιούμενα ἢ μαχόμενα ἐφέλκεσθαι, ὥσπερ ἐν ἐκείνῳ τῷ μύθῳ, ὅτι Ζεὺς πρὸ πάντων ἐγένετο καὶ θεῶν ἁπάντων ἐστὶ πατήρ, καὶ τὴν Θέμιν οὖσαν τοῦ Κρόνου τὸ παλαιὸν γυναῖκα

342

---

[3] συνόψει PZ: συνάψει coni. Jacobs, Bursian
[4] suppl. RW: ἀπὸ <τῶν> αὐτῶν Heeren
[5] RW: τοῦ P: τοι Bursian
[6] ἄλλοτε δ' Bursian: ἀλλ' ὅτε P: ἄλλως δ' RW

---

[10] The reference is obscure and no such synopsis (if the text is correct) is known. The association of Logos with Zeus is un-

1.8. FICTIVE HYMNS

1. The following points must be understood about fictive hymns (*peplasmenoi*). First, they cannot easily be composed for eminent gods and those whose genealogies and powers are obvious, but usually for lesser known gods and divinities (*daimones*). For example, Plato depicts Eros at one point as born before the earth existed,[1] at another point as Aphrodite's son,[2] and yet at a later point, resorting to fiction, as the son of Plenty and Poverty.[3] Then too, he says that Eros' power presides over the medical art,[4] and that the god unites the severed halves of our bodies.[5] He has contrived these hymns with great variety, whether they concern Eros' nature, power, or birth.[6] 2. This license too comes to prose writers from poets, for poets fashion Terror (Deimos) and Fear (Phobos) as the squires of Ares;[7] Flight (Phygē)[8] as the friend of Fear; and Sleep (Hypnos) as the brother of Death (Thanatos)[9]—and, in

---

[4] 186be. The insertions of Pausanias here (incorrectly for Eryximachus) and Aristophanes in the following clause are rightly deleted as intrusive glosses.   [5] *Symp.* 189d–91d, Aristophanes speaking.   [6] Agathon's speech treats Eros' nature, Eryximachus' his power, and Socrates' his birth.

[7] Cf. Hom. *Il.* 4.439–40 and 15.119. At Hes. *Theog.* 933–34, Deimos and Phobos are Ares' sons by Aphrodite; at Hom. *Il.* 13.298–300, Phobos is called Ares' son.

[8] RW cite Hom. *Il.* 9.2 as the closest parallel.

[9] Cf. Hom. *Il.* 14.231 and 16.672 (twins).

fact, I too have fashioned Logos as the brother of Zeus, as in an ethical synopsis.[10]

3. We must next discuss what to keep in mind regarding fictive hymns. First, care must be taken to make fictive hymns consistent and not discontinuous. This can be achieved if the invention is derived from ‹the subject matter›[11] itself and is not remote from it.[12] Secondly, the invention should not be distasteful, but urbane and refined, such as the Muses being the daughters of Memory (Mnemosynē), and the like. 4. Some fictions are disagreeable even to hear, such as Athena springing from the head of Zeus, for this is perhaps acceptable if spoken allegorically and with reference to something else, but in other circumstances such fiction is disagreeable. Thirdly, we must lend all our fictions credibility by drawing on actual occurrences, as I myself have done,[13] and as Homer often does.

5. Again, fictive hymns must be consistent within themselves and not bring in contradictory or conflicting details, as in that myth claiming that Zeus was born before everything and is the father of all the gods, yet he married Themis, who long before had been the wife of Cronus. For

doubtedly Stoic in origin, but nowhere else is he called Zeus' brother. Jacobs' emendation "as in an ethical connection" would imply an allegorical affinity. M. refers to other writings of his own at 1.3.5 (a hymn to Apollo) and below in §4. There are no such self-references in Treatise II.

11 This is added by RW, apparently from τὰ πράγματα in §7.

12 RW interpret "not remote from it" as "recondite."

13 Presumably in his piece on Logos and Zeus, mentioned in §2.

ἠγάγετο. εἰ μὲν γὰρ ἦν πρὸ πάντων καὶ πρὸ Θέμιδος· εἰ δ' ἦν πρὸ Διὸς Θέμις, οὐ πρὸ πάντων.

6. Ἔτι πρὸς τούτῳ φυλακτέον ἐν τοῖς πεπλασμένοις ὕμνοις τὸ μῆκος καὶ τὴν περιεργίαν. ἤδη γάρ τινες τῶν νεωτέρων, ἀναπλάσαντες δαίμονά τινα νέον Ζηλοτυπίαν, κρήδεμνον μὲν αὐτῇ Φθόνον προσέθεσαν, ζώνην δ' αὖ Ἔριν. καὶ μάλιστα ὁ Παυσανίας ἐπιφορὰς ἔχει πρὸς τὴν κατὰ μέρος ταύτην περιεργίαν. ἔστι δὲ †εντ . . . ουσαν†[7] ἀρχαῖον καὶ νέον ἐν ποιήσει μέν, μάλιστα δὲ ἐν συγγραφῇ.

7. Τὴν ἑρμηνείαν δὲ προσάξεις τοῖς τοιούτοις ὕμνοις πρὸς τὰ πράγματα ὁρῶν, εἰ μὲν ἀνθρώπινόν τι ἀναπλάττοις, ἀφελεστέραν καὶ κομψοτέραν, λέγω δὲ ἀνθρώπινα ὅσα οὐ παντάπασιν φρικώδη καὶ θεῖα, οἷον Πενίαν καὶ Ἀγρυπνίαν, καὶ ὅσα τοιαῦτα. εἰ δὲ ἀναπλάττοις θεῖα, οὕτω καὶ τὴν ἑρμηνείαν σεμνοτέραν προσάξεις. χρὴ δὲ εἰδέναι, ὅτι γονιμώτατος καὶ ἐπινοίας ἐστὶ σημεῖον ὁ τοιοῦτος ὕμνος.

[7] εντ ουσαν P: obel. RW: καὶ ἑνῶσαι coni. Jacobs, Walz, Spengel

if he existed before everything, then he existed before
Themis, but if Themis existed before Zeus, then he did
not exist before everything.

6. Again, in fictive hymns one must guard against
excessive length and overelaboration. Some recent authors[14] have in fact created a new divinity called Jealousy
(Zēlotypia), and then given her Envy (Phthonos) as a veil
and Strife (Eris) as a sash. Pausanias[15] above all has a
propensity toward this overelaboration of parts. And there
is . . . ancient and new in poetry, but especially in prose.[16]

7. In such fictive hymns you should adopt a style with
a view to your subject matter. If your invention concerns
something human, the style should be simpler and more
refined. By "human subjects" I mean things not completely frightening or divine, but inventions like Poverty
(Penia), Insomnia (Agrypnia), and the like. If, however,
you are inventing divine subjects, then you should employ
a more dignified style. You should be aware that this sort
of hymn is the most creative[17] and is an indication of in-
ventiveness.

[14] These remain unknown.

[15] A sophist from Caesarea in Cappadocia (2nd c. AD). A brief
account of his declamation style is given at Philostr. VS 2.13.

[16] Jacobs, followed by Walz and Spengel, proposed the conjecture καὶ ἑνῶσαι: "it is possible to unite the ancient and new in
poetry," but it was rejected by Bursian and RW.

[17] That is, it allows the greatest creativity. RW translate
γονιμώτατος as "most powerful."

1.9. ΠΕΡΙ ΑΠΕΥΚΤΙΚΩΝ ΚΑΙ
ΠΡΟΣΕΥΚΤΙΚΩΝ

1. Οἱ δὲ ἀπευκτικοὶ καὶ προσευκτικοὶ ὕμνοι σχεδὸν μέν, ὥσπερ ἐφάσκομεν, πᾶσι τοῖς προειρημένοις εἰσὶν ἀναπεπλεγμένοι, ἢ τοῖς γε πλείστοις αὐτῶν. ἅπαντες γὰρ ἀνυμνοῦντες τοὺς θεοὺς εἰς εὐχὰς ἐγκλείουσι τοὺς λόγους. ἤδη δέ τινες καὶ ἀποτόμως καθ' αὑτοὺς γεγόνασιν, ἀπευκτικὸς μὲν ὁ τοιοῦτος·

Ζεῦ κύδιστε μέγιστε, κελαινεφές, αἰθέρι ναίων,
μὴ πρὶν ἐπ' ἠέλιον δῦναι καὶ ἐπὶ κνέφας ἐλθεῖν·

προσευκτικὸς δέ·

343   κλῦθί μευ αἰγιόχοιο Διὸς τέκος, ἥτε μοι αἰεὶ
ἐν πάντεσσι πόνοισι παρίστασαι·

καὶ παρὰ Πλάτωνι, "ὦ φίλε Πὰν" καὶ ὅσα ἐν τῷ Φαίδρῳ εὔχεται. 2. δεῖ δὲ τοὺς τοιούτους ὕμνους μὴ κατακορεῖς εἶναι. τὰς μὲν γὰρ εὐχὰς δικαίας εἶναι χρή, καὶ [ἀπευχὰς][1] δικαίας οὔσας καὶ ἁπλᾶς εἶναι δεῖ, τὸ δεῖνα γενέσθαι, εἶναι δὲ [ἁπλᾶς][2] καὶ βραχείας, ἔτι δὲ

---

[1] secl. Bursian, RW   [2] secl. Walz, Spengel, RW

---

[1] Cf. 1.2.1 and 8.   [2] ἐγκλείουσι here apparently = κατακλείουσι (cf. [DH] 5.2). Here and in the following section,

1.9. DEPRECATORY AND
PRECATORY HYMNS

1. Hymns that pray against something (*apeuktikoi*) or for something (*proseuktikoi*) are, as we said,[1] embedded in nearly all—or at least most—of the aforementioned types, for all who hymn the gods conclude their speeches with prayers.[2] To be sure, some are completely self-contained, like this deprecatory example:[3]

> Zeus, most glorious, greatest one, lord of dark clouds,
>   dwelling in the sky,
> do not let the sun go down nor darkness come over
>   us before . . .

or like this precatory one:[4]

> Hear me, daughter of aegis-bearing Zeus, you who
>   always
> stand by me in all my toils . . .

and in Plato's *Phaedrus*, the prayer that begins with "O dear Pan."[5] 2. Hymns such as these should not be tediously long, for prayers must be just and, being just, should also be straightforward—that such and such may happen—and also be brief. Besides, the point is not to instruct the gods,

M. conflates hymns (ὕμνοι) and prayers (εὐχαί). Of M.'s treatments, only the sendoff hymn (1.4) ends with a prayer.

[3] Hom. *Il.* 2.412–13 (Agamemnon speaking).

[4] Hom. *Il.* 10.278–79 (Odysseus speaking).

[5] 279bc, also cited at 1.2.8.

οὐ διδάσκειν τοὺς θεούς, ἀλλ' αἰτεῖν ἅπερ ἀκριβῶς
ἴσασιν. ἔτι δὲ καὶ πάσας εὐχὰς καὶ συγγραφέων
ἐπιὼν τὰς αἰτήσεις εἰς τοὺς πολίτας³ βραχείας οὔσας
εὑρήσεις. 3. ἤδη δὲ καὶ εἰς τοὺς πολιτικοὺς τὸ μέρος
τοῦτο τῶν ὕμνων κατῆλθε, πλήν γε ὡς ἐπιμαρτυρίας·
τὸ γὰρ "πρῶτον μὲν ὦ ἄνδρες Ἀθηναῖοι, τοῖς θεοῖς
εὔχομαι" καὶ τὰ ἑξῆς, καὶ τὸ "καλῶ δὲ τὸν Ἀπόλλω
τὸν Πύθιον," τῶν εὐκτικῶν καὶ ἀπευκτικῶν ὕμνων μετ-
είληφεν ἴχνη.

4. Οὐκ ἀγνοῶ δὲ ὅτι ἀπορητικούς τινες τεθείκασι
καὶ διαπορητικοὺς καθ' ἕκαστον τῶν μερῶν, οἷον δι-
ηπόρησαν περὶ γενεαλογίαν, περὶ Ἔρωτος εὐθύς, εἴτε
ἐκ χάους ἐγένετο, εἴτε ἐξ Ἀφροδίτης, καὶ πολλὰ τοιαῦτα. καὶ πάλιν περὶ δύναμιν, εἴτε ἀνθρώπιναι πράξεις καὶ διοικήσεις, εἴτε θεῖαι. καὶ συνορᾷς δὴ τοῦτο
τὸ εἶδος ὅ φημι πᾶν, ἀλλὰ τὸν τοιοῦτον ὕμνον τῷ μὲν
σχήματι διαφέρειν φημί, τῇ δὲ φύσει τὸν αὐτὸν εἶναι
ἐκείνων ἑκάστῳ, ὥσπερ καὶ τὴν Τύχην Σοφοκλῆς
ὕμνησε διαπορῶν.

---

³ εἰς τοὺς πολίτας: secl. Kroll, RW.

---

6 Cf. the injunction at Matt. 6:7–8: "When you are praying, do
not heap up empty phrases as the Gentiles do . . . Do not be like
them, for your Father knows what you need before you ask him."
7 The following two examples from Demosthenes illustrate
prayers to the gods and appeals to the audience. RW bracket "to
their citizens." 8 Dem. *Or.* 18.1. 9 Dem. *Or.* 18.141.
10 The first example, at the beginning of Demosthenes'
speech, is precatory and appeals to the audience to give him a fair
hearing. The second example may exhibit traces of deprecatory

but to ask for what they already know full well.[6] Further-more, if you survey all the prayers and appeals made by prose writers to their citizens,[7] you will find that they are brief. 3. This type of hymn has actually entered into public speeches, but in the form of attestations. The two passages "First of all, O men of Athens, I pray to the gods . . ."[8] and "I call upon Pythian Apollo"[9] bear traces of precatory and deprecatory hymns.[10]

4. I am aware that some have proposed hymns that are dubitative (*aporētikoi*) and full of doubts (*diaporētikoi*) for each of these types. For example, writers have expressed doubts about genealogies. Eros provides a ready example, whether he was born from Chaos or from Aphrodite, and so on.[11] Likewise, concerning a god's power, whether his deeds and domains are human or divine. No doubt you fully grasp my point.[12] I maintain, however, that although such hymns[13] differ in form, by their nature they are the same as each of those other types. Thus, Sophocles expressed doubts in his Hymn to Fortune.[14]

style: "if I falsely charge him, may the gods deprive me of every-thing good."   [11] Schol. Ap. Rhod. 3.26b states that for Hesiod Eros was the son of Chaos; for Apollonius he was the son of Aphrodite; for Sappho he was the son of Earth and Sky; for Simonides he was the son of Aphrodite and Ares; for Ibycus he was the son of Aphrodite and Hephaestus. Cf. 1.8.1 for further speculation about Eros' genealogy.   [12] M. seems here to be making a distinction (as at 1.1.4 and 1.6.3) between a specific element of hymns (expressions of doubt concerning some aspect of the god's nature) and the generic type of hymn in which it occurs.

[13] That is, so-called aporetic hymns.

[14] Soph., Fr. 740 N²; 809 Pearson. Since this is the only reference to this hymn and does not cite any lines, we cannot know what aspect of Fortune was in doubt.

5. Ἔφην δὲ γενέσθαι τινὰς ὕμνους ἢ[4] ἐξ ὁμοίου
⟨ἐκ⟩[4] τούτων ἁπάντων ἢ τῶν πλείστων συντεθέντας,[4]
οἵπερ εἰσὶ καὶ τελειότατοι ἔπαινοι καὶ μάλιστα τοῖς
συγγραφεῦσι πρέποντες· τῷ μὲν γὰρ ποιητῇ ἐξαρκεῖ
καὶ μέρος τι ἀπολαβόντι καὶ κατακοσμήσαντι τῇ ποι-
ητικῇ κατασκευῇ πεπαῦσθαι, ὁ δὲ συγγραφεὺς πειρά-
σεται διὰ πάντων ἐλθεῖν. χαριέστατον δὲ τὸ τοιοῦτον
μέρος παρέσχηται ἐν τοῖς Μαντευτοῖς Ἀριστείδης.
οὗτος γὰρ τὸν Ἀσκληπιὸν καὶ τὴν Ὑγίειαν συγγέ-
γραφεν †οὐκέτι μοι ὥς†[5] ἐπαίνων ἀνθρωπίνην περι-
έργειαν ἔχοντας.

6. Τὸ μὲν δὴ περὶ τῶν εἰς τοὺς θεοὺς βιβλίον τέλος
εἴληφεν ἡμῖν, ἐξ ὧν ἡγούμεθα καὶ ποιητὰς καὶ συγ-
γραφέας καὶ ῥήτορας πάντας ἀνυμνεῖν θεοὺς ἐντέ-
χνως, καὶ ὅπως καὶ ἐν ὁποίοις καιροῖς. ἐφεξῆς δ' ἂν
εἴη περὶ χώρας καὶ πόλεως ἐπαίνων εἰπεῖν· οὕτως γὰρ
καὶ εἰς τοὺς τόμους ἀναγωγὴ[6] γεγένηται. καὶ πρῶτον
περὶ τῶν τῆς χώρας ἐγκωμίων, οὐχ ὡς ἀποτόμως τινὸς ἐγκωμιάσαντος χώραν ἄνευ πόλεως, ἀλλ' ἐν τοῖς
τῶν πόλεων ἐγκωμίοις καὶ τῶν περὶ χώρας ἐπαίνων
παραλαμβανομένων.

4 ἢ . . . ⟨ἐκ⟩ . . . συντεθέντας coni. Bursian praeeunte Walz:
καὶ ἐξ ὁμοίου τούτων ἁπάντων ἢ τῶν πλείστων συντεθέντων
codd.   5 obel. Bursian, RW   6 Bursian, RW: ἀνάγκη P

15 Cf. 1.2.6.   16 I have adopted Bursian's emendations
for the manuscripts' "similarly there exist some hymns with all or
most of these types combined."

5. I have said[15] that there exist some hymns similarly composed of all or most of these types,[16] such being the most complete encomia and the most appropriate for prose writers. For a poet it is sufficient to select some portion, elaborate it with poetic adornment, and then be done, whereas the prose writer should attempt to cover them all. Aristides has provided the most elegant example of such a type in his "Prophetic"[17] speeches, for he wrote about Asclepius and Health (Hygieia)[18] . . . they . . . no longer having an exposition of praises on a human level (?).[19]

6. This marks the end of our book on hymns to the gods, by means of which I think that poets, prose writers, and orators can all skillfully hymn the gods, showing both how to do so and under what circumstances. Next we shall discuss the praise of countries and cities, for that is how the division into volumes[20] has been set up. First comes the praise of countries, not because anyone has simply praised a country without including its city, but because praise of a country is included in the praise of cities.

[17] "Evidently the title of a collection of speeches suggested by dreams or prophecy: 38 (*Asclepiades*), 41 (*Dionysus*), 42 (*Asclepius*) were probably parts of this" (RW).

[18] This perhaps refers to *Or.* 42. No hymn to Hygieia is extant.

[19] No emendations have provided adequate sense here. RW conclude, "This corrupt sentence must contain a laudatory account of Aristides' achievement in these hymns; it is his 'workmanship' which is 'superhuman.'"

[20] Volume (*tomos*) is presumably another term for book (*biblion*). In this treatise, "Book I" comprises sections 1–9; "Book II," sections 10–15; "Book III" (incomplete), section 16.

1.10. ΠΩΣ ΧΡΗ ΧΩΡΑΝ ΕΠΑΙΝΕΙΝ

1. Ἔπαινος μὲν χώρας, ὡς ἀνωτάτω διελέσθαι, διττός, ἢ κατὰ φύσιν ἢ κατὰ θέσιν. ἢ γὰρ πῶς κεῖται ἐξετάσαντες ἀξίαν αὐτὴν ἐπαίνου ἀποφαίνομεν, ἢ ὅπως πέφυκε. θέσιν τοίνυν χώρας δοκιμάζομέν τε καὶ κρίνομεν ὅπως κεῖται πρὸς γῆν ἢ πρὸς θάλατταν ἢ πρὸς οὐρανόν· πρὸς μὲν γῆν, εἰ μεσόγειος εἴη καὶ πλέον ἢ ἔλαττον θαλάττης ἀπέχουσα, ἢ ἐπιθαλαττίδιος καὶ ἐπ᾽ αἰγιαλοῖς· πρὸς δὲ θάλατταν, εἰ νῆσος ἢ νήσῳ ἐοικυῖα· πρὸς δὲ οὐρανόν, εἰ ἐν δυσμαῖς, ἢ ἐν ἀνατολαῖς, ἢ ἐν μεσημβρίᾳ, ἢ ἐν ἄρκτῳ, ἢ ἐν τῷ μέσῳ τούτων. 2. ἤδη δέ τινες καὶ κατ᾽ αὐτοὺς τοὺς ἀστέρας τὴν θέσιν ὡρίσαντο, ὥσπερ οἱ ποιηταί, ὑπὸ Πλειάδας ἢ Ὑάδας, ἢ ὑπὸ Ἀρκτοῦρον ἀνίσχοντα, ἢ ὑπὸ Ἕσπερον. κατὰ γὰρ τοὺς τρεῖς κανόνας θέσιν χώρας δοκιμάζομεν· ἐν γὰρ τῷ περὶ οὐρανοῦ καὶ τὸ τῶν ὡρῶν συνείληπται.

3. Τὴν δὲ φύσιν τῆς χώρας δοκιμάζομεν ἁπάσης

---

[1] The word χώρα designates the country, land, territory, or countryside surrounding a city.

[BOOK 2]

1.10. HOW TO PRAISE A COUNTRY

1. Praise of a country,[1] in the most general analysis, has two aspects, nature and location, for we demonstrate its worthiness for praise by examining either its situation or its nature. We assess and evaluate the location of a country by its situation with respect to land, sea, or sky. With respect to the land, whether it is inland and how far distant from the sea, or coastal and situated on the shore. With respect to the sea, whether it is an island or a peninsula. And with respect to the sky, whether it is in the west or east, south or north, or in the middle. 2. Some writers, like the poets, have defined location according to the stars, as being beneath the Pleiades or Hyades,[2] or under rising Arcturus,[3] or under Hesperus.[4] These three[5] are the criteria by which we evaluate the location of a country, since the topic of seasons is included in that of the sky.

3. We assess the nature of a country as a whole on the

[2] Both constellations indicate stormy weather and perhaps a northern location.

[3] The heliacal rising of the Bear (Ursa Major) is mid-September; its geographical reference would be north.

[4] Hesperus, the evening star, rises in the west.

[5] That is, land, sea, and sky.

345 ἐκ τῶν ἐξ τόπων τούτων, ἢ γὰρ ὀρεινή τίς ἐστιν ἢ
πεδινή, ἢ ξηρὰ καὶ ἄνυδρος ἢ λιπαρὰ καὶ εὔυδρος,
καὶ ἢ εὔφορος καὶ πολυφόρος ἢ ἄφορος καὶ δύσφορος. ἀπὸ γὰρ τούτων χώρας ἀρετὴν καὶ κακίαν διαγι-
νώσκομεν. ἵνα δέ σοι τῶν θεωρημάτων τούτων ἀπάν-
των παραδείγματα ὑπάρχῃ, ἑκάστου ἐκθήσομαι, δύο
εἰπὼν πρότερον πρὸς ἅττα[1] κεφάλαια ἀνάγοντας ἐπαινεῖν δεῖ, πρὸς ἡδονὴν ἢ πρὸς ὠφέλειαν· 4. πρὸς γὰρ
ταῦτα τὰ κεφάλαια ὁρῶντα δεῖ τοὺς περὶ χώραν ἐπαίνους ποιεῖσθαι. οἷον εἰ μεσόγειον ἐπαινοίης, πρὸς μὲν
ἡδονήν, ὅτι τῶν ἀπὸ τῆς ἠπείρου ἀγαθῶν βεβαίως
ἀπόλαυσις καὶ τέρψις γίνεται, ὁρῶν πεδία περιλαμ-
βανόντων καὶ τῶν πεδίων ληΐοις κατεστεμμένων·
πρὸς δὲ ὠφέλειαν, διότι οἱ καρποί τε γνησιώτεροι ἀπὸ
τῆς γῆς ἅτ' οὐ κλυζομένης καὶ τῶν ἀπὸ τῆς θαλάττης
ταραχῶν ἀπεχούσης.

5. Εἰ δὲ ἐπιθαλάττιον ἐπαινοίης, ὅτι ὅσα καὶ ἐν γῇ
καὶ ἐν θαλάττῃ ἡδέα καὶ ὠφέλιμα, συνείληφεν ἡ
χώρα. εἰ δὲ νῆσον ἐπαινοίης, καὶ πρὸς ἡδονὴν καὶ
πρὸς ὠφέλειαν, ὥσπερ Ἀριστείδης ἐν τῷ Νησιωτικῷ.
εἰ δὲ νήσῳ ἐοικυῖαν, ἅ τε περὶ Τύρου Ἀριστόβουλος
ἱστόρησε καὶ περὶ Κυζίκου Ἀριστείδης ἐν τῷ πρὸς

---

[1] ἅττα tent. Bursian: ἃ τὰ codd.: τὰ κεφάλαια secl. RW

basis of the following six topics: whether it is mountainous
or level; whether it is dry and arid or lush and wet; and
whether it is fertile and productive or barren and unproductive. It is on the basis of these features that we determine the good and bad qualities of a country. I shall provide you with examples for each of these considerations,
but will first state the two general topics[6] to which we must
refer in our praise, namely pleasure and utility, 4. for these
are the main topics to keep in mind when composing
praise of a country. For example, when praising an inland
country, you should say with respect to pleasure that it has
the secure use and enjoyment of the blessings of the mainland, with mountains surrounding plains which are themselves crowned with grain. With respect to utility, say that
the land produces crops that are more true to kind[7] because it is not flooded with saltwater and is distant from
storms off the sea.

5. If you praise a country on the coast, say that it has at
its disposal all the pleasant and useful aspects of both land
and sea. If you praise an island, do so with respect to both
pleasure and utility, as Aristides does in his "Island
Speech."[8] If it is a peninsula, look to what Aristobulus[9]
recounts concerning Tyre and Aristides about Cyzicus in

[6] In this treatise, κεφάλαια refer to abstract topics like utility
or pleasure. In the second treatise, κεφάλαια refer to sections of
a speech containing related rhetorical topics.

[7] γνήσιος (genuine, legitimate) usually applies to offspring.
Nowhere else is it used of crops.

[8] No speech of this title exists.

[9] Aristobulus of Cassandreia (4th c. BC) accompanied Alexander on his campaigns. His description of Tyre is not extant.

Κυζικηνούς, καὶ Ξενοφῶν ἐν τοῖς Πόροις περὶ τῆς
Ἀττικῆς.

6. Καὶ μὴν εἰ μὲν ἀνατολικὴ εἴη, ὅτι πρώτη αὕτη
ἡλίῳ ἐντυγχάνει, καὶ ἡγεμών ἐστι φωτὸς ἄλλαις, εἰ
δὲ δυτικὴ εἴη, ὅτι ὥσπερ κορωνὶς ἐπίκειται, παραπέμ-
πουσα τὸν θεόν· εἰ δὲ μεσημβρινή, ὅτι ὥσπερ ἐπὶ
παρατάξεως τοῦ οὐρανοῦ τὸ μέσον κατείληφεν· εἰ δὲ
ἀρκτική, ὅτι τὸ ὑψηλότατον τῆς γῆς καὶ ὑπόβορρον
ὥσπερ ἀκρόπολις κατέχει· εἰ δὲ τὸ μεσαίτατον, ὃ δὴ
περὶ τῆς Ἀττικῆς καὶ τῆς Ἑλλάδος λέγουσιν, ὅτι περὶ
αὐτὴν ἡ πᾶσα γῆ κυκλεῖται, καὶ ὥραις[2] ἐστὶν εὔκρα-
τος.

7. Ἔτι τοίνυν εἰ μὲν ὀρεινὴ εἴη, ὅτι ἀνδρὶ ἐρρωμένῳ
346 ἔοικε νεύροις διειλημμένῳ· εἰ δὲ πεδινή, ὅτι εὔτακτός
ἐστι καὶ οὐκ ἀνώμαλος οὐδ᾽ ὀστώδης. καὶ μὴν εἰ μὲν
ξηρὰ καὶ ἄνυδρος, ὅτι διάπυρός ἐστι κατὰ τὸν περὶ
τοῦ αἰθέρος λόγον καὶ τοῦ οὐρανοῦ· πυρώδης γὰρ ὁ
οὐρανὸς καὶ ἐπίξηρος· εἰ δὲ λιπαρὰ καὶ εὔυδρος, καὶ
πρὸς τὴν ἡδονὴν καὶ πρὸς τὴν ὠφέλειαν εὐφυής. καὶ
εἰ μὲν πάμφορος, ὅτι γυναικὶ εὔπαιδι ἔοικεν· εἰ δὲ
ἄφορός τε καὶ δύσφορος, ὅτι φιλοσοφεῖν τε καὶ καρ-
τερεῖν διδάσκουσα.

[2] RW: ὡραία codd.

his speech "To the Cyzicenes,"[10] and what Xenophon says about Attica in his "Ways and Means."[11]

6. Furthermore, if it is located in the east, say that it is the first land to greet the sun and that it guides its light to other lands; if in the west, that it is set there like a coronis mark,[12] sending the Sun on his way; if in the south, that it holds the middle station, so to speak, in the battle line of heaven; and if in the north, that it occupies the highest and northernmost part of the earth, like an acropolis; and if in the middlemost point, as they say is true of Attica and Hellas, that the whole earth revolves around it and that it is well-tempered in its seasons.

7. Then too, if it is mountainous, say that it is like a robust man conspicuous for his muscles; if flat, that it is well ordered and neither uneven nor bony.[13] If it is dry and arid, say that it is fiery in the manner of the ether and the sky, for the sky is hot and dry; if it is lush and wet, that it is endowed by nature for both pleasure and utility. If it bears all kinds of crops, say that it is like a woman with many children; if it is barren and stinting, that it teaches philosophy and endurance.

[10] *Or.* 27. Cyzicus (the modern Kapıdağ Peninsula) is located in the Propontis (Sea of Marmara).

[11] The first chapter, which bears a close resemblance to M.'s analysis, describes the advantages of Attica's land, including its crops, growing seasons, and central location.

[12] The symbol marking the end of a text in papyri.

[13] All three terms can apply to a human being (orderly, not erratic, not bony) and continue the metaphorical comparison of lands and human bodies.

8. Ἐκεῖνό γε μὴν ἰστέον, ὅτι τῶν ἐγκωμίων τὰ μέν ἐστιν ἔνδοξα, τὰ δὲ ἄδοξα,[3] τὰ δὲ ἀμφίδοξα, τὰ δὲ παράδοξα. ἔνδοξα μὲν τὰ περὶ ἀγαθῶν ὁμολογουμένων, οἷον θεοῦ ἢ ἄλλου τινὸς ἀγαθοῦ φανεροῦ· ἄδοξα δὲ τὰ περὶ δαιμόνων καὶ κακοῦ φανεροῦ·[4] ἀμφίδοξα δὲ ὅσα πῆ μὲν ἔνδοξά ἐστι, πῆ δὲ ἄδοξα, ὃ ἐν τοῖς Παναθηναϊκοῖς εὑρίσκεται καὶ Ἰσοκράτους καὶ Ἀριστείδου· τὰ μὲν γάρ ἐστιν ἐπαινετά, τὰ δὲ ψεκτά, ὑπὲρ ὧν ἀπολογοῦνται· παράδοξα δὲ οἷον Ἀλκιδάμαντος τὸ τοῦ Θανάτου ἐγκώμιον, ἢ τὸ τῆς Πενίας Πρωτέως τοῦ κυνός.

9. Ἐνέταξα δὲ τὸ θεώρημα, ἐπειδὴ ἀφόρους καὶ δυσφόρους χώρας, καὶ τὰς ἀνύδρους καὶ ψαμμώδεις, ὅπως ἐπαινεῖν χρὴ ὑπέδειξα. ὅτι γὰρ τῶν τοιούτων [καὶ][5] παραδόξων καὶ ἀπολογίαν ἐξευρίσκειν ἔστιν, εἰς ἐγκώμιον ἐξαρκεῖ. χώρας μὲν ἀπὸ τούτων ἐγκωμιαστέον, πόλεις δὲ ἐξ ὧν δεῖ ἐπαινεῖν μετὰ ταῦτα ὑποδεικτέον, ἵνα ἡμῖν κατὰ τὴν τομὴν προΐῃ τὸ σύνταγμα.

---

[3] τὰ δὲ ἄδοξα secl. Heeren, Bursian, RW
[4] ἄδοξα δὲ τὰ περὶ δαιμόνων καὶ κακοῦ φανεροῦ secl. RW praeeunte Bursian
[5] secl. Bursian

8. You must also keep in mind that encomia can be classified as "worthy," "unworthy,"[14] "ambiguous," and "paradoxical." Worthy encomia involve undisputed goods, such as a god or some other manifestly good thing; unworthy encomia involve divinities and obvious evil.[15] Ambiguous encomia involve subjects that are worthy in some respects, unworthy in others, as are found in the Panathenaic orations of Isocrates and Aristides, for some elements therein deserve praise, others blame, and for the latter they offer a defense. Paradoxical is, for example, Alcidamas' encomium of Death[16] or the Cynic Proteus' praise of Poverty.[17]

9. I have included this consideration here, because I had indicated how to praise barren and unproductive countries, as well as ones that are arid and sandy. For the purposes of an encomium, it is sufficient if one can devise a defense for such paradoxical subjects. These then are the topics for praising countries. Next we must point out topics for praising cities, so that our treatise may progress according to its scheme.

[14] Heeren (followed by Bursian and RW) bracketed the "unworthy" category.

[15] Bursian conjectured that this clause was a Christian interpolation, on the grounds that "divinities" were "demons." RW bracketed it, but there are many "unworthy" *daimones* in Hesiod and Homer.

[16] A fourth-century rhetorician, opponent of Isocrates. This is the only mention of his encomium of Death.

[17] No writings are extant from Peregrinus Proteus, the Cynic philosopher who immolated himself at Olympia in 167 AD.

1.11. ΠΩΣ ΧΡΗ ΠΟΛΕΙΣ ΕΠΑΙΝΕΙΝ

1. Οἱ τοίνυν περὶ τὰς πόλεις ἔπαινοι μικτοί εἰσιν ἀπὸ κεφαλαίων τῶν περὶ χώρας εἰρημένων καὶ τῶν περὶ ἀνθρώπους. ἐκ μὲν γὰρ τῶν περὶ χώρας τὴν θέσιν ληπτέον, ἐκ δὲ τῶν περὶ ἀνθρώπους τὸ γένος, τὰς πράξεις, τὰς ἐπιτηδεύσεις· ἀπὸ γὰρ τούτων τὰς πόλεις ἐγκωμιάζομεν. ὅπως δὲ τῶν κεφαλαίων τούτων ἕκαστον ἐργαζόμεθα, ἐγὼ διδάξω καὶ φράσω.

2. Θέσιν πόλεως δοκιμάζομεν κατὰ τοὺς ἄνω τόπους[1] τοὺς εἰρημένους καὶ καθ᾽ ἑτέρους πλείονας, ἢ πρὸς οὐρανὸν καὶ ὥρας, ἢ πρὸς ἤπειρον, ἢ πρὸς θάλατταν, ἢ πρὸς τὴν χώραν ἐν ᾗ κεῖται, ἢ πρὸς τὰς περιοίκους χώρας καὶ πόλεις, ἢ πρὸς ὄρη, ἢ πρὸς πεδία. (τὸ γὰρ εὔυδρον εἶναι τὴν πόλιν ἢ ποταμοῖς περιειλῆφθαι ἔφην τῶν περὶ χώραν εἶναι.) αὐτῶν δὲ τούτων ἕκαστον καὶ πρὸς ἡδονὴν καὶ ὠφέλειαν κατὰ τὴν ἄνω γεγονυῖαν διαίρεσιν. 3. χρὴ δὲ καὶ καθ᾽ ἕκαστον τούτων ‹παραδείγματα ἐκθέσθαι πρὸς›[2] τὸ εὐμαθέστερον καὶ σαφέστερον γενέσθαι τὸ σύνταγμα. τὴν γὰρ θέσιν πρῶτον ἔφην κατὰ τὸν οὐρανὸν καὶ κατὰ τὰς ὥρας δεῖν θεωρεῖν. θεωρεῖται δὲ ἢ κατὰ ψύ-

---

[1] τόπους Bursian: τρόπους codd.
[2] lacunam suppl. Bursian

1.11. HOW TO PRAISE CITIES

1. The praise of cities takes the topics (*kephalaia*) we discussed about countries and combines them with those pertaining to people. Accordingly, we should select location from the topics concerning countries, but origin, deeds, and activities from the topics pertaining to people—these are what we praise cities for. I shall offer instructions and show how we can develop each of these topics.

2. We assess a city's location on the basis of the topics mentioned above[1] and on others as well, including its relationship to the sky and the seasons, to the mainland or sea, to the territory in which it lies, to neighboring countries and cities, to mountains or plains. (I have mentioned that a city's having abundant water or being surrounded by rivers is included in the attributes of a country.)[2] Furthermore, each of these should be treated with respect to pleasure and utility, according to our previous analysis.[3]

3. For each of these we must give examples to make our treatise clearer and more easily understood. I said that we must first consider a city's location with respect to the sky and its seasons. These considerations include cold or heat,

[1] At 1.10.1–2 M. discussed a country's relationship to the mainland, sea, and sky. [2] M. mentioned abundant water at 1.10.3, but not specifically rivers.

[3] Cf. 1.10.3–7.

ξιν ἢ κατὰ θάλψιν ἢ κατ' ἀχλὺν ἢ κατὰ καθαρότητα
ἢ κατὰ εὐαρμοστίαν πασῶν τῶν ὡρῶν. εἰ γάρ τις
κατὰ τὸν οὐρανὸν δοκιμάσει, γίγνεται θέσις πόλεως
ἢ κατὰ ταῦτα πάντα ἢ κατὰ τούτων τὰ πλεῖστα ἢ
ἔνια.

4. Ἂν μὲν οὖν περιῇ δεικνύειν τὴν πόλιν, ἣν ἐγκωμιάζομεν, κατὰ πάντα ταῦτα εὔθετον οὖσαν, θαυμα-
στὸν γίνεται τὸ χρῆμα καὶ πλείους αἱ ἀφορμαί. εἰ δὲ
μή, τὰ πλεῖστα τούτων πειρᾶσθαι δεῖ προσόντα αὐτῇ
ἀποδεικνύναι· εἰ δὲ μὴ τὰ πλεῖστα, ἀλλὰ τὰ ἰσχυρό-
τατα καὶ τὰ μέγιστα. εἰ δὲ παντάπασιν ἄμοιρος εἴη
ἡ πόλις ἐγκωμίων κατὰ τὴν θέσιν (ὅπερ σπανιώτατόν
ἐστιν· εὑρήσομεν γὰρ ἢ ἐν ψυχροῖς τόποις οὖσαν ἢ
ἐν θερμοῖς ἢ ἐν εὐαρμοστοῖς παρὰ τὴν κρᾶσιν τῶν
ὡρῶν), εἰ δέ τινες τὴν Ἄσκρην οἰκοῖεν, ἐχρῆν αὐτὸ
τοῦτο εἰς ἐγκώμιον λαμβάνειν,[3] [εἰ δ' αὖ ἄφορός τε
καὶ δύσφορος, ἐχρῆν αὐτὸ τοῦτο εἰς ἐγκώμιον λαμβά-
νειν],[4] ὅτι φιλοσοφεῖν ἀνάγκη τοὺς ἐνοικοῦντας καὶ
καρτερικοὺς εἶναι.

5. Κατὰ τὸν αὐτὸν δὲ ὅρον, εἰ μὲν θερμότερος εἴη
ὁ τόπος, τὰ ἐν τοῖς ψυχροῖς κακὰ λεκτέον· εἰ δὲ ψυ-
χρότερος, τὰ ἐν τοῖς θερμοτέροις. ἄριστα δὲ κεκραμέ-
νας χρὴ νομίζειν τὰς ἱκανὸν χρόνον μέρει ἑκάστῳ
παραμενούσας. αὐτῶν δὲ τῶν ὡρῶν αἱ μὲν ἐπὶ τὸ μᾶλ-

3 εἰ δέ τινες . . . λαμβάνειν MmW: om. PZ: secl. Bursian
4 secl. RW: om. MmW

cloudiness or clearness, or the harmonious balance of all its seasons. If one is going to assess a city with respect to the sky, its situation depends on all, most, or some of these considerations.

4. If we can show that the city we are praising is well situated with respect to all those factors, we have a marvelous subject and numerous starting points (*aphormai*). But if not, we must try to demonstrate that the city has most of them, and if not most, then the most compelling and important ones. If the city's location should be completely devoid of things to praise (which is extremely rare, since we are likely to find that the city is located in a cold place, or hot one, or temperate one with a mixture of seasons)— if, in a word, it is Ascra[4] that the people live in—then we must incorporate that very thing into our praise on the grounds that the inhabitants are thereby compelled to be philosophical and tough.[5]

5. By the same token, if the place is pretty hot, bring up the disadvantages of cold places; if it is pretty cold, bring up those of hot places. We should consider those cities to be most temperate that remain in each state[6] for a satisfactory length of time. Of the seasons themselves,

[4] Hesiod's hometown in Boeotia, which he describes at *Op.* 639–40 as "a miserable village . . . terrible in winter, horrible in summer, never good." Bursian brackets this reference to Ascra as an interpolation.

[5] A similar point is made at 1.10.7. RW rightly bracket εἰ δ' αὖ . . . λαμβάνειν (but if the land is barren and stinting one could incorporate that very thing into one's praise). The issue here is climate, not the productivity of the land.

[6] That is, hot or cold.

λον θεωροῦνται, αἱ δὲ ἐπὶ τὸ ἔλαττον. χειμὼν μὲν γὰρ
καὶ θέρος ἐπὶ τὸ ἔλαττον· μᾶλλον γὰρ ἐλάττους καὶ
ἀσθενεστέρας ἐπαινετέον. ἔαρ δὲ καὶ μετόπωρον ἐπὶ
τὸ μᾶλλον· μᾶλλον γὰρ ἰσχύειν τὰς ὥρας ταύτας
ἐπαίνου ἄξιον.

6. Ἐν δὲ τῷ περὶ τῶν ὡρῶν καὶ ἃ ἑκάστη φέρει
τακτέον, αὐτὰ ταῦτα δὲ ἐφ᾽ ἑκάστῃ κατὰ τὰ τρία
ταῦτα θεωρητέον, χρόνον ποιότητα ποσότητα·[5] χρόνον μὲν εἰ[6] ὅλον μένει ἀκήρατα, ἢ[7] πλεῖστον τοῦ ἔτους·
ποιότητα δὲ πρὸς ἡδονὴν καὶ ὠφέλειαν· ὠφέλειαν μὲν
εἰ ἀβλαβῆ ἐστιν, ἡδονὴν δὲ εἰ ταῖς αἰσθήσεσι τερ-
πνά, γεύσεσιν ὄψεσι καὶ ταῖς ἄλλαις·[8] ποσότητα δὲ εἰ
πολλὰ ταῦτα εἴη.

7. Περὶ μὲν τῆς θέσεως τῆς κατ᾽ οὐρανὸν καὶ ὥρας
ταῦτα, ἐξ ὧν ἄν τις ἐγκωμιάζοι πόλιν. ἐφεξῆς δὲ καὶ
περὶ τῶν ἄλλων τῶν τῆς θέσεως στοιχείων ἐπισκεψώμεθα. ἦν δὲ δεύτερον καὶ τρίτον στοιχεῖον, ὅπως
κεῖται πρὸς ἤπειρον, ὅπως πρὸς θάλασσαν. ἐὰν μὲν
τοίνυν ἠπειρωτικὴ ᾖ καὶ πλεῖστον ἀπέχῃ ἀπὸ τῆς θαλάσσης, τὴν ἀπὸ τῆς ἀποχωρήσεως ἀσφάλειαν ἐγκωμιάσεις, καὶ σοφῶν ἀνδρῶν παραθήσεις γνώμας, αἳ
τοὺς κατ᾽ ἤπειρον οἰκισμοὺς ἐπαινοῦσι καὶ τοὺς πλεῖστον ἀπὸ θαλάττης ἀπέχοντας, καὶ πάντα ἐρεῖς ὅσα

---

[5] χρόνον ποιότητα ποσότητα Heeren, RW: χρόνος ποιότης
ποσότης Z
[6] χρόνον μὲν εἰ RW: ἢ χρόνῳ μὲν P: εἰ χρόνον MmW
[7] Russell per litteras: εἰ codd.
[8] γεύσεσιν ὄψεσι καὶ ταῖς ἄλλαις obel. RW

some are viewed favorably for being longer, others for being shorter: winter and summer for being shorter, since in their case comparative brevity and lack of strength are commendable; spring and fall for being longer, since the predominance of these seasons is praiseworthy.

6. Within the category of seasons we should also include the things that each season produces, and in each case we should consider their products under the three headings of time, quality, and quantity. As regards time, consider whether they remain unimpaired for the entire year or most of it; as regards quality, whether they provide pleasure and utility—utility if they do no harm; pleasure if they are agreeable to the senses, taste, vision, etc.;—and as regards quantity, whether they are numerous.[7]

7. So much for location with respect to the sky and seasons as a basis for praising a city. Let us next examine the other elements involved in location. The second and third elements were its position in relation to the mainland and the sea.[8] If it is inland and very far from the sea, you should praise the security provided by this distance, and cite wise men's opinions[9] in praise of inland settlements and those farthest from the sea—and you should cite all

---

[7] I have adopted RW's plausible reconstruction of this entire sentence. They, however, obelize the manuscripts' γεύσεσιν ὄψεσι καὶ ταῖς ἄλλαις ("taste, vision, etc.") as an intrusive gloss on αἰσθήσεσι.

[8] Cf. §2.

[9] RW cite Plato's discussion of the ideal city's required distance from the sea at *Leg.* 4.704a–5b as indicative of the philosophical tradition implied by "wise men," and they note continuing discussions in orations of Libanius (11.35–38 and 18.187).

ἐν τῷ ἑτέρῳ κακά. 8. ἐὰν δὲ ἡ πόλις θαλαττία ᾖ ἢ νῆσος, τάς τε ἠπείρους ἐρεῖς κακῶς καὶ τοὺς ἠπειρωτικοὺς οἰκισμούς, καὶ ὅσα ἀγαθὰ ἀπὸ θαλάσσης ἀριθμήσῃ. ἰδίως δὲ καὶ περιεργάσῃ τὴν ἑκάστης νήσου ἢ τὴν ἑκάστης πόλεως θέσιν. τὸ γὰρ τοιοῦτον μέρος ἀδύνατον περιστοιχίζεσθαι διὰ τὸ ἄπειρον. ἐὰν δὲ παραθαλάττιος ᾖ καὶ ἐπ᾽ αἰγιαλοῖς, ὅτι ἀμφότερα ὑπάρχει τὰ ἀγαθά. ἐὰν δὲ ὀλίγον ἀπέχῃ ἀπὸ τοῦ αἰγιαλοῦ, ὅτι τὰ μὲν ἑκατέρωθεν ἐκπέφευγε λυπηρά, τὰ δ᾽ ἀμφοτέρων ἀγαθὰ ἀνείληφεν.

349

9. Ἑξῆς ἦν στοιχεῖα θέσεως, ὅπως ἔχει πρὸς τὴν περιοικίδα χώραν, καὶ ὅπως πρὸς τὰς ἀστυγείτονας χώρας. πρὸς μὲν τοίνυν τὴν περιοικίδα χώραν θεωρητέον, εἰ ἐπ᾽ ἀρχῆς κεῖται, ἢ ἐν μέσῳ, ἢ πρὸς τῷ τέλει. καὶ εἰ μὲν ἐπ᾽ ἀρχῆς κεῖται, ὥσπερ προσώπῳ ἀπεικαστέον, καὶ ὅτι ἐντὸς τὴν αὑτῆς χώραν φυλάττει, ὥσπερ μιᾶς οἰκίας προπύλαια. ἐὰν δὲ ἐν μέσῳ, ὅτι ὥσπερ βασίλεια ἢ ἀρχεῖα ἢ ὀμφαλὸς ἀσπίδος, ὥσπερ Ἀριστείδης εἶπε, ἢ ὥσπερ ἐν κύκλῳ μέσον σημεῖον. ἐὰν δὲ ἐπὶ τέλει, ὅτι ὥσπερ ἐραστὰς ἀποφυγοῦσα τοὺς προσιόντας.

10. Ἔτι δὲ ὀψόμεθα καὶ ζητήσομεν, πότερον τὰ σκληρὰ προβαλλομένη ἐν πεδινοῖς ἐστιν, ἢ ἐν τοῖς σκληροτάτοις τόποις κατῴκισται τὰ πεδία προβαλλομένη· καὶ ἐὰν ἐν πεδινοῖς ἱδρυμένη, ὅτι ἀποπειρᾶται τῶν ἀφικνουμένων, ὥσπερ ἀγῶνα προτιθεῖσα, ἢ ὅτι εὐερκής ἐστιν, ὥσπερ τείχους ἀνεστηκότος. ἐὰν δὲ τὰ πεδία προβαλλομένη ἐν τοῖς σκληροῖς φαίνηται ἱδρυ-

the drawbacks of the opposite situation. 8. If, on the other hand, the city is located on the sea or is an island, you should disparage inland regions and inland settlements and tally up all the advantages that come from the sea. You should elaborate what is special about the location of each island or city. (It is impossible to exhaust such a category as this because it is unlimited.) If the city is near the sea and in a coastal region, say that it enjoys the advantages of both land and sea. If it is a short distance from the shore, say that it has escaped the disadvantages of each, but has acquired the advantages of both.

9. Next among the elements of location was its relationship to the surrounding territory and bordering countries. With regard to the surrounding territory, you must consider whether the city lies at the front, in the middle, or at the back. If it lies in front, you should compare it to a façade and say that it guards the land within like the foregates of a single house. If in the middle, say that it is like a palace, a town hall, the boss on a shield (as Aristides put it),[10] or like the point at the center of a circle. If it is at the back, say that it has retreated from those who approach it as a girl does from her lovers.[11]

10. Furthermore, we should look to see whether it lies in a plain with rugged terrain in front of it, or is built on very rugged places with the plain in front. If it is built in a plain, say that it tests those who approach it, as if setting them a challenge, or that it is secure, as if a wall were in front of it. If it is built in full view on rugged terrain with

[10] Aristid. *Panath.* 16: εἰς ὀμφαλόν.
[11] For lovers of a city (Athens), cf. Thuc. 2.43.1.

μένη, ὅτι ἥμερός ἐστι πρὸς τοὺς ἀφικνουμένους, καὶ
ὥσπερ ἀκρόπολις ἀφ' ὑψηλοῦ πυρσεύουσα. ἐὰν δὲ
ἀναμὶξ ᾖ ταῦτα καὶ συγκεχυμένως φαίνηται διακεί-
μενα, τὴν ποικιλίαν ἐπαινετέον, ὥσπερ Ἀριστείδης
πεποίηκεν.

11. Ἔτι δὲ πρὸς τὰ ὕδατα τὰ ἐν τῇ χώρᾳ θεατέον.
ὑδάτων δὲ φύσεις τριχῇ δεῖ διαιρεῖν, ἢ ὡς πηγῶν, ἢ
ὡς ποταμῶν, ἢ ὡς λιμνῶν. κριτέον δ' αὐτὰ ὥσπερ καὶ
τὰ ἄλλα, πρὸς ἡδονὴν καὶ ὠφέλειαν, καὶ ἔτι πρὸς
ταύτῃ τῇ διαιρέσει πρὸς πλῆθος καὶ αὐτοφυΐαν· ἐνιαχοῦ γὰρ καὶ θερμαὶ πηγαὶ εὑρίσκονται.

12. Πρὸς τοίνυν τὰς ἐν γειτόνων θεωρητέον ἢ⁹ πόλεις ἢ χώρας, πότερον ἐν ἀρχῇ ἐστιν αὕτη, ἢ πρὸς
τῷ τέλει, ἢ πανταχόθεν μέση· καὶ χῶραι καὶ πόλεις
εἰ μικραὶ καὶ ἀφανεῖς, ἢ μεγάλαι καὶ ἐπιφανεῖς, καὶ
εἰ ἀρχαῖαι ἢ νέαι. πρὸς μὲν τοίνυν χώρας, οἷον εἰ
λέγοι τις, ὅτι [ἡ νῦν καλουμένη Ἀσία]¹⁰ παρῴκισται
μεγάλῳ ἔθνει, καὶ ὅμως ὑπὸ μεγέθους οὐ κρύπτεται·
πόλεις δ', ὥσπερ λέγουσι περὶ τῶν πόλεων τῶν Ἀσι-
ανῶν, ὅτι ἐγγὺς ἀλλήλων οὖσαι οὐκ ἀφαιροῦνται ἀλ-
λήλας τὸν κόσμον.

13. Καὶ εἰ μὲν ἐπ' ἀρχῆς τῶν ἄλλων ἐθνῶν, ὅτι
προβέβληται ἀντ' ἄλλου φυλακτηρίου, ὥσπερ ὁ

---

⁹ ὡς πρὸς post ἢ (bis) del. RW   ¹⁰ secl. RW

---

¹² Cf. Aristid. *Panath.* 22: "[Attica] is neither entirely flat nor
entirely mountainous, but variegated and shaped so as to take

a plain in front, say that it is gentle toward those who come to visit and is like an acropolis shining like a beacon from on high. If, however, these features are intermingled and present no clear distinction, you should praise its variety as Aristides did.[12]

11. Furthermore, you must consider the sources of water in the land and divide them into three categories: springs, rivers, and lakes. These you must evaluate, just like the rest, according to pleasure and utility, with the additional distinction in this case concerning volume and natural state, for in some places hot springs are also found.

12. With regard to neighboring cities or countries, we must consider whether our city is located at the front, at the back, or right in the middle, whether the other countries and cities are small and obscure or great and illustrious, and whether they are ancient or new. Thus with regard to countries, for example, one might say that it[13] was settled next to a great nation and yet is not overshadowed by that greatness. With regard to cities, on the other hand, one might mention what is said of cities in Asia,[14] that although they are near to one another, they do not detract from one another's splendor.

13. If our city is situated in front of other nations, one might say that it is set in front like another guard post, as

advantage of the usefulness of each kind of terrain in turn, as the mark of a perfect land that reproduces a kind of image of the whole world" (M. Trapp, trans.).

[13] RW bracket the manuscripts' ἡ νῦν καλουμένη Ἀσία (what is now called Asia). It is unclear to what cities or country this could refer. See their discussion ad loc.

[14] Presumably Asia Minor.

Ἀριστείδης· τοῦτο γάρ φησι περὶ τῶν Ἀθηνῶν. εἰ δὲ
μέση κέοιτο ἡ πόλις πολλῶν χωρῶν καὶ πόλεων
μεγάλων, ὅτι πανταχόθεν περιβέβληται καὶ ἀντὶ κόσμου προπύλαια καὶ εἰς ἀσφάλειαν περιβόλους. εἰ δὲ
πρὸς τέλει, ὅτι ἀντὶ κεφαλῆς ἐπίκειται ταῖς ἄλλαις
χώραις καὶ κορυφῆς.

14. Εἰ δ' ἔνδοξοι εἶεν αἱ πόλεις καὶ ἐπιφανεῖς, ὅτι
ἐνδόξων ἐνδοξοτέρα ἐστὶ καὶ ἐπιφανῶν ἐπιφανεστέρα,
ἢ ἐπιφανῶν οὐκ ἀφανεστέρα ἢ οὐ πολύ· εἰ δὲ ἄδοξοι
καὶ οὐκ ἐπιφανεῖς, ὅτι δι' αὐτὴν ἀλλ' οὖν ὀνόματος
καὶ φήμης τυγχάνουσιν. εἰ μὲν ἀρχαῖαι χῶραι εἴησαν, ὅτι ἀνάγκη καὶ αὐτὴν ἀρχαίαν εἶναι τὴν πρόσοι-
κον χώραν· εἰ δὲ πόλεις, ὅτι αἱ μὲν κεκμήκασι χρόνῳ,
ἡ δ' ἀνθεῖ· εἰ δ' αὖ νέα, ὅτι πρὸς φυλακὴν προβέβληται νεωστὶ γεγενημένη.

15. Σκεψώμεθα τοίνυν καὶ τὴν τοπικὴν καλουμένην
θέσιν, ἥπερ ἐστὶν ὑπόλοιπος. καλοῦσι δὲ τοπικὴν τὴν
τοῦ τόπου φύσιν, ἐν ᾧ ἡ πόλις ἵδρυται. πᾶσα πόλις,
ὡς ἀνωτάτω συλλαβεῖν, αὐτὰ γὰρ τὰ καθ' ἑκάστην
σχήματα ἀδύνατον περιλαβεῖν, ἢ πᾶσα ἐν ὄρει καὶ
γηλόφῳ ἢ πᾶσα ἐν πεδίῳ <ἢ πῇ μὲν ἐν ὄρει πῇ δὲ
ἐν πεδίῳ>.[11] ἂν μὲν τοίνυν πᾶσα ἐν ὄρει, καὶ πρὸς
ἀσφάλειαν καὶ πρὸς ἡδονὴν ἐπαινετέον ἐκ τούτου,
κατὰ μὲν εἰρήνην διὰ τὴν τοῦ ἀέρος τοῦ ὑποκειμένου
351 καθαρότητα, κατὰ δὲ πόλεμον ὅτι αὐτοφυὲς τεῖχος καὶ
ἀπρόσβατον κέκτηται.

11 suppl. RW praeeuntibus Heeren et Bursian

84

Aristides said of Athens.[15] If the city lies in the middle of many other countries and great cities, say that it is completely surrounded with gateways for adornment and encircling walls for security. If it is at the back, say that it lies atop the other lands like a head or peak.

14. If the cities are renowned and illustrious, say that ours is more renowned and more illustrious than they, or no less illustrious, or not much less. If they are neither famous nor illustrious, say that it is indeed thanks to our city that they come by their name and fame. If the countries are ancient, say that our adjacent country must be ancient as well. If the cities are ancient, say that they have grown weary over time, while ours is flourishing. If, instead, our city is new, say that having recently been established, it has been set in front of them for their protection.

15. Let us now examine the remaining topic, which is called "site" and refers to the nature of the place where the city is built. To speak in the most general terms (since it is impossible to include all the individual configurations), every city is either wholly on a mountain or on a hill, or wholly on a plain, or partially on a mountain and partially on a plain. If, then, it is wholly on a mountain, it should be praised for this reason on the grounds both of security and of pleasure, since in times of peace it enjoys pure air and in times of war it possesses a natural and unscalable wall.

[15] Aristid. *Panath*. 9: πρόκειται γὰρ ἀντ᾽ ἄλλου φυλακτηρίου (for it stands forth like another guard post).

16. Ἐλαττώματα δὲ τῶν ἐν γηλόφῳ κειμένων ψύχους ὑπερβολαί, ὁμίχλη, στενοχωρίαι. δεῖ οὖν ἀποφαίνειν οὐ προσόντα ταῦτα ἢ οὐ μάλιστα. ἐὰν δὲ ἐν πεδίῳ, δεῖ ἐπαινεῖν, ὅτι ἐν ὀφθαλμῷ ἡ πόλις φαίνεται, ὅτι οὐκ ἔστιν ἀνώμαλος τοῖς ἄρθροις, ὥσπερ σῶμα εὔρυθμον, ὅτι γεωργική τίς ἐστιν ἡ φύσις τῆς πόλεως, ὅτι ὑπ' ἀνδρείας οὐ πέφευγεν, ὥσπερ αἱ ἄλλαι πόλεις, εἰς ὄρη.

17. Τὰ ἐλαττώματα τῶν ἐν ὑψηλῷ πόλεων ἱδρυμένων ὀνειδιεῖς, τὰ δὲ τῶν ἐν πεδίῳ φεύξῃ.[12] ἔστι δὲ ἐλαττώματα αὐχμοὶ καὶ πνιγμοὶ καὶ ῥᾳστώνη ἐπιθέσεως, καὶ ὅσα τοιαῦτα. ταῦτα οὖν ἢ ὡς ἥκιστα ἢ ὡς ἐλάχιστα ἀποδεικνύναι χρὴ προσόντα. ἀλλὰ μὴν εἰ πῇ μὲν πεδινὴ εἴη ἡ πόλις, πῇ δὲ ἐν ὄρεσιν, τό τε πλῆθος ἐπαινέσεις καὶ τὴν ποικιλίαν, ὅτι ἅπερ ἀμφοτέραις ταῖς πόλεσι πρόσεστι, ταῦτα ἀμφότερα μόνη κέκτηται, καὶ ὅτι τὰ ἀμφοτέρων ἐλαττώματα ἐκπέφευγε· πειράσῃ δὲ ἀποδεικνύναι καὶ ὅτι πολλαῖς ἔοικε πόλεσιν. ἐκ τούτων καὶ περὶ ταῦτα ἡ μέθοδος.

---

[12] τὰ ἐλαττώματα . . . φεύξῃ secl. RW

16. The drawbacks of cities located on high ground are extreme cold, mist, and lack of room. It is therefore necessary to show that these conditions do not apply, or for the most part do not. If it lies in a plain, you should praise it by saying that the city lies open to view, that like a well-proportioned body it is not irregular in its parts, that the city's nature is like that of a farm, that because of its bravery it has not sought refuge in the mountains as other cities do.

17. You will criticize the shortcomings of cities built on heights, and avoid those of cities in the plain.[16] Shortcomings of the latter include droughts, stifling heat, openness to attack, and the like. One must accordingly demonstrate that such conditions are not present at all, or to the smallest degree possible. If the city is partially in a plain and partially in mountains, you should praise its magnitude and variety because that city alone possesses the advantages of the other two cities, while avoiding the shortcomings of each. You should also attempt to show that this city resembles many cities in one. Such are the topics on which our method draws and the subjects it treats.

[16] RW follow Bursian in bracketing this sentence.

[1.12. ΠΩΣ ΔΕΙ ΛΙΜΕΝΑΣ ΕΓΚΩΜΙΑΖΕΙΝ][1]

1. Ἐν τούτῳ δὲ τῷ μέρει καὶ τὸ περὶ λιμένων ἔγκειται. λιμένες δὲ ἢ ἐν μέσῳ τῆς πόλεως, καὶ φήσεις ὥσπερ κόλπῳ δέχεσθαι τοὺς καταπλέοντας ὑπὸ τὰς ἀγκάλας· ἢ ἐν ἀρχῇ τῆς θέσεως, καὶ φήσεις ὥσπερ ποσὶν ἐπιστηρίζεσθαι τῷ λιμένι. καὶ ἢ αὐτοφυεῖς εἰσιν ἢ χειροποίητοι. ἂν μὲν τοίνυν χειροποίητοι ὦσιν, ἐρεῖς ὅτι οὐχ ἡ πόλις δι' αὐτούς, ἀλλ' αὐτοὶ διὰ τὴν πόλιν γεγόνασιν· εἰ δ' αὐτοφυεῖς, ὅτι ἀπρόχωστοί εἰσι διὰ τὸ αὐτοφυεῖς εἶναι, ὅσοι δὲ χειροποίητοι, προχοῦνται.

2. Καὶ ἢ εἷς ἐστιν ἢ πολλοί. ἂν μὲν εἷς, ὅτι ὥσπερ σώματος εἷς κόλπος ἐστίν· ἐὰν δὲ πολλοί, ὅτι ὑπὸ 352 φιλανθρωπίας πολλὰς χεῖρας προτείνει τοῖς καταίρουσι. λιμένας δὲ ἐπαινέσεις ἢ ὡς ἀκλύστους, ἢ ὡς νηνέμους καὶ ὡς ἐπισκεπεῖς, ἢ ὡς πολύπλους, ἢ ὡς κατὰ πάντα ἄνεμον ἐκπέμποντας, ἢ ὡς πρὸ τῶν μεγάλων πελαγῶν προκειμένους, ἢ ὡς ἀγχιβαθεῖς.

[1] secl. Heeren

---

[1] That is, on cities. The manuscripts have divided harbors, gulfs, and acropoleis into separate sections. Heeren bracketed these titles, as have all subsequent editors.

[1.12. HOW TO PRAISE HARBORS]

1. In this section[1] also belongs the treatment of harbors. They lie either in the middle of the city (in which case you should say that it welcomes, as if to its breast, those sailing in under its arms), or at the entrance to the site (in which case you should say that the city rests, as it were, upon its harbor's feet).[2] In addition, harbors are either natural or man-made. If they are man-made, you should say that the city did not come into existence because of its harbors, but the harbors because of the city. If they are natural, you should say that because they are natural they do not silt up, whereas those that are man-made do.

2. Furthermore, harbors are either single or many. If there is only one, say that the city, like a body, has but a single bosom. If there are many, say that because of its humanity (*philanthrōpia*) the city extends many hands to those putting in to shore.[3] You should also praise harbors for being protected from the waves, or sheltered and free from winds, or full of traffic, or able to send out ships in any wind, or fronting open seas, or having deep water right up to shore.

[2] For other comparisons of geographical features to human bodies, cf. 1.10.7.

[3] Aristid. *Panath*. 10 describes Attica's humanity as if stretching forth its hand to welcome sailors from the sea (τοῖς ἐκ τοῦ πελάγους ὡσπερεὶ χεῖρα προτείνουσα εἰς ὑποδοχήν).

[1.13. ΠΩΣ ΔΕΙ ΚΟΛΠΟΥΣ ΕΠΑΙΝΕΙΝ]

1. Ἐν τούτῳ δὲ καὶ τὸ περὶ τῶν κόλπων. κόλπους ἐπαινέσεις εἰς μέγεθος καὶ κάλλος καὶ εὐρυθμίαν καὶ εἰς εὐλιμενότητα καὶ πολυλιμενότητα.

[1.14. ΠΩΣ ΔΕΙ ΑΚΡΟΠΟΛΙΝ ΕΓΚΩΜΙΑΖΕΙΝ]

1. Ἐν τούτῳ δὲ καὶ τὸ περὶ τῶν ἀκροπόλεων· αἱ μὲν ἐν μέσῳ πόλεών εἰσιν, αἱ δ' ἐν πλαγίῳ. καὶ αἱ μὲν ὑψηλαί, στεναὶ δὲ τὸ ἄνω δάπεδον, αἱ δὲ βραχεῖαι μέν, εὐρύχωροι δέ· καὶ αἱ μὲν εὔυδροι, αἱ δὲ ἄνυδροι· καὶ αἱ μὲν ἀνώμαλοι τὰς κορυφάς, αἱ δὲ πεδινώτεραι. ἥτις μὲν οὖν τὰς μὲν ἀρετὰς εἴληφεν τὰς δὲ κακίας ἐκπέφευγεν, αὕτη καλλίστη, ὅμως δ' ἐξ ὧν ἐπαινετέον τούτων ἑκάστην λεκτέον.

2. Ἂν μὲν τοίνυν ἐν πλαγίῳ τῆς πόλεως ᾖ, ὅτι ἀκριβῶς κεφάλῃ[1] ἔοικε· μετὰ γὰρ πᾶν τὸ σῶμα κεῖται. εἰ δ' ἐν μέσῳ, ὅτι περὶ αὐτὴν ἡ πόλις ἵδρυται, ὥσπερ

---

[1] Heeren: κέλητι codd.

[1.13. HOW TO PRAISE GULFS]

1. In this section also belongs the treatment of gulfs. You should praise gulfs for their size, beauty, fine proportions, and good and plentiful harbors.

[1.14. HOW TO PRAISE AN ACROPOLIS]

1. In this section also belongs the treatment of acropoleis. Some are in the middle of cities, some on one side. Some are lofty and have narrow summits, others are low and spacious; some have abundant water, others have none; some are uneven on top, others more level. The one then that lays claim to the virtues and avoids the drawbacks is the best. Nevertheless, we must discuss how to praise each type of acropolis.

2. Thus, if it is on the side of the city, say that it is just like a head, because it lies beyond the entire body;[1] if it is in the middle, that the city is built around it like royal

---

[1] The text is much in doubt. The manuscripts have κέλητι (racehorse or skiff), which makes no sense. Heeren's conjecture relies on 1.11.13, where an acropolis at the back of a city is compared to a head. RW obelize μετὰ . . . κεῖται.

βασιλικαὶ περὶ ἱερὸν περιβολαί. ἂν δ' ὑψηλὴ μέν,
στενὴ δὲ τὸ ἄνω ἔδαφος, ὅτι ὥσπερ ἱερὸν τῷ ὄντι
ἅπαν ἀοίκητόν ἐστι πλὴν ὅσα τοῖς κατέχουσι θεοῖς.
εἰ δὲ βραχεῖα μέν, εὐρύχωρος δέ, ὅτι πόλει ἔοικεν ἡ
ἀκρόπολις ὑπ' εὐρυχωρίας.

3. Καὶ εἰ μὲν ἄνυδρος, ὅτι ὑπὸ ὕψους τοῦτο πέπον-
θεν, εἰ δὲ εὔυδρος, ὅτι καὶ ὑψηλὴ οὖσα καὶ πρὸς
χρείαν ἐστὶν αὐτάρκης. καὶ εἰ μὲν ἀνώμαλος, ὅτι
ὥσπερ ἄλλας ἀκροπόλεις ἐν αὐτῇ ἔχει· εἰ δὲ πεδινή,
ὅτι θέσεως ἕνεκα καὶ ῥᾳστώνης ὡς πόλις ᾠκίσθη.[2]
353 κράτιστον δὲ ὅπερ ἔφη τὰς ἀρετὰς παρούσας τὰς δὲ
κακίας ἀπούσας ἁπάσας δεικνύναι, ἢ πλείονας ἀρετὰς κακιῶν. ταῦτα καὶ περὶ ἀκροπόλεων θέσεως ἡμῖν
ἀποδεδείχθω.

[2] ὡς πόλις ᾠκίσθη Spengel ex Gudiano: καὶ πόλις vel καὶ
πόλει codd.: τῇ πόλει Bursian: lacunam post πόλις stat. RW

structures around a temple. If it is lofty but narrow on top, say that it is like a veritable sanctuary entirely unoccupied except by the gods who possess it; if it is low but spacious, that the acropolis is like a city in its expanse.

3. If it has no water, say that this happens because of its height; if it has abundant water, that in spite of its height it is self-sufficient for its needs. If it is uneven, say that it has, as it were, other acropoleis within itself; if it is level, that because of its location and ease of access it is built like a city.[2] The most important thing, as I said, is to point out the virtues that are present and all the drawbacks that are not—or at least to say that there are more virtues than drawbacks. So much for our treatment of the situation of acropoleis.

[2] The text is much in doubt. I have adopted Spengel's text based on one manuscript (Gudianus).

1.15. ΠΩΣ ΔΕΙ ΑΠΟ ΓΕΝΟΥΣ ΠΟΛΙΝ ΕΓΚΩΜΙΑΖΕΙΝ

1. Δεύτερος δ᾽ ἂν εἴη τόπος ὁ τοῦ γένους καλούμενος, διαιρεῖται δὲ εἰς οἰκιστάς, εἰς τοὺς οἰκήσαντας, εἰς τὸν χρόνον, εἰς τὰς μεταβολάς, εἰς τὰς αἰτίας ἀφ᾽ ὧν αἱ πόλεις οἰκοῦνται. τούτων δ᾽ αὖ ἕκαστον πολλαχῆ διαιρετέον, οἷον εὐθὺς εἰ τίς οἰκιστὴς ζητοῖμεν, εἰ θεός, εἰ ἥρως, εἰ ἄνθρωπος, καὶ πάλιν κατὰ τύχας στρατηγὸς ἢ βασιλεὺς ἢ ἰδιώτης.

2. Ἐὰν μὲν τοίνυν θεὸς ᾖ, μέγιστον τὸ ἐγκώμιον, ὥσπερ ἐπ᾽ ἐνίων λέγεται, ὡς περὶ Ἑρμουπόλεως καὶ Ἡλιουπόλεως καὶ τῶν τοιούτων. ἐὰν δὲ ἡμιθέων καὶ ἡρώων ᾖ καὶ μετὰ ταῦτα θεὸς γενόμενος, ἔλαττον μὲν τὸ ἐγκώμιον, ἔνδοξον δὲ καὶ οὕτως, ὥσπερ ἐφ᾽ Ἡρακλείας τῆς πόλεως, καὶ ὅσας ἢ Σαρπηδὼν ἢ Μίνως ᾤκισεν ἢ ἄλλοι ἥρωες. ἐὰν δὲ ἄνθρωπος, ἐὰν μὲν ᾖ στρατηγὸς ἢ βασιλεύς, ἔνδοξον, ἐὰν δὲ ἰδιώτης, ἄδοξον καὶ οὐκ ἐπιφανές.

3. Χρὴ οὖν, ὅτε τὸ περὶ τῶν οἰκιστῶν ἡμῖν διῄρηται, ἐκεῖνο τὸ θεώρημα [καὶ τὸ στοιχεῖον][1] κατὰ πάσης

---

[1] secl. Spengel, RW

---

[1] That is, after location; cf. 1.11.1.

1.15. HOW TO PRAISE A CITY FOR
ITS ORIGIN

1. The second topic[1] is called "origin" (*genos*) and is divided into founders, settlers, date, changes, and causes for settling cities. Each of these has many subdivisions. For instance, if we investigate who the founder was, we must determine whether he was a god, a hero, or a man, and in this last case, his station in life, whether he was a general, a king, or a private individual.

2. If the founder is a god—as is said of some cities such as Hermopolis, Heliopolis, and the like—the encomium is grandest. If he is a demigod or a hero who subsequently became a god, the encomium is less grand, but even so belongs to the "worthy"[2] type, as is the case with the city of Heraclea[3] and the various cities founded by Sarpedon, Minos, and other heroes.[4] If he is a man and also a general or a king, the encomium is still of the worthy type; if, on the other hand, he is a private individual, the encomium is of the unworthy type and lacks distinction.

3. It is therefore necessary, now that we have subdivided the section on founders, to recognize this principle

[2] For the types of encomia as "worthy" or "unworthy," see 1.10.8.   [3] Heraclea Pontica, mentioned below in §26, was the most prominent of many so-named cities.

[4] According to Ephorus, Sarpedon colonized Miletus from Crete (cf. Strabo 14.1.6). Minos colonized many cities in the Cyclades, including Rheneia, mentioned below in §25.

τῆς διαιρέσεως εἰδέναι, ὡς εἰ μὲν ἔνδοξος εἴη ὁ κατοι-
κίσας, τά τε ἄλλα αὐτοῦ ἐγκωμιαστέον ἐν βραχυτάτοις, καὶ ὅτι τὴν πόλιν ᾤκισεν ἣν ἂν ἐπαινῶμεν. ἐὰν
δὲ ἄδοξος καὶ ἡ διαδοχὴ ἄδοξος, γίνεται[2] ἢ τῷ αἰ-
σχρὰν ἔχειν δόξαν, ἢ τῷ μηδ' ὅλως ἔχειν· ἐὰν μὲν
τοίνυν μηδ' ὅλως ἔχῃ, φατέον μόνον, ὅτι ἀπὸ τῆς κτί-
σεως τῆς πόλεως, ὥσπερ ἐξαρκοῦν, ἠξίωσε γνωρίζε-
σθαι· εἰ δὲ φαύλην δόξαν εἰληφώς, ὅτι ἀπολογίαν
ἱκανὴν ταύτην ἐπὶ τοῖς ἄλλοις ἐξεῦρεν. ἀπὸ μὲν τῆς
τομῆς ταύτης τὸν οἰκιστὴν γνωριοῦμεν.

4. Τοὺς δὲ οἰκήσαντας διαιρήσομεν μιᾷ μὲν τομῇ
354 Ἑλλήνων καὶ βαρβάρων, δευτέρᾳ δὲ βαρβάρων μὲν
ἢ τῶν ἀρχαιοτάτων, ὥσπερ Φρυγῶν, ἢ βασιλικωτά-
των, ὥσπερ Λυδῶν ἢ Μήδων ἢ Περσῶν ἢ Αἰθιόπων
ἢ Σκυθῶν. καὶ ὅλως δήλη ἐστὶν ἡ ὁδὸς τῷ προϊόντι
κατὰ τὸ ἀποδοθὲν θεώρημα. δεῖ γὰρ ἀποφαίνειν τὰ
οἰκήσαντα γένη τὴν βάρβαρον πόλιν, ἣν ἂν ἐπαινέ-
σῃς, ἢ πρεσβύτατα ἢ σοφώτατα ἢ ἀρχικώτατα ἢ
ὅλως ἀρετήν τινα σχόντα, ἢ μίαν, ἢ πολλάς, ἢ πάσας, ἢ μάλιστα.

5. Ἑλλήνων δ' αὖ τῶν εὐγενεστάτων νομιζομένων
γενῶν· γένη δὲ τὰ ἀνωτάτω καὶ γνωριμώτατα τρία, τὸ
Δωριέων, Αἰολέων, Ἰώνων. τὸ μὲν τοίνυν Αἰολέων

---

[2] ἐὰν δὲ ἄδοξος καὶ ἡ διαδοχὴ ἄδοξος, γίνεται RW: ἐὰν
δὲ ἄδοξος ᾖ, καὶ ἡ διαδοχὴ ἄδοξος γίνεται codd.: ἐὰν δὲ
ἄδοξος ᾖ, ἡ διαδοχὴ ἄδοξος γίνεται Spengel: lacunam post
γίνεται indic. Bursian

throughout the entire process of division, that if the founder is famous, we should very briefly praise his other accomplishments and state that he founded the city that we are praising. But if neither he nor his descendants are famous—which happens either by having a disgraceful reputation or none at all[5]—if, then, he has no reputation at all, we should merely say that he expected to be recognized for founding the city as if that was sufficient in itself. If he has acquired a bad reputation, say that thereby he has found a sufficient defense for his other faults. Such is the analysis that we shall use to commend the founder.

4. We shall divide the settlers into Greeks and barbarians. The barbarians we shall divide into the most ancient, such as the Phrygians,[6] or else the most regal, such as the Lydians, Medes, Persians, Ethiopians, and Scythians. In general, the way to proceed in keeping with the scheme just laid out is clear: you must show that the races that settled the barbarian city you are praising are either the oldest, wisest, or most regal—or, generally speaking, in possession of some virtue, whether one, many, all, or to the greatest degree.

5. Of the Greeks, we take the races that are regarded as most noble. The foremost and best known of these are three in number: Dorian, Aeolian, and Ionian. The Aeo-

---

[5] This sentence is beyond repair. I have adopted RW's text.

[6] Herodotus (2.2) tells of the famous experiment by Psammetichus the Egyptian king that determined the Phrygians to be the oldest race.

πολὺ ἰσχυρότατον, τὸ δὲ Δωριέων ἀνδρικώτατον, τὸ
δὲ Ἰώνων ἐλλογιμώτατον. χρὴ οὖν ἀποφαίνειν τὴν
Ἑλληνίδα πόλιν ἐκ τούτων οὖσαν τῶν γενῶν.

6. Καὶ οὕτως μὲν τὰ γένη τῶν ἐνοικούντων διαγνω-
σόμεθα, καὶ τοὺς ἐπαίνους, οὓς ἂν περὶ τῶν γενῶν
εἴπωμεν, νομιοῦμεν προσήκειν τοῖς οἰκήσασιν, ὥσπερ
εἰ λέγοιμεν, ὅτι ἡ Σμύρνα ἢ Ἔφεσος τοῦ ἐλλογιμω-
τάτου μέρους ἐστίν, ἢ τῶν ἐν Κρήτῃ πόλεων πολλαὶ
καὶ Ῥόδος τοῦ ἀνδρικωτάτου (Δωρικαὶ γάρ εἰσι) καὶ
ἐπὶ τῶν ἄλλων ὡσαύτως.

7. Τρίτον ἔφαμεν τοῦ γένους εἶναι τὸν χρόνον, τρισὶ
διαιρούμενον ὅροις· ἢ τῶν παλαιοτάτων, ὅταν ἢ πρὸ
ἄστρων ἢ μετὰ τῶν ἄστρων φάσκωμεν, ἢ πρὸ κατα-
κλυσμοῦ ἢ μετὰ κατακλυσμὸν φάσκωμεν οἰκισθῆναι
ἢ πόλιν ἢ χώραν, ὥσπερ Ἀθηναῖοι μεθ' ἡλίου γενέσθαι φασίν, Ἀρκάδες δὲ πρὸ σελήνης, Δελφοὶ δὲ
μετὰ τὸν κατακλυσμὸν εὐθύς· διαστήματα γὰρ καὶ
ὥσπερ ἀρχαὶ αὗται τοῦ αἰῶνος.

8. Ἢ μέσῳ ὅρῳ λογιούμεθα, οἷον ὅτ' ἤνθησεν ἡ
Ἑλλὰς ἢ ἡ Περσῶν δύναμις ἢ Ἀσσυρίων ἢ Μήδων,
ὥσπερ Συρακοῦσαι καὶ ἔνιαι τῶν ἐν Ἰωνίᾳ πόλεων
καὶ πλεῖσται τῆς Ἑλλάδος καὶ τῆς βαρβάρου· τῶν δὲ
355 ἐσχάτων καὶ νεωτάτων αἱ ἐπὶ Ῥωμαίων· ὅσαι γὰρ
νεώταται πόλεις, παρὰ τούτων ἐκτίσθησαν.

---

7 The Athenians claimed to have sprung from their native soil;
cf. Pl. *Menex.* 237b. There is no other reference to their being
born when the sun was created.

lian race is much the strongest, the Dorian the bravest, and the Ionian the most highly regarded. You must therefore show that a Greek city comes from one of these races.

6. That is how we should distinguish the races of the inhabitants, and we shall deem the praises we bestow on the races to apply as well to the settlers. For example, if we say that Smyrna or Ephesus belongs to the most highly regarded group, or that Rhodes and many of the cities in Crete, being Doric, belong to the bravest, and likewise for the others.

7. The third topic mentioned within origin was date, which is divided into three periods. The most ancient pertains when we say that a city or country was settled before there were stars or at the time they were being formed, or before the flood or after it. Thus the Athenians claim to have come into existence along with the sun,[7] the Arcadians before the moon,[8] and the Delphians right after the flood.[9] These events represent fixed intervals and, as it were, the starting points of time.

8. In the middle period we shall reckon, for example, the time when Greece flourished or when the Persians, Assyrians, or Medes were in power. Syracuse for instance dates from this time, as do some of the cities in Ionia and the majority of cities in Greek or barbarian lands. To the last and most recent period belong cities founded in the time of the Romans, for it was by them that all the most recent cities were established.

[8] Cf. Ap. Rhod. 4.264–65: "The Arcadians are said to have existed before the moon did."

[9] Pyrrha and Deucalion founded a new race of people beneath Mount Parnassus after the flood; cf. Pind. *Ol.* 9.43–46.

9. Ἐὰν μὲν τοίνυν ἀρχαιοτάτη ἡ πόλις ᾖ, φήσεις τὸ πρεσβύτατον τιμιώτατον εἶναι καὶ ὅτι αἰώνιός ἐστιν ἡ πόλις, ὥσπερ οἱ θεοί. ἐὰν δὲ τοῦ μέσου ὅρου, ὅτι οὔθ' ὑπορρεῖ καὶ γεγήρακεν ὥστε πεπονηκέναι, οὔτε νεωστὶ ἀνέστηκεν. ἐὰν δὲ νεωτέρα ᾖ, ὅτι ἀνθεῖ καθάπερ κόρη ἀκμάζουσα, καὶ ὅτι μετὰ πλειόνων καὶ βελτιόνων ἐλπίδων οἰκεῖται. χρὴ δὲ τὰς νεωτέρας μηδὲν ἐλαττουμένας σεμνότητι τῶν παλαιοτέρων δεικνύειν, τὰς δὲ ἀπὸ τοῦ μέσου ὅρου πρὸς ἀμφοτέρας αὐτάρκεις. τοσαῦτα καὶ περὶ χρόνου τῶν πόλεων δεδόσθω.

10. Τέταρτος τόπος ὁ τῶν μεταβολῶν, διαιρεῖται δὲ κατὰ τάδε· ἢ γὰρ ἀπῳκίσθη, ἢ συνῳκίσθη, ἢ μετῳκίσθη, ἢ ἐπηυξήθη, ἢ ὅλως οὐκ οὖσα πρότερον ῳκίσθη. ἀπῳκίσθη μέν, ὥσπερ αἱ πλεῖσται τῶν Ἑλληνίδων, αἱ ἐν Ἰωνίᾳ, αἱ ἐν Ἑλλησπόντῳ, αἱ νῆσοι· συνῳκίσθη δέ, ὥσπερ Μεγάλη πόλις ἐν Ἀρκαδίᾳ· μετῳκίσθη δέ, ὥσπερ περὶ Σμύρνης Ἀριστείδης, φησὶ γὰρ αὐτὴν τρὶς ἀλλάξαι τὸν τόπον· ἐπηυξήθη δέ, ὥσπερ ὅσας πρότερον κώμας οὔσας πόλεις πεποιήκασι βασιλεῖς· ῳκίσθησαν δέ, ὅσας πρότερον οὐδ' οὔσας ὅλως πόλεις τινὲς ἀπέφηναν.

11. Μεταβολὴ δὲ παρὰ ταύτας ἁπάσας γίνεται ἐπ' ἐνίων πολλάκις περὶ τὸ ὄνομα· τὴν γὰρ αὐτὴν πόλιν ἢ χώραν ποτὲ μὲν Κραναάν, ποτὲ δὲ Κεκροπίαν, ποτὲ δὲ Ἀκτήν, ποτὲ δὲ Ἀττικήν, ποτὲ δὲ Ἀθήνας κεκλήκασι· καὶ Πελοπόννησον ποτὲ μὲν Πελασγίαν, ποτὲ δὲ Ἀπίαν, ποτὲ δὲ ἄλλο τι τοιοῦτον. ἀλλὰ τὸ τοιοῦτον

9. If, then, the city is very ancient, you will say that what is oldest is most esteemed, and that the city is everlasting like the gods. If it belongs to the middle period, say that neither does it decline and grow old to the point of exhaustion, nor has it just now arisen. If it is recent, say that it blossoms like a maiden in her prime, and that it is governed with hopes for more and better things. You must show that the newer cities are not at all inferior in dignity to those that are more ancient, and that those of the middle period can hold their own against both. Let this suffice for the date of cities.

10. The fourth topic is that of changes and is divided as follows: either a city was created through colonization, or formed through unification (*synoecism*), or was settled by migration, or developed through a process of growth, or came into being through settlement with no prior existence at all. Colonization produced the majority of Greek cities in Ionia, the Hellespont, and the islands. Unification can be illustrated by Megalopolis in Arcadia, migration by Smyrna, of which Aristides says that it changed its location three times.[10] Growth can be seen where kings have turned former villages into cities. Cities come into being through settlement when people make them appear where previously they did not exist at all.

11. In addition to all these changes, there are often cases in which cities undergo a change of name. In this way one and the same city or land has at different times been called Cranaa, Cecropia, Acte, Attica, and Athens, while the Peloponnesus has been variously called Pelasgia, Apia, or something else. However, this sort of change does

[10] Aristid. *Or*. 17.2–4 ("Smyrnaean Oration I").

τῆς μεταβολῆς εἶδος οὐκ ἔχει πρόφασιν ἐπαίνου,
πλὴν εἴ τις τοὺς ἄνδρας ἐπαινοίη ἢ θεούς, ἀφ' ὧν αἱ
πόλεις ὀνομάζονται. ὅπως δὲ τῶν μεταβολῶν ἕκαστον
356 εἶδος ἐπαινεσόμεθα, διδάξω.

12. Ἐὰν μὲν ἀποικίαν, ὅτι ἀπὸ μεγίστης πόλεως
ἀπῴκησαν καὶ ἐνδοξοτάτης, ὅτι ἀπῴκισται ἐνδόξως,
ὅτι δυνάμει κατέσχε τὸν τόπον, ὅτι κατὰ φιλίαν
ἀπῳκίσθησαν, οὐχὶ στάσει καὶ πολέμοις ἐκπεσόντες,
καὶ ὅλως ὑποδέδεικταί σοι πρὸς ἃ χρὴ βλέπειν κἂν
τοῖς τῶν ἀπῳκισμένων πόλεων ἐπαίνοις.

13. Εἰ δὲ συνῳκισμένην πόλιν ἐπαινοίης, καὶ τὰ
μέρη αὐτὰ καθ' ἑαυτὰ μέγιστα ἀποφανεῖς· ὅσῳ γὰρ
ἂν μειζόνως ἐπαινοίης, μειζόνως τὴν συνῳκισμένην
πόλιν ἐγκωμιάσεις, τὴν δὲ πρόφασιν τοῦ συνοικι-
σμοῦ ἐξετάσεις καὶ τοὺς συνοικήσαντας, οἵτινες
ἦσαν· καὶ πάλιν ἡ τούτων ἰδέα σοι ἐπιδέδεικται.

14. Εἰ δὲ μετῳκισμένη εἴη ἡ πόλις, δεῖ σε δεικνύναι
ὅτι οὐ κατὰ συμφορὰς ἀλλὰ πρὸς κάλλος μεταβα-
λοῦσα τὸν τόπον, ὅτι μετοικιζομένη μείζων καὶ καλ-
λίων ἐγένετο, καὶ περιεργάσῃ εἴτε ἅπαξ εἴτε πολλά-
κις· κἂν μὲν ἅπαξ ἢ δίς, ἔκτυπα αὐτῆς πρότερον
καταθέσθαι· εἰ δὲ πολλάκις, ὅτι κινουμένη καὶ βαδι-
ζούσῃ ἔοικεν ἡ πόλις. 15. καὶ τῶν μετοικισμῶν τὰς
αἰτίας, εἰ μὲν εἴησαν φαῦλαι, συγκρύψεις ὡς δυνατόν,
οἷον σεισμοὺς ἢ πορθήσεις ἢ λοιμοὺς ἢ τὰ τοιαῦτα·
εἰ δ' εἴησαν ἀγαθαί, ἐγκωμιάσεις καὶ ἀπὸ τούτων.
τοιαῦτά σοι περὶ τούτων ἀποδέδεικται.

not provide a reason for praise, unless one praises the men or gods for whom the cities are so named. I shall now give instructions on how we may praise each type of change.

12. If the city in question is a colony, say that the colonizers came from a very great and distinguished city, that it was settled in an admirable fashion, that it[11] took possession of its site by force, and that the settlers left from home amid conditions of friendship, not as refugees from internal strife or war. You have been shown in general terms what things to look for when praising colonized cities.

13. If you praise a city created by unification, you should make clear that its individual parts also are very great, for the more abundantly you praise them, the more you will praise the unified city. You should consider the reason for the unification and who they were that brought it about. Once again, the model for this subject has been shown to you.

14. If the city was established by a wholesale migration, you must show that the change of location occurred not because of disasters, but for beauty's sake, and that by means of its migration the city became bigger and more beautiful. Moreover, you should investigate whether this happened just once or often. If it was only once or twice, say that the city began by setting forth prototypes of itself; if it happened many times, say that it is like a city that moves and walks. 15. If the reasons for migration are unfortunate, such as earthquakes, sacks, plagues, and the like, you should conceal them as much as possible; if, however, they are good, you should use them as material for praise. You have been shown enough on this subject.

[11] Presumably the colonizing city.

16. Εἰ δ' ἐπηυξημένη ἡ πόλις εἴη, οὐ χαλεπὸν συν-
ιδεῖν, ἀφ' ὧν ἄν τις ἐγκωμιάζοι. ὥσπερ γὰρ σῶμα
αὐξανόμενον, τῷ χρόνῳ φήσεις προεληλυθέναι αὐτὴν
εἰς μέγεθος, καὶ διὰ τοῦτο προσδοκᾶν αὐτὴν καὶ ἔτι
μᾶλλον προελεύσεσθαι.

17. Εἰ δ' ἡ πόλις ἦν ἐπαινεῖς ἅμα οἰκοδομηθεῖσα
καὶ πόλις ἦν γενομένη, τὸ ἐκ διαφορᾶς πρὸς τὰς ἐκ
κωμῶν μεταβαλούσας πολλὰς ἄν σοι παράσχοι προ-
φάσεις ἐπαίνων, ὅτι, ὥσπερ ἔνιοι ἅμα τῷ τεχθῆναι ἐν
ἀξιώματί εἰσι καὶ οὐ πρότερον δοῦλοι εἶτα ἐλεύθεροι,
357 οὐδὲ πρότερον ἰδιῶται εἶτα ἄρχοντες, οὕτως αἱ τοιαῦται πόλεις. καὶ αὕτη ἡ περὶ ταῦτα μέθοδος.

18. Εἰ δ' ἐκ κώμης εἴη μεταβεβληκυῖα, ὅτι, ὥσπερ
ἐν στρατοπέδῳ οὗτος ἄριστος στρατηγός, ὅστις χιλίαρχος πρότερον ἐγένετο, καὶ χιλίαρχος ὅστις λοχα-
γός, καὶ λοχαγὸς ὅστις στρατιώτης, οὕτω καὶ πόλις
ἀρίστη, ἥτις ἐν πείραις ἐξητάσθη.

19. Καὶ ὅλως οὐκ ἀπορήσεις, κατὰ τοῦτο ἰὼν τὸ
ἴχνος, ἐξ ὧν ἄν ἐπαινοίης. τοσαῦτά σοι καὶ περὶ τῶν
μεταβολῶν καὶ τῶν εἰδῶν τῆς μεταβολῆς <εἰρήσθω.
τὴν δὲ περὶ τὸ ὄνομα μεταβολήν>[3] φημι οὐδὲν μέγα
πρὸς ἐγκώμιον ἔχειν ἢ βραχύ, ἐπαινούντων ἡμῶν ἢ
θεὸν ἢ ἄνθρωπον τὸν ἐπώνυμον.

20. Ἦν δὲ μετὰ τὰς μεταβολὰς τόπος ὁ τῶν αἰτίων,
πενταχῇ δὲ καὶ οὗτος διαιρεῖται· καὶ πῶς τὴν διαίρεσιν ποιησάμενοι τοὺς ἐπαίνους ἂν προσαγάγοιμεν
ἑξῆς ἂν εἴη ἀποδεῖξαι. αἰτίαι τοίνυν οἰκισμῶν πόλεων
ἢ θεῖαι ἢ ἡρωικαὶ ἢ ἀνθρώπιναι. καὶ πάλιν ἢ ἐπ' εὐ-

16. If the city has grown, it is not difficult to see what topics to use for praise. You can say that like a developing body it has grown to its great size over time, and that you expect it for that reason to progress even further.

17. If the city you are praising became a city at the same time it was founded, its difference from cities that developed out of villages can give you many grounds for praise. For example, you may say that just as some men are held in esteem right from the moment of birth instead of previously being slaves and then becoming free, or previously being citizens and then becoming rulers—so it is with cities of this sort. Such is the procedure for this subject.

18. If the city has been transformed from a village, say that just as in an army the best general is a former colonel, and the best colonel a former captain, and the best captain a former soldier, so that city is best which has been tested through experience.

19. All in all, if you follow this line you will not lack topics for your praise. Let this be sufficient treatment of change and its various types. As for change of name, I do not think that it provides anything of importance for praise, or only a little if we praise the god or man for whom it is named.

20. After changes came the topic of causes, which is divided into five parts. After making these divisions, the next step will be to show how to marshal our praises. Now, the causes of city settlements are either divine, heroic, or human. Then again, they involve occasions either of hap-

---

[3] suppl. Finckh, RW praeeunte Heeren

φροσύνη ἢ πένθει· καὶ πάλιν κατὰ τὰ τελικὰ καλούμενα κεφάλαια, ⟨ἢ ὡς διὰ τὸ δίκαιον ἢ ὡς διὰ τὸ
καλὸν⟩[4] ἢ ὡς διὰ τὸ συμφέρον, ἢ ὡς διὰ τὸ ἀναγκαῖον.

21. Χρὴ δὲ τούτων τὰ παραδείγματα ἐκθέσθαι. θεία
μὲν τοίνυν αἰτία ἐστίν, ὁποία περὶ Ῥόδου ἢ Δήλου·
περὶ μὲν Ῥόδου ὅτι διαλαχόντες ὁ Ζεὺς καὶ ὁ Ποσειδῶν καὶ Ἅιδης τὰ πάντα Ἡλίῳ μοῖραν οὐ κατέλιπον,
ἀναμνησθέντες δὲ ἔμελλον ἀνακληροῦσθαι, ὁ δ'
Ἥλιος ἀρκεῖν αὐτῷ ἔφη εἰ φανερὰν ποιήσειαν τὴν
Ῥόδον· περὶ δὲ Δήλου, ὅτι διὰ τὴν Ἀπόλλωνος καὶ
Ἀρτέμιδος γένεσιν ἀνέδραμεν ἐκ θαλάττης.

22. Ἡρωϊκαὶ δ' αἰτίαι αἱ περὶ Σαλαμῖνος τῆς ἐν
Κύπρῳ, ἢ Ἄργους τοῦ Ἀμφιλοχικοῦ· τὴν μὲν γὰρ ὁ
Τεῦκρος ᾤκισεν ἐκπεσών, τὴν δὲ Ἀμφίλοχος ὁ Ἀμ-
φιάρεω, καὶ πολλαὶ πόλεις τῶν Ἑλληνίδων τοιαύτας
ἔχουσιν αἰτίας ἡρωϊκάς. ἀνθρώπιναι δέ, ὁποῖαι αἱ
περὶ Βαβυλῶνος λεγόμεναι, †οἷον νυινουν†[5] Σεμίραμις
ᾠκοδόμησεν [βασίλειαν εἶναί φησι].[6] καὶ Ῥωμαϊκαὶ

358

---

[4] suppl. Finckh, Bursian, RW
[5] obel. RW: οἷον Νῖνον Spengel, Bursian   [6] secl. RW

---

[12] "Definitive topics" (literally, "final headings") are only mentioned here and below in §§25 and 27. They consist of broad,
abstract categories such as utility and pleasure (cf. 1.10.3–4), as
well as justice, honor, and necessity, mentioned here.

[13] The island of Rhodes had previously been submerged under the sea. This account derives almost verbatim from Pind. Ol.
7.54–71.

piness or of grief. Finally, they can be viewed in terms of the so-called definitive topics (*telika kephalaia*),[12] i.e., as actuated by justice, honor, utility, or necessity.

21. We must set forth examples of these. Divine causation is like that seen in connection with Rhodes or Delos. In the former case, when Zeus, Poseidon, and Hades had divided up the universe, they did not reserve a share for Helios. Being reminded of that fact, they were about to make a new distribution, but Helios said that he would be satisfied if they made Rhodes appear.[13] As for Delos, it rose up from the sea for the birth of Apollo and Artemis.[14]

22. Heroic causes are to be seen in connection with Salamis in Cyprus or Amphilochian Argos, the former being founded by Teucer as an exile,[15] the latter by Amphilochus the son of Amphiaraus.[16] Indeed many Greek cities have heroic causes of this sort. Human causes are reflected in the stories told about Babylon and its founding by Semiramis.[17] Then too, all the Roman cities founded by

[14] Delos had been a wandering island before Leto arrived and gave birth to Apollo and Artemis; cf. Pind., Fr. 33d. This account conflates the stories of Delos and Rhodes.

[15] Because he did not save his half brother Ajax at Troy, Teucer went into exile and founded a new Salamis on Cyprus.

[16] Cf. Thuc. 2.68.3: "Amphilochus son of Amphiaraus, when he returned home after the Trojan war, was dissatisfied with the state of affairs at Argos, and therefore founded Amphilochian Argos on the Ambracian gulf" (C. F. Smith, trans.).

[17] A queen of Assyria (historically associated with Sammuramat, the late ninth-century BC queen of Assyria). In Greek legend she was the wife of Ninos, the eponymous king of Nineveh, and built Babylon. For a full discussion of the textual difficulties in this passage, see RW ad loc.

δὲ πᾶσαι πόλεις, ἃς Ῥωμαίων ᾤκισαν βασιλεῖς,
τοιαύτας ἔχουσι τὰς αἰτίας. αὕτη μὲν δὴ πρώτη διαίρεσις.

23. Ἡ δὲ δευτέρα, ὅτι αἱ μὲν ἐπ᾽ εὐφροσύνῃ, αἱ δὲ
ἐπὶ πένθει. εὐφροσύνῃ μέν, οἷον γάμῳ γενέσει νίκῃ
καὶ τοῖς τοιούτοις. δεῖ δὲ καὶ τούτων παραδείγματα
γράψαι. γάμων μὲν τοίνυν, ὥς φασι τὴν Μέμφιν ἐπὶ
τῷ γάμῳ τῆς Ἀφροδίτης καὶ τοῦ Ἡφαίστου. νίκης δέ,
οἷόν φασι τὴν Θεσσαλονίκην ἐπὶ τῇ νίκῃ τῶν Θεσ-
σαλῶν οἰκισθῆναι ὑπὸ Μακεδόνων· καὶ τὴν ἐπὶ Ἀκτίῳ
Νικόπολιν ὑπὸ Ῥωμαίων ἐπὶ τῇ νίκῃ τῇ κατὰ Κλεο-
πάτρας. 24. ἐπὶ πένθει δὲ καὶ οἴκτῳ, ὡς ἱστοροῦσι
Βουκέφαλον τὴν ἐν Ἰνδοῖς πόλιν ἐπὶ τῷ ἵππῳ τοῦ
Ἀλεξάνδρου τῷ Βουκεφάλῳ ἀνοικισθῆναι· τὴν Ἀντινόου δὲ ἐν Αἰγύπτῳ ⟨ἐπὶ τῷ⟩[7] Ἀντινόου θανάτῳ ὑπὸ
Ἀδριανοῦ. καὶ δῆλον ἡγοῦμαί σοι γεγενῆσθαι καὶ τὸ
τῆς διαιρέσεως ταύτης θεώρημα.

25. Ἦν δὲ ἡ τρίτη διαίρεσις κατὰ τὰ τελικὰ κεφάλαια καλούμενα. τοῦ μὲν τοίνυν δικαίου τὸ κατὰ Ῥή-
νειαν, ὅτι οἰκίσας αὐτὴν ὁ Μίνως ἀνέθηκε τῷ Ἀπόλλωνι εὐσεβείᾳ, τὸ δ᾽ εὐσεβὲς δίκαιον. τοῦ δὲ καλοῦ,

[7] suppl. Finckh, RW

Roman emperors have similar causes. So much for the first division.

23. The second division concerns causes occasioned by happiness or grief. Occasions of happiness include marriage, birth, victory, and the like, and of these too, I must give examples. As an instance of marriage, they say that Memphis[18] commemorates the wedding of Aphrodite and Hephaestus; of victory, that Thessalonica was founded by the Macedonians on the occasion of their victory over the Thessalians,[19] and that Nicopolis at Actium was founded by the Romans upon their victory over Cleopatra.[20] 24. As for occasions of grief and lamentation, it is reported that the city of Bucephalus in India was founded to commemorate Bucephalus, Alexander's horse,[21] and that the city of Antinous in Egypt was founded by Hadrian upon the death of Antinous.[22] I think that the general principle of this analysis too has been made clear to you.

25. The third division was that involving the so-called definitive topics. An instance of justice, accordingly, is to be seen in the case of Rheneia,[23] since Minos founded it and dedicated it to Apollo out of piety (for piety is a form of justice). An instance of honor is offered by Alexandria,

[18] In Egypt.   [19] Cassander actually founded the city by unification (*synoecism*) and named it for his wife, Thessalonica (daughter of Philip II), in the late fourth century.

[20] Octavian defeated Antony and Cleopatra at Actium in 31 BC.   [21] Alexander the Great founded the city upon the death of his favorite horse in 326 BC.

[22] Antinoöpolis was founded in 130 AD.

[23] A small island west of Delos.

ὡς τὸ κατὰ Ἀλεξάνδρειαν, ὅτι εὐδοξίας ἕνεκα καὶ
κλέους ὁ Ἀλέξανδρος μεγίστην τῶν ὑφ' ἡλίῳ πόλεων
ἠβουλήθη κατοικίσαι. 26. τοῦ δὲ συμφέροντος, ὡς τὸ
καθ' Ἡράκλειαν τὴν ἐν Πόντῳ, ὅτι τοὺς βαρβάρους
ἀναστέλλων Ἡρακλῆς τὸν ἐκεῖ τόπον κατῴκισε. τοῦ
δ' ἀναγκαίου, ὡς τὸ κατὰ τὰς πόλεις τὰς κατ' Ἴστρον
ποταμὸν ὑπὸ Ῥωμαίων κατοικισθείσας, τὰς καλου-
μένας Καρπίας, ὡς μὴ διαβαίνοντες οἱ βάρβαροι
κακουργοῖεν.

27. Οὐσῶν δὲ τούτων τῶν αἰτιῶν καὶ τοιουτοτρόπων
εἰδέναι σε χρὴ ὅτι ἐνδοξόταται μὲν αἱ θεῖαι, δεύτεραι
δὲ αἱ ἡρωϊκαί, τρίται δὲ αἱ ἀνθρωπικαί· καὶ πάλιν
πρῶται μὲν αἱ ἐπ' εὐφροσύνῃ, δεύτεραι δὲ αἱ ἐπὶ πέν-
θει· καὶ πάλιν ἐνδοξότεραι μὲν αἱ ἐκ περιουσίας τῶν
τελικῶν κεφαλαίων, χρησιμώτεραι δὲ αἱ ἀπὸ τῶν
ἀναγκαίων καὶ συμφερόντων.

28. Ἐν μὲν οὖν ταῖς ἐνδοξοτέραις ἐπὶ πλέον διατρι-
πτέον, ἐν δὲ ταῖς ἀδόξοις ἐπ' ἔλαττον· ὁ μέντοι τόπος
ἀναγκαιότατος πρὸς ἔπαινον πόλεων ῥήτορι πανταχοῦ. αὐτῶν δὲ τούτων τῶν αἰτιῶν μυθώδεις μὲν αἱ
θεῖαι καὶ ἡρωϊκαί, πιθανώτεραι δὲ αἱ ἀνθρωπικαί. τὰς
μὲν τοίνυν ἀνθρωπικὰς αὐξητέον, τὰς δὲ ἡρωϊκὰς καὶ

---

24 In 331 BC.

25 See above, §2.   26 A Dacian people, perhaps those re-
settled by Aurelian or Galerius in the late third century AD.

27 The topic involves choosing to use one's resources for noble
ends. At *Top.* 3.118a Aristotle contrasts a life of abundant re-

because it was for the sake of fame and glory that Alexander wished to found it as the greatest city under the sun.[24]
26. Utility is at issue in the case of Heraclea in Pontus, because Heracles settled that place while repulsing the barbarians.[25] Necessity is to be seen in the case of the cities known as Carpian,[26] which were founded by the Romans on the Danube in order to prevent the barbarians from crossing the river and causing harm.

27. Such being these causes, you must also be aware that divine causes are the most esteemed, with heroic coming second, and human third; then too, happy causes rank first, grievous ones second. Finally, of the definitive topics, causes arising from an abundance of resources (*ek periousias*)[27] are more esteemed, while those required by necessity or expediency are more utilitarian.[28]

28. Accordingly, more time should be spent on the more esteemed causes, less on those without esteem. This topic is absolutely essential for a rhetor when praising cities in any situation. Of the causes themselves, the divine and the heroic lie in the realm of myth, while human causes are more plausible. For this reason human causes

sources with one of bare necessities and concludes: τὸ δ᾽ ἐκ περιουσίας ἐστίν, ὅταν ὑπαρχόντων τῶν ἀναγκαίων ἄλλα τινὰ προσκατασκευάζηταί τις τῶν καλῶν. (The condition of abundance exists, when, already possessing the necessities of life, a man is prepared to gain other things that are noble.) The topic reappears at 1.16.23.

[28] A similar contrast is made at 1.16.23, where deeds performed because one has the resources (ἐκ περιουσίας) are more glorious, those out of necessity (ἐξ ἀνάγκης) more just.

θείας καὶ πιστωτέον καὶ αὐξητέον. τοσαῦτά σοι καὶ
περὶ τῆς τοῦ γένους ἐπιχειρήσεως ἔχομεν συμβαλέ-
σθαι. τρίτον τοίνυν ἡμῖν βιβλίον γραφέσθω τόδε
περὶ ἐπιτηδεύσεων καὶ πράξεων· καὶ γὰρ ἀπὸ τούτων
δεῖν ἔφαμεν τὰς πόλεις ἐγκωμιάζειν.

must simply be amplified, heroic and divine ones both confirmed and amplified. That is as much as we can contribute to the handling of origin as a topic. Our third book, accordingly, will deal with activities and deeds, for as we stated,[29] the praise of cities must draw on those as well.

[29] Cf. 1.11.1.

1.16. ΠΩΣ ΔΕΙ ΑΠΟ ΕΠΙΤΗΔΕΥΣΕΩΝ ΤΑΣ ΠΟΛΕΙΣ ΕΓΚΩΜΙΑΖΕΙΝ

1. Τῶν τοίνυν ἐπιτηδεύσεων αἱ μὲν κατὰ τὴν τῆς πολιτείας κατάστασιν θεωροῦνται, αἱ δὲ κατὰ τὰς ἐπιστήμας, αἱ δὲ κατὰ τὰς τέχνας, αἱ δὲ κατὰ τὰς δυνάμεις. αὐτῶν δὲ τούτων τῶν μερῶν ἢ εἰδῶν ὅ τι χρὴ διαιρεῖσθαι, πειράσομαι ποιῆσαι καταφανές.

2. Πολιτεῖαι μέν εἰσι τρεῖς, βασιλεία, ἀριστοκρατία, δημοκρατία, ταύταις δὲ παρακείμεναί εἰσι κακίαι, βασιλείᾳ μὲν τυραννίς, ἀριστοκρατίᾳ δὲ ὀλιγαρχία καὶ πλουτοκρατία λεγομένη, δημοκρατίᾳ δὲ λαοκρατία. παρὰ πάσας δὲ ταύτας ἡ μικτὴ ἐκ πάντων τούτων, ὁποία ἥ τε Ῥωμαϊκὴ καὶ ἡ Λακωνικὴ τὸ παλαιόν.

3. Εἰ τοίνυν ἐπαινοίης πόλιν, εἰ μὲν τυραννουμένην, ὡς βασιλευομένην ἐπαινεῖν δεῖ, ὡς ἐν τοῖς Νικοκλείοις ὁ Ἰσοκράτης πεποίηκεν, εἰ δὲ λαοκρατουμένην, ὡς

---

[1] ἐπιτηδεύσεις are activities, practices, pursuits, and accomplishments that help define a people's character, as opposed to actual deeds (πράξεις). Its equivalent, ἐπιτηδεύματα, is much

[BOOK 3]

1.16. HOW TO PRAISE CITIES FOR
THEIR ACTIVITIES

1. Some activities[1] are to be viewed in relation to a city's governance, others to branches of knowledge, others to skills, and still others to abilities. I shall attempt to make clear how these types or kinds are to be analyzed.

2. Governments assume three different forms: kingship, aristocracy, and democracy. Corresponding to these are bad forms: tyranny to kingship; oligarchy and so-called plutocracy to aristocracy; and mob rule (*laocratia*)[2] to democracy. In addition to all these is a mixed form that combines them all,[3] exemplified by the governments of Rome and ancient Sparta.

3. If, therefore, you are praising a city that is a tyranny, you must praise it as if it were a kingship, as Isocrates did in his speeches to Nicocles;[4] if it is ruled by a mob, praise

---

more common. In fact, with two exceptions, at 1.11.1 and 1.15.28, ἐπιτηδεύσεις occurs only in this section and nowhere in Treatise II.

[2] The term appears only here (and below in §3 as a verb) in extant Greek texts.   [3] That is, all the good forms.

[4] *Orr.* 2 and 3 to Nicocles, son of Evagoras (ca. 435–374 BC) ruler of Cyprus.

360 δημοκρατουμένην, ὡς ἐν τῷ Παναθηναϊκῷ Ἰσοκράτης καὶ Πλάτων ἐν τῷ ἐπιταφίῳ· εἰ δὲ πλουτοκρατουμένην, ὡς ἀριστοκρατουμένην· εἰ δὲ μικτήν, ὅτι ἐξ ἁπασῶν εἴληφε τὰ κάλλιστα. τοῦτο δὲ ὁ Πλάτων περὶ τῆς Λακωνικῆς πολιτείας ἐν τοῖς Νόμοις εἴρηκεν καὶ Ἀριστείδης ἐν τῷ Ῥωμαϊκῷ.

4. Εἴησαν δ' ⟨ἂν⟩[1] ἐπαίνων ἀφορμαὶ παρὰ ταύτας ἁπάσας δεῖξαι πόλιν μὴ κατὰ τοὺς αὐτοὺς χρόνους ἁπάσαις κεχρημένην ἀλλ' ἄλλοτε ἄλλῃ, ὅπερ Ἰσοκράτης περὶ τῆς τῶν Ἀθηναίων πόλεως εἴρηκε καὶ Ἀριστείδης ἐν τῷ Παναθηναϊκῷ.

5. Δεῖ δὲ νομίζειν περὶ πολιτείας ἄριστον εἶναι τὸ ἑκοῦσαν ἀλλὰ μὴ ἄκουσαν ἄρχεσθαι τὴν πόλιν, καὶ τὸ ἀκριβῶς φυλάττειν τοὺς νόμους, ἥκιστα δὲ νόμων δεῖσθαι. τοῦτο δὲ τὸ μέρος τῶν ἐπαίνων κινδυνεύει σχεδὸν ἀργὸν εἶναι· ὑπὸ γὰρ μιᾶς αἱ Ῥωμαϊκαὶ ἅπασαι νῦν διοικοῦνται πόλεις, τελειότητος δὲ ἕνεκεν ἐχρῆν περὶ αὐτοῦ μνησθῆναι.

6. Αἱ δὲ κατὰ τὰς ἐπιστήμας ἐπιτηδεύσεις, εἰ κατὰ πόλιν εἴησαν εὐδόκιμοι, ἀστρολογία καὶ γεωμετρία ἢ μουσικὴ ἢ γραμματικὴ ἢ φιλοσοφία· αἱ γὰρ τοιαῦταί εἰσιν αἱ κατ' ἐπιστήμην ἐπιτηδεύσεις. φασὶ γὰρ τοὺς Μυτιληναίους ἐπὶ κιθαρῳδίᾳ μέγιστον φρονῆσαι, Θηβαίους δὲ ἐπὶ αὐλητικῇ, Δηλίους ἐπὶ χοροστατικῇ, ἔτι

[1] suppl. RW

5 *Panath.* 114–50.   6 Cf. *Menex.* 238c–39a.

it as if it were a democracy, as Isocrates did in his Panathenaic oration[5] and Plato in his *Epitaphius*;[6] and if it is a
plutocracy, praise it as if it were an aristocracy. If it is of
mixed form, say that it has taken the best features from
them all, a claim made by Plato in the *Laws* concerning
the Spartan constitution[7] and by Aristides in his speech
"On Rome."[8]

4. Besides all these, starting points for praise may be
found by showing that a city did not make use of all the
forms at the same time, but different ones at different
times, as Isocrates and Aristides say of Athens in their
Panathenaic orations.[9]

5. You must judge that the best feature of a government
is that it rules a willing city, not a resisting one, and that it
scrupulously keeps its laws while being least in need of
them. This aspect of praise could seem to be more or less
useless, since all Roman cities are now under a single government, but for the sake of completeness it was necessary
to mention it.

6. Activities within branches of knowledge (*epistēmai*),
if a city holds them in esteem, are astronomy and geometry, music, literary scholarship (*grammatikē*), and philosophy, for such are the activities within the field of
knowledge. For example, they say that the Mytilenians
take great pride in their lyre playing, the Thebans in their
pipe playing, the Delians in choral dancing,[10] and the Al-

---

[7] *Leg.* 4.712ce.   [8] *Or.* 26.90.

[9] Isoc. *Panath.* 114ff., and Aristid. *Panath.* 383–86.

[10] Cf. *Hymn Hom. Ap.* 146–50. Bursian and RW delete this
example as an interpolation because it lacks a connective and is
not included in the preceding list.

δὲ καὶ νῦν τοὺς Ἀλεξανδρέας ἐπὶ γραμματικῇ καὶ γε-
ωμετρίᾳ καὶ φιλοσοφίᾳ.

7. Αἱ δὲ κατὰ τὰς τέχνας ἐπιτηδεύσεις αἱ μέν εἰσι
βάναυσοι, αἱ δὲ ἐλευθέριοι. βάναυσοι μὲν χρυσο-
χοϊκὴ καὶ χαλκευτικὴ καὶ τεκτονικὴ καὶ ὅσαι τοιαῦται. ἔστιν οὖν καὶ ἀπὸ τούτων ἐπαινέσαι πόλιν ἢ εἰς
πλῆθος ἢ εἰς ἀκρίβειαν. . . .² φασὶ γὰρ Ἀθηναίους
μὲν ἐπὶ ἀγαλματοποιίᾳ καὶ ζωγραφίᾳ, καὶ Κροτωνιά-
τας ἐπὶ ἰατρικῇ μέγιστον φρονῆσαι, καὶ ἄλλους ἐπ'
ἄλλαις τέχναις.

361   8. Αἱ δὲ κατὰ τὰς δυνάμεις ἐπιτηδεύσεις ῥητορικὴ
καὶ ἀθλητικὴ καὶ ὅσαι τοιαῦται. Αἰγινῆται μὲν γὰρ
ἐπὶ ἀθλητικῇ καὶ Ἑρμουπολῖται ⟨ἐπὶ ῥητορικῇ⟩³ με-
γαλοφρονοῦσι.

9. Παρὰ πάσας δὲ ταύτας τὰς ἐπιτηδεύσεις καὶ τὰ
ἐνεργήματα σκοπούμεθα,⁴ εἰ κοσμίως διοικεῖται ἡ πό-
λις· ἀνήκει δὲ ἐπὶ τὴν τῶν ἀνδρῶν καὶ τὴν τῶν γυναικῶν δίαιταν καὶ τὴν τῶν παίδων ἀγωγήν. δεῖ γὰρ τὸ
αὐτὸ ἀποφαίνειν προσῆκον καὶ γυναιξὶ καὶ ἀνδράσι
καὶ παισὶν ἐπὶ διαίτῃ ἀπονενεμημένον, ὅπερ ὁ Δίων
ἐν τῷ Ταρσικῷ ἐπιγραφομένῳ πεποίηκεν.

---

² lacunam stat. Walz, Bursian: ἐλευθέριοι δὲ οἷον ἀγαλμα-
τοποιία καὶ ζωγραφία καὶ ἰατρική coni. Heeren
   ³ suppl. RW   ⁴ Finckh, RW: κοσμούμεθα codd.

---

¹¹ Apparently, a list of liberal skills is missing here. Heeren's
conjecture would fill the requirement: "whereas liberal skills include, for example, sculpture, painting, and medicine."

exandrians even to this day in their literary scholarship, geometry, and philosophy.

7. Some activities involving skills (*technai*) are manual (*banausoi*), others liberal (*eleutherioi*). Manual skills include gold working, bronze working, construction, and the like. Therefore it is possible to praise a city for these also in terms either of quantity or of quality.[11] For they say that the Athenians take great pride their sculpture and painting, the Crotoniates in their medicine,[12] and others in other skills.

8. Activities involving abilities (*dynameis*) include rhetoric, athletics, and the like. For instance, the Aeginetans pride themselves on their athletic ability,[13] and the Hermopolitans ⟨on their rhetoric⟩.[14]

9. In addition to all these activities, we also consider behaviors, in order to see whether the city is governed in an orderly fashion. This pertains to the comportment of men and women and the education of children, for one must show that appropriate conduct has been assigned to women, men, and children with regard to daily life,[15] as Dio Chrysostom did in his speech entitled "For Tarsus."[16]

---

[12] Democedes of Croton was called the most skillful physician of his time at Hdt. 3.125.   [13] Aeginetan prowess in athletics is well documented in Pindar's eleven odes for Aeginetan victors.

[14] There is no indication that Hermopolis was an athletic center. RW add ἐπὶ ῥητορικῇ (on their rhetoric) and note (p. 262): "in P. Berol. 21849 the town at which Victor asks his brother Theognostus to hand over some rhetorical books (including M.'s τέχνη etc.) is in fact Hermoupolis."   [15] This sentence is corrupt and no satisfactory emendation has been proposed.

[16] *Or.* 33.48 praises Tarsus for its orderliness (*eutaxia*) and the modesty (*sōphrosynē*) of its women but does not mention men or children.

10. Ἀπὸ μὲν δὴ τούτων τὰς τῶν πόλεων ἐπιτηδεύσεις δοκιμαστέον, τὰς δὲ πράξεις κατὰ τὰς ἀρετὰς
καὶ τὰ μέρη αὐτῶν. χρὴ δὲ καὶ περὶ τούτων σοι διελέσθαι. οὐκοῦν ἀρεταὶ μέν, ὥσπερ ἔφαμεν, τέσσαρες·
ἀνδρεία, δικαιοσύνη, σωφροσύνη, φρόνησις. πράξεις
δὲ πᾶσαι, ὅσας ἢ ἰδιῶται ἢ πόλεις ἀποδείκνυνται,
κατὰ ταύτας δοκιμάζονται, καὶ αὐτὰς καὶ τὰ μέρη
αὐτῶν.

11. Ἔστι δὲ δικαιοσύνης μὲν μέρη εὐσέβεια, δικαιοπραγία καὶ ὁσιότης. εὐσέβεια μὲν περὶ τοὺς θεούς,
δικαιοπραγία δὲ περὶ τοὺς ἀνθρώπους, ὁσιότης δὲ
περὶ τοὺς κατοιχομένους. τῆς δ' αὖ περὶ τοὺς θεοὺς
εὐσεβείας τὸ μέν τί ἐστι θεοφιλότης, τὸ δὲ φιλοθεότης. θεοφιλότης μὲν τὸ ὑπὸ τῶν θεῶν φιλεῖσθαι καὶ
παρὰ τῶν θεῶν πολλῶν τυγχάνειν, φιλοθεότης δὲ τὸ
φιλεῖν τοὺς θεοὺς καὶ φιλίαν ἔχειν περὶ αὐτούς. τῆς
δ' αὖ φιλοθεότητος τὸ μέν τί ἐστιν ἐν λόγοις, τὸ δέ τι
ἐν ἔργοις. ἔργα δ' ἢ ἴδια ἢ δημόσια, καὶ κατ' εἰρήνην
ἢ πόλεμον· ἄλλως γὰρ οὐκ ἂν εὐσέβεια φανείη πόλεως.

12. Δεῖ δὲ καὶ τούτων παραδείγματα ἑκάστων ἐκθέσθαι. τῆς μὲν θεοφιλότητος ἐκεῖνα ἐγκώμια ἃ περὶ
Ἀθηναίων καὶ Ῥοδίων καὶ Κορινθίων ⟨καὶ Δελφῶν⟩[5]
λέγεται. περὶ Ἀθηναίων μέν, ὅτι Ἀθηνᾶ καὶ Ποσειδῶν
362 ἤρισαν περὶ γῆς αὐτῶν, περὶ δὲ Ῥοδίων, ὅτι ὖσεν ὁ

[5] suppl. Spengel, Bursian, RW

10. Such are the topics by which to assess the activities of cities. Their actions (*praxeis*), on the other hand, are assessed in terms of the virtues and their subdivisions, which I must now analyze for you. The virtues, as we have said,[17] are four in number: courage, justice, moderation, and intelligence.[18] All actions, whether displayed by individuals or by cities, are assessed in terms of these virtues, both in themselves and in their subdivisions.

11. The subdivisions of justice are piety, fair-dealing (*dikaiopragia*), and reverence. Piety is concerned with the gods, fair-dealing with men, and reverence with the departed. Piety toward the gods, in turn, has two aspects, the quality of being "god-loved" (*theophilotēs*) and the quality of being "god-loving" (*philotheotēs*). The former consists in being loved by the gods and obtaining many benefits from them, the latter in loving the gods and being on friendly terms with them. Loving the gods in turn has two components, one involving words and the other deeds. Deeds are either private or public and are performed in peace or in war, for in no other way can a city's piety be manifested.

12. We must provide examples for each of these. The quality of being god-loved is exemplified in the praises spoken of the Athenians, Rhodians, Corinthians, and Delphians. Concerning the Athenians, it is said that Athena and Poseidon quarreled over possession of their land;[19]

---

[17] There has been no previous mention of the canonical four virtues in this treatise. They are, however, listed in 2.1.21, 2.2.27, 2.4.11, and 2.9.5.   [18] *Phronēsis* (practical intelligence) has replaced the broader term *sophia* (wisdom), familiar from Plato.

[19] The contest was depicted on the west pediment of the Parthenon. Cf. Hdt. 8.55 and Aristid. *Panath*. 40.

Ζεὺς χρυσῷ, περὶ δὲ Κορινθίων καὶ Ἰσθμοῦ, ὅτι
Ἥλιος καὶ Ποσειδῶν ἤρισαν, περὶ δὲ Δελφῶν Ἀπόλλων καὶ Ποσειδῶν καὶ Θέμις καὶ Νύξ.

13. Ἐν δὲ τούτῳ τῷ μέρει ἢ τοὺς πλείστους ἢ τοὺς
ἀρίστους τῶν θεῶν ταῖς μεγίσταις τῶν τιμῶν ἢ ταῖς
πρώταις ἢ ταῖς πλείσταις ἢ ταῖς ἀναγκαιοτάταις ἀποφαίνειν χρὴ τετιμηκότας· πλείστους μέν, ὡς περὶ
Ἀθηναίων λέγεται· καὶ γὰρ Διόνυσον καὶ Ἀπόλλωνα
καὶ Ποσειδῶνα καὶ Ἀθηνᾶν καὶ Ἥφαιστον καὶ Ἄρην
ἢ πάντας αὐτοὺς ἢ τοὺς πλείστους τετιμηκέναι λέ-
γουσι· τοὺς ἀρίστους δέ, ὥσπερ Ὀλυμπίαν τὸν Δία
καὶ Νεμέαν· 14. ταῖς δὲ μεγίσταις, ὡς περὶ Ἀθηναίων,
ὅτι σῖτον αὐτοῖς ἐδωρήσαντο· πλείσταις δέ, ὡς περὶ
Ἀθηναίων· σχεδὸν γὰρ ἅπασαν τοῦ βίου τὴν κατασκευὴν αὐτοῖς ἀξιοῦσι παρὰ τῶν θεῶν γεγενῆσθαι·
ταῖς δὲ ἀναγκαιοτάταις, ὡς τὸ περὶ Αἰγυπτίων·
ἀστρολογίαν γὰρ καὶ γεωμετρίαν ἀξιοῦσι παρ' αὐτῶν
γεγενῆσθαι. καὶ μάλιστα ὡς τὸ περὶ λόγων καὶ φιλο-
σοφίας· Ἀθηναίοις γὰρ μάλιστα ταῦτα ὑπάρξαι δοκεῖ. οὕτως μὲν οὖν τὴν θεοφιλότητα ὡρίκαμεν[6] τῆς
τεχνικῆς ἕνεκα χρείας [ἐπισκεπτέον].[7]

15. Τὴν δ' αὖ φιλοθεότητα,[8] ὥσπερ ἔφην, κριτέον
ἰδίᾳ μέν, εἰ τῶν πολιτῶν ἕκαστος τῆς περὶ τοὺς θεοὺς

[6] τὴν θεοφιλότητα ὡρίκαμεν coni. Bursian: ἡ θεοφιλότης
ὠνομάσθη, ἣν τῆς τεχνικῆς ἕνεκα χρείας ἐπισκεπτέον codd.:
totam sententiam obel. RW   [7] seclusi
[8] τὴν δ' αὖ φιλοθεότητα M: ἐπισκεπτέον δ' αὖ περὶ θεό-
τητα ὥσπερ ἔφην κριτέον P

concerning the Rhodians, that Zeus showered them with gold;[20] concerning the Corinthians and the Isthmus, that Helios and Poseidon quarreled over them;[21] and concerning the Delphians, that Apollo, Poseidon, Themis, and Night did likewise.[22]

13. In this section, we must show that either the greatest number or the best of the gods have bestowed on them the greatest, the first, the most abundant, or the most essential honors. On the score of "most numerous gods," it is said of the Athenians that Dionysus, Apollo, Poseidon, Athena, Hephaestus, and Ares—either all of these or the majority—have done them honor. The category of "best gods" applies to Zeus in his relation to Olympia and Nemea. 14. "Greatest honors" is exemplified by the Athenians, to whom the gods gave grain,[23] and so too is "most numerous honors," since the Athenians claim that almost every asset in life has come to them from the gods. As for "most essential honors," those are evident in the case of the Egyptians, who claim that astronomy and geometry came from the gods, while literature and philosophy are said to belong especially to the Athenians. Such, then, is the way we have defined "being god-loved" for the purposes of rhetoric.

15. Next, "loving the gods" must be judged, as I said,[24] both on an individual basis, considering whether each of the citizens engages in worship of the gods, and by its

---

[20] Cf. Pind. *Ol*. 7.34, 49–50.

[21] Cf. Paus. 2.1.6.

[22] Cf. Aesch. *Eum*. 1–8.

[23] Cf. Aristid. *Panath*. 34 and 336. This incident is also referred to at 2.2.24.   [24] Cf. §11.

θεραπείας ἐπιμελεῖται, δημοσίᾳ δὲ κατὰ πολλοὺς τρόπους, εἰ τελετὰς κατεστήσαντο, εἰ πολλὰς ἑορτὰς ἐνό-
μισαν, εἰ πλείστας θυσίας ἢ ἀκριβεστάτας, εἰ πλεῖστα ἱερὰ ᾠκοδόμησαν ἢ πάντων θεῶν ἢ πολλὰ
ἑκάστου, εἰ τὰς ἱερωσύνας ἀκριβῶς ποιοῦνται· ἀπὸ
γὰρ τούτων αἱ τῶν πόλεων φιλοθεότητες σκοποῦνται.
16. τὴν μὲν οὖν τῶν καθ᾽ ἕνα σπάνιον ἐν τοῖς νῦν
χρόνοις εὑρεῖν, τῆς δὲ κοινῆς εὐσεβείας καὶ περὶ τοὺς
θεοὺς σπουδῆς πολλαὶ ἀντιποιοῦνται πόλεις, ὥστ᾽, εἰ
363   τούτων μίαν ἀποφαίνοις τὴν ἐγκωμιαζομένην, ἱκανὴν
εὐφημίαν ἔσῃ πεπορισμένος. καὶ περὶ μὲν τῆς εἰς
τοὺς θεοὺς εὐσεβείας ταῦτα.

17. Ἡ δ᾽ αὖ δικαιοπραγία διαιρεῖται εἴς τε τοὺς
ἀφικνουμένους ξένους καὶ εἰς ἀλλήλους, μέρος δ᾽ αὐτῆς καὶ τὸ τοῖς ἔθεσιν ἴσοις καὶ φιλανθρώποις καὶ τὸ
νόμοις ἀκριβέσι καὶ δικαίοις χρῆσθαι. 18. εἰ γὰρ μήτε
ξένους ἀδικοῖεν μήτε ἀλλήλους κακουργοῖεν, τοῖς δ᾽
ἔθεσιν ἴσοις καὶ κοινοῖς καὶ τοῖς νόμοις χρῶντο δικαίοις, οἱ πολῖται ἄριστα καὶ δικαιότατα τὰς πόλεις
οἰκήσονται. ἀλλὰ τὸ τῶν νόμων ἐν τοῖς νῦν χρόνοις
ἄχρηστον· κατὰ γὰρ τοὺς κοινοὺς τῶν Ῥωμαίων νόμους πολιτευόμεθα, ἔθεσι δ᾽ ἄλλη πόλις ἄλλοις χρῆ-
ται, ἐξ ὧν προσῆκεν ἐγκωμιάζειν.

19. Τῆς τοίνυν ὁσιότητος διττὸς τρόπος· ἢ γὰρ περὶ
τὴν ἐκφορὰν τῶν τετελευτηκότων αἱ τιμαὶ γίνονται ἢ
περὶ τὰ νομιζόμενα κατὰ τὰ μνήματα καὶ τοὺς τά-
φους. περὶ μὲν δὴ τὴν ἐκφοράν, ὡς τὸ Ἀθήνησι πρὸ
ἡλίου ἀνίσχοντος, ἢ ἐν Θουρίοις νύκτωρ ἡ πρόθεσις,

many public forms, noting whether they have established mysteries, whether they have instituted many festivals, whether they perform the most numerous or most scrupulous sacrifices, whether they have built the greatest number of temples, either for all the gods together or numerous ones for each, and whether they maintain priesthoods in a scrupulous manner. It is by these criteria that a city's "god-loving" qualities are examined. 16. Acts of individual god-loving are rarely found in the present times, but many cities lay claim to public piety and zeal for the gods. If then you can show that the city being praised is one of them, you will have praised it sufficiently. So much for piety toward the gods.

17. Fair-dealing is divided into treatment of visiting foreigners and treatment of fellow citizens. A part of it also involves observing customs that are fair and humane and laws that are precise and just. 18. If citizens neither treat foreigners unjustly nor mistreat one another, and if they observe fair and equally shared customs and just laws, they will govern their cities most nobly and justly. In these times, however, the topic of laws is irrelevant, for we govern our cities[25] according to the universal laws of the Romans. Customs, on the other hand, differ from city to city and so provide appropriate material for praise.

19. Reverence for the departed has two aspects, since honors are paid to the dead in connection either with the funeral or with the customs that pertain to memorials and tombs. With regard to the funeral, we must consider whether the display of the body takes place before sunrise as in Athens or at night as in Thurii, and whether there is

---

[25] Or, "conduct our public lives."

ἢ προθέσεως ἡμέρα τακτή, ὡς τὸ Ἀθήνησι καὶ ὅσα
ἄλλα τοιαῦτα. περὶ δὲ τὰ ἐτήσια, τίνος ἀπάγουσι
χοάς, πόσας τινάς, μέχρι τίνος, ἐν ποίᾳ ἡλικίᾳ, τίνες
αἱ ἀποφράδες ἡμέραι· πάντα γὰρ ταῦτα ὁσιότητός
εἰσιν. αὕτη τῆς δικαιοσύνης ἡ διαίρεσις αὐτῆς καὶ
τῶν μερῶν, πρὸς ἣν τὸν ἐγκωμιάζοντα εἰς δικαιοσύνην ἡντινοῦν τῶν πόλεων δεῖ βλέπειν.

20. Μετὰ δὲ τὴν δικαιοσύνην [καὶ]⁹ τὴν σωφροσύνην καὶ τὴν φρόνησιν ἐπισκεψώμεθα. σωφροσύνης
μὲν οὖν διττὸς ἔλεγχος, ἔν τε τῇ κοινῇ πολιτείᾳ καὶ
τοῖς ἰδίοις οἴκοις. ἐν πολιτείᾳ μὲν κοινῇ περί τε παίδων ἀγωγῆς καὶ παρθένων καὶ γάμων καὶ συνοική-
σεων καὶ τῶν νομίμων τῶν ἐπὶ τοῖς ἁμαρτήμασιν τοῖς
ἀκόσμοις. καὶ γὰρ γυναικονόμους πολλαὶ τῶν πόλεων
εἰσὶν αἱ χειροτονοῦσιν. 21. ἐν ἄλλαις δὲ τῶν πόλεων
οὔτε πρὸ πληθούσης ἀγορᾶς νέον φαίνεσθαι οὔτε
μετὰ δείλην ὀψίαν καλόν, οὐδὲ γυναῖκα καπηλεύειν ἢ
ἄλλο τι ποιεῖν τῶν κατὰ τὴν ἀγοράν. ἐν ἐνίαις δὲ
πανηγύρεσιν οὐδὲ γυναῖκες φαίνονται, ὥσπερ ἐν
Ὀλυμπίᾳ. χρὴ τοίνυν καὶ ταῦτα ἐν τοῖς ἐγκωμίοις πα-
ρατηρεῖν· ἐν δὲ τοῖς ἰδίοις βίοις ἤδη καὶ εἰ ἐλάχιστα
μοιχεία καὶ ἄλλα ἁμαρτήματα ἐν τῇ πόλει φαίνεται.

22. Φρονήσεως δὲ κατὰ τὸν αὐτὸν τρόπον· ἐν μὲν
τοῖς κοινοῖς εἰ τὰ νόμιμα καὶ περὶ ὧν οἱ νόμοι τίθεται
ἀκριβῶς ἡ πόλις, κλῆρον ἐπικλήρων, καὶ ὅσα ἄλλα
μέρη νόμων· ἀλλὰ καὶ τοῦτο τὸ μέρος διὰ τὸ τοῖς
κοινοῖς χρῆσθαι τῶν Ῥωμαίων νόμοις ἄχρηστον.
ἰδίως δέ, εἰ πολλοὶ ἐλλόγιμοι γεγόνασιν ἀπὸ τῆς πό-

a fixed day for the display as in Athens, and so forth. As regards annual observances, we must consider what the libations consist of, how many are offered, for how long, by what age-groups, and which days are ill-omened, for these are all aspects of reverence. This concludes the analysis of justice and its subdivisions, to which we must pay attention when praising the justice of any city.

20. After justice, let us consider moderation and intelligence. There are two areas in which to assess moderation, in public governance and in private homes. Under public governance fall the education of boys and girls, marriages and cohabitations, and laws regarding crimes against good order. Then too, many cities elect overseers of women's behavior (*gynaikonomoi*). 21. In other cities, it is improper for a young person to appear in public before mid-morning or after dark, or for a woman to sell goods or conduct any other business in the marketplace. At some civic festivals, such as at Olympia, women cannot appear at all. We must therefore pay close attention to these matters in encomia. In private lives as well, consider whether adultery and other wrongdoings very seldom occur in the city.

22. Intelligence is treated in the same fashion. With respect to public affairs, we should consider whether the city establishes precise rules for customs and legal issues such as inheritance and all other areas of the law—although this facet too is irrelevant because we are subject to the universal laws of the Romans. As for individuals, we must consider whether many highly regarded rhetori-

---

[9] secl. Spengel, RW

λεως ῥήτορες, σοφισταί, γεωμέτραι, καὶ ὅσαι ἐπι-
στῆμαι φρονήσεως ἤρτηνται.

23. Ἡ δ᾽ ἀνδρεία κατ᾽ εἰρήνην καὶ κατὰ πόλεμον
δοκιμάζεται· κατὰ μὲν εἰρήνην πρὸς τὰς ἐκ τοῦ δαι-
μονίου συντυχίας, σεισμούς, λιμούς, λοιμούς, αὐ-
χμούς, καὶ ὅσα τοιαῦτα. κατὰ δὲ πόλεμον πρὸς τὰς
ἐν τοῖς ὅπλοις πράξεις. πρὸς τὰ τέλη γὰρ νίκην ἢ
ἧτταν ἀναγκαῖον γενέσθαι, χρὴ τοίνυν ἧτταν μὲν
ἐρρωμένως, νίκην δὲ ἀνθρωπίνως ἀποφαίνειν ἐνηνο-
χυῖαν τὴν πόλιν. τῶν δ᾽ ἐν τοῖς ὅπλοις πράξεων αἱ
μὲν πρὸς Ἕλληνας, αἱ δὲ πρὸς βαρβάρους· ἔτι δὲ αἱ
μὲν ἐκ περιουσίας, αἱ δ᾽ ἐξ ἀνάγκης. ἐνδοξότεραι μὲν
τοίνυν αἱ ἐκ περιουσίας, δικαιότεραι δὲ αἱ ἐξ ἀνάγκης.

24. Τῶν δὲ πράξεων αἱ μὲν ἔνδοξοι, αἱ δὲ ἀμφίδο-
ξοι, αἱ δὲ ἄδοξοι. ἔνδοξοι μέν, ὧν καὶ ἡ πρόφασις
καλὴ καὶ τὸ τέλος, ὡς ἡ ἐν Μαραθῶνι· καὶ γὰρ τὸ
τέλος καὶ ἡ πρόφασις τῆς βελτίστης μοίρας. ἀμφίδο-
ξοι δέ, ὧν τὸ μὲν τέλος φαῦλον, ἡ δ᾽ αἰτία καλή, ὡς
τὸ ἐν Θερμοπύλαις Λακεδαιμονίων ἔργον· ἢ τὸ μὲν
τέλος ἀγαθόν, ἡ δ᾽ αἰτία φαύλη, ὡς τὸ περὶ Μηλίους

365

---

26 See 2.1.27 for an emperor's humane treatment after a victory.

27 At 1.15.27 M. divided the causes of city-founding into those
done because abundant resources were available (ἐκ περιουσίας)
as opposed to those required by necessity or expedience (ἀπὸ τῶν
ἀναγκαίων καὶ συμφερόντων), like the glorious founding of Alexandria in contrast to the utilitarian founding of towns along the

cians, sophists, and geometricians have come from the city, and practitioners of all types of knowledge (*epistēmai*) that require intelligence.

23. Courage is assessed in times of peace and war—in peacetime, with respect to acts of god like earthquakes, famines, plagues, droughts, and the like; in wartime, with respect to deeds in combat. Since outcomes necessarily result in victory or defeat, we must therefore show that the city has borne defeat with fortitude and victory with humanity (*anthrōpinōs*).[26] Some deeds in combat are committed against Greeks, others against barbarians. In addition, some are performed because one has the resources, others out of necessity.[27] Deeds performed because one has the resources are more glorious; those performed out of necessity are more justified.

24. Some deeds are glorious, some ambiguous, some infamous. Glorious are those whose justification and outcome are noble, like the battle of Marathon,[28] since its outcome and justification were of the best class. Ambiguous are ones whose outcome is bad but the cause is noble, like the action of the Spartans at Thermopylae,[29] or else the outcome is good but the cause is bad, like the operation of the Athenians at Melos.[30] Infamous are those of

Danube. For the use of one's resources for noble ends, cf. Arist. *Top.* 3.118a (quoted at 1.15.27).

[28] In 490 BC, when the Athenians defeated the invading Persians.

[29] In 480 BC, when the three hundred Spartans temporarily held off the Persian army.

[30] In 416–15 BC, when the Athenians destroyed Melos because it refused to join the Athenian empire.

Ἀθηναίων ἔργον. ἄδοξοι δέ, ὧν καὶ ἡ αἰτία καὶ τὸ τέλος φαῦλον, ὡς τὸ Λακεδαιμονίων περὶ Καδμείαν ἔργον. 25. αὐτῶν δὲ τῶν πράξεων[10] αἱ μὲν κοιναί, αἱ δὲ ἴδιαι· ἴδιαι μέν, ὡς τὸ περὶ Θυρέαν Λακεδαιμονίου ἔργον, κοιναὶ δέ, ὡς τὸ ἐν Θερμοπύλαις Λακεδαιμονίων ἔργον. ἐνδοξότεραι τοίνυν αἱ κοιναί. ὡς δὲ χρὴ ταύτας τάττειν, ἐν ἄλλοις δείξομεν.

26. Δοκεῖ δὲ ἴδιος τόπος εἶναι παρὰ τούτους ὁ ἀπὸ τῶν τιμῶν, ὧν τετυχήκασιν αἱ πόλεις παρὰ βασιλέων ἢ ἀρχόντων ἢ γνωρίμων ἀνδρῶν, οἷον ὅτι αὐτονόμους ἀφῆκαν ἐνίας πόλεις οἱ Ῥωμαῖοι καὶ ἐλευθέρας. ἀλλὰ τοῦτο ἐπιχείρημα ἂν εἴη μᾶλλον ἢ τόπος γενικός· ἔστι γὰρ τὸ[11] ἀπὸ κρίσεως ἐνδόξου. ἔσται δέ σοι ἡ περὶ ταῦτα ἔφοδος γνωριμωτέρα ⟨ἐκ τοῦ περὶ⟩ ἐπιχειρημάτων συγγράμματος· ἡμῖν δὲ νῦν οὐ ⟨περὶ τούτων ὁ λόγος ἀλλὰ⟩[12] περὶ τῶν γενικῶν καὶ ἀνωτάτω τόπων, ἀφ᾽ ὧν πόλεις ἔστιν ἐπαινεῖν.

27. Χρὴ δέ σε μηδ᾽ ἐκεῖνο ἀγνοεῖν, ὅτι καὶ ἐπὶ μέρει τούτων ὅλαι ὑποθέσεις γίνονται. καὶ γὰρ ἐπὶ λουτροῦ μόνου κατασκευῇ καὶ ἐπὶ λιμένος καὶ ἐπὶ

---

[10] RW: ὑποθέσεων codd.

[11] τὸ Heeren: ὁ codd.

[12] ἔσται δέ σοι . . . ἀλλὰ suppl e.g. RW: ἡμῖν δὲ νῦν οὐκ ἐπιχειρημάτων συγγράμματος ἔσται σοι ἡ περὶ ταῦτα ἔφοδος, γνωριμωτέρα δὲ ἡ codd.: alii alia

---

[31] In 382 BC, when the Spartan Phoebidas treacherously seized the Theban acropolis. Cf. Xen. *Hell*. 5.2.25ff.

which both the cause and the outcome are bad, like the Spartans' attack on the Theban Cadmea.[31] 25. Among actions themselves, some are performed by groups, others by individuals; the latter are exemplified by the single Spartan's exploit at Thyrea,[32] the former by the Spartan action at Thermopylae. Greater esteem is attached to actions by groups. Elsewhere I shall show how to arrange these subjects.[33]

26. Besides these topics, there is thought to be a specific one concerning the honors that cities have received from emperors, governors, or famous men, as, for example, when the Romans have granted some cities autonomy and freedom. This, however, would be a particular argument (*epicheirēma*), namely one based on authoritative judgment,[34] rather than a general topic. Such an approach to this material will be clearer to you from a treatise on arguments; our present work, however, is not about that but about generic and general topics to be used in praising cities.[35]

27. You must also not forget that entire subjects may be based on one part of a city. For example, it is possible to make an oration on the construction of a single bath or

[32] Othryades was the sole Spartan survivor in the "Battle of the 300" against the Argives, circa 546 BC; cf. Hdt. 1.82.

[33] This claim is not fulfilled in either treatise.

[34] For the argument, ἀπὸ κρίσεως ἐνδόξου (from authoritative judgment), RW cite Minucianus' περὶ ἐπιχειρημάτων (1.423.29–33 Sp.). [DH] cites the authoritative judgment of Homer at 4.3.

[35] The text of this sentence is corrupt; I have adopted the reconstructions of RW.

μέρει τινὶ τῆς πόλεως ἀνοικοδομηθέντι ἔστι προσφωνεῖν. ἐπὶ μέντοι τούτων διαμέμνησο μὴ τελέως τέ-
μνειν, ἀλλὰ μόνον τὸ προσταχθέν, ἄλλα δὲ ὡς βραχύτατα ἐπιδραμεῖν.[13]

28. Ἔτι τοῖς τῶν πόλεων ἐγκωμίοις κἀκεῖνο χρὴ
ἐπισημήνασθαι, ὅτι τὰ ἐγκώμια γίγνεται τὰ μὲν
κοινὰ παντὸς τοῦ χρόνου, τὰ δ᾽ ἴδια καιρῶν, ⟨ἴδια μὲν
καιρῶν⟩[14] ὅταν ἐν ἑορταῖς ἢ πανηγύρεσιν οἱ λόγοι
γίγνωνται, ἢ ἐν ἀγῶνι, ἢ ἐν μονομαχίαις· κοινὰ δέ,
ὅταν μηδεμίαν τοιαύτην πρόφασιν ἔχῃ. χρὴ τοίνυν
τῶν πανηγυρικῶν πλείστην διατριβὴν περὶ τὸν καιρὸν ἕκαστον ποιεῖσθαι, οἷον εἰ ἑορτὴ εἴη ἢ πανήγυρις
ἢ σύνοδος ἐν ἀγῶνι ἢ ἐνοπλίῳ ἢ γυμνικῷ ἢ μουσικῷ.

29. Ὅπως δὲ χρὴ τούτων ἕκαστον ἐπαινεῖν, νῦν ἤδη
ἄκουε. ἐπαινεῖν χρὴ τὰς συνόδους καὶ πανηγύρεις ἢ
ἐκ τῶν ἰδίων ἢ ἐκ τῶν κοινῶν· κοινῶν μὲν τῶν θετι-
κῶν, ὅσα ἀγαθὰ ἐκ συνόδων γίνεται ἀνθρώποις· ἰδίων
δὲ ⟨κατὰ⟩[15] τὰ περιστατικὰ καλούμενα μόρια, ἀπὸ
προσώπου τριχῶς, θεῶν εἰ ἑορταὶ ἢ ἡρώων ἢ βασιλέων, τίνες οἱ συνάγοντές εἰσι, τίνες οἱ συνιόντες·
ἀπὸ τοῦ τόπου, εἰ ἐν εὐκαιρίᾳ κεῖται ὁ τόπος, ἔνθα ἡ
σύνοδος, ἢ καὶ ἀπὸ τόπων πλεῖστον ἀπεχόντων συν-

366

[13] conieci praeeunte Jacobs: ἀλλὰ μόνον τὸ προσταχθὲν
ἀναγκαίως βραχύτατα ἐπιδραμεῖν M
[14] suppl. Heeren, Walz, RW
[15] suppl. Finckh, Bursian: τὰ . . . μόρια secl. RW

harbor, or on the restoration of some sector of a city. On these occasions, however, you should remember not to make this an entire division, but ‹to treat› only the subject matter that has been assigned, while touching on the rest as briefly as possible.[36]

28. A further point to note while praising cities is that some encomia are common to all times, others specific to particular occasions. Encomia for specific occasions are speeches delivered during feasts (*heortai*) or festivals (*panēgyreis*), at competitions, or at gladiatorial shows. Encomia are general when they lack any such pretext. Accordingly, in festival speeches (*panēgyrikoi*) one must spend most of the time on the particular occasion, which may be, for example, a feast, a festival, or a gathering for the purpose of competition, whether gladiatorial, athletic, or musical.

29. Now let me tell you how to praise each of these. You should praise gatherings and festivals on either particular or general grounds. General topics include all the benefits that people derive from gatherings. Particular ones, in accordance with the so-called circumstantial components,[37] relate (a) to the persons involved, considered under three aspects, i.e., whether the festivals celebrate gods, heroes, or emperors; who the organizers are; and who attend it; (b) to location, i.e., whether the gathering place is conveniently located, or if people come from faraway places (for things sought after with great effort are

---

[36] The text of this sentence is doubtful. RW obelize everything after "but."

[37] These include "who, what, when, where, why," etc.

ἔρχονται· τὰ γὰρ περισπούδαστα τίμια· ἀπὸ δὲ χρόνου, εἰ τοῦ ἔτους ἐν τῷ ὑγιεινοτάτῳ καὶ ἡδίστῳ καιρῷ·
ἀπὸ δὲ αἰτίας, εἰ οἴονται ἡδίους καὶ βελτίους ἔσεσθαι·
ἀπὸ ὕλης δέ, ἂν πολυτελεῖς καὶ σεμναί.

30. Δεῖ δ' ἴσως καὶ παραδείγματα τούτων εἰπεῖν, ἵν'
ὑπάρχῃ ῥᾴδιον παρακολουθῆσαι. τῶν μὲν τοίνυν κοινῶν ἐστιν, οἷον τὸ Ἰσοκράτους, "τῶν τοίνυν τὰς πανηγύρεις καταστησάντων δικαίως ἐπαινουμένων." ⟨τῶν
δὲ ἰδίων ἀπὸ προσώπου· εἰ⟩[16] ἡ μὲν πανήγυρις ἄγεται
θεῷ, ὡς Ὀλύμπια τῷ Διΐ· ἥρωϊ δὲ τὰ Ἴσθμια Παλαί-
μονι, καὶ Νέμεα Ἀρχεμόρῳ· βασιλεῖ δέ, ὡς τὰ Σεβά-
στεια πολλαχοῦ. τῶν δὲ συναγόντων, ὡς τῶν Ἀθηναίων ἢ Ῥωμαίων· συμβάλλεται γὰρ ἐπὶ δόξαν τῇ
πανηγύρει καὶ τὸ ἐνδόξους εἶναι τοὺς ἐπαγγέλλοντας
τὴν σύνοδον. 31. τῶν δὲ συνιόντων ὡς πλείστων ἢ ὡς
ἐνδοξοτάτων, ἐνδοξοτάτων μέν, ὡς οἱ Ὀλυμπίαζε· οἱ
γὰρ γνωριμώτεροι συνέρχονται· πλείστων δέ, ὡς τὸ
περὶ τὴν πανήγυριν τῶν Ἑβραίων ἐπὶ τὴν Συρίαν τὴν
Παλαιστίνην· ἐξ ἐθνῶν γὰρ πλείστων συλλέγονται.

32. Κατὰ δὲ τὸν τόπον, ἔνθα μὲν ἡ πανήγυρις, ὡς
τὸ περὶ Δελφῶν, ὅτι ἐν ὀμφαλῷ τῆς γῆς κεῖται· ὅθεν
δὲ ὁρμῶνται οἱ συνιόντες, ὡς ἐπὶ τοῦ Πυθικοῦ ἀγῶ-
νος· ἐκ περάτων γὰρ τῆς γῆς συνίασι· δι' οὗ δὲ τόπου

---

[16] suppl. Bursian praeeuntibus Heeren, Walz

valued); (c) to time, i.e., whether it takes place in the healthiest and most pleasant season of the year; (d) to motivation, i.e., whether those who attend think that they will become happier and better; and (e) to material outlay, i.e., whether the celebrations are lavish and dignified.

30. Perhaps I ought to give examples of these to make this easier to follow. An example of a general proposition is Isocrates' "Now the founders of public festivals are justly praised."[38] Particular propositions include citing the person involved, if[39] the public festival is held for a god, as the Olympic games are for Zeus; or for a hero, as the Isthmian games are for Palaemon and the Nemean games for Archemorus; or for an emperor, like the Sebasteia that are held in many places. Organizers may be cited, like Athenians or Romans, because it adds to the prestige of a festival that those who announce the gathering are themselves held in high repute. 31. The attendance may be cited for its large numbers or great distinction: of great distinction like those who go to Olympia, because the most notable gather there; in large numbers like those at the festival of the Hebrews in Syrian Palestine, because they gather from the greatest number of nations.

32. The location of the festival may serve as a basis for praise, as when one says of Delphi that it lies at the "navel" of the earth; or where the people attending come from, as when one says of the Pythian games that people gather there from the ends of the earth; or what places they pass

[38] *Paneg.* 43.
[39] I have tentatively accepted Bursian's supplements.

367 συνέρχονται, ὡς τὸ περὶ Ὀλυμπίων· χαλεπωτάτη γὰρ
ἡ ἄνοδος, ὅμως δὲ παραβάλλονται οἱ ἄνθρωποι.

33. Ἀπὸ δὲ χρόνου κατὰ μὲν τὴν περίοδον, ἐὰν μὲν
ᾖ ἐνιαύσιος, ὅτι οὐ σπανιότητί ἐστι περισπούδαστος,
ὥσπερ αἱ ἄλλαι, καὶ συνεχῶς γινομένη οὐδὲν ἐκείνων
ἀπολείπεται σεμνότητι, ὡς τὰ Λήναια, ὡς Ἐλευσί-
νια . . .[17] καὶ Νέμεα καὶ Ἴσθμια· ἐν δὲ πενταετηρικῇ
ἢ τετραετηρικῇ ἢ <διὰ>[18] πλειόνων, ὡς τὰ Πύθια καὶ
Ὀλύμπια καὶ Δαίδαλα ἐν Πλαταιαῖς· δι᾽ ἑξήκοντα
γὰρ ἐτῶν ἄγεται.

[17] lacunam stat. RW
[18] suppl. Bursian, RW

through along the way, as when one says of the Olympic games that although the journey there is very difficult, nevertheless men take the risk.[40]

33. As regards a festival's timing, if it is annual, say that it is not because of its infrequency that it is much sought after, as with other festivals, and though occurring regularly it is in no way inferior to them in dignity. Examples include the Lenaea,[41] the Eleusinia[42] . . .[43] and the Nemean and Isthmian festivals; and in ones occurring every three or four years, or at longer intervals, like the Pythian and Olympic games[44] and the Daedalian festival in Plataea, which is held every sixty years.[45]

[40] Safe travel to Olympia in the northwest corner of the Peloponnesus was ensured by the declaration of the Olympic Truce a month before the games opened. "We can find no explanation why M. should say that the road to Olympia was so difficult" RW (270).

[41] An annual Athenian festival with a dramatic competition.

[42] Initiations into the cult of Demeter and Persephone were celebrated annually at Eleusis.

[43] RW detect a lacuna here, because the Nemean and Isthmian games were biennial.

[44] According to inclusive reckoning, the Pythian and Olympian games were celebrated every five years.

[45] Paus. 9.3.5 states that the Greater Daedalian festival was held at an interval of sixty years. The treatise breaks off without treating the benefits and expenses of festivals.

2.1. ΠΕΡΙ ΒΑΣΙΛΙΚΟΥ

1. Ὁ βασιλικὸς λόγος ἐγκώμιόν ἐστι βασιλέως·
οὐκοῦν αὔξησιν ὁμολογουμένην περιέξει τῶν προσόντων ἀγαθῶν βασιλεῖ, οὐδὲν δὲ ἀμφίβολον καὶ ἀμφι-
σβητούμενον ἐπιδέχεται διὰ τὸ ἄγαν ἔνδοξον τὸ
πρόσωπον εἶναι, ἀλλ' ὡς ἐφ' ὁμολογουμένοις ἀγαθοῖς
τὴν ἐργασίαν ποιήσῃ.

2. Λήψῃ τοίνυν ἐν τούτῳ τὰ προοίμια δηλονότι ἀπὸ
τῆς αὐξήσεως, μέγεθος περιτιθεὶς τῇ ὑποθέσει, ὅτι
δυσέφικτος, καὶ ὅτι καθῆκας ἑαυτὸν εἰς ἀγῶνα οὐ ῥάδιον κατορθωθῆναι λόγῳ, ἢ τοὺς ἑαυτοῦ λόγους μα-
καριεῖς, ὅτι καθῆκαν εἰς πεῖραν πραγμάτων μετ' ἀγα-
θῆς καὶ λαμπρᾶς τῆς τύχης, ἧς εἰ τύχοιεν,[1] μεγίστην
ἄρασθαι δυνήσονται δόξαν· ἢ ὅτι ἄτοπόν ἐστι τοσούτων ἀγαθῶν παρὰ βασιλέων πειρωμένους μὴ τὸν πρέ-
ποντα καὶ ὀφειλόμενον αὐτοῖς ἔρανον ἀποδιδόναι· 3. ἢ
ὅτι δύο τὰ μέγιστα τῶν ὑπαρχόντων ἐν τῷ βίῳ τῶν
ἀνθρώπων ἐστὶν εὐσέβεια περὶ τὸ θεῖον καὶ τιμὴ περὶ
βασιλέας, ἃ προσήκει καὶ θαυμάζειν καὶ ὑμνεῖν κατὰ
δύναμιν.

4. Δέχεται δὲ τὰ προοίμια τοῦ λόγου καὶ ἐκ παρα-
δειγμάτων ἀορίστων αὐξήσεις, οἷον ὡς ἂν εἰ λέγοι-

---

[1] τύχοιεν PZp: λόγοι ἐπιτύχοιεν cett.

2.1. THE ROYAL ORATION

1. The royal oration (*basilikos logos*) is an encomium of the emperor. Consequently, it will contain generally agreed-upon amplification of the good things pertaining to the emperor, and, because of such a person's great prestige, it excludes anything ambiguous or disputed. In short, you must base your composition on qualities acknowledged to be good.

2. In it you should obviously derive your introduction from topics of amplification and endow your subject with importance by noting how difficult it is to undertake and by claiming that you are engaged in a contest of words by no means easy to win. Or else, you can count your own words blessed and say, "They have engaged in a trial of deeds thanks to splendid good fortune, and should they have its blessing, they stand to win the greatest glory." Or else: "Since we enjoy so many benefits from the emperors, it is unreasonable not to repay them with our due and proper contribution." 3. Or else: "The two most important things in human life are reverence for the gods and respect for emperors, and these oblige us to venerate and hymn them to the best of our ability."

4. The oration's introductions also permit amplification derived from indefinite examples,[1] as when we might say,

---

[1] Indefinite examples contain no specific names or details. Cf. Hermog. *Id.* 1.11.102 (282.1 Rabe).

μεν, ὥσπερ δὲ πελάγους ἀπείρου τοῖς ὀφθαλμοῖς μέ-
369 τρον οὐκ ἔστι λαβεῖν, οὕτω καὶ βασιλέως εὐφημίαν
λόγῳ περιλαβεῖν οὐ ῥᾴδιον. οὐ μόνον δὲ ἐπὶ τοῦ βα-
σιλικοῦ τοῦτο εὕροις ἄν, ἀλλὰ καὶ ἐπὶ πάσης ἐπιδει-
κτικῆς ὑποθέσεως, καὶ μάλιστα ἐν τοῖς συντόνοις τῶν
ἐπιδεικτικῶν. ὥσπερ οὖν τὸ κρεῖττον ὕμνοις καὶ ἀρεταῖς ἱλασκόμεθα, οὕτω καὶ βασιλέα λόγοις.

5. Λήψει δὲ δευτέρων προοιμίων ἐννοίας, ὅταν αὐξήσεως ἕνεκα παραλαμβάνηται, ἢ ἀπὸ Ὁμήρου τῆς
μεγαλοφωνίας, ὅτι ταύτης μόνης ἐδεῖτο ἡ ὑπόθεσις, ἢ
ἀπὸ Ὀρφέως τοῦ Καλλιόπης ἢ ἀπὸ τῶν Μουσῶν
αὐτῶν, ὅτι μόλις ἂν καὶ αὗται πρὸς ἀξίαν τῆς ὑποθέσεως εἰπεῖν ἠδυνήθησαν, ὅμως δὲ οὐδὲν κωλύει καὶ
ἡμᾶς ἐγχειρῆσαι πρὸς δύναμιν. 6. ἡ τρίτη δὲ τοῦ προ-
οιμίου ἔννοια (καθόλου δὲ τούτου μέμνησο τοῦ παραγ-
γέλματος) προκαταρκτικὴ γενέσθω τῶν κεφαλαίων,
οἷον[2] ὡς διαποροῦντος τοῦ λέγοντος ὅθεν χρὴ τὴν
ἀρχὴν τῶν ἐγκωμίων ποιήσασθαι.

7. Μετὰ τὰ προοίμια ἐπὶ τὴν πατρίδα ἥξεις. ἐνταῦθα
δὲ διασκέψῃ κατὰ σαυτόν, πότερον ἔνδοξός ἐστιν ἢ
οὔ [καὶ πότερον πατρίδος περιβλέπτου καὶ λαμπρᾶς

---

[2] οἷον RW: λοιπὸν codd.: om. Pm

---

[2] Literally, "intense" (*syntonos*), in contrast to the "relaxed"
(*anetos*) or "casual" (*syngraphikos*) style of informal speeches or
talks. This distinction, primarily relating to the use or not of a
periodic style, is further discussed at 2.5.2–4.

140

"Just as our eyes cannot take in the extent of the limitless sea, so to encompass praise of the emperor in speech is no easy task." You may find that this applies not only to a royal oration but to every epideictic subject, especially in the case of formal[2] epideictic speeches. "Consequently, just as we propitiate divinities with hymns and virtues,[3] we do the same for the emperor with speeches."

5. When second introductions are added for the sake of amplification, you may derive topics from the magnificence either of Homer ("this alone was what the subject required"), or of Orpheus, Calliope's son, or of the Muses themselves: "Even they could scarcely have spoken worthily of this subject; yet nothing prevents me from giving it my best effort." 6. The third topic of the introduction (and in general keep this rule in mind) must prepare for the sections[4] to come, when, for example, the speaker expresses doubt as to where he should begin his praises.[5]

7. After these introductions move on to his homeland.[6] Here you should take into consideration whether or not it is famous. If it is famous, you should comment on it first,

---

[3] The compressed phrase ὕμνοις καὶ ἀρεταῖς implies "hymns and [recitals of their] virtues." M. provides an extensive example of a hymn detailing the *aretai* of a god (Sminthian Apollo) at 2.16.12–23.

[4] κεφάλαια, literally, "headings," are the main sections of topics into which an oration is divided.

[5] M. provides an example of searching for a beginning in his Sminthian Oration at 2.16.3. There is a brief discussion of aporetic passages in hymns at 1.9.4, where the god's parentage is at issue.   [6] In the following sections, πατρίς varies in meaning between homeland and hometown (πόλις); ἔθνος refers to the nation or race, γένος to the family, lineage, or race.

141

ἢ οὔ].[3] κἂν μὲν ἔνδοξος ἡ πατρὶς τυγχάνῃ, προθήσεις
τὸν περὶ ταύτης λόγον, καὶ πρὸ τοῦ γένους ἐρεῖς, οὐκ
ἐνδιατρίβων μὲν εἰς τὸ τοιοῦτον οὐδὲ προχέων ἐνταῦθα
πολλοὺς τοὺς λόγους· οὐ γὰρ ἴδιον τοῦτο μόνον βασιλέως τὸ ἐγκώμιον, ἀλλὰ κοινὸν πρὸς πάντας τοὺς
οἰκοῦντας τὴν πόλιν· διόπερ τὰ μὴ ἀναγκαῖα λυσιτελεῖ παρατρέχειν. 8. ἂν δὲ μὴ ἡ πόλις ἔνδοξος ᾖ, ζητήσεις τὸ ἔθνος ἅπαν, εἰ ἀνδρεῖον ὑπείληπται καὶ
ἄλκιμον, εἰ περὶ λόγους ἔχει ἢ κτῆσιν ἀρετῶν, ὡς τὸ
Ἑλληνικόν, εἴτε νόμιμον, ὡς τὸ Ἰταλικόν, ἢ ἀνδρεῖον,
ὡς τὸ τῶν Γαλατῶν καὶ Παιόνων, καὶ ἀντὶ τῆς πατρί-
370 δος ἀπὸ τοῦ ἔθνους λήψῃ βραχέα, προσοικειῶν κἀνταῦθα τοῦ βασιλέως τὸν ἔπαινον καὶ κατασκευάζων,
ὅτι ἀναγκαῖον τὸν ἐκ [τῆς τοιαύτης πόλεως ἢ][4] τοῦ
τοιούτου ἔθνους τοιοῦτον εἶναι, καὶ ὅτι τῶν ὁμοφύλων
πάντων ἐπαινετῶν ὄντων αὐτὸς μόνος διήνεγκεν· οὗτος γοῦν καὶ μόνος ἠξιώθη τῆς βασιλείας· εἶτα ἐξ
ἱστορίας παραδείγματα, ὅτι πάντων ὄντων ἀνδρείων
Θετταλῶν ὁ Πηλέως ἠξιώθη τῆς ἡγεμονίας τοῦ γένους, δηλονότι τῷ πάντων διαφέρειν.

9. Ἐὰν δὲ μήτε ἡ πατρὶς μήτε τὸ ἔθνος τυγχάνῃ
περίβλεπτον, ἀφήσεις μὲν τοῦτο, θεωρήσεις δὲ πάλιν,
πότερον ἔνδοξον αὐτοῦ τὸ γένος ἢ οὔ. κἂν μὲν ἔνδοξον ᾖ, ἐξεργάσῃ τὰ περὶ τούτου, ἐὰν δὲ ἄδοξον ᾖ ἢ
εὐτελές, μεθεὶς καὶ τοῦτο ἀπ' αὐτοῦ τοῦ βασιλέως τὴν
ἀρχὴν ποιήσῃ, ὡς Καλλίνικος ἐποίησεν ἐν τῷ με-

---

[3] secl. Bursian, RW   [4] secl. RW

even before you speak of his lineage. Do not, however, expend much time or many words on such a subject, because this praise is not limited to the emperor alone, but pertains to all the inhabitants of the city. Consequently, it is wise to skim over nonessential details. 8. If, however, the city is not famous, ascertain whether the nation as a whole is considered courageous and valiant, or excels in oratory or possesses virtues like the Greeks, or is renowned for its law like the Italians, or courageous like the Galatians and Paeonians.[7] In this case, you should select a few characteristics from his nation instead of from his hometown and associate the emperor's praise with them as well, by asserting that one from such a nation must have similar qualities, while noting: "Although all his countrymen are praiseworthy, he alone excels, because he alone was deemed worthy of being emperor." Then you may add historical examples. "Although all the Thessalians were brave, only Peleus' son[8] was deemed worthy to rule the race, clearly because he excelled them all."

9. If neither his hometown nor his nation is well regarded, you must omit this topic and consider next whether or not his lineage is famous. If it is famous, you should develop the topics concerning it, but if it is undistinguished or lowly, you should omit this as well and begin with the emperor himself, as Callinicus did in his great

---

[7] That is, Gauls and Pannonians.
[8] Achilles.

γάλῳ βασιλικῷ· 10. ἢ ἄλλως τοιαῦτα ἄττα περὶ τοῦ
γένους ἐρεῖς, ὅτι εἴχομεν εἰπεῖν τι περὶ τοῦ γένους,
ἐπεὶ δὲ νικᾷ τὰ τοῦ βασιλέως, σπεύδωμεν ἐπὶ βασιλέα. οἱ μὲν οὖν ἄλλοι γένη κοσμείτωσαν καὶ λεγόντων περὶ αὐτῶν ἃ βούλονται, ἐγὼ δὲ μόνον ἐπαινέσω
τοῦτον ἄνευ τοῦ γένους· ἀρκεῖ γὰρ αὐτὸς χωρὶς ἐπει-
σάκτου τινὸς εὐφημίας ἔξωθεν. 11. ἢ οὕτως· πολλοὶ τῷ
μὲν δοκεῖν ἐξ ἀνθρώπων εἰσί, τῇ δ' ἀληθείᾳ παρὰ τοῦ
θεοῦ καταπέμπονται καί εἰσιν ἀπόρροιαι ὄντως τοῦ
κρείττονος· καὶ γὰρ Ἡρακλῆς ἐνομίζετο μὲν Ἀμφι-
τρύωνος, τῇ δ' ἀληθείᾳ ἦν Διός· οὕτω καὶ βασιλεὺς ὁ
ἡμέτερος τῷ μὲν δοκεῖν ἐξ ἀνθρώπων, τῇ δ' ἀληθείᾳ
τὴν καταβολὴν οὐρανόθεν ἔχει. οὐ γὰρ ἂν τοσούτου
κτήματος καὶ τοσαύτης ἀξίας ἔτυχε, μὴ οὐχὶ ὡς
κρείττων γεγονὼς τῶν τῇδε.

12. Ταῦτα καὶ τὰ τοιαῦτα περὶ τοῦ γένους ἀφοσιω-
σάμενος πάλιν ζήτει τὰ περὶ γενέσεως αὐτοῦ τοῦ βασιλέως. εἰδέναι δὲ χρὴ τοῦτο ἀκριβῶς, ὅτι, ἐὰν μὲν
ἔχωμεν μεθόδῳ τινὶ κρύψαι τὸ ἄδοξον, ὥσπερ ἐπὶ τοῦ
371 γένους εἰρήκαμεν ὅτι, ἐὰν μὴ ὑπάρχῃ τοῦτο ἔνδοξον,
ἐρεῖς αὐτὸν ἐκ θεῶν γενέσθαι, καὶ δὴ τοῦτο ποιήσο-
μεν· εἰ δὲ μή, παρελευσόμεθα.

13. Οὐκοῦν ἔστω σοι μετὰ τὴν πατρίδα καὶ μετὰ
τὸ γένος τρίτον κεφάλαιον τὸ περὶ τῆς γενέσεως, ὡς
ἔφαμεν, ⟨καὶ⟩[5] εἴ τι σύμβολον γέγονε περὶ τὸν τόκον

[5] suppl. RW

"Royal Oration."[9] 10. Or else, you may treat his lineage in the following way: "We could have talked about his lineage, but since the emperor's qualities are so compelling, let us proceed directly to the emperor. So, let others extol people's families and say about them what they will, but I shall praise him alone, without reference to his lineage, for he is sufficient unto himself and needs no praise fetched from elsewhere." 11. Or else: "Many men seem to have human parents, but in reality are sent down from god and are actually emanations of the divine. For example, Heracles was thought to be the son of Amphitryon, but in reality was the son of Zeus. Likewise, our emperor appears to have human parents, but in reality he has his origin in heaven, for he would not have obtained such great possession and honor, unless he had been born superior to men here on earth."

12. After duly treating such topics concerning his lineage, next look into the circumstances surrounding the birth of the emperor himself. Be well aware that if, by some tactic, we are able to conceal a lack of prestige (as we said, if his lineage is not illustrious, you should claim that he was born of the gods), we shall do just that; but if we cannot do so, we should simply pass the topic by.

13. So, as we stated,[10] after his hometown and lineage should come a third section concerning his birth. If any portent connected with his birth appeared on land, in the

---

[9] A late third-century AD historian and orator of whom little is known. Nothing remains of his "Royal Oration." He is credited with a *prosphonētikos* to the emperor Gallienus (r. 253–268 AD). He is also mentioned in passing as a model at 2.2.33.

[10] There is no such previous discussion in this treatise. These encomiastic topics are, however, listed at 2.7.2 and 2.10.8.

ἢ κατὰ γῆν ἢ κατ' οὐρανὸν ἢ κατὰ θάλασσαν, [καὶ]⁶
ἀντεξέτασον τοῖς περὶ τὸν Ῥωμύλον καὶ Κῦρον καὶ
τοιούτοις τισί. [τὰ]⁷ κατὰ τὴν γένεσιν [καὶ]⁸ γὰρ κἀκεί-
νοις συνέβη τινὰ θαυμάσια, τῷ μὲν Κύρῳ τὰ τῆς
μητρὸς ὀνείρατα, τῷ δὲ τὰ περὶ τὴν λύκαιναν· κἂν μὲν
ᾖ τι τοιοῦτον περὶ τὸν βασιλέα, ἐξέργασαι, ἐὰν δὲ
οἷόν τε ᾖ καὶ πλάσαι καὶ ποιεῖν τοῦτο πιθανῶς, μὴ
κατόκνει· δίδωσι γὰρ ἡ ὑπόθεσις διὰ τὸ τοὺς ἀκούοντας ἀνάγκην ἔχειν ἀβασανίστως δέχεσθαι τὰ ἐγκώμια. 14. μετὰ τὴν γένεσιν ἐρεῖς τι καὶ περὶ φύσεως,
οἷον ὅτι ἐξέλαμψεν ἐξ ὠδίνων εὐειδὴς τῷ κάλλει κατα-
λάμπων τὸ φαινόμενον ἀστέρι καλλίστῳ τῶν κατ' οὐρανὸν ἐφάμιλλος.

Ἑξῆς δὲ κεφάλαιόν ἐστιν ἡ ἀνατροφή, εἰ ἐν βασι-
λείοις ἀνετράφη, εἰ ἁλουργίδες τὰ σπάργανα, εἰ ἐκ
πρώτης βλάστης ἐν βασιλικοῖς ἀνετράφη κόλποις· ἢ
οὐχ οὕτως μέν, ἀνελήφθη δὲ εἰς βασιλείαν νέος ὢν
ὑπό τινος μοίρας εὐτυχοῦς. 15. κἀνταῦθα θήσεις
παραδείγματα ζητήσας ὅμοια, ἐὰν ᾖ· ἐὰν δὲ μὴ τὴν
ἀνατροφὴν ἔνδοξον ἔχῃ, ὡς Ἀχιλλεὺς παρὰ Χείρωνι,
ζητήσεις τὴν παιδείαν καὶ ἐνταῦθα προσεπισημαί-
νων, ὅτι βούλομαι⁹ δὲ ἐπὶ τοῖς εἰρημένοις καὶ τὴν
φύσιν τῆς ψυχῆς αὐτοῦ διεξελθεῖν, ἐν ᾧ ἐρεῖς τὴν
φιλομάθειαν, τὴν ὀξύτητα, τὴν περὶ τὰ μαθήματα
σπουδήν, τὴν ῥᾳδίαν κατάληψιν τῶν διδασκομένων.

⁶ secl. RW   ⁷ secl. RW   ⁸ secl. RW
⁹ RW: βούλει codd.

sky, or at sea, compare it to those that appeared for Romulus and Cyrus and others of that sort. For certain miracles occurred in connection with their births: in the case of Cyrus, his mother's dreams;[11] in that of Romulus, his suckling by the mother wolf. If anything similar happened regarding the emperor, expound on it, and if you can invent a story and make it plausible, do not hesitate to do so; the subject permits it, since the audience is obligated to accept your praise because they cannot put it to the test. 14. After the topic of birth, say something about his nature, as for example, "He shone forth from the womb resplendent with beauty and lighting up the world, a match for the fairest star in heaven."[12]

Next comes the section on upbringing—whether he was reared in the palace, swaddled in purple robes, or nursed in the royal bosom from the day of his birth; or if instead he ascended to the throne as a young man by some stroke of good fortune. 15. At this point, if you can find any similar examples, provide them, but if he does not have an illustrious rearing as Achilles had with Chiron, then you should look instead to his education and add at this point: "In addition to what I have said, I wish[13] to elaborate on the nature of his soul." Here you can mention his love of learning, his intellectual sharpness, his zeal for his studies, and his facility for grasping what he is taught.

---

[11] Hdt. 1.107–8. Actually, Astyages has the two dreams about Cyrus' mother and the child she will bear.   [12] Presumably the morning star, synonymous with youth and beauty.

[13] RW's βούλομαι makes the sentence into a direct quotation. The manuscripts' βούλει (you wish) would make it indirect. The δέ tells in favor of RW's emendation.

κἂν μὲν ἐν λόγοις ᾖ καὶ φιλοσοφίᾳ καὶ λόγων γνώ-
σει, τοῦτο ἐπαινέσεις· ἐὰν δ' ἐν μελέτῃ πολέμων καὶ
ὅπλων, τοῦτο θαυμάσεις, ὡς ἀγαθῇ μοίρᾳ γενόμενον
προμνηστευσαμένης αὐτῷ τῆς τύχης τὰ μέλλοντα·
372 καὶ ὅτι ἐν οἷς ἐπαιδεύετο διαφέρων τῶν ἡλίκων ἐφαίνετο, ὡς Ἀχιλλεύς, ὡς Ἡρακλῆς, ὡς οἱ Διόσκουροι.

16. Τὰ δὲ ἐπιτηδεύματα χώραν ἐξετάσεως ἕξει, ἐπιτηδεύματα δ' ἐστὶν ἄνευ ἀγωνιστικῶν πράξεων ἤθη·
τὰ γὰρ ἐπιτηδεύματα ἤθους ἔμφασιν περιέχει, οἷον
ὅτι δίκαιος ἐγένετο ἢ σώφρων ἐν τῇ νεότητι, καθάπερ
καὶ Ἰσοκράτης ἐποίησεν ἐν τῷ Εὐαγόρᾳ, ἐν οἷς καὶ
μικρὸν προελθὼν εἶπεν, "ἀνδρὶ δὲ γενομένῳ ταῦτά τε
πάντα συνηυξήθη καὶ ἄλλα προσεγένετο," ὡς καὶ
Ἀριστείδης ἐν τῷ Παναθηναϊκῷ, ὅτι φιλάνθρωπος ἡ
πόλις (ὡς ἐπιτήδευμα γὰρ τοῦτο ἐξήτασεν) ὑποδεχο-
μένη τοὺς καταφεύγοντας.

17. Ἀκολουθεῖ τοίνυν τοῖς ἐπιτηδεύμασι λοιπὸν ὁ
περὶ τῶν πράξεων λόγος. χρὴ δὲ γινώσκειν καὶ φυλάττειν τὸ παράγγελμα ὅτι, ὅταν μέλλῃς ἀπὸ κεφαλαίου μεταβαίνειν εἰς κεφάλαιον, δεῖ προοιμιάζεσθαι
περὶ οὗ μέλλεις ἐγχειρεῖν, ἵνα προσεκτικὸν τὸν ἀκροατὴν ἐργάσῃ καὶ μὴ ἐᾷς λανθάνειν μηδὲ κλέπτεσθαι
τῶν κεφαλαίων τὴν ζήτησιν· αὐξήσεως γὰρ οἰκεῖον τὸ
προσεκτικὸν ποιεῖν τὸν ἀκροατὴν καὶ ἐπιστρέφειν ὡς
περὶ μεγίστων ἀκούειν μέλλοντα. 18. τίθει δὲ καὶ σύγκρισιν ἐφ' ἑκάστῳ τῶν κεφαλαίων τούτων, ἀεὶ συγκρίνων φύσιν φύσει καὶ ἀνατροφὴν ἀνατροφῇ καὶ

If it involves oratory, philosophy, or knowledge of literature, you will praise that. But if it involves the practice of warfare and arms, you will marvel at his auspicious birth and the good fortune that ordained his future. "In the disciplines which he was being taught, he clearly stood out from his age mates like Achilles, Heracles, or the Dioscuri."

16. His activities[14] will have a place for exposition, activities being character traits apart from competitive deeds, for activities entail an indication of character. For example, mention that he was just or moderate in his youth, as Isocrates did in the *Evagoras*, where he went right on to say, "and when he became a man, all those qualities increased as he matured, while other virtues were added to them."[15] Similarly, in his Panathenaic oration Aristides said that Athens was humane for taking in fugitives (for he treated that as an activity).[16]

17. Following activities comes an account of his deeds. It is necessary to recognize and observe this rule: when about to proceed from one section to another, you must introduce what you are going to treat, in order to make your listener attentive and not allow the sequence of the sections to go unnoticed or be obscured, for it is a feature of amplification to make the listener attentive and aware that what he is about to hear is very important. 18. Then too, in each of these sections add a comparison, always comparing nature with nature, upbringing with upbring-

---

[14] *epitēdeumata* are activities or pursuits, in contrast to deeds or accomplishments (*praxeis*).   [15] *Evag.* 23. Evagoras' modesty (*sōphronynē*) was mentioned in *Evag.* 22.   [16] *Panath.* 49–50 praises Athens' *philanthrōpia* in harboring refugees, the most famous being the Heraclidae, mentioned at 52–54.

παιδείαν παιδείᾳ καὶ τὰ τοιαῦτα, ἀνευρὼν καὶ παραδείγματα, οἷον Ῥωμαίων βασιλέων καὶ στρατηγῶν καὶ Ἑλλήνων ἐνδοξοτάτων.

19. Τὰς τοιαύτας τοίνυν πράξεις διαιρήσεις δίχα εἴς τε τὰ κατ᾽ εἰρήνην καὶ τὰ κατὰ πόλεμον. καὶ προθήσεις τὰς κατὰ τὸν πόλεμον, ἐὰν ἐν ταύταις λαμπρὸς ὁ ἐπαινούμενος φαίνηται· δεῖ γὰρ τὰς τῆς ἀνδρείας πράξεις πρώτας παραλαμβάνειν ἐπὶ τῶν τοιούτων ὑποθέσεων εἰς ἐξέτασιν· γνωρίζει γὰρ βασιλέα πλέον ἡ ἀνδρεία. 20. ἐὰν δὲ μηδὲ εἷς πόλεμος αὐτῷ πεπραγμένος τύχῃ, ὅπερ σπάνιον, ἥξεις ἐπὶ τὰ
373 τῆς εἰρήνης ἀναγκαίως. εἰ μὲν οὖν τὰ κατὰ τὸν πόλεμον ἐγκωμιάζεις, ἀπὸ τῆς ἀνδρείας ἐρεῖς μόνον, οὐκ ἀφ᾽ ἑτέρων τινῶν· εἰ δὲ τὰ κατὰ τὴν εἰρήνην, τῆς μὲν ἀνδρείας οὐκέτι, ἑτέρων δέ τινων· 21. διαίρει γὰρ ἀπανταχοῦ τὰς πράξεις ὧν ἂν μέλλῃς ἐγκωμιάζειν εἰς τὰς ἀρετάς (ἀρεταὶ δὲ τέσσαρές εἰσιν, ἀνδρεία, δικαιοσύνη, σωφροσύνη, φρόνησις) καὶ ὅρα τίνων ἀρετῶν εἰσιν αἱ πράξεις, καὶ εἰ κοιναί τινές εἰσι τῶν πράξεων τῶν τε κατὰ τὸν πόλεμον καὶ κατ᾽ εἰρήνην ἀρετῆς μιᾶς, ὥσπερ ἐπὶ τῆς φρονήσεως· φρονήσεως γάρ ἐστι καὶ τὸ στρατηγεῖν καλῶς ἐν τοῖς πολέμοις, φρονήσεως δὲ καὶ τὸ καλῶς νομοθετεῖν καὶ τὸ συμφερόντως διατιθέναι καὶ διοικεῖν τὰ κατὰ τοὺς ὑπηκόους. οὐκοῦν ἐν ταῖς πράξεσι τοῦ πολέμου τὰ κατὰ τὴν ἀνδρείαν ἐρεῖς καὶ τὰ τῆς φρονήσεως, ὅσα τῶν κατὰ τὸν πόλεμον οἰκεῖα ταύτῃ.

ing, education with education, and so forth, having come up with examples of such figures as Roman emperors, generals, or very famous Greeks.

19. You should then divide such deeds into two categories, those performed in peacetime and those performed in war, giving priority to the latter if the honorand is distinguished for them. Deeds of courage must be considered first in the case of such subjects, because courage commends an emperor more than other virtues do. 20. If, however, he happens never to have fought a single war (which is rare), you will be forced to proceed to deeds of peace. Now if you are praising deeds in war, speak only of courage and no other virtues, but if you are praising deeds of peace, no longer speak of courage but of other virtues instead. 21. Everywhere divide the deeds you are going to praise according to the four virtues (courage, justice, moderation, and intelligence),[17] and consider to which virtues the deeds belong and whether some deeds in war and in peace share a single virtue, as for example intelligence. For it takes intelligence to be a successful general in war, and it also takes intelligence to make good laws and to arrange and administer the affairs of one's subjects to their benefit.[18] Therefore, concerning deeds of war you should speak of those involving courage and those dependent on intelligence—to the extent that wartime deeds do involve the latter.

[17] Of the four canonical virtues, M. cites φρόνησις (practical intelligence) rather the more theoretical σοφία (wisdom).

[18] Cf. §31 below, where M. contrasts the tyrant who uses his intelligence to legislate for his own benefit with the emperor who uses his to legislate for his subjects' benefit.

22. Διαγράψεις δὲ ἐν ταῖς πράξεσι ταῖς τοῦ πολέμου καὶ φύσεις καὶ θέσεις χωρίων ἐν οἷς οἱ πόλεμοι, καὶ ποταμῶν δὲ καὶ λιμένων καὶ ὀρῶν καὶ πεδίων, καὶ εἰ ψιλοὶ ἢ δασεῖς οἱ χῶροι, καὶ εἰ <λεῖοι ἢ>[10] κρημνώδεις. ἐκφράσεις δὲ καὶ λόχους καὶ ἐνέδρας καὶ τοῦ βασιλέως κατὰ τῶν πολεμίων καὶ τῶν ἐναντίων κατὰ τοῦ βασιλέως· εἶτα ἐρεῖς, ὅτι σὺ μὲν τοὺς ἐκείνων λόχους καὶ τὰς ἐνέδρας διὰ φρόνησιν ἐγίνωσκες, ἐκεῖνοι δὲ τῶν ὑπὸ σοῦ πραττομένων οὐδὲν συνίεσαν.

23. Καὶ μὴν καὶ πεζομαχίας ἐκφράσεις καὶ ἱππέων διασκευὰς εἰς ἱππομαχίαν καὶ ὅλου στρατοπέδου πρὸς ὅλον στρατόπεδον μάχην, ἤδη δέ που καὶ ναυμαχίαν, εἰ γένοιτο· οἷα πολλὰ παρὰ τοῖς συγγραφεῦσιν, ἐν τοῖς Μηδικοῖς παρὰ Ἡροδότῳ, παρὰ Θουκυδίδῃ πάλιν ἐν τοῖς Πελοποννησιακοῖς, καὶ παρὰ Θεοπόμπῳ ἐν τοῖς Φιλιππικοῖς καὶ Ξενοφῶντι ἐν τῇ Ἀναβάσει καὶ τοῖς Ἑλληνικοῖς βιβλίοις. 24. καὶ μὴν καὶ αὐτοῦ τοῦ βασιλέως ἐκφράσεις μάχας καὶ περιθήσεις ἅπασαν ἰδέαν καὶ ἐπιστήμην, ὡς Ἀχιλλεῖ, ὡς Ἕκτορι, ὡς Αἴαντι περιτίθησιν ὁ ποιητής. διαγράψεις δὲ καὶ πανοπλίαν βασιλέως καὶ ἐπιστρατείας, ἐπιτείνας μὲν τῷ καιρῷ τῆς ἀριστείας καὶ τῆς συμπλοκῆς, ὅταν βασιλέως ἀριστείαν ἐκφράζῃς.

25. Ἐνταῦθα καιρὸν ἕξεις καὶ ἀνεῖναι κατὰ μέσον τὸν λόγον (καὶ γὰρ τοῦτο παρειλήφαμεν παρὰ τῶν

[10] suppl. RW

22. In treating deeds of war, depict the nature and location of the places where the wars took place, including rivers, harbors, mountains and plains, and whether the locales were barren or wooded, flat or steep. You should also describe ambushes and surprise attacks both by the emperor against the enemy and by the enemy against the emperor. Then you may say, "Through your intelligence, you were aware of their ambushes and surprise attacks, whereas they understood nothing about your operations."

23. In addition, describe infantry battles and formations[19] of cavalry for combat and the battle of entire army against army—and perhaps a sea battle as well, if any occurred. There are many such examples in the historians: in Herodotus' *Persian Wars*, Thucydides' *Peloponnesian War*, Theopompus' *Philippica*, and Xenophon's *Anabasis* and *Hellenica*. 24. In particular, you should describe the emperor's own combats and bestow on him all impressive appearance and expertise, as Homer does for Achilles, Hector, and Ajax. You should also describe the emperor's armor and that of the expedition,[20] intensifying the narrative[21] when you describe the emperor's valor at the moment of his prowess in combat.

25. Here you will also have the opportunity to relax the narrative[22] in the middle of this account (an innovation we

---

[19] Or, "the equipment."   [20] Or, reading ἐπιστρατείας as an accusative plural, (describe) "his expeditions."

[21] ἐπιτείνειν (its nominal form is ἐπίτασις) here involves close-up, detailed descriptions of hand-to-hand combat (as in Homeric battle scenes).   [22] ἀνεῖναι (and its nominal form ἄνεσις, used below) here apparently involves stopping the action by shifting the focus to a speaking character. It is not known who the recent authors mentioned are.

153

νεωτέρων καινοτομηθέν) καὶ φωνὴν καθάπερ ἐν δρά-
ματι ἢ χώρᾳ ἢ ποταμῷ περιτιθέναι· ποταμῷ μέν, ὡς
ὁ ποιητής,

ὦ Ἀχιλεῦ, πέρι μὲν κρατέεις, πέρι δ' αἴσυλα
ῥέξεις

χώρᾳ δὲ ὁμοίως, ὅταν εἴπωμεν ἐκείνην καταμέμφε-
σθαι τὴν θρασύτητα τὴν τῶν τολμησάντων ἀντιστῆ-
ναι, καὶ ὅτι ἐστενοχωρεῖτο τοῖς τῶν πεσόντων σώμα-
σιν· οἷον κἀμοὶ δοκεῖν, εἰ ποιητικὸς ἦν ὁ Ἴστρος,
ὥσπερ ὁ ποταμὸς ἐκεῖνος ὁ ποιητικὸς Σκάμανδρος,
εἶπεν ἄν,

ἐξ ἐμέθεν γ' ἐλάσας πεδίον κάτα μέρμερα ῥέζε·
πλήθει γὰρ δή μοι νεκύων ἐρατεινὰ ῥέεθρα,
οὐδέ τι πῇ δύναμαι προχέειν ῥόον

καὶ τὰ τοιαῦτα.

26. Μετὰ δὲ τὴν ἄνεσιν ἐπάξεις πάλιν καὶ ἄλλα
κατορθώματα, καὶ τρόπαια τροπαίοις συνάψεις, καὶ
νίκας νίκαις, ἱππέων φυγάς, πεζῶν φόνους. ἐνταῦθα
δὲ καιρὸν ἕξεις καὶ ἐπισυνάψαι περὶ φρονήσεως, ὅτι
αὐτὸς ἦν ὁ διατατόμενος, αὐτὸς ὁ στρατηγῶν, αὐτὸς
ὁ τὸν καιρὸν τῆς συμβολῆς εὑρίσκων, σύμβουλος
θαυμαστός, ἀριστεύς, στρατηγός, δημηγόρος.[11]

27. Μετὰ τὸ τέλος τῶν πράξεων ἢ καὶ πρὸς τῷ
τέλει τῶν πράξεων ἐρεῖς τι καὶ περὶ τρίτης ἀρετῆς,

[11] δημιουργός P

have adopted from recent authors) and, just as in drama, to give voice to a country or river—to a river, as when Homer says,

> O Achilles, you surpass men in might, and you
> surpass them in evil deeds.[23]

Similarly to a country, when we say that it blames the audacity of those who have dared to resist, and was crowded with the corpses of the fallen. For example, "It seems to me that if the Ister[24] were in epic, it would have said, like the Scamander of epic,

> At least drive them from me and wreak evil on the
> plain,
> for my lovely streams are full of corpses
> and there is no way that I can pour forth my
> flow . . ."[25]

and so on.

26. After this relaxation, you should introduce other successes, adding trophies to trophies, victories to victories, cavalry routs, and infantry carnage. Here you will also have the opportunity to add something about his intelligence. "He personally drew up the troops, he personally commanded them and determined the right time to engage in combat—a wondrous counselor, champion, general, and orator."

27. At or near the conclusion of wartime deeds, you should say something about a third virtue, namely his hu-

---

[23] *Il.* 21.214 (Scamander speaking).   [24] The Danube, the site of imperial campaigns from Trajan on.

[25] *Il.* 21.217–19.

λέγω δὴ τῆς φιλανθρωπίας, μόριον δὲ τῆς φιλανθρωπίας ἡ δικαιοσύνη· ὅτι νικήσας ὁ βασιλεὺς οὐ τοῖς
ὁμοίοις ἠμύνατο τοὺς ἄρξαντας ἀδίκων ἔργων, ἀλλ᾽
ἐμέρισε κατὰ τὸ δίκαιον τὰς πράξεις τιμωρίᾳ καὶ φιλανθρωπίᾳ, καὶ ὅσα ἡγεῖτο πρὸς σωφρονισμὸν ἀρ-
375   κεῖν ἐργασάμενος, ἐνταῦθα στήσας φιλανθρωπίᾳ τὰς
πράξεις ἀνῆκε συγχωρήσας τὸ λείψανον τοῦ γένους
σώζεσθαι, ἅμα μὲν ἵνα μνημεῖον τοῦ πάθους τοῦ γεγονότος σώζηται τὸ λειπόμενον, ἅμα δὲ ἵνα καὶ τὴν
φιλανθρωπίαν ἐνδείξηται.

28. Τέλος δ᾽ ἐπιθεὶς ταῖς κατὰ τὸν πόλεμον πράξεσι
μεταβήσῃ λοιπὸν ἐπὶ τὸν λόγον τὸν περὶ τῆς εἰρήνης.
τοῦτον δὲ διαιρήσεις εἰς σωφροσύνην, εἰς δικαιοσύνην καὶ εἰς φρόνησιν. καὶ ἐν μὲν τῇ δικαιοσύνῃ τὸ
ἥμερον τὸ πρὸς τοὺς ὑπηκόους ἐπαινέσεις, τὴν πρὸς
τοὺς δεομένους φιλανθρωπίαν, τὸ εὐπρόσοδον. 29. οὕτως οὐ μόνον ἐν τοῖς κατὰ τὸν πόλεμον ἔργοις ὁ βασιλεὺς ἡμῖν θαυμάσιος, ἀλλὰ καὶ ἐν τοῖς κατ᾽ εἰρήνην
θαυμασιώτερος· τίς γὰρ οὐκ ἂν ἀγάσαιτο τῶν ἔργων;
καὶ προσθήσεις ὅτι καθάπερ οἱ Ἀσκληπιάδαι σώ-
ζουσι τοὺς ἀρρωστοῦντας, ἢ καθάπερ τοὺς καταφεύγοντας ἐπὶ τὰ ἄσυλα τεμένη τοῦ κρείττονος ἔστιν
ἰδεῖν ῥᾳστώνης τυγχάνοντας (οὐ γὰρ ἀποσπᾶν ἐπι-
χειροῦμεν οὐδένα) οὕτως ὁ βασιλέως ὄψεσιν ἐντυχὼν
τῶν δεινῶν ἀπήλλακται. 30. καὶ ἐρεῖς ὅτι δικαίους ἄρχοντας κατὰ ἔθνη καὶ γένη καὶ πόλεις ἐκπέμπει φύ-
λακας τῶν νόμων καὶ τῆς τοῦ βασιλέως δικαιοσύνης
ἀξίους, <οὐ>[12] συλλογέας πλούτου. ἐρεῖς ἔτι καὶ περὶ

manity (*philanthrōpia*), an aspect of which is justice.
"When victorious, the emperor did not punish the perpe-
trators of the unjust deeds with retribution in kind, but
justly divided his actions between punishment and humanity, and after carrying out everything he considered
sufficient for punishment, he stopped at that point out of
humanity, relented, and allowed the rest of the people to
live, so that the remnant would survive as a reminder of
the defeat they had suffered, and at the same time so that
he might demonstrate his humanity."

28. After concluding the deeds in war, you should proceed to the part of your speech concerning peace, which
you will divide under the rubrics of moderation, justice,
and intelligence. In the portion on justice, praise his gentleness toward his subjects, his humanity to those in need,
and his approachableness. 29. "Thus not only in deeds of
war is our emperor admirable, but even more so in deeds
of peace: who would not marvel at his deeds?" You may
add, "Just as the sons of Asclepius rescue those who are
sick, or just as we see refugees finding safety in the invio-
late sanctuaries of the gods (because we make no attempt
to drag anyone out), so anyone who obtains an audience
with the emperor is relieved of his troubles." 30. You may
also say, "He sends out just governors to the nations, races,
and cities who are guardians of the laws and worthy of the
emperor's justice, not collectors of wealth." Furthermore,

---

12 οὐ Rhak.: om. codd.: ἀξίους τινας συλλογέας p

τῶν φόρων οὓς ἐπιτάττει καὶ τοῦ σιτηρεσίου τῶν
στρατευμάτων ὅτι[13] στοχάζεται καὶ τοῦ κούφως καὶ
ῥᾳδίως δύνασθαι φέρειν τοὺς ὑπηκόους.

31. Ἐρεῖς τι καὶ περὶ νομοθεσίας, ὅτι νομοθετεῖ τὰ
δίκαια, καὶ τοὺς μὲν ἀδίκους τῶν νόμων διαγράφει,
δικαίους δὲ αὐτὸς θεσπίζει· τοιγάρτοι νομιμώτεροι
μὲν οἱ νόμοι,[14] δικαιότερα δὲ τὰ συμβόλαια τῶν ἀνθρώπων πρὸς ἀλλήλους. ἂν δέ τις ὑπολάβῃ τὴν νο-
μοθεσίαν φρονήσεως εἶναι μόνης, γινωσκέτω ὅτι τὸ
μὲν νομοθετῆσαι μόνης φρονήσεως, τὸ δὲ προστάτ-
τειν πράττειν τὰ δέοντα δικαιοσύνης, οἷον ὁ μὲν τύ-
ραννος πολλάκις συνίησι διὰ φρόνησιν ἃ συμφέρει
376 αὐτῷ νομοθετεῖν ἢ μή, νομοθετεῖ δὲ τὰ ἄδικα, ὁ δὲ
βασιλεὺς τὰ δίκαια.

32. Μετὰ τὴν δικαιοσύνην ἐπαινέσεις αὐτοῦ τὴν
σωφροσύνην· ἀκολουθεῖ γὰρ μάλιστα τῇ δικαιοσύνῃ
ἡ σωφροσύνη· τί οὖν ἐνταῦθα ἐρεῖς; ὅτι διὰ βασιλέα[15]
σώφρονες μὲν οἱ γάμοι, γνήσιοι δὲ τοῖς πατράσιν οἱ
παῖδες, θέαι δὲ καὶ πανηγύρεις καὶ ἀγῶνες μετὰ τοῦ
προσήκοντος κόσμου καὶ τῆς πρεπούσης σωφροσύνης γίνονται· οἷον γὰρ ὁρῶσι τὸν βασιλέως βίον,
τοιοῦτον ἐπανῄρηνται. 33. εἰ δὲ ἐπ᾽ ἀξίας εἴη καὶ τιμῆς
μεγίστης ἡ βασιλίς, ἐρεῖς τι καὶ κατὰ καιρὸν ἐνθάδε·
ἣν θαυμάσας ἠγάπησε, ταύτην[16] κοινωνὸν τῆς ἑαυτοῦ
βασιλείας πεποίηται, καὶ οὐδ᾽ εἰ ἔστιν ἄλλο οἶδε γυ-
ναικεῖον φῦλον.

[13] hic RW: ante τοῦ σιτηρεσίου codd.
[14] νόμοι PZp: γάμοι cett.

with regard to the taxes he levies and the provisioning of his armies, you may say, "He also takes care that his subjects can bear them lightly and easily."

31. You should also say something about his lawmaking. "He is a just lawmaker. He rescinds unjust laws and decrees just ones himself. As a result, his laws[26] are more legitimate and transactions between men more just. And anyone who thinks that legislation is solely a function of intelligence should recognize that while framing laws is indeed a function of intelligence alone, prescribing what ought to be done is a function of justice. For example, a tyrant often understands by intelligence what is expedient or not for him to legislate, but then enacts unjust laws, whereas the emperor enacts just ones."

32. After justice, praise his moderation, for moderation goes hand in hand with justice. What then should you say here? "Thanks to our emperor, marriages are chaste and fathers have legitimate children; then too, spectacles, festivals, and contests are conducted with proper solemnity and fitting moderation, for the people emulate the conduct they see in their emperor." 33. And if the empress is held in highest honor and respect, you may appropriately say something here. "The woman he admired and loved, he has made the partner[27] of his empire, and he is unaware that the rest of womankind exists."

---

[26] The alternate reading γάμοι (marriages) avoids the tautology of νομιμώτεροι . . . νόμοι, but the issue of marriage is intrusive here and is taken up in the following section on moderation.

[27] Several manuscripts add "and the sole (partner)."

---

[15] βασιλέα PZ: τοὺς βασιλέας p
[16] καὶ μόνην post ταύτην add. PZp

Ἥξεις ἐπὶ τὴν φρόνησιν μετὰ ταῦτα. ἀεὶ δὲ μέλλων ἄρχεσθαι ἑκάστης τῶν ἀρετῶν χρῶ προοιμιακαῖς ἐννοίαις, ὡς ἔφαμεν. 34. ἐρεῖς τοίνυν ἐπὶ τῇ φρονήσει, ὅτι σύμπαντα ταῦτα οὐκ ἂν ἤρκεσε πρᾶξαι βασιλεύς, οὐδ᾽ ἂν τοσούτων πραγμάτων ὄγκον διήνεγκεν, εἰ μὴ φρονήσει καὶ συνέσει τῶν ἐπὶ γῆς ὑπερέφερε, δι᾽ ἣν καὶ νομοθεσίαι καὶ σωφροσύναι καὶ αἱ λοιπαὶ κατορθοῦσθαι πεφύκασιν ἀρεταί· εἶτα ὀξὺς ἰδεῖν, ἐνθυμηθῆναι δεινός, προϊδέσθαι τὸ μέλλον κρείττων μάντεως, ἄριστος γνώμων κρῖναι τὴν ἑτέρων εὐβουλίαν, ἱκανὸς τὰ δυσχερῆ καὶ ῥάδια γνῶναι.

35. Ἐπὶ τούτοις μὲν καταπαύσεις τὸν λόγον τὸν περὶ τούτων, μνημονεύσεις δὲ μετὰ τοῦτο τῆς τύχης, λέγων ὅτι συμπαρομαρτεῖν δὲ ἔοικεν ἐφ᾽ ἅπασι καὶ πράξεσι καὶ λόγοις τῷ βασιλεῖ τῷ μεγάλῳ τύχη λαμπρά· κατορθοῖ γὰρ ἕκαστον κρεῖττον εὐχῆς, καὶ ὅτι παίδων γένεσις αὐτῷ δεδώρηται, ἂν οὕτω τύχῃ, καὶ φίλοι πάντες εὖνοι καὶ δορυφόροι κινδυνεύειν[17] ὑπὲρ αὐτοῦ πρόθυμοι.

36. Ἥξεις δὲ ἐπὶ τὴν τελειοτάτην σύγκρισιν, ἀντεξετάζων τὴν αὐτοῦ βασιλείαν πρὸς τὰς πρὸ αὐτοῦ 377 βασιλείας, οὐ καθαιρῶν ἐκείνας (ἄτεχνον γάρ) ἀλλὰ θαυμάζων μὲν ἐκείνας, τὸ δὲ τέλειον ἀποδιδοὺς τῇ παρούσῃ. οὐκ ἐπιλήσῃ δὲ τοῦ προειρημένου θεωρήματος, ὅτι ἐν ἑκάστῳ τῶν κεφαλαίων ποιήσεις συγκρίσεις, ἀλλ᾽ ἐκεῖναι μὲν ἔσονται μερικαί, οἷον παι-

17 ἅπαντες post κινδυνεύειν add. mW

Last comes intelligence. As we said,[28] always provide introductory topics when embarking on each of the virtues. 34. Thus, with regard to intelligence, say, "The emperor could not have accomplished all those things, nor could he have borne the weight of so many affairs, did he not surpass men on earth in intelligence and understanding, which enable lawmaking, moderation, and all the other virtues to flourish." Then add, "He is quick to perceive, a powerful thinker, better than a seer at anticipating the future, a superlative expert at judging the good counsel of others, and adept at distinguishing what is difficult from what is easy."

35. Here you should end your discussion of these topics and next mention fortune. "It appears that splendid good fortune accompanies our great emperor in all his endeavors, both deeds and words, because he succeeds in everything beyond expectation. He has been granted the birth of children (if such is the case), all his friends wish him well, and his bodyguards are eager to face danger on his behalf."[29]

36. You will come next to the comprehensive comparison, when you compare his rule with those that came before, not disparaging them (for that is unprofessional), but admiring them while assigning perfection to the present one. You must not neglect the aforementioned precept[30] to make comparisons in each of the sections, but those will

[28] Cf. §§6 and 17.

[29] The addition of ἅπαντες, "all" (his bodyguards), in some manuscripts perhaps reflects concern for the constant danger to emperors from disloyal members of the praetorian guard.

[30] Cf. §18.

δείας πρὸς παιδείαν ἢ σωφροσύνης πρὸς σωφροσύνην,
αὗται δὲ περὶ ὅλης ἔσονται τῆς ὑποθέσεως, ὡσανεὶ
βασιλείαν ὅλην ἀθρόως καὶ ἐν κεφαλαίῳ πρὸς ὅλην
βασιλείαν συγκρίνομεν, οἷον τὴν Ἀλεξάνδρου πρὸς
τὴν παροῦσαν.

37. Μετὰ τὴν σύγκρισιν οἱ ἐπίλογοι. ἐν τούτοις
ἐρεῖς τὰς εὐετηρίας, τὰς εὐδαιμονίας τῶν πόλεων, ὅτι
πλήρεις μὲν ὠνίων αἱ ἀγοραί, πλήρεις δὲ ἑορτῶν καὶ
πανηγύρεων αἱ πόλεις, γεωργεῖται μετ᾽ εἰρήνης ἡ γῆ,
πλεῖται ἡ θάλασσα ἀκινδύνως, εὐσέβεια δὲ ἡ περὶ τὸ
θεῖον ηὔξηται, τιμαὶ δὲ κατὰ τὸ προσῆκον ἑκάστοις
νέμονται, οὐ δεδοίκαμεν βαρβάρους, οὐ πολεμίους,
ὀχυρώτερον τοῖς βασιλέως ὅπλοις τετειχίσμεθα ἢ
τοῖς τείχεσιν αἱ πόλεις, αἰχμαλώτους οἰκέτας κεκτήμεθα αὐτοὶ μὴ πολεμοῦντες, παρὰ δὲ τῆς βασιλέως
χειρὸς νικώσης δεχόμενοι. 38. τίνας οὖν εὐχὰς εὔχε-
σθαι δεῖ τῷ κρείττονι τὰς πόλεις ἢ ὑπὲρ βασιλέως
ἀεί; τί δὲ μεῖζον αἰτεῖν παρὰ τῶν θεῶν ἢ βασιλέα
σώζεσθαι; ὄμβροι γὰρ κατὰ καιρὸν καὶ θαλάσσης
φοραὶ καὶ καρπῶν εὐφορίαι διὰ τὴν βασιλέως δικαιοσύνην ἡμῖν εὐτυχοῦνται· τοιγάρτοι καὶ ἀμειβόμεναι
αὐτὸν αἱ πόλεις καὶ ἔθνη καὶ γένη καὶ φυλαὶ στεφα-
νοῦμεν, ὑμνοῦμεν, γράφομεν, πλήρεις εἰκόνων αἱ πόλεις, αἱ μὲν πινάκων γραπτῶν, αἱ δέ που καὶ τιμωτέ-
ρας ὕλης. ἐπὶ τούτοις εὐχὴν ἐρεῖς αἰτῶν παρὰ θεοῦ εἰς
μήκιστον χρόνον προελθεῖν τὴν βασιλείαν, διαδοθῆ-
ναι εἰς παῖδας, παραδοθῆναι τῷ γένει.

be partial ones, such as comparing education with education or moderation with moderation, whereas this will be of the whole subject, as when we compare an entire reign collectively with another, such as that of Alexander with the present one.

37. After this comparison come the concluding remarks. Among these you should mention the prosperity and happiness of the cities. "The markets abound with goods for sale, the cities are full of feasts and festivals, the land is farmed in peace and the sea sailed without danger, piety for the gods has increased, honors are deservedly allotted to individuals; we do not fear barbarians or enemies; we are more securely defended by our emperor's armies than our cities by their walls; we possess captured slaves in our homes, not by going to war ourselves, but by receiving them from the conquering hand of our emperor. 38. What prayers, then, should the cities address to the gods except always for our emperor? What greater thing to ask from the gods than the safety of our emperor? For rains in season, abundance from the sea, and bountiful crops are ours to enjoy because of our emperor's justice.[31] And so, in return, we cities, nations, races, and tribes crown him,[32] compose hymns to him, write about him; our cities are full of his likenesses, some of painted wood, others of more precious material." Thereupon, you should utter a prayer, requesting of the gods that his reign may last as long as possible, be passed on to his children, and be handed down to his posterity.

[31] A commonplace; cf. Hom. *Od*. 19.109–14 and Hes. *Op*. 225–37.

[32] Cf. the crown speech (2.11).

2.2. ΠΕΡΙ ΕΠΙΒΑΤΗΡΙΟΥ

1. Ἐπιβατήριον ὁ βουλόμενος λέγειν δῆλός ἐστι βου-
378 λόμενος προσφωνῆσαι ἢ τὴν ἑαυτοῦ πατρίδα ἐξ ἀποδημίας ἥκων, ἢ πόλιν ἑτέραν, εἰς ἣν ἂν ἀφίκηται, ἢ
καὶ ἄρχοντα ἐπιστάντα τῇ πόλει. οὐκοῦν ἐν τούτοις
ἅπασι τὸ προοίμιον ἐκ περιχαρείας εὐθύς· δεῖ γὰρ
συνηδόμενον φαίνεσθαι ἢ ταῖς πόλεσιν, ὅτι θαυμά-
σιόν τινα καὶ ἐπαινούμενον ἄρχοντα δέχονται, ἢ τῷ
ἄρχοντι, ὅτι ἐπ᾽ ἀγαθῇ μοίρᾳ ἥκει, ἢ καὶ αὐτὸν ἑαυτῷ
τὸν λέγοντα ὅτι τεθέαται ἢ πόλιν ἢ ἄρχοντα, ὃν πάλαι τε καὶ ἐκ πλείονος ἰδεῖν ἐπεπόθει.

2. Κἂν μὲν ἄρχοντα, εὐθὺς ἐρεῖς· ἀλλ᾽ ἥκεις μὲν ἐπ᾽
αἰσίοις συμβόλοις ἐκ βασιλέως λαμπρός, ὥσπερ
ἡλίου φαιδρά τις ἀκτὶς ἄνωθεν ἡμῖν ὀφθεῖσα· οὕτω
πάλαι μὲν ἀγαθὴ φήμη διήγγειλε τὴν ἐπ᾽ αἰσίοις
ἄφιξιν καὶ εὐκταιοτάτην μοῖραν τῶν ὑπηκόων· εἶτα
κατασκευάσεις ὅτι βεβαιοῖς ἐν ἔργῳ τὴν φήμην, ἢ ὅτι
ὑπερβάλλεις τὴν φήμην, ἢ ὡς ἂν ὁ καιρὸς διδῷ.

3. Εἶτα μετὰ τὸ προοίμιον τοῦτο ἥξεις εἰς τὸν περὶ
τῶν ὑπηκόων λόγον. διπλοῦς δ᾽ οὗτος· ἢ γὰρ κακῶς
πεπονθότων αὐτῶν παρὰ τοῦ μικρῷ πρόσθεν ἄρχον-

2.2. THE ARRIVAL SPEECH

1. Anyone proposing to deliver an arrival speech (*epiba-tērios logos*) obviously intends to address either his own hometown when arriving from abroad; another city to which he has come; or else a governor who has come to his city.[1] In all these cases, the introduction begins immediately with expressions of joy, for the speaker must show that he is rejoicing with the cities (because they are receiving an admired and acclaimed governor), or with the governor (because he has come under auspicious circumstances), or is expressing his own joy (because he beholds the city or governor he had long desired to see).

2. If you are addressing a governor, say right off, "It is with favorable omens that you have come from the emperor, as splendid as a bright ray of sunshine appearing to us from on high. For a welcome report long ago announced your auspicious arrival and the good fortune that your subjects had fervently prayed for." Then you can assert, "You confirm the report in fact," or "You surpass the report"—or whatever the situation permits.

3. After this introduction, you should speak of the governor's subjects. This takes two forms. Either you will vividly describe how badly they suffered under the recent

---

[1] M. treats this third type first in §§2–15 and the first type in §§16–33 (including a sample "Trojan Oration" in §§34–37). He does not treat the second type, addressing a foreign city.

165

τος διατυπώσεις καὶ αὐξήσεις τὰ δυσχερῆ, μηδὲν
βλασφημῶν τὸν παυσάμενον, ἀλλὰ ἁπλῶς τὴν δυσ-
τυχίαν τῶν ὑπηκόων λέγων, εἶτα ἐπάξεις ὅτι ὥσπερ
νυκτὸς καὶ ζόφου τὰ πάντα κατειληφότος αὐτὸς καθάπερ ἥλιος ὀφθεὶς πάντα ἀθρόως τὰ δυσχερῆ διέλυ-
σας, καὶ ἐργάσῃ τοῦτο καὶ οὐ παραδραμεῖς, ὅτι τοίνυν ἀνέπνευσαν ἅπαντες ὥσπερ νέφους τινὸς τῶν
δεινῶν παρελθόντων·[1] ἢ οὐδὲν πεπονθότων ἐρεῖς·
αὐτίκα μὲν ἐπαυσάμεθα μεγίστας εὐεργεσίας ὁμολο-
γοῦντες τῷ ἄρχοντι, ἄρτι δὲ ἀκούσαντες ἀγαθῶν ἀγ-
γελίαν καὶ μέλλοντες ἀφ’ ἱερῶν ἐφ’ ἱερά, ὡς ἂν εἴποι
τις, καὶ ἐκ τῶν ‹καλῶν ἐπὶ τὰ›[2] καλλίονα φαιδροὶ καὶ
γεγηθότες προαπηντήκαμεν. 4. εἶτα μετὰ ταῦτα πάλιν
ἐρεῖς ὅτι τάς τε ἄλλας χάριτας μεγίστας τοῖς βασιλεῦσιν ὀφείλοντες, ἐφ’ οἷς ὑπὲρ ἡμῶν ἀθλοῦσι, καὶ
ἐπὶ τούτοις ἂν δικαίως μείζους ὁμολογήσαιμεν, ὅτι
τοιοῦτον ἡμῖν κατέπεμψαν. πειρῶ δ’ ἐν τοῖς τοιούτοις
λόγοις ἀεὶ συντέμνειν τὰ βασιλέως ἐγκώμια, καὶ μηδὲν διατρίβειν, ἵνα μὴ διπλῆν ποιήσῃς τὴν ὑπόθεσιν.

5. Ἐὰν μὲν οὖν ἔχῃς πράξεις εἰπεῖν τοῦ ἄρχοντος,
ἐρεῖς· εἰ δὲ μή, περιέργως ἢ πατρίδα ἢ ἔθνος ἐκφρά-

379

---

[1] παρελθόντων RW ex Dem. 18.188: παραδραμόντων codd.
[2] suppl. Bursian: καλῶν ἐμπεσεῖν εἰς RW

governor and amplify their hardships—without slandering the previous one, but simply stating the unhappiness of the subjects. Then you should add, "Just as if night and darkness had held the world in its grip, you appeared like the sun to our eyes and scattered all our hardships at once." You should not skim over this, but elaborate it, by saying, "And so, all the people have breathed a sigh of relief, now that our afflictions have passed by like a cloud."[2] Or, if they have not suffered, say, "We have just now ceased crediting that governor with our greatest benefactions, having just heard the good news, and—like people, as they say, about to go from one holy place to another[3] or from good things to better ones[4]—we have come forth to greet you beaming with joy." 4. Next you can say, "We owe the greatest gratitude to the emperors[5] for their other efforts on our behalf, but we would justly agree that more gratitude is owed them on this occasion for dispatching such a governor to us." In speeches like this always try to keep praise of the emperor brief and not dwell on it, to avoid making your subject twofold.

5. If you have deeds of the governor to mention, you should do so, but if not, describe in considerable detail his

---

[2] Perhaps an adaptation of Dem. 18.188: κίνδυνον παρελθεῖν ἐποίησεν ὥσπερ νέφος (it made the danger pass away like a cloud).

[3] RW translate ἱερά as "festivals." Although ἱερά can denote "sacrifices," elsewhere in M. it refers to "temples."

[4] The text is corrupt. I have adopted Bursian's emendation.

[5] The plural implies joint emperors. Cf. also §§13 and 18 ("the present emperors") and the similar passage at 2.9.3. At other times M. uses the singular (e.g., §7 below).

σεις καὶ χωρογραφήσεις τῷ λόγῳ ἀπὸ τῶν ἐπισημο-
τάτων καὶ θρυλουμένων περὶ τῆς χώρας ἢ τῆς πατρίδος, ⟨οἷον⟩[3] ὅτι Ἰταλιώτης, ἐκ ποιᾶς[4] δὲ χώρας ἢ
πόλεως περιωνύμου, οἷον τῆς Ῥώμης.

6. Ζητήσεις δὲ καὶ τοῦ γένους πράξεις. εἰ δὲ ἀπο-
ροίης πράξεων τοῦ ἐπαινουμένου, ἐκ τούτων θηράσεις
τὸν ἔπαινον, ὥστε μὴ αὐχμηρὰν καὶ ἄγονον παρα-
σχέσθαι τὴν ὑπόθεσιν. ἔπειτα λέγε· πείθομαι δὲ τὸν
ἐκ τοιούτων γεγονότα πρὸς τοὺς ἑαυτοῦ πατέρας
ἁμιλλώμενον ἀγαθὸν περὶ ἡμᾶς γενήσεσθαι καὶ δί-
καιον· καὶ γὰρ καὶ ἐκεῖνοι δίκαιοι· οὐκοῦν δικάσει μὲν
ἡμῖν ὑπὲρ τὸν Αἰακόν, ὑπὲρ τὸν Μίνωα, ὑπὲρ τὸν Ῥα-
δάμανθυν· καὶ τούτου ἄμεινον ἤδη προμαντεύομαι, ὦ
Ἕλληνες. 7. καὶ εἰπὼν τὰ τοιαῦτα καὶ πλείω περὶ δικαιοσύνης, ὅτι οὐδεὶς ἀδίκως οἰκήσει τὸ δεσμωτήριον
ἢ δίκην δώσει τῷ νόμῳ, οὐ προκριθήσεται πλούσιος,
οὐ χαμαὶ πεσεῖται λόγος τοῦ πένητος δίκαιος, πεπαύσθωσαν ἡμῖν οἱ πλούσιοι ταῖς περιουσίαις κομπού-
μενοι, πεπαύσθωσαν οἱ πένητες ὀδυρόμενοι τὴν ἀσθέ-
νειαν, ἥξεις ἐπὶ τὸν τῆς ἀνδρείας ἔπαινον, ὅτι
πρεσβεύσει πρὸς βασιλέα ὑπὲρ ἡμῶν τοῖς γράμμασι·
καὶ γὰρ οἱ πατέρες ἀεὶ ἐπρέσβευσαν αὐτοῦ, εἰ πολλάκις ἄρχοντας ἔχοις λέγειν. ἀντιστήσεται τοῖς δει-
νοῖς, ὥσπερ ἀγαθὸς κυβερνήτης ὑπὲρ τοῦ σκάφους
ὑπερέχοντος τοῦ κλύδωνος.

---

3 suppl. RW
4 corr. Bursian: ποίας codd.

hometown or nation and depict its landscape, drawing on the most salient and best-known features of his land or hometown—for example, that he is Italian and comes from such and such a region or a famous city like Rome.

6. Also take into consideration the deeds of his family, and if you lack any by the honorand himself, seek your praise from theirs instead, to keep your subject from being dry and sterile. Then say, "I am confident that someone born from such parents, who strives to match his forebears, will be good and just to us, because they were just. Therefore he will be a better judge for us than an Aeacus, Minos, or Rhadamanthys[6]—in fact I prophesy something even better than this, O Hellenes!" 7. Such statements and more can be made about justice. "No one will be imprisoned unjustly or punished unjustly by law; the rich man will not be favored; the just plea of the poor man will not fall to the ground; let the rich stop boasting to us of their riches and the poor cease lamenting their powerlessness." You should turn next to the praise of his courage. "He will petition the emperor in writing on our behalf, for his forefathers continually served as ambassadors"—if, that is, you can say that they often performed that function. "He will face dire threats like a good helmsman to save his ship when the waves rise high against it."

[6] The three just judges in the underworld.

8. Καὶ τὰς ἀρετὰς δὲ τὰς ἄλλας οὕτως ἐκ μεθόδου προάξεις, προλέγων ὅτι τοιόσδε δὲ ἔσται καὶ τοιόσδε, οἷον ὅτι σώφρων τυγχάνων ἔσται κρείττων κέρδους,

380 κρείττων ἡδονῶν· καὶ ἐπάξεις μετὰ ταῦτα τὸν περὶ τῆς φρονήσεως λόγον, ἐπισφραγιζόμενος τὰ προειρημένα, ὅτι πάντα δὲ ταῦτα ποιήσει διὰ φρόνησιν καὶ σύνεσιν· ὃς γὰρ ἀγνοεῖ τῶν προσηκόντων οὐδέν, περὶ πάντων δὲ ἀκριβῶς ἐπισκέπτεται, πῶς οὐ δῆλός ἐστιν ὁμολογουμένως μέλλων ἄρχειν ἐπ' ἀγαθῷ τῶν ὑπηκόων καλῶς; 9. τάξεις δ' ἀεὶ τὰς ἀρετὰς ἐν ἁπάσῃ ὑποθέσει, ὡς ἄν σοι συμφέρειν ὁρᾷς, καὶ ὡς ἂν ἴδῃς ἐπιδεχομένην τὴν ἀκολουθίαν τοῦ λόγου.

Ἐπειδὴ δὲ συγκρίσεις οὐ δυνάμεθα τάττειν πρὸς τὰς πράξεις διὰ τὸ μηδέπω πεφηνέναι τοῦ ἄρχοντος πράξεις, συγκρίνομεν αὐτοῦ τὸ γένος γένει ἐνδόξῳ ἢ τῶν Ἡρακλειδῶν ἢ τῶν Αἰακιδῶν. ἐν δὲ ταῖς ἀρεταῖς οὐ συγκρίνομεν· τί γὰρ ἂν καὶ συγκρίναιμεν μηδέπω μηδενὸς γεγονότος; 10. ἐκ μεθόδου δὲ εἰσάξομεν, ἐν μὲν τῇ δικαιοσύνῃ οὕτως· οὐ γὰρ δὴ Φωκίων μὲν καὶ Ἀριστείδης καὶ εἴ τις τοιοῦτος ἕτερος τῆς ἐκ τῶν ἔργων εὐδοξίας ἐπεθύμησαν, ὁ δὲ ἡμέτερος παρόψεται τὴν ἐκ τούτων εὔκλειαν, ἀλλ' ὥσπερ ἐκεῖνοι δι' ἀρετὴν ἀείμνηστοι γεγόνασιν, οὕτως καὶ αὐτὸς ἐπιθυμήσει

---

7 M. is wary of intelligence (*phronēsis*) alone, when separated from other virtues. Here it is paired with understanding (*synesis*). Cf. 2.1.31, where intelligence must be combined with justice (*dikaiosynē*) in order to make good laws.

8. You may treat the other virtues by using the technique of predicting that such and such a person will act accordingly. For example, "Being moderate, he will be superior to the allure of gain or pleasures." Finally, bring up his intelligence and confirm all you have said. "He will do all these things with intelligence and understanding, for if someone knows all that is fitting and proper, and carefully takes everything into consideration, how is he not clearly and undeniably going to rule well and for the good of his subjects?"[7] 9. In every subject, you must always arrange the virtues as you see to your advantage, and as you find the train of thought permits.

Since we cannot bring in comparisons of the governor's deeds, because he does not yet have any to show, we can compare his family to a famous family like the Heraclidae[8] or Aeacidae.[9] In this section on virtues, however, we cannot make any comparisons, for what might we compare when nothing has yet happened? 10. We can, though, introduce comparisons by using the following technique, as in the case of justice. "Indeed since Phocion,[10] Aristides,[11] and others like them desired fame for their deeds, our governor will certainly not overlook such fame, but just as they have earned everlasting fame on account of their virtue, he will likewise aspire to leave in our minds the mem-

[8] The lineage includes Heracles' son Hyllus and his descendants who became rulers in the Peloponnesus.

[9] Aeacus' sons and grandsons included Peleus, Achilles, and Neoptolemus.   [10] Fourth-century Athenian statesman, known as "The Good."

[11] Early fifth-century Athenian statesman, known as "The Just." The same two statesmen are paired at 2.9.6.

μνήμην καλλίστων ἔργων ἐν ταῖς διανοίαις ταῖς ἡμε-
τέραις καταλιπεῖν, ζηλώσει τὸν Μίνωα, μιμήσεται
τὸν Ῥαδάμανθυν, ἁμιλληθήσεται πρὸς τὸν Αἰακόν·
καὶ καθ' ἑκάστην τῶν ἀρετῶν οὕτως ποιήσεις, ἀπὸ
τοῦ μέλλοντος κατ' εἰκασμὸν καὶ κατὰ τὸ ἀκόλουθον
τὸν ἔπαινον ἐργαζόμενος.

11. Τὰς δὲ συγκρίσεις τὰς πρὸς ὅλην τὴν ὑπόθεσιν
ἐργασόμεθα οὕτως· ὅσοι μὲν οὖν γεγόνασιν ἄρχοντες
καὶ παρ' ἡμῖν καὶ παρ' ἑτέροις, ἢ τῷ γένει μόνῳ σεμνύνεσθαι ἔδοξαν, ἢ φρόνησιν προὐβάλλοντο ἢ τῶν
ἄλλων μίαν ἀρετῶν· οὗτος δὲ ὅτι τῷ γένει πάντων
κρείττων ἐστί, καθάπερ καὶ ὁ <ἥλιος>[5] τῶν ἀστέρων
δέδεικται, μετὰ μικρὸν δὲ καὶ ἐπὶ ταῖς ἀρεταῖς θαυμα-
381   σθήσεται, κρείττων μὲν ἐν δικαιοσύνῃ τῶν ἐπὶ δικαιοσύνῃ φρονούντων ὀφθείς, κρείττων δὲ ἐν ἀνδρείᾳ,
καὶ [κρείττων δὲ][6] ἐν φρονήσει <καὶ>[7] σωφροσύνῃ,
ἢ οὐκ ἐλάττων τῶν ἐπὶ τοῖς ἔργοις τοῖς ἐκ τούτων
δοξάντων μέγα φρονεῖν. ἐξέσται δέ σοι καὶ ἡμιθέων
καὶ στρατηγῶν μνημονεῦσαι ἐν τῇ συγκρίσει πάσας
ἐνταῦθα τὰς ἀρετὰς ἀθρόως συγκρίνοντι.

12. Τοὺς δὲ ἐπιλόγους ἐργάσῃ, ὡς ἀπὸ τοῦ σκοποῦ
τῆς ὑποθέσεως δεικύμενος[8] τοὺς ὑπηκόους, οἷον ὅτι
προαπηντήκαμεν δέ σοι ἅπαντες ὁλοκλήροις τοῖς γένεσι, παῖδες, πρεσβῦται, ἄνδρες, ἱερέων γένη, πολιτευομένων συστήματα, δῆμος περιχαρῶς δεξιούμενοι,
πάντες φιλοφρονούμενοι ταῖς εὐφημίαις, σωτῆρα καὶ
τεῖχος, ἀστέρα φανότατον ὀνομάζοντες, οἱ δὲ παῖδες
τροφέα μὲν ἑαυτῶν, σωτῆρα δὲ τῶν πατέρων· 13. εἰ δὲ

ory of his outstanding accomplishments. He will emulate Minos, he will imitate Rhadamanthys, he will compete with Aeacus." You can treat each of the virtues in a similar fashion, composing your praise on the basis of future prospects by means of conjecture and likelihood.

11. We should construct comparisons of the entire subject in the following way. "Now previous governors, both here and elsewhere, have thought fit to pride themselves on their lineage alone, or have displayed their intelligence or some other single virtue. But because ours surpasses all others in lineage—as the sun outshines the stars—very soon he will be admired as well for his virtues, being seen as superior in justice to those who pride themselves on justice, superior in courage, intelligence, and moderation—or at least not inferior to those known to have prided themselves on the deeds resulting from their virtues." In this comparison you will be able to mention demigods and generals, since in this instance you are comparing all the virtues together.

12. You should construct the epilogue with a view to your subject by representing his subjects. For example, "We have come forth to meet you, all of us, with entire families—children, elders, adults, clans of priests, organizations of citizens, ordinary people, welcoming you with joy, all greeting you with praises, calling you their savior and protector and brightest star, while the children call you their provider and the savior of their fathers. 13. And

---

δυνατὸν ἦν καὶ ταῖς πόλεσιν ἀφεῖναι φωνὴν καὶ σχήματα λαβεῖν γυναικῶν ὥσπερ ἐν δράμασι, εἶπον ἄν·
ὦ μεγίστης ἀρχῆς, ἡδίστης δὲ ἡμέρας, καθ᾽ ἣν ἐπέ-
στης· νῦν ἡλίου φῶς φαιδρότερον· νῦν ὥσπερ ἔκ τινος
ζόφου προσβλέπειν δοκοῦμεν λευκὴν ἡμέραν· μετὰ
μικρὸν ἀναθήσομεν εἰκόνας, μετὰ μικρὸν ποιηταὶ καὶ
λογοποιοὶ καὶ ῥήτορες ᾄσουσι τὰς ἀρετὰς καὶ διαδώ-
σουσιν εἰς γένη πάντων ἀνθρώπων· ἀνοιγέσθω θέατρα, πανηγύρεις ἄγωμεν· ὁμολογῶμεν χάριτας καὶ
βασιλεῦσι καὶ κρείττοσι.

14. Καὶ ταῦτα μὲν περὶ ἄρχοντος ἄρτι τοῖς ὑπηκό-
οις ἐπιστάντος εἰρήκαμεν, ἐὰν δέ τινος λέγωμεν ἐπιβατήριον ἄρχοντος μὲν πάλαι τοῦ ἔθνους, ἄρτι δὲ
ἐπιστάντος τῇ ἡμετέρᾳ, τὰ μὲν αὐτά, οἷα καὶ ἐκ περιχαρείας εἰρήκαμεν, δεῖ λαμβάνειν· ἐρεῖς δὲ τὰς πράξεις καθ᾽ ἑκάστην μὲν τῶν ἀρετῶν, μετὰ δὲ τὰ ἐκ
περιχαρείας. οὕτω δὲ διαιρήσεις τὸν λόγον· βασιλέως
δι᾽ ὀλίγων ἐρεῖς ἐγκώμιον, γένος ἐὰν ἔχῃ λαμπρόν,
διὰ βραχέων ὁμοίως καὶ τοῦτο, εἶτα τὰς πράξεις καθ᾽
ἑκάστην τῶν ἀρετῶν ἰδίᾳ συγκρινεῖς, εἶτα ἀθρόαν
382   σύγκρισιν, εἶτα τοὺς ἐπιλόγους.

15. Δοκεῖ δὲ περιττὸν ἔχειν ὁ ἐπιβατήριος λόγος
κατὰ τοῦ προσφωνητικοῦ τὸ ἐκ περιχαρείας κεφάλαιον μετὰ τὰ προοίμια, καὶ ταῦτα ἐκ περιχαρείας
λαμβανόμενα· ὅμως οὐδὲν κωλύει μετὰ τὰ προοίμια
τελείαν ἐργασίαν τῶν κεφαλαίων δίδοσθαι. χρήσῃ δὲ

if our cities could take on the form of living women and speak as they do in drama,[12] they would say, 'O greatest of governorships, O sweetest of days, this day on which you have arrived! Now the sun shines more brightly, now as if emerging from darkness we seem to behold a bright day.[13] Soon we shall erect statues, soon poets, historians, and orators will sing of your virtues and pass them on to all mankind. Let the theaters be opened, let us celebrate festivals, let us acknowledge our gratitude to the emperors and to the gods.'"

14. What we have said applies to a governor coming to his subjects for the first time. If, however, we deliver an arrival speech for a governor who has long ruled the nation but only now comes to our city, we must adopt what we said about expressing joy. After these expressions of joy, you should speak of his deeds according to each of the virtues. Divide the speech as follows. First praise the emperor succinctly. If the governor has an illustrious lineage, praise it briefly as well. Then make specific comparisons of his deeds under each of the virtues. After this, make a comprehensive comparison and add the epilogue.

15. It is thought that the arrival speech, in contrast to an address (*prosphōnētikos logos*),[14] has an additional section consisting of expressions of joy after the introductions (themselves also based on joyfulness). However, that does not prevent you from providing a complete treatment of the sections that follow the introductions.[15] With such

---

[12] Broadly construed to include epic poetry.

[13] A play on λευκός as both "bright" and "lucky."

[14] The address is treated at 2.9.

[15] These include the encomiastic portions outlined in §14.

ἐν ταῖς τοιαύταις ὑποθέσεσι ταῖς τῶν προσφωνητικῶν
καὶ τῶν ἐπιβατηρίων ἢ ἑνὶ προοιμίῳ ἢ καὶ δευτέρῳ
πολλάκις, ἔστι δὲ ὅτε καὶ τρισὶ χρήσῃ, ὅταν ἀπαιτῇ
καὶ τοῦτο ἡ ὑπόθεσις.

16. Ἐὰν δέ τις τῷ εἴδει τούτῳ [τῷ ἐπιβατηρίῳ][9] καὶ
πρὸς πόλιν θέλῃ χρήσασθαι, ἴστω ὅτι ἀπὸ τῆς διαθέσεως καὶ τῆς εὐνοίας τῆς περὶ τὴν πόλιν, ἣν ἔχει,
καὶ ἀπὸ τῆς ὄψεως τῆς φανερᾶς τῆς πόλεως λήψεται
τὴν χορηγίαν τοῦ λόγου ἐκ μεθόδου καὶ τῶν πατρίων
μεμνημένος· οἷον ἐπόθουν μὲν πάλαι καὶ γυμνάσια
καὶ θέατρα ταῦτα καὶ ἱερῶν κάλλη καὶ λιμένων τῆσδε
τῆς πόλεως· τίς γὰρ οὐκ ἂν ἀγάσαιτο τῶν παρ' ἡμῖν
ἐξαιρέτων τὰς ὑπερβολάς; εἶδον δὲ καὶ νῦν ἀσμένως
καὶ γέγηθα τῇ ψυχῇ τὰ ἐξαίρετα. 17. ἄλλοι μὲν γὰρ
ἄλλοις χαίρουσιν, οἱ μὲν ἵπποις, οἱ δὲ ὅπλοις, ἐγὼ δὲ
ἀγαπῶ τὴν ἐμαυτοῦ πατρίδα καὶ νομίζω μηδὲν διαφέρειν τὴν περὶ ταύτην ἐπιθυμίαν τῆς περὶ τὴν ἀκτῖνα,
ἣν ὁ ἥλιος ἐξ ὠκεανοῦ ἐκτείνει φανείς· τί γὰρ ἂν γένοιτο μεῖζον πόλεως, ἣν ὁ δεῖνα ἔκτισεν;

18. Εἶτα ἔπαινον ἐρεῖς διὰ βραχέων τοῦ κτίσαντος,
κἂν μὲν βασιλέως ἔργον ἡ πόλις τυγχάνῃ, συνῳδοὶ
δ' ὦσιν οἱ νῦν βασιλεύοντες τῷ τότε, ἐρεῖς ὅτι ὁ τούτων πρόγονος ἔκτισεν· ἡ γὰρ βασιλεία καὶ τὸ ἀξίωμα
συνάπτει τὰ γένη· ἐὰν δὲ ὡς τύραννον μισῶσιν, ὅτι

[9] secl. RW

176

subject matter as exists in both addresses and arrival speeches, you may employ one introduction, often two, and sometimes even three, when the subject requires it.

16. Anyone intending to use this genre[16] to address a city should make sure to base the bulk of the speech on his favorable attitude and the goodwill he has for the city and on the city's visible appearance, mentioning as well its ancestral traditions using the following technique. For example, "Long have I yearned for this city's gymnasia, theaters, beautiful temples, and harbors, for who would not marvel at the superlative qualities of our exceptional attractions? And now once more I have seen those attractions with gladness and joy in my soul. 17. Thus it is that different people delight in different things: some in horses, others in weapons, but I love my own hometown[17] and I believe that my desire for it is no less than my desire for the rays spreading from the sun when it appears from the Ocean. For what could be greater than the city that 'so and so' founded?"

18. At this point, briefly praise the founder. If the city happens to be the handiwork of an emperor, and if the present emperors are well-disposed to the former one, you can say that *their* ancestor founded it, for the office and distinction of being emperor unites families. If, on the other hand, they detest the founder as a tyrant, say that

[16] That is, the arrival speech (the addition τῷ ἐπιβατηρίῳ is probably a gloss). This portion takes up the first type in §1.

[17] This priamel is formally similar to Sappho, Fr. 16.1–4 ("Some say an array of horsemen, others of infantry . . ."), but its climax is reminiscent of Hom. *Od.* 9.28: "So nothing is sweeter than one's own land (ἧς γαίης)."

πάσης τῆς οἰκουμένης ἡ πόλις, καὶ ὅτι τινὰς μὲν τῶν πόλεων ἀνὴρ εἷς ἢ βασιλεὺς εἷς ἔκτισε, ταύτην δὲ ἡ οἰκουμένη σύμπασα.

19. Οὐκοῦν μετὰ τὰ προοίμια ὄντα ἐκ περιχαρείας κεφάλαιον ἐργάσῃ ἔχον ἐναντίου αὔξησιν οὕτως· ὅτι ἐδυσχέραινον δὲ ὡς ἔοικεν τὸν παρελθόντα χρόνον καὶ ἠνιώμην ἀθεάμων ὑπάρχων κάλλεων τοσούτων καὶ πόλεως, ἣν μόνην καλλίστην πόλεων ὁ ἥλιος ἐφορᾷ· ἐπειδὴ δὲ εἶδον, ἐπαυσάμην τῆς λύπης, ἀπεσεισάμην δὲ τὴν ἀνίαν, ὁρῶ δὲ ἅπαντα ὧν ἐπόθουν τὴν θέαν, οὐκ ὀνειράτων εἰκόνας οὐδὲ ὥσπερ ἐν κατόπτρῳ σκιάς, ἀλλ' αὐτὰ τὰ τεμένη, αὐτὴν τὴν ἀκρόπολιν, αὐτοὺς τοὺς νεὼς καὶ λιμένας καὶ στοάς.

20. Δεύτερον δὲ κεφάλαιον ἐρεῖς μετὰ τοῦτο αὐτοῦ τοῦ κτίσαντος ἔπαινον σύμμετρον. τρίτον κεφάλαιον, ἐν ᾧ τὴν φύσιν τῆς χώρας ἐκφράσεις, ὅπως μὲν ἔχει πρὸς θάλασσαν, ὅπως δὲ πρὸς ἤπειρον, ὅπως δὲ πρὸς ἀέρας· διεξεργάσῃ δὲ τούτων ἕκαστον συμμέτρως, καὶ ἐν μὲν τῷ κατ' ἤπειρον ἐκφράσεις πεδίων κάλλη, ποταμῶν, λιμένων, ὀρῶν· ἐν δὲ τῷ κατὰ θάλατταν, ὅπως ἐπιτηδείως ἔχει πρὸς τοὺς καταίροντας καὶ τίσι πελάγεσι περικλύζεται, ἐν ᾧ καὶ ἔκφρασις πελάγους· ἐν δὲ τῷ κατὰ τοὺς ἀέρας, ὅτι ὑγιεινῶς ἔχει. καὶ συγκρινεῖς τούτων ἕκαστον, τὴν μὲν χώραν ἑτέρᾳ χώρᾳ, οἷον ὅτι ἐν καλῷ μὲν κεῖται, καθάπερ ἡ Ἰταλία, διαφέρει δὲ τῷ

city belongs to the whole world,[18] and add, "Some cities were founded by a single man or a single emperor, but this one was founded by the whole world."

19. After these introductory expressions of joy, you should compose a section containing amplification of the opposite emotion in the following way. "In the past I was troubled, as you might expect, and pained at being unable to behold all these beautiful features and the city that is the single most beautiful city under the sun, but when I saw it, my distress ceased and I shook off my pain, and I see all the things I longed to see—not as phantoms in dreams or reflections in a mirror, but the very sanctuaries, the very acropolis, the very temples and harbors and colonnades."

20. After this, add a second section consisting of a brief encomium of the founder himself. In a third section, you should describe the physical nature of the land and its location vis-à-vis sea, mainland, and climate.[19] You must work up each of these at moderate length. In the portion concerning the mainland, describe the beauties of the plains, rivers, harbors, and mountains. In regard to the sea, tell how convenient the place is for those putting in and by what seas it is washed, along with a description of the sea. In regard to the climate, say how healthful it is. You should make comparisons when treating each of these topics. For example, in comparing your land with another one, say, "Like Italy, this land has a beautiful location, but

---

[18] "World" here and elsewhere in this treatise translates ἡ οἰκουμένη (γῆ), signifying the inhabited world.

[19] The topics of a land's (or a city's) location and nature are covered extensively in 1.11.

ἐκείνην μὲν ἐν μέρει τινὶ τῆς οἰκουμένης πλησίον
βαρβάρων κεῖσθαι ἢ καὶ πρὸς τῷ τέλει τῆς οἰκουμένης, ταύτην δὲ ἢ πλησίον Ἑλλάδος εἶναι ἢ κατὰ τὸ
μέσον τῆς οἰκουμένης, καὶ εὐφυέστερον ἔχειν πρὸς
ἤπειρον καὶ πρὸς θάλασσαν· τὸ δὲ πρὸς ἀέρας ἢ πρὸς
τοὺς Ἀθηναίων ἀέρας ἢ πρὸς τοὺς Ἰώνων.

21. Εἶτα μετὰ τὰς συγκρίσεις ταύτας καὶ τὴν ἐργασίαν τῶν ἐπιχειρημάτων συνάψεις τὰ κατὰ τὴν πόλιν, ὅπως ἔχει καὶ αὐτὴ θέσεως ἐν τῇ χώρᾳ· ἀκολουθεῖ γὰρ τῷ λόγῳ τῷ περὶ φύσεως τῆς χώρας καὶ ὁ
λόγος ὁ περὶ τῆς θέσεως τῆς πόλεως, ἐν ᾧ ἐρεῖς, πότερον ἐν μέσῳ κεῖται τῆς χώρας, ἢ πρὸς θάλασσαν
μᾶλλον, ἢ πρὸς τοῖς ὄρεσιν.

384   22. Ἰδίαν μέντοι ἐργασίαν ὁ περὶ τῆς θέσεως τῆς
πόλεως ἕξει, ἄμφω δὲ εἰς ἓν κεφάλαιον ἀνάγειν τό τε
κατὰ τὴν φύσιν τῆς χώρας καὶ τὸ κατὰ τὴν θέσιν τῆς
πόλεως οὐδὲν κωλύει, λέγω δὲ εἰς τὸ τῆς φύσεως κε-
φάλαιον· ταὐτὸν γάρ ἐστιν ἐπὶ τῆς χώρας καὶ φύσις
καὶ θέσις, πλὴν ὅτι ἡ μὲν θέσις τὸ κεῖσθαι σημαίνει,
ἡ δὲ φύσις τὰ ἐν τῇ θέσει, ὥσπερ βλαστήματα καὶ
ὄρη καὶ πεδία καὶ ποταμοὺς καὶ φυτά, ὥστε ἡ μὲν
θέσις ἔσται καὶ φύσις, οὐ πάντως δὲ ἡ φύσις θέσις·
23. φυτὰ γὰρ καὶ ποταμοὺς καὶ ὀρῶν ὑπεροχὰς καὶ τὰ
τοιαῦτα ὁ τῆς φύσεως περιέχει λόγος· ἵνα δὲ συντόμως εἴπω, ὁ περὶ τῆς φύσεως τῆς χώρας λόγος διττός
ἐστιν· ὁ μὲν γάρ ἐστι τῆς θέσεως, ὡς ἔχει πρὸς ἑκάτερον τῶν στοιχείων, ὁ δὲ τῶν ἐν τῇ χώρᾳ βλαστη-
μάτων.

it is superior because Italy lies in a portion of the world near barbarians or at the end of the world, whereas this land is near Hellas or in the middle of the world, and is more naturally suited as regards both mainland and sea." As for the climate, compare it to that of Athens or Ionia.

21. After these comparisons and supporting arguments, you should add comments on the city's location within the land, because treatment of the city's location naturally follows treatment of the land's physical nature. Here you should say whether the city lies in the middle of the land, more toward the sea, or near the mountains.

22. To be sure, the topic of the city's location will have its own treatment, but nothing prevents combining the nature of the land and the location of the city into one section, namely that on "nature." For the land's nature and its location are the same, except that location indicates position, whereas nature indicates what exists in that location, such as crops, mountains, plains, rivers, and vegetation. The result is that location will include nature, but nature will not necessarily include location, 23. because the treatment of nature includes vegetation, rivers, high mountains, and the like. In short, treatment of the land's nature has two aspects: one involves its location with respect to each of the other elements,[20] the other involves what grows on the land.

[20] That is, land, sea, and air.

24. Μετὰ δὲ τὸν περὶ τῆς φύσεως λόγον τὸν περὶ τῆς ἀνατροφῆς θήσεις, ἐὰν ἔχῃς ἐν πατρίοις, ὡς ὁ Ἀριστείδης εὐπόρησεν εἰπὼν ὡς Ἀθηναῖοι παρὰ τῆς Δήμητρος τοὺς καρποὺς ἔλαβον καὶ λαβόντες τοῖς ἄλλοις μετέδοσαν· ἐὰν δὲ μὴ ἔχῃς, ἐπαίνεσον τὰ ἔθη, ὡς ἐν κεφαλαίῳ τῶν ἐπιτηδευμάτων· ἐπιτηδεύματα γάρ ἐστιν ἔνδειξις τοῦ ἤθους καὶ τῆς προαιρέσεως τῶν ἀνδρῶν ἄνευ πράξεων ἀγωνιστικῶν. ἐρεῖς οὖν ὅτι πρὸς τοὺς ξένους φιλάνθρωποι, ὅτι πρὸς τὰ συμβόλαια νόμιμοι, ὅτι μεθ᾽ ὁμονοίας συνοικοῦσιν ἀλλήλοις, καὶ ὅτι ὁποῖοι πρὸς ἀλλήλους, τοιοῦτοι καὶ πρὸς τοὺς ἔξωθεν.

25. Ἐφ᾽ ἅπασι δὲ τούτοις τοῖς κεφαλαίοις, ἐπειδήπερ ἐπιβατήριον ὑπεθέμεθα, προσθήσεις ἐκεῖνα συχνότερον, ἵνα μὴ ἀπάδῃ τῆς ἐπαγγελίας ὁ λόγος· ταῦτά με ἦν τὰ ἐφελκόμενα, ταῦτα ἐπόθουν, διὰ τοῦτο οὔτε νύκτωρ οὔτε μεθ᾽ ἡμέραν ἐδόκουν ἡσυχάζειν φλεγόμενος τοῖς περὶ ταῦτα ἔρωσι· καὶ οὐ ταῦτά με μόνον πρὸς τὸν πόθον διήγειρεν, ἀλλὰ τούτων πλείω καὶ θαυμασιώτερα, οἷς συνάψεις τὰ ἑξῆς ἐγκώμια.

385 26. Ἐὰν δὲ μὴ ἐπιβατήριος ὁ λόγος ᾖ, ἄλλως δὲ πάτριος, περὶ μὲν ἐρώτων καὶ περιχαρείας ἐρεῖς οὐδέν, ἁπλῶς δὲ ἄνευ τῆς τοιαύτης προσθήκης ἐργάσῃ τὸ ἐγκώμιον πᾶσι[10] χρώμενος τοῖς κεφαλαίοις ἐφεξῆς,

---

10 πᾶσι coni. RW: πατρίοις codd.: πατρίδος coni. Bursian

24. After the section on nature, you should add one on nurture—if, that is, you have material in its traditions, as Aristides did so successfully when he remarked that the Athenians were given their crops by Demeter but then shared them with everyone else.[21] But if you do not have any such material, praise their ethical behavior, as in the section on activities, for activities are an indication of character and of the choices that people make apart from competitive deeds.[22] You can say, then, that they are humane to strangers, law-abiding in contracts, live together in concord, and treat outsiders as they treat one another.

25. Since we have undertaken an arrival speech, in each of these sections you should frequently add the following remarks, so that the speech does not stray from its expressed purpose. "These are the things that drew me here, these are what I longed for, these are the reasons why neither night nor day did I feel at peace, because I was burning with love for them. And not these alone aroused longing in me, but even more wondrous things," to which you should add the ensuing praise.

26. If, however, it is not an arrival speech, but solely a patriotic speech (*patrios logos*),[23] say nothing about love and joy; simply omit such additions and compose your praise by employing all the sections in order, as previously

[21] *Panath.* 34 and 336. This incident is also referred to at 1.16.14. [22] A similar argument was made at 2.1.16. The idea that choice (*proairesis*) reveals character (*ēthos*) goes back at least to Aristotle's discussion of tragedy at *Poet.* 50b8–10.

[23] M. does not treat such a speech, nor does an analysis of one exist elsewhere. Presumably it is one like Isocrates' Panathenaic oration, spoken by a local rhetorician, so that the topics of arrival are inapplicable.

ὡς προείρηται καὶ ῥηθήσεται. ἔστι δὲ κεφάλαια
ἐκεῖνα περὶ ὧν εἰρήκαμεν, φύσις, ἀνατροφή, ἐπιτηδεύματα, ἰδιάζον δὲ κεφάλαιον τοῦ ἐπιβατηρίου τὸ ἐκ
περιχαρείας, τὰ δὲ λοιπὰ κοινά.

27. Μετὰ τοίνυν τὰ ἐπιτηδεύματα διαιρήσεις τὰς
πράξεις εἰς τέσσαρας ἀρετάς. δικαιοσύνην· ἐν ᾗ μαρ-
τυρίαν λήψῃ τῶν περιοίκων, ὅτι ταύτην ἡγούμενοι τὴν
πόλιν ὅρον εἶναι δικαιοσύνης ἥκουσι παρ' ἡμᾶς δικα-
σόμενοι· καθάπερ οἱ Ἀθηναῖοι τὸν Ἄρειον πάγον δικαιοσύνης ἀγωνιστήριον παρειλήφασιν, οὕτω καὶ τὴν
πόλιν τὴν ἡμετέραν οἱ ἀστυγείτονες, καὶ οὐδεὶς ἐνε-
κάλεσεν οὔτε ξένος οὔτε ἰδιώτης τῶν παρ' ἡμῖν οὔτε
ἀστυγειτόνων πόλις τῇ ἡμετέρᾳ οὔτε περιοίκων, οὔτε
περὶ ὅρων, οὔτε περὶ ὧν εἰώθασιν ἀμφισβητεῖν αἱ
πόλεις· 28. εἶτα ἀπὸ τῶν καταπλεόντων ἐμπόρων, ὅτι
αἱροῦνται τὰς ἄλλας πόλεις καταλιπόντες εἰς τὴν
ἡμετέραν καταίρειν πεπειραμένοι τῆς ἡμετέρας φιλαν-
θρωπίας· εἶτα κατασκευάσεις ὅτι μὴ τὸ τέλος φορτικὸν εἰσπραττόμεθα, ὅτι μηδὲ ζημιοῦνται παρὰ τοὺς
νόμους.

29. Τὴν δὲ σωφροσύνην ἀπὸ ἐγκρατείας ἐρεῖς, ἀπὸ
τῆς τῶν νέων ἀγωγῆς, καὶ κατασκευάσεις ὅτι οἱ μὲν
περὶ λόγους καὶ φιλοσοφίαν ἔχουσιν, οἱ δὲ περὶ τέχνας καὶ ἄλλας ἐπιστήμας. ἀνάγκη δὲ τοὺς περὶ
ταῦτα ἔχοντας Ἀφροδίτης μὲν ἀτόπων νόμων ὑπερο-
ρᾶν, παρασκευάζειν δὲ τὴν ψυχὴν τὰ βελτίω περιεργάζεσθαι.

30. Περὶ δὲ τῆς φρονήσεως οὕτως ἐρεῖς, ὅτι θαυμά-

discussed or soon to be. Those sections we have already covered are nature, nurture, and activities. Particular to the arrival speech is the section on joy; all the rest is common to both types.

27. After "activities," then, you should divide "deeds" according to the four virtues. For justice, you may cite the testimony of neighboring people. "They consider this city to be the very definition of justice and come to us to seek judgments. And just as the Athenians were bequeathed the Areopagus as their court of justice, so have our neighbors come to regard our city, and no foreigner or private citizen of our own, no neighboring city or one in the surrounding area, has brought a charge against our city, whether over boundaries or over such disputes as cities normally have." 28. Then say of merchants who sail here, "They prefer to leave other cities and put in at ours, because they have experienced our humaneness."[24] Then you may assert, "We do not impose tariffs, nor are merchants unlawfully fined."

29. You should base your discussion of moderation on self-control (*enkrateia*)[25] and the upbringing of the young, and argue, "Some engage in oratory and philosophy, others in skills or other kinds of knowledge. People engaged in those activities necessarily disdain Aphrodite's perverse ways and train their souls to be concerned with higher things."

30. As for intelligence, say, "Those who share our na-

[24] For *philanthrōpia* as an aspect of justice, see 2.1.27.

[25] ἐγκράτεια connotes mastery of one's passions, especially sexual ones.

ζοντες οἳ τὸ αὐτὸ ἔθνος καὶ γένος εἰλήχασι παρ᾽ ἡμᾶς
ἥκουσι συσκεψόμενοι περὶ τῶν κοινῶν, ὥσπερ τὸ παλαιὸν παρ᾽ Ἀθηναίους οἱ Ἕλληνες, καὶ κοινόν ἐστι
386 συνέδριον καὶ βουλευτήριον τοῦ [κοινοῦ][11] γένους ἡ
ἡμετέρα πόλις· καὶ ὅτι εἰ ἔδει νῦν νομοθετεῖν, ἐνομο-
θέτησεν ἂν τῷ κοινῷ γένει τῶν ἀνθρώπων, ὥσπερ τὸ
παλαιὸν ἡ τῶν Λακεδαιμονίων καὶ Ἀθηναίων τοῖς
Ἕλλησι· ποῦ μὲν γὰρ Σόλωνες πλείους τῶν παρ᾽
ἡμῖν; ποῦ δὲ Λυκοῦργοι βελτίους; ποῦ δὲ Μίνωες καὶ
Ῥαδαμάνθυες, οἱ τῶν Κρητῶν νομοθέται;

31. Περὶ δ᾽ ἀνδρείας ἐρεῖς ὅτι πολλῶν πολλάκις
πρεσβειῶν πρὸς βασιλέα καὶ ἐκ πολλῶν ἐθνῶν γενο-
μένων οὐδένες μετὰ πλείονος παρρησίας καὶ σεμνό-
τητος διελέχθησαν τῶν ἀπὸ τῆς ἡμετέρας.

32. Εἶτα ἐφ᾽ ἑκάστῃ τῶν ἀρετῶν συγκρίσεις ἐργάσῃ, ἰδίαν μὲν καθ᾽ ἑκάστην, μετὰ δὲ ταύτην ἐφ᾽
ἁπάσαις αὐταῖς ἀθρόαν σύγκρισιν ἐργάσῃ πόλεως
πρὸς πόλιν, συλλαμβάνων ἅπαντα καὶ τὰ πρὸ τούτων
ὁμοίως, φύσιν, ἀνατροφήν, ἐπιτηδεύματα, πράξεις·
καὶ ἐν οἷς μὲν ἂν τούτων εὕρῃς σωζομένην τὴν ἰσό-
τητα ἢ καὶ πλεονεξίαν παρὰ τῇ πόλει ἣν ἐπαινεῖς,
ταῦτα ἀντεξετάσεις ἐν τῇ συγκρίσει, ἐν οἷς δ᾽ ἂν εὑρί-
σκῃς αὐτὴν ἐλαττουμένην, ταῦτα παραδραμεῖς· καὶ
γὰρ Ἰσοκράτης συγκρίνων Θησέα Ἡρακλεῖ, ἐν οἷς
μὲν εὗρεν αὐτὸν πλεονεκτοῦντα, ἀντεξήτασεν, ἐν οἷς
δὲ τὸν Ἡρακλέα, ταῦτα ἐσίγησε.

[11] secl. RW

tionality and race come to us out of admiration, in order to deliberate together on affairs of common concern, just as long ago the Greeks came to Athens. Our city too is the shared assembly place and council chamber of our race. And were there need for making laws today, it would have legislated for all mankind, just as Sparta and Athens did long ago for the Greeks. For where are there more Solons than here with us? Where better Lycurguses? Where better Minoses or Rhadamanthyses, those lawmakers of Crete?"[26]

31. Concerning courage, say, "Although many embassies have frequently come to the emperor from many nations, no ambassadors have argued with greater frankness or dignity than those from our city."[27]

32. You should draw specific comparisons when treating each of the virtues, but thereafter compose a comprehensive comparison of city with city, one that combines all the virtues and includes all the sections previously mentioned, namely nature, nurture, activities, and deeds. In this comparison you should draw contrasts for those qualities in which you find that the city you are praising maintains equality or even superiority, but skim over those in which you find your city to be inferior. For example, when Isocrates compared Theseus with Heracles, he contrasted those qualities wherein he found Theseus to hold the advantage, but said nothing of those wherein Heracles was superior.[28]

---

[26] Bursian unnecessarily bracketed the last clause as a gloss. It distinguishes the two Greek lawgivers from the two Cretan ones.   [27] Courage and frankness ($\pi\alpha\rho\rho\eta\sigma\acute{\iota}\alpha$) toward the emperor are also praised at 2.9.9.   [28] *Helen* 23–31.

33. Μετὰ τὴν σύγκρισιν ἥξεις ἐπὶ τοὺς ἐπιλόγους, ἐν οἷς διαγράψεις αὐτὸ τὸ σχῆμα τῆς πόλεως, καὶ ἐρεῖς στοάς, ἱερά, λιμένας, εὐετηρίας, ἀφθονίαν, τὰ ἐκ τῆς θαλάσσης ἐπεισαγόμενα ἀγαθά, ἵππων δρόμους, ἂν ἔχῃ, ἀγώνων διαθέσεις, λουτρῶν ἀπολαύσεις, ὑδάτων ἐπιρροάς, ἄλση ἐν αὐτῇ τῇ πόλει, τὰ περὶ τὴν πόλιν, οἷον ἂν ἱερὸν πλησίον πολυτελὲς ᾖ, ἂν μαντεῖον, ἂν τέμενος θεοῖς ἀνακείμενον· καὶ γὰρ ταῦτα συντελεῖ πρὸς κόσμον τῇ πόλει.

Ἐφ’ ἅπασι δὲ τούτοις τοῖς παραγγέλμασιν ἐντεύξει Καλλινίκου λόγοις καὶ Ἀριστείδου καὶ Πολέμωνος καὶ Ἁδριανοῦ, καὶ μιμήσῃ τὰς ἐργασίας ἐν μὲν τῷ τῆς φύσεως τόπῳ, ἐν δὲ τοῖς λοιποῖς ὡσαύτως· οὐχ ἧττον δὲ κἂν τοῖς ἐπιλόγοις τὸν ἐκείνων τρόπον ζηλώσεις.

34. Τὰ μὲν οὖν εἰρημένα καθολικῶς εἴρηται περὶ τοῦ πατρίου καὶ ἐπιβατηρίου· καὶ διακέκριται τὸ ἴδιον ἑκάστου ἐν τῇ διαιρέσει, ἐὰν δέ ποτε βουληθῇς εἰπεῖν, ὦ γλυκύτατε τῶν ἑταίρων, καὶ Τρωϊκόν, ⟨ἐρεῖς⟩[12] μὲν ἐγκώμιον τῆς χώρας πρῶτον, οὐδὲν δ’ ἄλλο ἐστὶν ἢ λόγος περιέχων ἔκφρασιν τῆς φύσεως καὶ τῆς θέσεως αὐτῆς ὅπως ἔχει πρὸς τὴν παρακειμένην ἤπειρον, ὅπως ἔχει πρὸς τὴν γειτνιῶσαν θάλασσαν, ὅπως ἀέ-

[12] suppl. Bursian, RW

[29] A late third-century AD historian and orator, also mentioned in 2.1.9.

33. After this comparison comes the epilogue, in which you should describe the distinct character of the city and speak of its colonnades, temples, harbors, prosperity, abundance, goods imported from the sea, hippodromes (if it has any), athletic contests, pleasant baths, aqueducts, and groves in the city itself, as well as features outside the city, for example, a richly appointed temple nearby, oracular shrine, or sanctuary dedicated to the gods, for these too contribute to the city's adornment.

In addition to all these instructions, you should read the speeches of Callinicus,[29] Aristides,[30] Polemon,[31] and Hadrian,[32] and imitate their treatments of the topic of nature and the other topics as well, and especially emulate their manner in the epilogue.

34. These instructions apply in general to both patriotic and arrival speeches. What is particular to each has been distinguished in our analysis.[33] But if ever you wish to deliver a Trojan oration, my dearest companion,[34] you should first praise the land, which is nothing less than a speech containing a description of its nature and its location in relation to the adjoining land, neighboring sea, and

[30] Publius Aelius Aristides (ca. 117–181 AD) is frequently mentioned and quoted as a model in both treatises.

[31] Marcus Antonius Polemon (ca. 88–144 AD) of Laodicea, an orator and sophist (cf. Philostr. VS 1.25). [32] Hadrianus of Tyre (ca. 113–193 AD), a student of Herodes Atticus (cf. Philostr. VS 2.10). [33] Cf. §26. [34] The identity of this person (the only such addressee in either treatise) is unknown. If indeed M. hails from Laodicea, the Troad would lie about two hundred miles northwest. The Troad is also the site of M.'s Invitation Speech (2.13.10–16) and Sminthian Oration (2.16).

ρων ἔχει εὐκρασίας, εἶτα ἐπὶ τούτοις λαμπρῶς καὶ
διειργασμένως ἐκφράσεις, ἐρεῖς δὲ καὶ περὶ ποταμῶν
καὶ ὀρῶν καὶ ἵππων[13] καὶ πεδίων καὶ σπερμάτων καὶ
δένδρων, ὅπως ἐπιτηδείως ἔχει πρὸς ταῦτα σύμπαντα,
καὶ ὅτι τούτων οὐδενός ἐστιν ἐνδεής.

35. Καὶ τοῦτο μὲν δὴ κεφάλαιον περὶ τῆς θέσεως,
πρὸς δὲ ἀπόδειξιν τούτου τοῦ κεφαλαίου λήψῃ ἀρ-
χαῖα διηγήματα πρὸς πίστιν λέγων οὕτως· τοιγάρτοι
διὰ τοῦτο καὶ κατὰ τοὺς παλαιοὺς χρόνους βασιλείας
μεγίστας καὶ περιβοήτους εὐτυχήσαμεν,[14] Δαρδάνου
τοῦ Τρωὸς τὴν ἀρχὴν ⟨λαβόντος⟩[15] τοῦ Λαομέδοντος,
καὶ οἱ πατέρες ἡμῶν ἦρξαν οὐ μικρῶν θαλάσσης μέ-
τρων, οὐδὲ νήσων τινῶν [ἄρχουσιν],[16] οὐδὲ περιγε-
γραμμένων τόπων, καθάπερ ἡ Πελοπόννησος, ἀλλ'
ἦρξαν μὲν Λυδίας, ἐπῆρξαν δὲ Καρίας, καὶ προῆλθον
τὴν ἑῴαν ἅπασαν καταστρεφόμενοι, καὶ ὡμολόγησαν
ἡμῖν δουλεύειν Αἰγύπτιοι καὶ Βλέμμυες καὶ Ἐρεμβῶν
γένη, εἴπερ αὐτοὶ καὶ ἐν τοῖς τελευταίοις χρόνοις φαίνονται ὑπακούοντες ἡμῖν ἐν ταῖς συμμαχίαις καὶ κλή-
σεσιν.

36. Ἡ μὲν οὖν ἀπόδειξις τοῦ κεφαλαίου τοιαύτη,
ὥστε συμπεπλήρωται τὸ κεφάλαιον τοῦτο τὸ περὶ τῆς
φύσεως καὶ θέσεως τῆς χώρας ἀπὸ τῆς ἱστορίας.

[13] καὶ ἵππων secl. Spengel, RW
[14] Bursian: εὐτυχήσαντας codd.: εὐτυχήσαντας . . . Λαομέδοντος obel. RW
[15] suppl. RW   [16] secl. Bursian, RW

climate. Then, you should provide splendidly detailed descriptions and speak of rivers, mountains, horses,[35] plains, crops, and trees, and say how well provided the land is in regard to all of these and how it lacks none of them.

35. So much for the section on location, but to offer proof and confirm its validity, you should include some ancient stories. For example, "It was for this reason, therefore, that even in olden times, when Laomedon took the reign from Tros, son[36] of Dardanus, we acquired the greatest and most famous kingdoms, and our forefathers ruled no small extent of the sea, or some few islands, or limited territories like the Peloponnesus, but ruled over Lydia, governed Caria, and proceeded to subdue the entire East, and the Egyptians, Blemmyes,[37] and tribes of the Erembi[38] were acknowledged to be under our rule, since they were clearly our subordinates in the final days in the alliances and levies."[39]

36. Such, then, is the confirmation of this section, and by this means the section on the nature and location of the land is filled out with historical material. After this, insert

---

[35] Spengel and RW bracketed καὶ ἵππων. Bursian suggested καὶ λιμένων, "and harbors," as in §20. But since the discussion includes plants, horses could figure in descriptions of plains, especially since fine horses are a prominent aspect of Trojan lore, and hippodromes were singled out in §33.

[36] Actually, grandson.

[37] A nomadic people of Nubia, south of Egypt.

[38] Mentioned as a people visited by Menelaus in his travels around Egypt and Libya at Hom. *Od.* 4.84.

[39] These are supposedly Trojan allies during the last days before the fall of Troy. This passage has multiple textual difficulties. For a full discussion, see RW ad loc.

μετὰ ταῦτα ἐμβαλεῖς τὸν περὶ τῆς πόλεως λόγον οὕτω
πως· τὸ μὲν οὖν παλαιὸν ἐρασθέντες τῆς χώρας θεοὶ
καὶ Ποσειδῶν καὶ Ἀπόλλων μικρὸν ἀνωτέρω θαλάττης τὸ Ἴλιον τειχίζουσιν, ὥσπερ τῆς ὅλης χώρας
ἀκρόπολιν. εἴπερ οὖν περὶ τῶν Ἀθηναίων ἐρίζοις, εἶτα
τὴν ἐκ κοινῆς γνώμης κατασκευήν, οὐ δι᾽ ἀπεχθείας
ἀλλήλοις ἥκοντες, ὥσπερ ἐπὶ τῆς Ἀθηναίων πόλεως,
ἀλλ᾽ ὁμογνωμονοῦντες ἀμφότεροι ὥσπερ οὐδὲν κάλλιον νομίζοντες. 37. Ἀλέξανδρος δὲ μετὰ ταῦτα, ὁ
μηδὲ Ἡρακλέους λειπόμενος μηδὲ Διονύσου νομι-
σθεὶς εἶναι χείρων, ὁ τῆς οἰκουμένης τὸ μέγιστον καὶ
πλεῖστον μέρος μιᾷ χειρὶ Διὸς παῖς ὄντως χειρωσά-
μενος, ἐπιτηδειότατον τοῦτον χῶρον ὑπολαβών, μεγίστην πόλιν καὶ ὁμώνυμον αὐτῷ κατασκευάσας, εἰς
ταύτην τὴν ἡμετέραν ἤγειρε. μετὰ ταῦτα ἐρεῖς καὶ
περὶ τῆς πόλεως, ὅπως καὶ αὐτὴ ἐν μέσῃ τῇ χώρᾳ
κεῖται ἢ μικρὸν ἐπικλίνει πρὸς τὴν θάλασσαν, εἶθ᾽
ἐξῆς ὥσπερ ἔχει σύμπασα ἡ διαίρεσις.

an account of the city along these lines. "Long ago when the gods fell in love with this land, Poseidon and Apollo built the walls of Ilium a short way inland from the sea, like an acropolis of the entire land." Then, if you are drawing a contrast with Athens, employ an argument based on shared intention. "It was not because of mutual hatred that they[40] came together, as in the case of Athens,[41] but because both agreed that they considered nothing to be more noble. 37. Later on, Alexander—who was no second to Heracles, nor considered inferior to Dionysus, and who was truly the son of Zeus—after singlehandedly subduing the greatest and most extensive part of the world, deemed this site to be perfectly suited, and, founding a great city named for himself, raised it into this city of ours."[42] After this, say how the city lies in the middle of the land, or slopes down a bit toward the sea, and so on, according to the division of topics as a whole.

[40] Poseidon and Apollo.

[41] Over which Poseidon and Athena quarreled.

[42] M. ahistorically attributes the foundation of Alexandria Troas to Alexander the Great.

2.3. ΠΕΡΙ ΛΑΛΙΑΣ

1. Τὸ τῆς λαλιᾶς εἶδος χρησιμώτατόν ἐστιν ἀνδρὶ σο-
φιστῇ, καὶ ἔοικε δύο εἴδεσι τῆς ῥητορικῆς ὑποπίπτειν
τῷ τε συμβουλευτικῷ καὶ τῷ ἐπιδεικτικῷ· πληροῖ γὰρ
ἑκατέρου τὴν χρείαν· καὶ γὰρ ἄρχοντα ἐὰν ἐγκωμιάσαι βουλώμεθα, πολλῶν ἐγκωμίων παρέχει τὴν ἀφθο-
νίαν· καὶ γὰρ δικαιοσύνην αὐτῷ καὶ φρόνησιν καὶ τὰς
λοιπὰς ἀρετὰς διὰ τῆς λαλιᾶς καταμηνύειν δυνάμεθα.
2. καὶ μὴν καὶ συμβουλεῦσαι διὰ λαλιᾶς ὅλῃ πόλει
καὶ ἀκροαταῖς πᾶσι καὶ ἄρχοντι, εἰ βουλοίμεθα,
προσδραμόντι πρὸς τὴν ἀκρόασιν ῥάδιον. καὶ μὴν
καὶ αὐτοῦ καταμηνῦσαί τινα ὀργὴν ἢ λύπην ἢ ἡδονὴν
πρὸς τοὺς ἀκροατὰς διὰ λαλιᾶς οὐ κεκώλυται, ἔξεστι
δὲ καὶ σχηματίσαι διάνοιαν ὅλην ἢ ἀποσκώπτοντα ἢ
κωμῳδεῖν ἐπιχειροῦντα ἦθός τινος [προαιρούμενον],[1]
ἢ ψέγοντα βίον, ἢ ἄλλο τι τῶν τοιούτων. εἰπόντες δὲ
τούτων παραδείγματα πειρασόμεθα καὶ περὶ τῶν ὑπο-
λοίπων τοῦ γένους διεξελθεῖν.
3. Ἄρχοντός τινος ἔθνους διὰ λαλιᾶς πρόκειται
ἡμῖν ἐγκώμιον. οὐκοῦν ζητήσομεν ὁποῖός ἐστι περὶ
βασιλέας, ὁποῖός ἐστι περὶ κατασκευὰς τῶν πόλεων
καὶ τῶν δημοσίων οἰκοδομημάτων, περὶ τὰς κρίσεις
τῶν ἰδιωτῶν, ὁποῖος δὲ καὶ καθ᾽ ἑαυτὸν τὸν τρόπον,

389

194

2.3. THE TALK

1. The genre of the talk (*lalia*) is especially useful for a sophist. It naturally falls under two branches of rhetoric, the deliberative and the epideictic, because it makes use of both. For example, if we wish to praise a governor, epideictic rhetoric provides an abundance of encomiastic topics, since in a talk we are able to point out his justice, intelligence, and other virtues. 2. Then too, it is easy in a talk to give advice to an entire city and all the audience, including the governor, if, that is, he is in attendance and should we wish to do so. Furthermore, in a talk nothing prevents the speaker from expressing to the audience some anger, pain, or pleasure that he feels. It is even possible to shape one's purpose as a whole by mocking or attempting to make fun of someone's character, by criticizing either his way of life or some other such trait. After citing examples of these, we shall attempt to survey the remaining features of this genre.

3. Our first task for a talk is an encomium of a provincial governor. Accordingly, we shall take into consideration where he stands with respect to emperors, to the physical condition of cities and public buildings, and to the trials of private citizens, and also whether his personal manner

---

1 secl. Bursian, RW

ὁμιλητικὸς καὶ πρᾶος ἢ τοὐναντίον αὐστηρὸς καὶ
κατεστυμμένος. 4. οὐκοῦν ληψόμεθα πρὸς τοῦτο [τὸ]²
παράδειγμα ἱστορίαν ἀρχαίαν ἢ πλάσαντες αὐτοί,
ἵνα μὴ δοκῶμεν αὐτοῖς γυμνοῖς τοῖς πράγμασιν ἐγ-
χειρεῖν· οὐ γὰρ ἔχει τοῦτο ἡδονήν· χαίρει γὰρ τὸ τῆς
λαλιᾶς εἶδος τῇ γλυκύτητι καὶ τῇ τῶν διηγημάτων
ἁβρότητι. παραγένοιτο δ᾿ ἂν ἡ γλυκύτης τῷ λόγῳ, εἰ
παραδείγματα λέγοιμεν δι᾿ ὧν ἐμφανιοῦμεν ὃ προαι-
ρούμεθα, ἱστορίας ἡδίστας τοῖς ἀκροαταῖς μαθεῖν
ἐκλεγόμενοι, οἷον περὶ θεῶν, ὅτι καὶ θεοὶ πεφύκασιν
ἐπιμελεῖσθαι τῶν ἀνθρώπων, οἷον εἰ Ἡρακλέους μνη-
μονεύοιμεν ὡς πειθομένου μὲν ἀεὶ τῷ Διῒ προστάτ-
τοντι, ἀθλοῦντος δὲ ὑπὲρ τοῦ βίου τῶν ἀνθρώπων, καὶ
τοὺς μὲν ἀδίκους ἐξαιροῦντος, τοὺς ἀγαθοὺς δὲ ἐγ-
καθιστάντος πρὸς ἐπιμέλειαν τῶν πόλεων, 5. ⟨ἢ⟩³ εἰ
Ἀγησίλαον λέγοιμεν, ὡς πειθόμενον Λακεδαιμονίων
τοῖς προστάγμασιν, ἄρξαντα δὲ τῆς Ἰωνίας καὶ τοῦ
Ἑλλησπόντου λαμπρῶς καὶ θαυμασθέντα οὕτως
ὥστε καὶ ταινίαις ἀναδεθῆναι παρὰ τῶν ὑπηκόων καὶ
ἄνθεσι βάλλεσθαι ταῖς πόλεσιν ἐπιδημοῦντα. μεστὴ
δὲ καὶ ἡ ἱστορία Ἡροδότου γλυκέων διηγημάτων· ἐν
οἷς ἡδονὴ παντοδαπὴς παραγίνεται τῷ λόγῳ, οὐ μόνον ἀπὸ τῆς ξένης τῶν διηγημάτων ἀκοῆς, ἀλλὰ καὶ
ἀπὸ τῆς ποιᾶς συνθέσεως, ὅταν μὴ τραχείᾳ χρώμεθα

² secl. Bursian, RW
³ suppl. Bursian, RW

is affable and tolerant or aloof and scornful. 4. To support this, we should adduce an example—either an ancient legend or one we invent ourselves—to avoid the impression of dealing with bare facts, because there is no pleasure in that and because the genre of the talk takes delight in sweetness (*glykytēs*)[1] and the delicacy (*habrotēs*)[2] that narratives provide. The speech can acquire sweetness if we relate examples that get our point across, while selecting the most pleasant stories for the listeners to learn. For example, we could tell how the gods are naturally inclined to care for humans, or bring up Heracles and tell how he always obeyed Zeus' commands, how he labored on behalf of human life, and how he did away with unjust men while installing good men to care for their cities.[3] 5. Additionally, we could tell how Agesilaus[4] obeyed the commands of the Lacedaemonians, ruled splendidly over Ionia and the Hellespont, and was so admired that his subjects crowned him with fillets and showered him with flowers whenever he visited their cities. Herodotus' *Histories* are also full of sweet narratives, which add every kind of pleasure to the writing, not only because of the novel storytelling, but also because of the particular type of exposition—

[1] For a full account of the style and subject matter appropriate to sweetness, see Hermog. *Id*. 330–39.   [2] Cf. 1.3.5 and especially 2.4.1 concerning the charm (*charis*) and delicacy of old stories.   [3] There is an implied equivalence of Zeus ≈ emperor(s), Heracles ≈ governor. The three examples (including Agesilaus) also mirror the eulogistic trilogy of gods, heroes, and men; cf. Pind., *Ol*. 2.1–2.   [4] Agesilaus (ca. 444–ca. 360 BC) was a highly regarded king of Sparta. See Xenophon's *Agesilaus* and Plutarch's *Life of Agesilaus*. Once again, Lacedaemonians ≈ emperor(s), Agesilaus ≈ governor.

τῇ ἐξαγγελίᾳ, μηδὲ περιόδους ἐχούσῃ καὶ ἐνθυμή-
ματα, ἀλλ' ὅταν ἁπλουστέρα τυγχάνῃ καὶ ἀφελε-
390 στέρα, οἷα ἡ Ξενοφῶντος καὶ Νικοστράτου καὶ Δίωνος τοῦ Χρυσοστόμου καὶ Φιλοστράτου τοῦ τὸν
Ἡρωικὸν καὶ τὰς Εἰκόνας γράψαντος ἐρριμμένη καὶ
ἀκατασκεύαστος.

6. Χρὴ δὲ καὶ ὀνείρατα πλάττειν καὶ ἀκοήν τινα
προσποιεῖσθαι ἀκηκοέναι, καὶ ταύτην βούλεσθαι
ἐξαγγέλλειν τοῖς ἀκούουσιν· ὀνείρατα μέν, ὡς εἰ λέγοιμεν ὅτι παραστὰς νύκτωρ ὁ Ἑρμῆς προσέταττε
κηρύττειν τὸν ἄριστον τῶν ἀρχόντων, καὶ πειθόμενος
τοῖς ἐκείνου προστάγμασιν ἐρῶ κατὰ μέσον θέατρον
ἅπερ ἐκείνου λέγοντος ἤκουσα· ἀκοὴν δέ, ὡς εἰ λέγοιμεν οὕτως, ὅτι ἀπήγγειλέ τις ἐμοὶ τῶν ἀπὸ ἀστυγεί-
τονος πόλεως πολλὰς ἀρετὰς καὶ θαυμαστάς, ἃς ἐν
ὑμῖν, εἰ σχολὴν ἀκούειν ἄγοιτε, φράσαι προαιροῦμαι.

7. Συμβουλεύσεις δὲ διὰ λαλιᾶς περὶ ὁμονοίας πόλει, ἀκροαταῖς, φίλοις, ἀντιπολιτευομένοις καὶ ταράτ-
τουσι συναγαγεῖν αὐτοὺς εἰς εὔνοιαν τὴν πρὸς ἀλλή-
λους· συμβουλεύσεις δέ ποτε καὶ ἐθέλειν ἀκούειν

---

5 As, for example, Thucydides' style, notorious for its syntacti-
cal complexity and logical arguments.

6 Literally, "tossed off" (*errimenē*). Demetr. *Eloc.* 12 describes
such a style (Demetrius cites Herodotus and Hecataeus as examples) as one in which "clauses seem thrown one on top of the
other in a heap without the connections or buttressing or mutual
support which we find in periods" (D. C. Innes, trans.).

7 Second-century AD sophist from Macedonia. No works survive.

a style we can employ that is neither rough nor full of periods and logical arguments (*enthymēmata*)[5] but rather plainer and simpler, like the loosely structured[6] and unadorned style of Xenophon, Nicostratus,[7] Dio Chrystostom,[8] and Philostratus,[9] the author of the *Heroïcus* and *Portraits*.

6. You should also make up dreams or claim to have heard some report that you wish to announce to the audience. In the case of dreams, we might say, "Hermes appeared during the night and ordered me to proclaim the best of governors, and in obedience to his orders I shall say in the middle of the theater[10] what I heard him tell me." In the case of a report, we might say, "Someone from a neighboring city related to me the governor's many marvelous virtues, which, if you have the leisure to hear, I propose to set forth in your midst."

7. In a talk on the subject of concord, you can advise a city, the audience, friends, political opponents and rabble-rousers alike, to come together in goodwill with one another. You may also advise them, on occasion, to be willing to listen to speeches, if you are aware that they are averse

[8] Dio of Prusa, the "Golden-Mouthed" (Chrysostom), circa 40–ca. 110 AD. Some eighty speeches survive, many epideictic, on a wide variety of subjects, often composed in a conversational style.

[9] One of three Philostrati of Lemnos of the second and third centuries AD. The two works cited are extant and probably belong to the author of the *Life of Apollonius of Tyana*, who flourished in the early third century.

[10] Either, literally, a theater (where public addresses often took place) or, metaphorically, the audience; cf. also §13.

λόγων, εἰ μισολόγους γινώσκεις καὶ δυσχερῶς συν-
ιόντας. 8. ἐξαγγελεῖς δὲ σαυτοῦ πάθος, οἷον ὡς ἐν
ὑποδείγματι, εἰ λέγοις ὅτι οὐκ ἀπαιτοῦσιν συνεχῶς αἱ
ἀκροάσεις οὐδὲ ἀναγκάζουσι λέγειν, πλάσας τοιοῦτον
λόγον, ὅτι Ἀπόλλων πολὺς ἦν θεσπίζων περὶ τοὺς
τρίποδας καὶ καταλαβὼν Κασταλίαν καὶ τοὺς Δελφοὺς ἐπλήρου τὴν προφῆτιν μαντικοῦ [τοῦ]⁴ πνεύμα-
τος, τῶν δὲ Μουσῶν ἠμέλει· χαλεπαίνουσαι οὖν αἱ
Μοῦσαι ἀξιοῦσι μαθεῖν τὴν αἰτίαν, διότι οὐ μετέχει
χορείας τῆς ἐν Ἑλικῶνι μετὰ Μουσῶν, ἰδίᾳ δὲ φοιβά-
ζει Μουσῶν⁵ ἐν τοῖς ἀδύτοις καὶ ποθεῖ μᾶλλον τοὺς
τρίποδας. 9. σχηματίζων δὲ πρός τε σαυτὸν ἐρεῖς
ταῦτα καὶ πρὸς τοὺς ἀκροατάς, ὅτι Ζεὺς ᾐτιᾶτο τὰς
Μούσας, ὅτι οὐ προτρέπουσι τὸν Ἀπόλλωνα συγχο-
ρεύειν αὐταῖς καὶ πλήττειν τὴν λύραν· ἐμφανιεῖς δὲ
391 καὶ ἡδονὴν σεαυτοῦ πρὸς τοὺς ἀκούοντας οὕτως, ὅταν
ἀποδέχῃ τὴν ἀκοὴν αὐτῶν ὡς κριτικῶς ἀκροωμένων,
ὅτι ἤσθης ἐπὶ τῇ τοιαύτῃ διαθέσει τῶν ἀκροατῶν,
ὥσπερ Ἰσοκράτης ἤσθη τοῖς Ἕλλησιν ἀναγνοὺς ἐν
Ὀλυμπίᾳ τὸν πανηγυρικὸν λόγον, αἰσθανόμενος ὅτι
κατεῖδον ἀκριβῶς τὸ μεγαλεῖον τοῦ λόγου.

10. Ἀποσκώψεις δὲ πολλάκις καὶ ψέξεις ἀνωνύμως
ὑπογράφων τὸ πρόσωπον, εἰ βούλοιο, καὶ τὸ ἦθος

---

⁴ secl. RW   ⁵ secl. RW fortasse recte

11 For such a situation, cf. Diodotus' speech at Thuc. 3.42.43.
RW also cite Dio Chrys. *Or.* 32 (see esp. §§1–13).

200

to speechmaking or annoyed to be gathering.[11] 8. You may also express your own feelings by saying, for example, that audiences do not often invite you or force you to speak, and then invent a story like this. "Apollo was very busy prophesying amid his tripods. Having taken possession of Castalia and Delphi,[12] he was filling the priestess[13] with prophetic inspiration, but neglecting the Muses. As a result, the Muses were upset and decided to find out why Apollo was shunning their choruses on Helicon and was prophesying all by himself in his shrine, more enamored of his tripods than of the Muses." 9. Applying this to yourself and to your audience, say, "Zeus actually blamed the Muses for not encouraging Apollo to dance with them and play his lyre." You should also express your own pleasure to the audience when you accept their attention as discerning listeners, saying that you are pleased that they have such an attitude, just as Isocrates was pleased when he read his *Panegyricus* to the Greeks at Olympia, because he sensed that they accurately discerned the grandeur of his speech.[14]

10. You should often employ criticism and censure by sketching an anonymous person, if you wish, and castigat-

---

[12] Apollo secured the oracular site of Delphi and the Castalian spring by slaying the snake that guarded it. Cf. the *Homeric Hymn to Apollo*.

[13] The Pythia who pronounced his oracles.

[14] At the conclusion of the *Panegyricus*, Isocrates says (disingenuously) that he failed to attain the grandeur ($\tau o \hat{v} \ \mu \epsilon \gamma \acute{a} \theta o v s$, 187) he had aspired to and invites his listeners to imagine their happiness if they follow his advice. His speech also promotes concord (*homonoia*), the theme of this section.

διαβάλλων, καὶ ὥσπερ ἐν τῷ ἐπαινεῖν ἐξῆν ἐκ πάσης ἀρετῆς λαμβάνειν τὰ ἐγκώμια, οὕτως ἔξεστί σοι ἀπὸ πάσης κακίας διαβάλλειν καὶ ψέγειν, ὅταν ἐθελήσῃς.

11. Ἔστι δέ ποτε καὶ ἀπολογήσασθαι καὶ διαθεῖναι τὸν ἀκροατὴν ἐπὶ παρόδου, ἣν μέλλεις[6] ποιεῖσθαι, πολλάκις μὲν ἠθικῶς μετριάζοντα, ὅτι τέττιξ μιμεῖται τοὺς ᾠδικοὺς τῶν ὀρνίθων, πολλάκις δὲ αἰτήσεις συγγνώμην φάσκων ἐξ ὑπογύου σοι γεγενῆσθαι τὸ σπούδασμα, ἢ ὅτι τῶν λόγων τὰς ἀπαρχὰς ἀνατίθης τῇ πατρίδι καὶ τοῖς πολίταις, ὥσπερ τῇ Δήμητρι καὶ τῷ Διονύσῳ οἱ γεωργοὶ τὰ θαλύσια.

12. Ἁπλῶς δὲ χρὴ γινώσκειν, ὅτι λαλιὰ τάξιν μὲν οὐδεμίαν θέλει σῴζειν καθάπερ οἱ λοιποὶ τῶν λόγων, ἀλλὰ ἄτακτον ἐπιδέχεται τὴν ἐργασίαν τῶν λεγομένων· ἃ γὰρ βούλει τάξεις πρῶτα καὶ δεύτερα, καὶ ἔστιν ἀρίστη τάξις τῆς λαλιᾶς τὸ μὴ κατὰ τῶν αὐτῶν βαδίζειν συνεχῶς, ἀλλ᾽ ἀτακτεῖν ἀεί· ἀπὸ τοῦ γένους ποτὲ ἐγκωμιάσεις, ἄλλοτε πάλιν ἀπὸ προαιρέσεως ἐγκωμιάσεις, ἄλλοτε ἀπὸ τῶν χθὲς καὶ πρώην συμβεβηκότων περὶ αὐτόν. καὶ ἀπὸ τύχης ἐγκωμιάσεις ἄλλοτε καὶ ἀπὸ πράξεως μιᾶς ἄλλοτε.

13. Καὶ ταῦτα μὲν περὶ τούτων, λεχθήσεται δὲ καὶ ἕτερα. ἐρεῖς τι καὶ εἰς τὴν σεαυτοῦ πατρίδα ὡς χρονίως μὲν ἐπανελθὼν ἐπ᾽ αὐτήν, ἀσμενέστατα δὲ αὐτὴν θεασάμενος, καὶ τὸ Ὁμηρικὸν ἐπιφωνήσεις

6 Bursian: μέλλει codd.

ing his moral character. Just as in praising it was possible to draw on any given virtue for your encomium, so it is possible for you to criticize and censure by drawing on any vice, when that is your intention.

11. Sometimes it is also possible to make an apology and prepare the audience for the performance you are about to make, often by showing your modest character ("a cricket is imitating songbirds"), often too by asking for forbearance, claiming that this assignment has come upon you on the spur of the moment, or that you are dedicating the first fruits of your words to your hometown and its citizens, just as farmers offer first fruits to Demeter and Dionysus.

12. As a general rule, you must recognize that a talk does not aim to preserve any particular order as other speeches do, but permits a disorderly presentation of its contents. You may thus put first or second whichever topics you wish. Indeed, the best way to arrange a talk is to avoid marching through topics in strict sequence and instead maintain a certain disorder. At one point, you can praise your subject for his birth, at another for his choices,[15] and at another for what happened to him just recently. Sometimes you can praise him for his good luck, at other times for a single accomplishment.

13. So much for this; other aspects need to be taken up.[16] In addressing your homeland upon returning after a long absence and beholding her with great joy, you can cite the words of Homer:

[15] Choice indicates one's ethical character; cf. 2.2.24.
[16] Specifically, the topics of an arrival talk.

392   κῦσε δὲ ζείδωρον ἄρουραν,
χαίρων ᾗ γαίῃ πατρῴῃ

καὶ ἀσπάσῃ τῷ λόγῳ τῶν ἀκροατῶν τὸ θέατρον,
⟨καὶ⟩[7] κοινῇ πάντας καὶ καθ᾽ ἕνα ἕκαστον, ἀνωνύμως
μέντοι, ὡς μὴ ἐκ τοῦ προφανοῦς ὄνομα λέγειν, ἀλλὰ
συγχαίρειν ἑαυτῷ ὅτι πρεσβύτας εἶδες οὓς κατέλιπες
ἀκμάζοντας, καὶ εἰς ἄνδρας τελοῦντας οὓς ἐν ἐφήβοις
εἴασας, καὶ νεανίσκους εἶδες τελοῦντας εἰς παῖδας,
καὶ ὅτι

   οὐδὲν γλύκιον ἧς πατρίδος οὐδὲ τοκήων
γίνεται.

14. Ἁπλῶς δὲ χρὴ γιγνώσκειν περὶ λαλιᾶς, ὅτι
πάντα ὅσα βουληθῶμεν ἐμφανίσαι δι᾽ αὐτῆς, ταῦτα
ἔξεστιν ἡμῖν λέγειν τάξιν μηδεμίαν ἐκ τέχνης φυλάτ-
τουσιν, ἀλλ᾽ ὡς ἂν προσπίπτῃ. στοχάζεσθαι μέντοι
δεῖ ἑκάστου καιροῦ τῶν λεγομένων καὶ συνιέναι ποῖον
χρήσιμον εἰπεῖν πρῶτον, ποῖον δὲ δεύτερον.

15. Χρὴ δὲ καὶ μνημονεύειν αὐτῶν Ἀθηνῶν, ἐξ ὧν
ἡ πάροδος, καὶ ἱεροφαντῶν καὶ δᾳδούχων καὶ Πανα-
θηναίων καὶ λόγων ἀγώνων καὶ μουσείων καὶ παιδευτῶν καὶ νεολαίας· φέρει γὰρ ταῦτα πολλὴν γλυκύτητα. 16. χρὴ δέ σε καὶ κιθαρῳδῶν ὀνόματα διαφόρων
εἰδέναι, Ὀρφέως, Ἀρίονος, Ἀμφίονος καὶ τῶν περὶ
αὔλησιν εὐδοκίμων καὶ μάντεων, καὶ ὅλως ἐνδόξων

       [7] suppl. RW

He kissed the life-giving earth . . .
rejoicing in his native land.[17]

In your speech you should greet the throng of listeners both as a group and individually, but without naming anyone openly. Instead, express your joy upon seeing elders you had left in their prime, grown men you had left as ephebes, young men you had left as children, and add:

nothing is sweeter than one's homeland and parents.[18]

14. As a general rule, it is necessary to recognize that in a talk we can say everything we wish to express without adhering to any systematic order, but as it occurs to us. Nonetheless, one must aim for the right moment to make each point and understand what is advantageous to put first and what second.

15. You must also mention Athens itself, where you are coming from—the hierophants and torchbearers,[19] the Panathenaic festivals and contests of oratory, the schools and instructors, and bands of pupils—for these provide considerable sweetness.[20] 16. You also need to know the names of famous lyre players like Orpheus, Arion, Amphion, and famous pipe players and prophets, and in

[17] The first part of this quotation comes from *Od*. 5.463, the second from 13.251.

[18] *Od*. 9.34–35, also quoted at 2.14.11 (in the leave-taking speech).

[19] Celebrants of the annual Eleusinian mysteries; cf. 2.14.4.

[20] Hermog. *Id*. 330 indicates that a major aspect of sweetness is subject matter that is pleasant.

τεχνιτῶν πλεονεκτήματα ἐρεῖς· 17. ἔτι δὲ περὶ ὀρῶν
ἐπισήμων, Ὀλύμπου, Πιερίας, Ἴδης, Ἑλικῶνος, Παρ-
νασοῦ· πλείστην γὰρ ἡδονὴν ταῦτα παρέξει τῷ εἴδει
τῆς λαλιᾶς. πολὺς δὲ καὶ ὁ Διόνυσος ἔστω καὶ χο-
ρεῖαι καὶ Σειληνοὶ καὶ Σάτυροι, καὶ Ὠκεανὸς ποταμὸς
καὶ Νεῖλος καὶ Ἴστρος καὶ Ἀχελῷος καὶ Εὐρυμέδων
καὶ Θύμβρις, καὶ εἴ τις ἄλλος ἐπίσημος. 18. χρησιμώ-
τατοι δὲ πρὸς λαλιὰν καὶ οἱ Πλουτάρχειοι βίοι,
ὥσπερ εἰς ἄλλην πολλὴν καὶ παντοδαπὴ παίδευσιν·
καὶ γὰρ πλήρεις εἰσὶν ἱστοριῶν καὶ ἀποφθεγμάτων
καὶ παροιμιῶν καὶ χρειῶν· ταῦτα γὰρ πάντα καταμι-
393 γνύναι ταῖς λαλιαῖς χρήσιμον, ἵνα πανταχόθεν τὴν
ἡδονὴν θηρεύσωμεν.

19. Δεῖ δὲ ζητεῖν καὶ μεταμορφώσεις φυτῶν καὶ
ὀρνέων. γέγραπται δὲ καὶ Νέστορι ποιητῇ καὶ σοφι-
σταῖς μεταμορφώσεις φυτῶν καὶ ὀρνέων· τούτοις δὲ
τοῖς συγγράμμασιν ἐντυγχάνειν πάνυ λυσιτελεῖ. 20.
ἔχειν δὲ δεῖ σε μνήμην καὶ ποιητῶν ἐπισήμων Ὁμήρου, Ἡσιόδου, τῶν λυρικῶν. αὐτοί τε γὰρ καθ᾽ ἑαυτοὺς ἄξιοι μνήμης, καὶ πολλοὺς μὲν ἐνεκωμίασαν,
πολλοὺς δὲ ἔψεξαν, παρ᾽ ὧν δυνήσῃ λαβεῖν παραδείγματα. 21. καὶ Ἀρχιλόχου δὲ οὐκ ἀμελήσεις, ἱκανῶς
κολάσαντος τοὺς ἐχθροὺς τῇ ποιήσει, ἵνα καὶ αὐτὸς
ὅταν ἐθέλῃς ψέγειν τινάς, ἔχῃς ἀποχρήσασθαι τἀν-
δρί. καλοὶ μὲν γὰρ αὐτοὶ καθ᾽ ἑαυτούς, ἀεὶ συνόντες
βασιλεῦσι καὶ τυράννοις συμβουλεύοντες τὰ ἄριστα,

---

[21] That is, of Bacchants.   [22] The Tiber.

general you should mention the masterpieces of famous artists. 17. In addition, mention famous mountains like Olympus, Pieria, Ida, Helicon, and Parnassus, for these can add enormous pleasure to a talk. Also make much of Dionysus and his choruses,[21] Silenuses and Satyrs, and rivers like Ocean, Nile, Ister, Achelous, Eurymedon, Thymbris,[22] and any others that are famous. 18. Plutarch's *Lives* are also very useful for a talk, as they are for many other kinds of instruction, for they are full of stories, sayings, maxims, and anecdotes. It is useful to include all these in talks, in order to seek out pleasure from every source.

19. One should also be on the lookout for metamorphoses of plants and birds. Nestor the poet[23] and some sophists[24] have written *Metamorphoses* of plants and birds, and it is very worthwhile to read these writings. 20. You should also mention famous poets like Homer, Hesiod, and the lyrists. Not only are they worth mentioning in and of themselves, but they have also praised and blamed many people, from whom you can take examples. 21. Also, you should not neglect Archilochus,[25] who ably chastised his enemies in his poetry. You can draw on him if you wish to censure any people. These poets are good in and of themselves, as they were always associating with kings and

[23] Lucius Septimius Nestor of Laranda (early 3rd c. AD) wrote a *Metamorphoses* in hexameters. Some verses are apparently quoted in *Anth. Pal.* 9.129 and 364.

[24] Probably prose writers such as Hadrian (mentioned at 2.2.33).

[25] A seventh-century BC lyric poet, famous for his personal attacks on enemies.

καλὴ δὲ καὶ ἡ ἀπὸ τῶν ποιημάτων αὐτῶν ἐπιφώνησις
καὶ μνήμη· γλυκεῖς γὰρ οἱ ἄνδρες καὶ ἡδονὴν ἐμποιῆσαι λόγῳ μάλιστα προσφορώτατοι.

22. Ὅτι μὲν οὖν ἐγκωμιάζειν καὶ ψέγειν καὶ ⟨προ-
τρέπειν καὶ⟩[8] ἀποτρέπειν διὰ λαλιᾶς ἔξεστι, καὶ ὅτι
διαθέσεις τῆς ψυχῆς καταμηνύειν δέδοται διὰ τῆς λαλιᾶς, οἷον λύπην ἡδονὴν ὀργὴν ἤ τι τῶν τοιούτων,
ἱκανῶς ἡμῖν προείρηται· ὁποῖον δὲ δεῖ τὸ εἶδος τῆς
ἀπαγγελίας εἶναι, καὶ τοῦτο προστέθειται, ὅτι ἁπλοῦν
καὶ ἀφελὲς καὶ ἀκατάσκευον· καὶ ὅτι οὐδεμίαν τάξιν
ἀπὸ τῆς τέχνης νενομοθετημένην ἐπιδέχεται, καὶ
τοῦτο μεμαθήκαμεν. 23. προσκείσθω δὲ ὅτι οὐδὲ μα-
κρὰς τὰς λαλιὰς εἶναι δεῖ, πλὴν εἰ μή τις δι' αὐτῶν
ἐθέλοι μόνων τὴν ἐπίδειξιν ποιήσασθαι· καλὸν γὰρ ἡ
συμμετρία, καθάπερ τὸ ἀδολεσχεῖν καὶ πολλοὺς ἀνα-
λίσκειν λόγους, ἱστορίας ἱστορίαις συνάπτοντα καὶ
μύθους μύθοις καὶ διηγήματα διηγήμασιν, ἀπειρόκαλον εἶναι πεπίστευται.

24. Ἔστι δὲ καὶ συντακτικὴ λαλιά, ὡς ἐὰν μέλλοντες ἀνάγεσθαι ἀπὸ τῶν Ἀθηνῶν ἐπὶ τὴν ἐνεγκοῦσαν
394 ἢ αὖ πάλιν ἀπὸ τῆς ἐνεγκούσης ἐπὶ τὰς Ἀθήνας ἐμ-
φανίζωμεν ὅτι δυσχεραίνομεν τὴν ἀπόλειψιν, ἐνδει-
κνύμενοι ἑαυτοὺς[9] ἀνιωμένους· εἶτα ἐκ μεθόδου ἥξομεν
ἐπὶ τὰ ἐγκώμια τῆς πόλεως, ἣν ἂν ἀπολιπεῖν μέλλω-
μεν, οἷον τίς ἂν ἕλοιτο ἀδακρυτὶ παραλιπεῖν—ὡς
εἰ ἐπ' Ἀθηνῶν λέγοις—μυστήρια, κηρύγματα ἱερὰ
Ἐλευσῖνάδε προστάττοντα βαδίζειν, καὶ ἄστυδε πά-

---

[8] suppl. RW   [9] Nitsche: τοὺς codd.

tyrants and giving them the best counsel. Also good are references to and quotations from their poems, for these poets are "sweet" and especially well-suited to make your speech enjoyable.

22. We have now adequately explained how it is possible in a talk to praise or blame, encourage or dissuade,[26] and how it is permitted to express one's personal feelings such as pain, pleasure, anger, and the like. Furthermore, we have explained the type of style it must have, namely one that is plain (*haplous*), simple (*apheles*), and unadorned (*akataskeuos*).[27] We also learned that it permits no order prescribed by systematic rules.[28] 23. It should be added that talks must not be long, unless someone intends to make them the entire presentation, for concision (*symmetria*) is good, just as babbling on and wasting many words by adding stories to stories, myths to myths, and narratives to narratives is acknowledged to be in bad taste.

24. There also exists a leave-taking talk (*syntaktikē lalia*).[29] For example, if we are about to sail home from Athens or to Athens from home,[30] we should declare how sad we are to leave and display our grief. Next comes regular praise of the city we are going to leave. For example, in the case of Athens, "Who could choose to leave, without tears in their eyes, the mysteries, the holy proclamations commanding the procession to Eleusis and back

[26] The first pair pertains to epideictic rhetoric, the second to deliberative; cf. §1.   [27] See §5.   [28] See §14.

[29] In this talk the speaker himself is leaving, as distinct from the following sendoff talk (*propemptikē lalia*) at 2.4, which bids farewell to another person who is departing. Cf. 2.14, the leave-taking speech (*syntaktikos logos*).   [30] Home is presumably Alexandria Troas, as elsewhere in this treatise.

λιν ἀπ' Ἐλευσῖνος· τίς δ' ἂν ἀνάσχοιτο ἀκροπόλεως
τοιαύτης κάλλος καταλιπεῖν, ἱερά, Διονύσια, Παναθή-
ναια, ἄνδρας λογάδας σοφίας καὶ ἀρετῆς τροφίμους;
καὶ ὅλως ἐφαρμόσομεν τὰ τῆς πόλεως ἐξαίρετα, τὰ
κάλλη τῶν οἰκοδομημάτων καὶ πανηγύρεων πολυτε-
λείας.

25. Ἔστι δὲ καὶ ἐπιβατήριον εἰπεῖν λαλιὰν εὐθὺς
ἐπιστάντα τῇ πατρίδι, ὡς μικρῷ πρόσθεν ἐμνημονεύσαμεν, ἐν οἷς περὶ τῶν ἐπιφωνήσεων τῶν Ὁμηρικῶν
ἐλέγομεν, ἐν ᾗ πάντως τὸν ἔρωτα τὸν περὶ τὴν πόλιν
ἐνδείξεται ὁ λέγων ἀπὸ τοῦ παρεστῶτος χρόνου λαβὼν τὴν ἀρχήν, ὡς γεγηθώς, ὡς ἄσμενος προσέπλευ-
σεν τοῖς λιμέσιν, ὡς εἶδε κάλλη πεδίων, ὡς προσέβα-
λεν ἀκροπόλει, ὡς περιεπτύξατο τῶν πολιτῶν ἅπαντας
καὶ ἕκαστον καὶ ἔργῳ καὶ λόγῳ, ὡς πάντας ἐνόμισεν
ἀδελφοὺς εἶναι αὐτοῦ τοὺς ἡλικιώτας καὶ πατραδέλ-
φους τοὺς ἄλλους, καὶ γένος ἓν πᾶσαν τὴν πόλιν, καὶ
ὅτι οὐκ ἐπελέληστο τῆς πατρίδος ἀποδημῶν προσθή-
σει·[10] 26. ἀλλ' ἄγε διηγοῦ τὰ ἐξαίρετα καὶ πάτρια, οἷα
ταῖς ἄλλαις οὐ πρόσεστι πόλεσιν. εἶτα ἥξεις εἰς
ἐγκώμιον ἄρχοντος, ἐὰν ὁ ἄρχων παρῇ, ἐπὶ τὸ τοῦ
πατρὸς ἢ ἐπὶ τὸ τῆς πολιτείας, ὅτι τίς οὐκ ἂν ἐρα-
σθείη τοιαύτης πολιτείας, ἐν ᾗ ὁμόνοια καὶ φιλία καὶ
πάντες ἀρετῇ σύντροφοι, καὶ ὅσα τοιαῦτα. καὶ ἁπλῶς
πολυσχιδὴς ἡ τῆς λαλιᾶς χρεία. οἶδε γὰρ καὶ πᾶσαν
ὑπόθεσιν πρέπουσαν ἀνδρὶ πολιτικῷ περιεργάζεσθαι.

---

10 ἐπελέληστο . . . προσθήσει Walz: ἐπελέλησο . . . προσθήσεις Spengel: alia alii

again from Eleusis to the city? Who could bear to leave behind the beauty of such an acropolis, the temples, the Dionysiac and Panathenaic festivals, the select men nurtured in wisdom and virtue?" In short, we should work in the outstanding features of the city, the beautiful buildings and the lavish celebrations.

25. It is also possible to deliver an arrival talk (*epibatērios lalia*) directly upon coming home, as we mentioned above in discussing quotations from Homer.[31] Here the speaker proclaims his wholehearted love for his city, and, beginning with the present occasion, expresses how glad and joyful he was to sail into the harbor, to behold the beauty of the countryside, to approach the acropolis, to greet his citizens, one and all, with embraces and salutations, to consider all his age mates his brothers and the elders his uncles,[32] and how the whole city was one family, adding how he never forgot his hometown while away.[33] 26. Go on to describe the city's outstanding features and traditions that other cities do not possess. Proceed next to the praise of the governor, if he is present, of his father,[34] or of the governance of the city. "Who would not fall in love with such a polity, in which there is concord and friendship and where all the citizens are nurtured for virtue?" and so on. Simply put, a talk has all sorts of uses, for it has the ability to elaborate every subject appropriate for a public orator.[35]

[31] In §13.   [32] Literally, foster fathers.

[33] Or, following Spengel, "you will add that you had not forgotten." RW obelize προσθήσεις· ἀλλ' ἄγε διηγοῦ.

[34] The text is in doubt as to whose father is meant. RW propose that it is the speaker's father.

[35] That is, as distinct from a judicial orator.

2.4. ΠΕΡΙ ΠΡΟΠΕΜΠΤΙΚΗΣ

395 1. Ἡ προπεμπτικὴ λαλιὰ λόγος ἐστὶ μετ᾽ εὐφημίας τινὸς προπέμπων τὸν ἀπαίροντα. χαίρει δὲ ἁβρότητι καὶ διηγημάτων ἀρχαίων χάρισι. πολλοὶ δὲ τῆς προπεμπτικῆς τρόποι. εἷς μὲν ὁ δυνάμενος συμβουλὴν κατὰ μέρος δέξασθαι, τῶν λοιπῶν μερῶν δεχομένων καὶ ἐγκώμια καὶ λόγους ἐρωτικούς, εἰ βούλεται προστιθέναι καὶ ταῦτα ὁ λέγων· δύναται δὲ συμβουλὴν ἐπιδέξασθαι, ὅταν ὁ πολλῷ κρείττων προπέμπῃ τὸν ἥττονα, ὡς ὅταν ὁ παιδευτὴς προπέμπῃ τὸν ἀκροατήν· δίδωσι γὰρ αὐτῷ συμβουλευτικὸν ἦθος τὸ οἰκεῖον ἀξίωμα.

2. Ἕτερος δὲ τρόπος ἂν γένοιτο, ἐν ᾧ δυνήσεταί τις ἐνδείξασθαι ἦθος ἐρωτικὸν καὶ διάπυρον περὶ τὸν προπεμπόμενον, συμβουλὴν μὴ καταμιγνύς, τῆς ἀξίας ὑπαρχούσης ἐφαμίλλου καὶ τῆς δόξης ἴσης τῷ προπέμποντι καὶ τῷ προπεμπομένῳ, ὡς ὅταν ἑταῖρος ἑταῖρον προπέμπῃ· καὶ γὰρ εἰ βελτίων εἴη ὁ προπέμπων ἐνταῦθα τοῦ ἀπαίροντος, ἀλλ᾽ οὖν ἡ κοινωνία τοῦ ὀνόματος καὶ τὸ ἀμφοτέρους εἶναι φίλους ἀφαιρεῖται τὸ ἀξίωμα τῆς συμβουλῆς τὸν λέγοντα.

3. Γένοιτο δ᾽ ἂν καὶ ἄλλος τρόπος πλείονα διατριβὴν ἔχων περὶ τὰ ἐγκώμια μᾶλλον, σχεδὸν δὲ εἰπεῖν

2.4. THE SENDOFF TALK

1. The sendoff talk (*propemptikē lalia*) is a laudatory speech that bids farewell to a person who is departing. It delights in delicacy (*habrotēs*)[1] and the charm (*charis*) of old stories. There are many types of sendoff talks. One type contains advice in one part, while the remaining parts contain praise and expressions of love (should the speaker wish to add them). It can admit advice when a much more important person is sending off an inferior, as when a teacher sends off a student, for his particular status grants him the character of an advisor.

2. There can be a second type, in which the speaker is able to display a loving and passionate attitude toward the one departing without including any advice. This occurs when the status and reputation of the two parties are equal, as when a friend is sending off his friend. For even if the one bidding farewell in this case is superior to the one departing, nonetheless the title they share as mutual friends deprives the speaker of his advisory status.

3. Yet a third type spends much more time on praise (indeed, one might say almost the entire time), when the

---

[1] Cf. 2.3.4, where the delicacy of ancient legends is combined with sweetness.

μικροῦ σύμπασαν, ὅταν ἐθέλῃ προΐστασθαι τῷ μὲν
δοκεῖν προπεμπτικὸν λόγον, τῇ δ' ἀληθείᾳ ἐγκώμιον,
ὥσπερ ἂν εἰ μέλλοιμεν προπέμπειν ἄρχοντα ἢ τῆς
ἀρχῆς πεπαυμένον ἢ ἀφ' ἑτέρας εἰς ἑτέραν πόλιν μέλλοντα ἀπιέναι.

4. Λέγω δὲ ταῦτα οὐκ ἀποστερῶν οὐδένα τῶν προειρημένων τρόπων τῆς προπεμπτικῆς τῶν ἐρωτικῶν
παθῶν—χαίρει γὰρ ἡ προπεμπτικὴ πανταχοῦ τούτοις—ἀλλ' ἐνδεικνύμενος ὅτι ὅπου μὲν μᾶλλόν ἐστιν
αὐτοῖς καταχρῆσθαι, ὅπου δὲ ἐπ' ἔλαττον. παραλήψῃ
δὲ ἐπὶ τοῦ ἄρχοντος καὶ πόθον πόλεων ὁλοκλήρων
περὶ αὐτὸν καὶ ἔρωτας.

396   5. Διαιρήσεις δὲ τὴν προπεμπτικὴν οὑτωσί πως·
ὑποκείσθω δὲ ἡμῖν νέος συνήθης προπέμπων φίλον.
οὐκοῦν ὁ τοιοῦτος ἐνταῦθα ὥσπερ τι πεπονθὼς τῶν
ἀτόπων καὶ ἀπροσδοκήτων σχετλιάσει πρὸς τὴν τύχην ἢ πρὸς τοὺς ἔρωτας, ὅτι μὴ συγχωροῦσι θεσμὸν
φιλίας διαμένειν βέβαιον, ἀλλ' ἄλλοτε ἄλλους πό-
θους ἐμβάλλοντες παρασκευάζουσι τὸν πάλαι συνθέ-
μενον καὶ ὁμολογήσαντα φιλίαν ἄλυτον διαφυλάξειν
πάλιν ἐρᾶν πατρίδος, πάλιν γονέων ἐπιθυμεῖν, ὥσπερ
ἐπιλανθανόμενον τῶν πρὸς τὸν φίλον αὐτῷ περὶ φιλίας συνθηκῶν· 6. ἢ εἰσελεύσεται πρὸς τοὺς ἀκροατὰς
ὥσπερ πρός τινας δικαστὰς γραφὴν ἀποφέρων κατὰ
τοῦ φίλου, προσποιούμενος δῆθεν κατὰ τὴν πρὸς τὸν
ἑταῖρον συνθήκην. καὶ ἐπάξεις πάλιν παρακαλῶν
τοὺς ἀκροατὰς μὴ περιορᾶν παραβαίνοντα. ἐν οἷς καὶ
ἱστορίας ἐρεῖς καὶ παραδείγματα· ἱστορίας μέν, ὅτι

speaker pretends to offer a sendoff talk that is really an encomium. Such can occur when we are sending off a governor who has either concluded his tenure or is about to leave one city for another.

4. I say all this not to exclude emotions of love from any of the aforementioned types, because the sendoff talk always delights in those emotions. My point is that there are occasions for greater or lesser use of them. In the case of a governor, you may include the longing and love that whole cities feel for him.

5. You may divide the sendoff talk somewhat along the following lines. Let us assume that a young companion is sending off his friend. In this case, he will complain to Fortune or to the Love Gods, as though he has suffered something unreasonable and unexpected, because they do not allow the bond of friendship to remain secure. Instead, they keep instilling ever-changing desires and cause a person who has promised all along to maintain an unbroken friendship, again to love his hometown or again to long for his parents, as if forgetting the pact of friendship he had with his friend. 6. Alternatively, he may face the audience as if they were jurors and pretend that he is charging his friend with a breach of contract. You will then plead with your audience not to let him break the law. Here you can cite stories and examples. You can tell stories

Θησεὺς καὶ Ἡρακλῆς ἑταῖροι γενόμενοι καὶ Διομήδης καὶ Σθένελος καὶ Εὐρύαλος δυσαπαλλάκτως ἀλλήλων εἶχον· 7. ἐξ ἀλόγων δὲ παραδείγματα, ὅτι κἂν ταῖς ἀγέλαις καὶ ἵπποι καὶ μόσχοι συναφθέντες ἀλλήλοις συνηθείᾳ καὶ ὄρνιθες δυσχερῶς ἀλλήλων χωρίζονται. προϊὼν δὲ τῷ λόγῳ ὑπομνησθήσῃ, ἂν οὕτω τύχῃ, καὶ ἀσκήσεως κοινῆς καὶ παλαίστρας καὶ γυμνασίων τῶν αὐτῶν.

8. Μετὰ τὸν πρὸς τοὺς ἀκροατὰς λόγον, οὓς ὥσπερ δικαστὰς ὑπεθέμεθα, τρίτον ἐπὶ τούτοις εἰσάξεις πρὸς ἐποχὴν δῆθεν καὶ τὰ τῆς πόλεως ἐγκώμια· οὐδ᾽ οὕτως ὁ τῶν Ἀθηναίων αἱρεῖ σε πόθος, οὐδὲ μυστηρίων καὶ τελετῶν, οὐδὲ μουσεῖα καὶ θέατρα λόγων, οὐδὲ παιδευτῶν φιλοτιμίαι περὶ τοὺς λόγους; . . . Ἄρειος δὲ πάγος καὶ Λύκειον καὶ Ἀκαδημία καὶ ἀκροπόλεως κάλλος, ἃ διείργασται φιλοπόνως ἅμα καὶ χαριέντως . . . ἀνέραστος ἄρα ὡς ἔοικεν ἦσθα·

397 πῇ δὴ συνθεσίαι τε καὶ ὅρκια βήσεται ἡμῖν;

9. οἷος γὰρ ἦν ἄρα μεγαλοφρονῶν ἐπὶ φίλοις ἐγώ, οἷον δὲ τεῖχος ἐδόκουν περιβεβλῆσθαι τὸν φίλον· νῦν δὲ γεγύμνωμαι καὶ περιήρημαι καθάπερ Αἴας τῆς ἀσπίδος, οἰκήσω τόπους ἐρήμους [καὶ ἐρημίας]¹ μισάνθρωπος ἐπικληθείς, ὥσπερ τὸν Τίμωνά φασι· τί γάρ μοι συντίθεσθαι φιλίαν, ἵνα πάλιν καὶ παραβαίνοντος ἀνιαθῶ; μακαρίζω τῶν θηρίων ἐκεῖνα ὅσα τὸν μονήρη βίον ἔοικεν ἀγαπᾶν.

of how the companions Theseus and Heracles were inseparable, as were Diomedes, Sthenelus, and Euryalus.[2] 7. Examples can come from animals, telling how horses and heifers accustomed to living together in herds, as well as birds, find separation from one another painful. Further on in your speech, you can bring up (if it is true) the exercises you shared in the same wrestling and gymnastic schools.

8. After this address to the audience as jurors, you may introduce a third topic, praise of the city, ostensibly to make him hesitant to leave. "Does not desire then for Athens hold you back? not her mysteries and initiations? not her schools and lecture halls, not the literary rivalries of professors? . . . the Areopagus and Lyceum and Academy and the beautiful Acropolis, all constructed with such care and charm . . . Apparently, you weren't in love after all.[3]

What then will come of our agreements and oaths?[4]

9. How truly proud I was of my friends and what a stalwart defender I considered this friend to be! But here I am defenseless and stripped of my shield like an Ajax. I shall go live in deserted places and be called a misanthrope as Timon was said to be. Why, I ask, consent to friendship, only to suffer when he betrays it? I envy those animals content to live a solitary life."

---

[2] For the latter three, cf. Hom. *Il.* 2.563–65.
[3] The text is fragmentary, but the topics are clear.
[4] Hom. *Il.* 2.339 (Nestor speaking).

---

[1] secl. RW

10. Ταῦτα μὲν οὖν καὶ τὰ τοιαῦτα τὸ πρῶτον μέρος τῆς προπεμπτικῆς ἕξει, καὶ τοιοῦτον ἦθος ἐνδείξῃ πρὸς[2] συνήθη καὶ φίλον τὰ ἐρωτικὰ εἰπὼν ἐν τούτοις τῆς προπεμπτικῆς κατὰ ⟨τὴν⟩[3] διαίρεσιν. ἐπειδὰν δὲ ἐπὶ τὸ λειπόμενον μέρος ἔλθῃς τῆς λαλιᾶς, σχετλιάσεις πάλιν ὡς βουληθεὶς πεῖσαι εἶτα ἀποτυχών, καὶ ἐπάξεις λέγων· οὐκοῦν ἐπειδὴ δέδοκται καὶ νενίκημαι, φέρε δὴ καὶ τῇ βουλήσει συνδράμωμεν.

11. Ἐνταῦθα τοίνυν ἥξεις ἐπὶ τὰ ἐγκώμια ἐκ μεθόδου, ὡς εὐτυχεῖς μὲν οἱ γονεῖς τῆς βλάστης, εὐδαίμων δὲ καὶ ἡ πόλις ἐπὶ σοί· τοὺς μὲν γὰρ εὐφρανεῖς ταῖς ἀρεταῖς, τῆς δὲ προστήσῃ ἐν δικανικαῖς ἀγοραῖς, ἐν ῥητόρων ἀγῶσιν, ἐν πρεσβείαις καὶ λόγων φιλοτιμίαις. ἵνα δὲ σύστασιν λάβῃ ταῦτα, ἐρεῖς ὅτι σύνοιδας αὐτῷ δικαιοσύνην καὶ σωφροσύνην καὶ φρόνησιν καὶ ἀνδρείαν καὶ ἀρετὴν ἐκ λόγων, καὶ οὐκ αὐτὸς μόνος, ἀλλὰ καὶ οἱ παιδευταὶ καὶ ὅσοι συνήθεις γεγόνασιν. 12. ἐν οἷς καὶ πράξεις ἐρεῖς πρὸς ἀπόδειξιν τῶν ἀγαθῶν, ἂν εὐπορῇς καὶ πράξεων· καὶ ὅτι βασιλεῦσι χρήσιμος ἔσται γνωσθεὶς διὰ τὴν ἀρετήν, καὶ ὅτι παιδευτηρίων προστήσεται ἴσως, οὐ μέντοι Ἰσοκράτης ἢ Ἰσαῖος ἢ Λυσίας ἤ τις τοιοῦτος ὅμοιος ἔσται.

13. Ἐρεῖς δὲ ταῦτα, ἐὰν πάνυ πεπαιδευμένον ὄντα λόγων προπέμπῃς τινά· τούτῳ γὰρ ἁρμόσει τὸ τοιοῦτον ἐγκώμιον, ὅτι προστήσεται τυχὸν καὶ λόγων

---

[2] ἐνδείξῃ πρὸς Bursian, RW: ἐνδείξεται καὶ codd.
[3] suppl. Bursian, RW

10. That sort of material should occupy the first portion of the sendoff talk. And, according to our analysis, such is the attitude you should display in this portion of the talk as you express your love for your bosom friend. When you come to the remaining portion of the talk, you should again complain of having failed to persuade him as you had wished, and conclude, "Well, since his mind is made up and I must concede, let us then concur with his wish."

11. At this point you will come to the regular praises. "How fortunate are the parents for bearing such a child, and how blessed is the city to have you! You will delight your parents with your virtues and will be the city's champion in the law courts, in contests of oratory, on embassies, and in literary rivalries." To confirm this, you can say that you have firsthand knowledge of his justice, moderation, intelligence, courage, and excellence in speaking—not you alone, but all his teachers and companions as well. 12. Here you should cite his deeds (if you have some at hand) as proof of his good qualities. You can say that emperors will find him useful once he becomes recognized for his excellence, and that he may one day become head of a school—although he will be no Isocrates, Isaeus, Lysias, or anyone like them.[5]

13. You must say these things only if you are sending off someone well educated in oratory, because such praises about how he will perhaps be a master of rhetoric and

[5] RW ad loc. point out that "these orators did not take part openly in public life . . . So they are not fit models for a future sophist who is also to be a political figure."

398 καὶ παιδεύσει νέους· ἐὰν γὰρ τῶν μὴ προσόντων αὐτῷ
μνησθῇς, ἃ πάντες ἴσασιν ὅτι τούτων οὐδὲν αὐτῷ
πρόσεστιν, καὶ ἀπίθανον εἶναι δοκεῖ καὶ περὶ τῶν ἄλλων λόγων ὕποπτον καταστήσεις σεαυτὸν ἐκ τούτου
καὶ προσάντη τὸν ἀκροατὴν τῷ λόγῳ. δεῖ γὰρ τοῖς
ὁμολογουμένοις πανταχοῦ συντρέχειν. 14. ἐρεῖς δὲ καὶ
ἐπὶ τῶν τοιούτων ὅτι καὶ ὅτε ἅμιλλαι λόγων ἐπὶ τῶν
μουσείων ἦσαν, ἐπῃνεῖτο παρὰ τῶν καθηγεμόνων τῶν
ἡλικιωτῶν μᾶλλον. καὶ ὥσπερ Ἔφορος ἐστεφανοῦτο
καὶ Θεόπομπος, οἱ μαθηταὶ Ἰσοκράτους, ὡς διαφέρον-
τες τῶν ἄλλων (καὶ γὰρ Ἰσοκράτης ἀρετῆς προὐτίθει
ἀγῶνα τοῖς ἀρίστοις τῶν ἀκροατῶν κατὰ μῆνα στέφανον), οὕτω καὶ οὗτος διαφέρων ἐφαίνετο καὶ ἐπαίνων ἠξιοῦτο οὐκ ἐλαττουμένων στεφάνων.

15. Ἐπειδὴ δὲ εἰς εὐδαιμονίαν συντελεῖ καὶ σώματος κάλλος, γράψον καὶ τὸν νεανίαν, οἷος μὲν ἰδεῖν,
οἷος δ᾽ ὀφθῆναι. ἐν ᾧ διαγράψεις αὐτοῦ καὶ ἴουλον καὶ
ὀφθαλμοὺς καὶ κόμην καὶ τὰ λοιπά. ἵνα δὲ τὸν λόγον
σεμνὸν ποιῇς τὸν περὶ τῆς γραφῆς καὶ τὴν διαβολὴν
ἐκφύγῃς τὴν ἐκ τοῦ κάλλους, ἀπέργασαι τὸ ἦθος σε-
μνότερον, λέγων ὅτι κοσμεῖ δὲ τὸ εἶδος τῇ τῶν ἠθῶν
ἐγκρατείᾳ, καὶ τῷ μὴ πολλοῖς ῥᾳδίως ἑαυτὸν ἐνδιδόναι, ἀλλὰ μόνοις συνεῖναι τῶν ἀνδρῶν τοῖς ἀρίστοις
καὶ λόγοις καὶ βιβλίοις.

teach the young will actually apply to him. For if you mention qualities he does not have and which everyone knows he does not possess, not only will it be judged incredible, but you will thereby make yourself suspect regarding everything else you say, and incline the audience against your speech. One must always stick to acknowledged facts. 14. In the case of well-educated persons, you can also say, "When oratorical competitions were held in the schools, he was praised by his masters above all his contemporaries. And just as Isocrates' students, Ephorus and Theopompus, won crowns because they surpassed the others (for Isocrates used to hold a competition of excellence every month with a crown for his best students), so he proved to be superior and was judged worthy of praise no less valuable than crowns."

15. Since physical beauty also contributes to happiness, describe the young man's looks and how others see him.[6] Here you will describe his youthful beard, eyes, hair, and so forth. But to keep this description dignified and avoid any slander arising from praising his beauty,[7] render his ethical character more dignified, by saying, "He adorns his good looks with his moral self-control (*enkrateia*). He does not mingle lightly with the crowd, but associates only with the best men, best speeches, and best books."

---

[6] The unusual phrase οἷος μὲν ἰδεῖν, οἷος δ' ὀφθῆναι recurs at 2.5.20. RW translate ἰδεῖν as "glance," that is, how he looks at others, but this is difficult to parallel; see their discussion ad loc. The epexegetical infinitive ἰδεῖν is frequent in such expressions. I have treated the phrase as pleonastic: his appearance and how he is perceived.   [7] Similar caution about praising physical beauty (of a bride) is expressed at 2.5.20.

221

16. Καιρὸν ἔχεις μετὰ ταῦτα καὶ τὴν πατρίδα ἐπαινέσαι τὴν ἐκείνου, ὅτι λαμπρὰ καὶ ἔνδοξος καὶ οὐ μείων τῶν πολυθρυλήτων, ἐν ᾗ λαμπρὸς ὀφθήσεται ἐν λαμπρᾷ καὶ εὐδαίμονι. εἶτα ἐπὶ τούτοις ἅπασιν ἀξιώσεις αὐτὸν μεμνῆσθαι τῆς πάλαι συνηθείας, τῆς εὐνοίας, τῆς φιλίας, καὶ παραμυθεῖσθαι τὴν ἀπόστασιν μνήμαις καὶ λόγοις.

Κἂν μὲν πεζεύειν μέλλῃ, διάγραφε τὴν ὁδὸν καὶ τὴν γῆν δι᾽ ἧς πορεύεται, οἷος μὲν ἔσται, ἐὰν οὕτω τύχῃ, διὰ τῆς Θρᾴκης διιών, ἐπαινούμενος καὶ προ-
399 πεμπόμενος, ἐπὶ τοῖς λόγοις θαυμαζόμενος, οἷος δὲ διὰ Λυδίας καὶ Φρυγίας· 17. ἐὰν δὲ διὰ θαλάττης ἀνάγηται, ἐκεῖ σοι μνήμη θαλαττίων ἔσται δαιμόνων, Αἰγυπτίου Πρωτέως, Ἀνθηδονίου Γλαύκου, Νηρέως, προπεμπόντων τε καὶ συνθεόντων τῇ νηΐ, καὶ συνηδομένων δελφίνων τε ἅμα καὶ κητῶν, τῶν μὲν σαινόντων, τῶν δὲ ὑποφευγόντων, ὡς Ποσειδῶνος αὐτοῦ τὴν ναῦν προπέμποντος· ἡ δὲ ναῦς θείτω θεοῖς ἐναλίγκιον ἄνδρα φέρουσα, ἕως ἂν προσαγάγῃς αὐτὸν τοῖς λιμέσι τῷ λόγῳ, καταστρέψεις δὲ εἰς εὐχὴν τὸν λόγον αἰτῶν αὐτῷ παρὰ τῶν θεῶν τὰ κάλλιστα.

16. After this, you will have an opportunity to praise his hometown, saying that it is no less splendid and famous than those highly vaunted cities, and that he will shine forth in that splendid and prosperous place. Finally, ask him to remember your longstanding companionship, goodwill, and friendship, and to assuage the pain of separation through memories and words.

If he is traveling overland, describe his route and the country through which he will pass. And if it so happens that he goes through Thrace, tell how he will be praised and escorted and admired for his oratory, and likewise how he will be regarded if passing through Lydia and Phrygia. 17. If he travels by sea, you should mention how the sea gods—Egyptian Proteus, Anthedonian Glaucus, and Nereus—will escort him as they speed beside the ship; how the dolphins and whales will share in the joy, some fawning, others fleeing, as Poseidon himself guides the ship. Let the ship speed on, carrying "a man like unto the gods,"[8] until you bring him into port in your speech. Then conclude it with a prayer, asking the gods to grant him the finest blessings.

---

[8] Said of Odysseus at Hom. *Od.* 13.89.

2.5. ΠΕΡΙ ΕΠΙΘΑΛΑΜΙΟΥ

1. Ὁ ἐπιθαλάμιος λέγεται ὑπό τινων καὶ γαμήλιος, λόγος δ᾿ ἐστὶν ὑμνῶν θαλάμους τε καὶ παστάδας καὶ νυμφίους καὶ γένος, καὶ πρό γε πάντων αὐτὸν τὸν θεὸν τῶν γάμων· χαίρει δὲ διηγήμασιν ἐπαφροδίτοις τε καὶ ἐρωτικοῖς· ταῦτα γὰρ οἰκεῖα τῇ ὑποθέσει.

2. Μετεχειρίσαντο δὲ τὸ εἶδος οἱ μὲν συντόνως, οἱ δὲ συγγραφικώτερον, καὶ δῆλον ὅτι ὁ μὲν σύντονος συνέστραπται λόγος ἅτε πολιτικῶς προϊών, καὶ ἕξει τὰς ἀρετὰς τοῦ πολιτικοῦ λόγου προοίμιά τε ἐγκατεσκευασμένα, ⟨ἐν οἷς⟩[1] ἢ μέγεθος περιθήσεις τῇ ὑποθέσει αὔξων αὐτὴν ἀπὸ τῶν προσώπων τῶν ζευγνυμένων, ἂν ὦσιν οἱ νυμφίοι τῶν ἐνδόξων, ἢ τὴν αἰτίαν ἐν αὐτοῖς ἐρεῖς, δι᾿ ἣν παρελήλυθας ἐπὶ τὸ λέγειν, ὅτι συγγενὴς τῶν γαμούντων, ὅτι παρακληθεὶς ἦλθον ἐπὶ τὸν λόγον, ὅτι ἔρανον ἀποδιδοὺς αὐτῷ προειληφὼς πρότερον χάριτας, ἢ καὶ ἄλλως, ὅτι φιλίᾳ χαριζόμενος, ἢ ὅ τι περ ἂν παραπέσῃ τοιοῦτον, ἢ ὅτι ἀρχόντων καὶ πόλεων καὶ ἐθνῶν συνελθόντων καὶ συνεορ-

---

[1] suppl. RW

---

[1] [DH] 2 treats marriage speeches.
[2] *thalamos* designates the chamber, while *pastas* is an alcove

224

2.5. THE EPITHALAMIUM

1. The epithalamium (*epithalamios logos*), which some call a marriage speech (*gamēlios logos*),[1] sings the praises of wedding chambers and bridal bedrooms,[2] brides and grooms, families—and above all the god of marriage himself.[3] It delights in stories that are charming and erotic, for they are germane to the subject.

2. Some have treated the genre formally, others more casually (*syngraphikōteron*).[4] Obviously the formal (*syntonos*)[5] speech is tightly constructed. It will proceed like a public oration and have the features of a public speech, including elaborate introductions, in which you may either invest the subject matter with importance and amplify it on the basis of the persons being married, if the bride and groom are distinguished people, or else you may explain why you have come forward to speak. "I am a relative of the wedding parties," or "I was invited to come speak," or "I am repaying him[6] for previous favors," or "I take delight in our friendship," or any such thing that occurs to you. Alternatively, "Since governors, cities, and nations have

or separate area in which the bed is located.   [3] That is, Hymenaeus (§22) or Gamos (§23).   [4] Literally, "more prosaically," indicating a looser, less elevated style.

[5] Literally, "intense," indicating an elevated, highly structured, usually periodic style. Cf. 2.6.26–27 and 2.14.15.

[6] Presumably the groom or the father hosting the wedding.

τάζειν αἱρουμένων ἄτοπον ἦν αὐτὸν σιγᾶν καὶ μὴ
χαρίζεσθαι τοσαύτῃ συνόδῳ καὶ συνεορτάζειν ἐθέλειν
400 τοῖς παροῦσιν ἅπασιν. 3. μὴ ἀμοιρείτω μέντοι τὰ προοίμια χάριτος, κἂν σύντονα τυγχάνῃ, ἀλλ' ἐχέτω μὲν
ἐννοίας ἡδίστας ὡς ἔνι μάλιστα πρεπούσας τῇ ὑπο-
θέσει· εἰ δὲ μή, ὀνόματα γοῦν ἐπαφρόδιτα καὶ κε-
χαρισμένα παστάδων, ὑμεναίων, γάμων, Ἀφροδίτης,
ἐρώτων, ἵνα καὶ οἰκεῖα γένηται τῇ ὑποθέσει καὶ τοῖς
ἀκούουσιν ἥδιστα.

4. Καὶ τὰ μὲν προοίμια τοῦ συντόνου ταῦτα καὶ
τούτοις παραπλήσια, τοῦ δὲ ἀνέτου καὶ συγγραφικοῦ
λόγου ἧττον μὲν ἐγκατάσκευα, οὐκ ἐμπερίβολα δέ,
ἀλλ' ὡς ἐν συγγραφῇ ἡπλωμένα μᾶλλον ἐννοίας
ἔχοντα τὰς αὐτάς. ἔστι δέ ποτε ἐν ἀνέτῳ λόγῳ καὶ
ἀπὸ διηγήματος ἄρξασθαι ἀνύοντά τι διὰ τοῦ διηγήματος τῶν προειρημένων ἐννοιῶν, οἷον εἰ λέγοις ὅτι
γαμοῦντος Διονύσου τὴν Ἀριάδνην παρῆν ὁ Ἀπόλλων νέος ὢν καὶ τὴν λύραν ἔπληττεν· ἢ ὅτι Πηλέως
γαμοῦντος παρῆσαν μὲν ἅπαντες οἱ θεοί, προσῆσαν
δὲ Μοῦσαι, καὶ οὐκ ἠμέλει τῶν παρόντων ἕκαστος
πρέπουσαν αὐτῷ δωρεὰν χαρίζεσθαι τῷ γάμῳ, ἀλλ'
ὁ μὲν ἐδίδου δῶρα, ὁ δὲ ἔπληττε λύραν, αἱ δὲ ᾖδον,
αἱ δὲ ᾖδον, Ἑρμῆς δὲ ἐκήρυττε τὸν ὑμέναιον· ὁρῶ δὲ
καὶ νῦν παρ' ἡμῖν ὅμοια. καὶ γὰρ οἱ μὲν σκιρτῶσιν,
οἱ δὲ ἀνευάζουσιν, ἐγὼ δὲ λέγω καὶ ᾄδω τοὺς γάμους.

---

7 Literally, "loose."

8 "Elaborate" here and above in §2 refers to arguments am-

gathered for the purpose of celebrating together, I have found it absurd for *me* to remain silent and not to grace so great a gathering nor wish to celebrate with all these present here." 3. All the same, even if your introductions are formal, do not allow them to lack charm. They should contain, as much as possible, very pleasant topics that are especially appropriate to the subject; but if not, at least they should contain lovely and charming words pertaining to bridal bedrooms, marriage songs, weddings, Aphrodite, and Loves, so they may be both germane to the subject and highly pleasing to the audience.

4. These and their like are the introductions of a formal speech. Those of a relaxed (*anetos*)[7] and casual (*syngraphikos*) speech are less elaborate[8] and lack extensive embellishment. Although they contain the same topics, they are simpler[9] as in casual prose. In a relaxed speech one may sometimes open with a narrative to convey one of the topics we mentioned. For example, you might say, "When Dionysus married Ariadne, young Apollo was present and played his lyre," or "At the wedding of Peleus, all the gods were present, including the Muses, and not one of the guests neglected to grace the wedding with a gift befitting his particular talents: one gave presents, another played the lyre, some women played pipes, others sang, and Hermes announced the wedding song. I see similar things here with us now: some are dancing, others are shouting for joy, and I am speaking and singing of the

plifying the importance of the wedding in a more elevated style. A similar point is made of the introductions to the bedtime speech at 2.6.20.

[9] That is, not containing periods.

5. ἢ ἄλλως· ὅτε ὁ Μεγακλῆς ἐγάμει τὴν Ἀγαρίστην καὶ συνῆλθον τῶν Ἑλλήνων οἱ ἄριστοι, τότε οὐδεὶς μὲν ποιητής, οὐδεὶς δὲ λογοποιὸς ὑστέρει, ἀλλ᾽ ὁ μὲν ῥήτωρ ἔλεγεν, ὁ δὲ συγγραφεὺς βίβλους ἐν μέσοις ἀνεγίνωσκε, ἅπαντες δὲ ἀνύμνουν τὸν γάμον· τῆς δὲ [τῆς]² Σικυωνίας οὐ χείρων ἡ παρ᾽ ἡμῖν, ὥστε καὶ ταῦτα δεύτερα γίνεσθαι.

6. Καὶ περὶ μὲν προοιμίων τοσαῦτα· δώσει γὰρ ἡμῖν ἡ ὑπόθεσις πρὸς τὰ τότε παρόντα πρόσφορα ἀληθεστέρας ἐννοίας καὶ μᾶλλον ἴσως οἰκείας· τὰ δὲ μετὰ τὰ προοίμια ἔστω περὶ τοῦ θεοῦ τοῦ γάμου λό-
401 γος ὥσπερ θετικὸς καθόλου τὴν ἐξέτασιν περιέχων ὅτι καλὸν ὁ γάμος, ἄρξῃ δὲ ἄνωθεν, ὅτι μετὰ τὴν λύσιν τοῦ χάους εὐθὺς ὑπὸ τῆς φύσεως ἐδημιουργήθη ὁ γάμος, εἰ δὲ βούλει, ὡς Ἐμπεδοκλῆς φησι, καὶ ὁ ἔρως. γενόμενος δὲ ὁ θεὸς οὗτος συνάπτει μὲν οὐρανὸν τῇ γῇ, συνάπτει δὲ Κρόνον τῇ Ῥέᾳ, συνεργοῦντος αὐτῷ πρὸς ταῦτα τοῦ ἔρωτος· 7. εἶτα ἐφεξῆς ἐρεῖς ὅτι ἡ τῶν ὅλων διακόσμησις διὰ τὸν γάμον γέγονεν, ἀέ-ρος, ἀστέρων, θαλάσσης· τοῦ γὰρ θεοῦ τούτου τὴν στάσιν παύσαντος καὶ συνάψαντος ὁμονοίᾳ καὶ τε-λετῇ γαμηλίῳ τὸν οὐρανὸν πρὸς τὴν γῆν, ἅπαντα διεκρίθη καὶ στάσιν οἰκείαν ἔλαβεν. ὑποβαίνων δὲ πάλιν ἐρεῖς ἐξ ἀκολουθίας ὅτι καὶ αὐτὸς τῇ βασιλείᾳ

² secl. RW

marriage." 5. Alternatively, "When Megacles married Agariste[10] and the most noble Greeks were in attendance, no poet, no writer was lacking then, but the orator declaimed, the historian stood in the middle and read his books, and everyone sang in praise of the wedding. Our bride is not inferior to the Sicyonian bride—so it is that things repeat themselves."

6. So much for the introductions. The subject itself will give us truer and perhaps more relevant topics for what is appropriate at any given time. After the introductions should come a kind of thematic passage on the god of marriage, including a general consideration of the thesis that marriage is a good thing. You should start from the very beginning, telling how Marriage (Gamos) was created by Nature right after Chaos was dispelled. You may add, if you wish, that Eros too was created then, as Empedocles says.[11] Once Marriage was born, he joined Sky (Uranus) to Earth (Gē) and Cronus to Rhea, with Eros assisting him in accomplishing this. 7. Next you should say that the ordering of the entire universe—air, stars, and sea—came about through Marriage, for when this god halted their strife and brought the sky together with the earth through concord and the rite of marriage, everything was sorted out and assumed its proper place. You may then continue the sequence of events. "Marriage himself also created Zeus and placed him in charge of the

---

[10] Hdt. 6.126–30 relates the famous contest of suitors to marry Agariste, the daughter of Cleisthenes of Sicyon, which Megacles of Athens won. M. adds many details not in Herodotus.

[11] Cf. DK B17, where, however, he speaks of Φιλότης, not Eros.

τῶν ὅλων τὸν Δία δημιουργήσας ἐπέστησε, καὶ οὐκ
ἄχρι τῶν θεῶν ἔστη μόνον, ἀλλὰ καὶ τοὺς ἡμιθέους
αὐτὸς παρήγαγεν πείσας θεοὺς συνελθεῖν τοὺς μὲν
γυναιξί, τοὺς δὲ νύμφαις.

8. Μετὰ ταῦτα πάλιν ἐρεῖς ὅτι αὐτὸς τὸν ἄνθρωπον
ὁμοίως φῦσαι παρεσκεύασε καὶ σχεδὸν ἀθάνατον
ἐφιλοτέχνησε, συμπαραπέμπων ἀεὶ τὰς διαδοχὰς τοῦ
γένους τῷ μήκει τοῦ χρόνου, καὶ ὅτι βελτίων Προμη-
θέως ἡμῖν· ὁ μὲν γὰρ τὸ πῦρ μόνον κλέψας ἔδωκεν, ὁ
δὲ γάμος ἀθανασίαν ἡμῖν πορίζεται.[3] 9. ἐμπλεονάσεις
δὲ τούτῳ τῷ μέρει δεικνὺς ὅτι δι᾽ αὐτὸν θάλαττα
πλεῖται, δι᾽ αὐτὸν γεωργεῖται γῆ, ὅτι φιλοσοφία καὶ
γνῶσις τῶν οὐρανίων δι᾽ ἐκεῖνόν ἐστι καὶ νόμοι καὶ
πολιτεῖαι καὶ πάντα ἁπλῶς τὰ ἀνθρώπινα· εἶτα οὐδὲ
μέχρι τούτων στήσῃ, ἀλλ᾽ ὅτι καὶ μέχρι πηγῶν καὶ
ποταμῶν διικνεῖται ὁ θεὸς καὶ νηκτῶν καὶ χερσαίων
καὶ ἀερίων.

10. Ἐν δὲ τούτοις ἅπασι διηγήματα θήσεις· ποταμῶν μέν, ὅτι Ἀλφειὸς ὁ Πισαῖος ἐρᾷ πηγῆς Σικελικῆς
Ἀρεθούσης, καὶ βιάζεται τὴν φύσιν, καὶ καθάπερ
νυμφίος ἐρωτικὸς κελαρύζων διὰ τῆς θαλάττης ἔπεισι
ζέων εἰς τὴν νῆσον τῆς Σικελίας, καὶ εἰς κόλπους
ἐμπίπτει τῆς ἐρωμένης Ἀρεθούσης καὶ μίγνυται· νηκτῶν δέ· δῆλον γὰρ ὅτι καὶ αὐτὰ τὰ ζῷα τὰ κατὰ
θάλατταν τελετὴν οἶδε γάμου, καὶ τὰ χερσαῖα καὶ τὰ
πετεινὰ πάντα, καὶ τὸν ἀνήμερον λέοντα καὶ φοβερὰ
βρυχώμενον ἤγαγεν εἰς τὴν τελετὴν καὶ ὑπέζευξεν
Ἀφροδίτης νόμῳ, καὶ τὰς ἀγριωτάτας παρδάλεις καὶ

402

230

kingdom of the universe. Nor did he stop with the gods; he also brought forth the demigods by persuading some gods to have intercourse with women and nymphs."

8. After that, you can say, "Marriage arranged for humans to be born in a similar way, and contrived to make them virtually immortal by continually sending forth successive generations through the length of time," and "Marriage is better for us than Prometheus, because he merely stole fire and gave it to us, whereas Marriage provides for our immortality." 9. You may develop this portion by pointing out, "Because of Marriage the sea is sailed and the earth is tilled, because of him philosophy and knowledge of the heavens exist, as do laws and constitutions—quite simply, all human things." Nor should you stop there. "The god reaches even springs and rivers and creatures in the sea, on land, and in the air."

10. For each of these you should provide stories. For rivers: "The Alpheus river in Pisa is in love with the Sicilian spring Arethusa, so it changes its nature and, like a bridegroom in love, goes gushing and seething through the sea to the island of Sicily and falls into the lap of its beloved Arethusa and makes love." For fish: "It is clear that the creatures in the sea know about the rite of marriage, as do all those on land and in the air. Marriage brings to his rite even the savage lion with its terrifying roar and yokes him to Aphrodite's law, along with the wildest leop-

---

3 πορίζεται RW: ὁρίζεται PWp: χαρίζεται m

ὅσα τοιαῦτα. 11. περὶ δὲ δένδρων ἐρεῖς, ὅτι κἀκεῖνα
οὐκ ἄμοιρα γάμων· οἱ γὰρ ἐπὶ ταῖς κόμαις σύνδεσμοι
φιλοτεχνήματα γαμούντων δένδρων εἰσί, καὶ τοῦ θεοῦ
ταῦτά ἐστιν εὑρήματα. ἔτι δὲ τούτου ἀνωτέρω ἐν τῇ
μνήμῃ τῶν θεῶν ἐρεῖς διηγήματα ἐν ᾗ καὶ δεύτερον,
ἢ περὶ Ποσειδῶνος γαμοῦντος τὴν Τυρὼ ἐν ταῖς προ-
χοαῖς Ἐνιπέως, ἢ περὶ Διὸς γήμαντος τὴν Εὐρώπην
καὶ τὴν Ἰὼ καὶ ὅσα παραπλήσια τούτοις. 12. πολλὴ
δὲ ἱστορία τοιαύτη παρὰ ποιηταῖς καὶ συγγραφεῦσι,
παρ' ὧν καὶ λήψῃ τὴν χορηγίαν, ἐπιφωνήσεις δὲ καὶ
τῶν Σαπφοῦς ἐρωτικῶν καὶ τῶν Ὁμήρου καὶ Ἡσιό-
δου· πολλὰ δὲ αὐτῷ ἐν τοῖς Καταλόγοις τῶν γυναικῶν
εἴρηται περὶ θεῶν συνουσίας καὶ γάμου.

13. Μετὰ τὸν περὶ τοῦ γάμου λόγον, ἐν ᾧ τὸν θεὸν
ὕμνησας, ἥξεις ἐπὶ τὰ τῶν γαμούντων ἐγκώμια. κοινὰ
δὲ τὰ προειρημένα πάντα καὶ τὰ ῥηθησόμενα τοῦ τε
συντόνου καὶ τοῦ ἀνέτου λόγου, διοίσουσι δὲ τῷ χα-
ρακτῆρι μόνῳ τῆς ἀπαγγελίας· 14. τὰ <δὲ>⁴ τοιαῦτα
ἐγκώμια διττὴν [δ']⁵ ἔχει τὴν μέθοδον· ἢ γὰρ γένος
γένει συνάψεις οὐ συγκρίνων, ἵνα μὴ δοκῇς τὸ μὲν
ἐλαττοῦν, τὸ δὲ αὔξειν, ἀλλὰ κατὰ ἀντεξέτασιν προάγων τὸν λόγον, ὅτι ὅμοιον ὁμοίῳ συνάπτεται· παρα-
κολουθεῖ δὲ τῷ εἴδει τούτῳ ἀσάφειά τις καὶ αὐχμηρό-
της διὰ τὴν μῖξιν, ἣν ὡς δυνατὸν φυλαττομένους χρὴ
προάγειν σαφηνείας φροντίζοντας. ἢ οὐ συνάψεις μὲν
οὐδ' ἀντεξετάσεις, ἰδίᾳ δὲ ἐπαινέσεις πρότερον μὲν τὸ
τοῦ νυμφίου, ἂν οὕτω τύχῃ, δεύτερον δὲ τὸ τῆς κόρης.

⁴ suppl. RW   ⁵ secl. RW

ards and all such beasts." 11. For trees: "Even they are no strangers to marriage, for tendrils on their foliage provide the means for trees to mate, and these are the inventions of Marriage." Even beyond this, when mentioning the gods,[12] you can recount one or two stories about Poseidon marrying Tyro in the outflow of the Enipeus river,[13] or Zeus' marriage to Europa and Io,[14] or the like. 12. There are many such stories in poets and prose writers to draw upon for material, and you can quote from the love poems of Sappho, from Homer, and from Hesiod, too, who has much to say in his *Catalogues of Women* about the love-making and marriages of the gods.

13. After that discussion of marriage, in which you sang the god's praises, you will come to the praise of those hosting the wedding. All of what has been said and will be said applies to both formal and relaxed speeches; they will differ only in the character of their styles. 14. There are two approaches to such praise. You may pair family with family without evaluating them, so as not to give the impression of slighting one while magnifying the other, nonetheless proceeding by means of comparisons, since like is being compared to like. However, this type of presentation entails a certain lack of clarity and dryness because of its complexity. We must guard against this as much as possible and keep clarity in mind as we proceed. Alternatively, you can neither pair nor compare them, but individually praise the groom's family first, if it so happens, and then the bride's.

[12] This subject was broached at the end of §7.

[13] Cf. Hom. *Od.* 11.235–56.

[14] The former is treated in Mosch. *Id.* 2, the latter in Aeschylus' *Prometheus Bound*.

15. Δεῖ δὲ ζητεῖν τὸ ἐνδοξότερον ἐν τούτοις τοῖς καιροῖς καὶ τοῦτο προτάττειν, οὐκ ἐνδιατρίψεις δὲ σφόδρα τῷ περὶ τοῦ γένους λόγῳ τὴν τοῦ μήκους ἀηδίαν προφυλαττόμενος καὶ τῷ μηδὲ ἐπάγγελμα τοῦτο[6] ἔχειν τὴν ὑπόθεσιν, ἀλλὰ τοὺς γάμους μᾶλλον καὶ τὴν παστάδα. 16. πρέπει δέ τί σοι ὀλίγα τεχνολογῆσαι περὶ τοῦ γένους. ἐὰν μὲν οὖν ἔνδοξα σφόδρα τυγχάνῃ τὰ γένη, αὔξειν δεῖ ταῦτα συλλαμβάνοντα ἀθρόως τὸν περὶ αὐτῶν λόγον δι᾽ ὀλίγων, εἶτα ἀπὸ τῶν ἰδίων πάλιν αὔξειν ἀεὶ πράξεις αὐτῶν λέγοντα καὶ φιλοτιμίας. ἐὰν δὲ τῶν μετρίων καὶ μὴ περιβλέπτων τυγχάνῃ, δεῖ ζητεῖν τοὺς ἐγγὺς πατέρας, εἰ λαμπροὶ εἶεν κατὰ τὴν πόλιν ἢ εὐδόκιμοι, καὶ ἀπὸ τούτων μᾶλλον ἐπιχειρεῖν. εἰ δὲ οἱ ἐγγὺς μὲν πατέρες ἀφανεῖς, τὸ δὲ γένος ἐπισημότερον, μᾶλλον ἀπὸ τοῦ γένους πειρᾶσθαι χρὴ τὰ ἐγκώμια παραλαμβάνειν· θηρευέτω γὰρ ὁ λόγος τὰ ἐνδοξότερα. 17. ἐὰν δὲ τὸ μὲν ἔνδοξον τῶν γενῶν τυγχάνῃ, τὸ δὲ μὴ πάνυ, ἀντίθες τῷ ἐνδόξῳ τὰς ἀρετάς, σωφροσύνην, ἐπιείκειαν τοῦ ἑτέρου γένους· οὐ γὰρ ἀπορήσεις ἀφορμῶν. εἰ δὲ μηδέτερον τῶν γενῶν ἔχοι μηδεμίαν λαμπρότητα, χρὴ τὸ ἦθος καὶ τὸν τρόπον καὶ τὴν ἐπιείκειαν ἐπαινέσαντα διὰ βραχέων καὶ παρακλέψαντα τὸν περὶ αὐτῶν λόγον ἀναδραμεῖν ἐπὶ τοὺς νυμφίους.

18. Τρίτος τόπος ἐστὶν ὁ ἀπὸ τῶν νυμφίων, χαριέστατος δ᾽ ἂν οὗτος γένοιτο εἰ κατὰ συμπλοκὴν ἀντεξεταστικῶς προέλθοι, ὅτι θαυμάσιος μὲν ὁ νεανίας, θαυμασία δὲ ἡ κόρη, ἐν παιδείᾳ σοφὸς οὗτος, ἐν

15. In such cases, you should determine the more prestigious family and put it first. But do not spend too much time talking about the family, to avoid being irritatingly long-winded. Furthermore, the subject of the speech does not have this topic as its object, but rather the wedding and the bridal bedroom. 16. All the same, it is fitting to give you a few rules on how to treat families. If both families are very famous, you should praise them in a brief comprehensive statement and then extol them for their individual achievements as you mention their deeds and benefactions. If their families are modest and not well known, then you must see if they have near relatives who are illustrious or well known in the city, and treat them instead. But if their near relatives are not well known, whereas the family is more famous, you should try to base your praises on the family instead, for your speech must seek what is more esteemed. 17. If one of the families is highly esteemed and the other less so, offset the famous family with the other family's virtues, by citing their moderation and sense of fairness. That way you will not lack for starting points. If, however, neither family possesses any esteem, briefly praise their character, way of life, and sense of fairness. Then subtly curtail the discussion of them and move on to the bride and groom.

18. The third topic concerns the bride and groom. It can be made most elegant, if it proceeds by interweaving contrasting comparisons. "The young man is marvelous, but marvelous too is the girl; he is well educated, skilled

---

6 τοῦτο RW: ταύτην codd.

λύρᾳ, καὶ ἐν μούσαις οὗτος ἀρίζηλος, ἐκείνη δὲ ἐν
σεμνότητι· εἰ δ' οὐκ ἔχοις τοῦτο, λέγε, ὅτι οὗτος μὲν
ἐν λόγοις, ἐκείνη δὲ ἐν ἱστουργίαις καὶ Ἀθηνᾶς καὶ
404 Χαρίτων ἔργοις. 19. καὶ ἄνευ μὲν ἀντεξετάσεως, κατὰ
συμπλοκὴν δὲ ἄλλως· ἀμφοτέρων δὲ τίς οὐκ ἂν τὰς
ἀρετὰς ἐπαινέσειε, καὶ τὴν προσοῦσαν σωφροσύνην,
καὶ τὴν ἐνυπάρχουσαν ἐπιείκειαν; δυνατὸν δὲ καὶ ἰδίᾳ
καὶ χωρὶς ἑκάστου διελόμενον τὸν ἔπαινον ἐπαινεῖν,
κάλλος δὲ παρ' ἀμφοῖν κατὰ ἀντεξέτασιν πάντως·
οὐχ ἡ μὲν φυτῶν καλλίστῳ ἐλαίᾳ, ὁ δὲ φοίνικι παρα-
πλήσιος; καὶ ὅτι ὁ μὲν ῥόδῳ προσέοικεν, ἡ δὲ μήλῳ.
20. διαγράψεις δὲ καὶ τὸν νεανίαν οἷος ἰδεῖν, οἷος
ὀφθῆναι, ὡς χαρίεις καὶ εὐπρόσωπος, ὡς ἰούλοις
κατάκομος, ὡς ἄρτι ἡβάσκων· τῆς παρθένου δὲ φυ-
λάξῃ διὰ τὰς ἀντιπιπτούσας διαβολὰς κάλλος ἐκφράζειν, πλὴν εἰ μὴ συγγενὴς εἴης καὶ ὡς εἰδὼς
ἀναγκαίως <λέγοις, ἢ>[7] λύοις τὸ ἀντίπιπτον τῷ λέγειν
"ἀκηκόαμεν ταῦτα."

21. Τέταρτος τόπος ἐστὶν ἀπὸ τοῦ <τὰ>[8] περὶ τὸν
θάλαμον καὶ παστάδας καὶ θεοὺς γαμηλίους ἐρεῖν, ὡς
ὅταν λέγωμεν, συνελήλυθε μὲν οὖν ἡ πόλις, συνεορτά-
ζει δὲ ἅπασα, πεπήγασι δὲ παστάδες οἷαι οὐχ ἑτέρῳ
ποτέ, θάλαμος δὲ πεποίκιλται ἄνθεσι καὶ γραφαῖς
παντοίαις, πολλὴν δὲ τὴν Ἀφροδίτην ἔχει· 22. πείθομαι δὲ καὶ ἔρωτας παρεῖναι τόξα μὲν ἐντειναμένους,
βέλη δὲ ἐφαρμόττοντας, φαρμάκοις πόθων τὰς ἀκί-

---

[7] suppl. Bursian, RW   [8] suppl. Bursian, RW

at lyre playing, and admired for his literary culture; she for her dignified manner." If you are unable to say this, you can say that he is admired for speaking, she for weaving and the works of Athena and the Graces. 19. Alternatively, interweaving but without drawing comparisons, say, "Who would not praise the virtues of them both, their attribute of moderation, their ingrained sense of fairness?" It is also possible to praise each one separately, but when it comes to the beauty of both, always use comparisons. "Is she not like the olive, the most beautiful plant? Is he not like a palm tree?" or "He resembles a rose, she an apple." 20. You can also describe how the groom looks and how others see him, how charming and handsome he is, how flowing his youthful beard, how recently he has reached maturity. But be careful when praising the bride's beauty because of the adverse slander it could cause,[15] unless, that is, you are a relative and can speak as one who unavoidably knew of it. If not, you can ward off disapproval by saying, "So we've heard."

21. The fourth topic consists of depictions of the wedding chamber, bridal bedrooms, and the gods of marriage. For example, "The city has gathered; everyone is celebrating. The bridal bedrooms have been prepared as never before for anyone else. The chamber has been decorated with flowers and paintings of all sorts and is full of Aphrodite's charm. 22. I am sure that the Loves are present with drawn bows, notching their arrows tipped with desire-

[15] Similar caution about praising male physical beauty is expressed at 2.4.15.

δας χρίσαντας, δι' ὧν τὰς ψυχὰς συγκυρώσουσιν
ἀναπνεῖν ἀλλήλαις, Ὑμέναιος δὲ ἀνάψει λαμπάδας
ἡμῖν καὶ δᾷδας γαμηλίῳ πυρί· χαρίτων τε μνημονεύσεις καὶ Ἀφροδίτης, καὶ μετὰ μικρὸν λοχείας Ἀρτέμιδος, ὅτι ὀλίγῳ ὕστερον διαδέξεται λοχεία Ἄρτεμις
καὶ μαιεύσεται, καὶ τέξετε παῖδας ὑμῖν τε ὁμοίους καὶ
ἐν ἀρετῇ λαμπρούς. εἶτα εἰς εὐχὴν καταστρέψεις τὸν
λόγον.

23. Ἐξέσται δέ σοί ποτε καὶ φιλοτιμουμένῳ τὸν
θεὸν τῶν γάμων ἐκφράσαι, οἷός ἐστι, κατ' ἀρχὰς τοῦ
λόγου ἐν τῇ θέσει, ὅτι νέος ἐστὶν ἀειθαλὴς ὁ Γάμος,
405   λαμπάδα φέρων ἐν ταῖν χεροῖν, ῥαδινός, ἐρυθήματι
τὸ πρόσωπον καταλαμπόμενος, ἵμερον ἀποστάζων ἐκ
τῶν ὀμμάτων καὶ τῶν ὀφρύων. 24. ἐξέσται δέ σοί ποτε
καὶ ἀντὶ τοῦ Γάμου τὸν Ἔρωτα ἐκφράσαι ἢ ἐν ἀρχῇ
τοῦ λόγου ἢ πρὸς τῷ τέλει· ἂν μὲν γὰρ τὸν Γάμον
ὑποστήσῃ κατ' ἀρχάς, τὸν Γάμον ἐκφράσεις δηλο-
νότι· ἐὰν δὲ τὸν Ἔρωτα, τοῦτον τὸν θεὸν ἐκφράσεις.
ἐκφράσεις δὲ ἀκολούθως ποτὲ χοροὺς παρθένων καὶ
χοροὺς ἠιθέων καὶ κυβιστῶντας, οἷα παρ' Ὁμήρῳ ἐν
τῇ ἀσπίδι· πρέποι δ' ἂν ταῦτα λέγειν πρὸς τῷ τέλει
τοῦ λόγου, ὅταν ὁ λόγος εἰς τὸν θάλαμον καταντήσῃ·
τοιούτων γὰρ ἐνταῦθα ὁ καιρός, ἐν δὲ τῷ θετικῷ λόγῳ
κατ' ἀρχὰς καιρὸν ἔχεις μᾶλλον ἐκφράζειν τὸν θεὸν
τῶν γάμων ἢ τὸν Ἔρωτα, ὁπότερον ἂν τούτων ὑποστήσῃ.

inducing drugs to make their souls breathe as one. Hymenaeus will light the lamps and torches with the marriage fire for us." You should mention the Graces and Aphrodite, and shortly thereafter Artemis, the goddess of childbirth. "Before long, Artemis will take over as midwife and you will bear children like yourselves, famous for their virtues." Then you should conclude your speech with a prayer.

23. It will also be possible on occasion, if you are ambitious, to describe the nature of the god of marriage at the beginning of the speech in the general thesis.[16] "Gamos is young and ever flourishing, carrying a torch in his hands, slender, lighting up his face with a blush, dripping desire from his eyes and brows." 24. On occasion, you can also describe Eros instead of Gamos, either at the beginning of the speech or at the end. If you propose Gamos as your subject at the beginning, you will obviously describe him, but if it is Eros, you will describe that god instead. Accordingly, you will sometimes describe choruses of maidens and youths and tumblers, like those on the shield in Homer.[17] However, the appropriate place for that may be at the end of the speech, when it comes to the wedding chamber, for then is the right time for such descriptions. At the beginning of the speech, however, when the general thesis is set forth, you will have a better place to describe Marriage or Eros, whichever of them you have chosen.

[16] That is, in §6.
[17] Cf. *Il*. 18.491–95 and 593–606.

2.6. ΠΕΡΙ ΚΑΤΕΥΝΑΣΤΙΚΟΥ

1. Ὁ κατευναστικὸς λόγος ἐστὶ συντομώτατος[1] διὰ τῶν καιρίων βαδίζων, καίρια δέ ἐστι τὰ πρόσφορα, πρόσφορα δέ ἐστιν ὅσα τῷ θαλάμῳ ἁρμόζει καὶ τῇ τοῦ νυμφίου συζυγίᾳ καὶ ταῖς παστάσι καὶ ἔρωσί τε καὶ ὑμεναίοις καὶ τελετῇ γάμου. οἱ μὲν οὖν ποιηταὶ διὰ τοῦ παρορμᾶν ἐπὶ τὸν θάλαμον καὶ προτρέπειν προάγουσι τὰ κατευναστικὰ ποιήματα, καὶ ἡμεῖς δὲ οὐ πόρρω τούτων στησόμεθα, ἀλλὰ παροξυνοῦμεν καὶ προτρέψομεν· ἔστι γὰρ ὁ κατευναστικὸς προτροπὴ πρὸς τὴν συμπλοκήν.

2. Ἐν τούτοις τοίνυν τὸν Ἡρακλέα παραλαμβάνωμεν καὶ ἕτερον εἴ τις ἀνδρεῖος περὶ γάμους γέγονεν, οὐ τῇ πάσῃ ἐπεξιόντες τοῦ Ἡρακλέος ἀλκῇ, ἀλλὰ τοῖς περὶ γάμων αὐτῷ καὶ γυναικῶν καὶ νυμφῶν πεπραγμένοις, ἵνα καὶ χάριτας ὁ λόγος ἔχειν δοκῇ. ἐροῦμεν δὲ ἐγκώμιον τῆς νύμφης διὰ βραχέων, οὐ τὸ ἀπὸ τῆς σωφροσύνης οὐδὲ τὸ ἀπὸ τῆς φρονήσεως οὐδὲ τῶν λοιπῶν ἀρετῶν τῆς ψυχῆς, ἀλλὰ τὸ ἀπὸ τῆς ὥρας καὶ τοῦ κάλλους—τοῦτο γὰρ οἰκεῖον καὶ πρόσφορον μόνον—τοῦ δὲ νεανίσκου τὴν ἀλκὴν καὶ τὴν ῥώμην, παραινοῦντες μὴ καταισχῦναι ταῦτα τοσούτων μαρτύρων γενησομένων τῇ ὑστεραίᾳ τῆς τελετῆς.

406

240

2.6. THE BEDTIME SPEECH

1. The bedtime speech (*kateunastikos logos*) is very brief and treats timely material that fits the occasion, that is, everything having to do with the wedding chamber, the joining of the couple, bridal bedrooms, gods of love, wedding songs, and the rite of marriage. Poets compose their bedtime poems by urging the couple on to the wedding chamber and by exhorting them, and we should closely follow them, for we too will spur them on and exhort them, because the bedtime speech is an exhortation to have intercourse.

2. Accordingly, let us include in them Heracles or some other manly marriage mate, without detailing all of Heracles' exploits, but only those achievements involving marriages with women and nymphs, so that the speech makes a charming impression. We should briefly praise the bride, not lauding her moderation, intelligence, or the other virtues of her soul, but her youth and beauty, for these alone are germane and appropriate. As for the groom, we shall praise his valor and strength, and urge him not to disgrace them, given how many witnesses will be on hand in the morning after his initiation.

---

1 Finckh, Bursian, RW: συντονώτατος codd.

3. Φυλακτέον δ' ἐν τούτῳ, μή τι τῶν αἰσχρῶν μηδὲ τῶν εὐτελῶν ἢ φαύλων λέγειν δόξωμεν, καθιέντες εἰς τὰ αἰσχρὰ καὶ μικρά, λέγειν γὰρ δεῖ ὅσα ἔνδοξά ἐστι καὶ ὅσα σεμνότητα φέρει καί ἐστιν εὐχαρῆ. ἄρξῃ δ' οὕτω πως· τὴν μὲν παρασκευὴν τοῦ γάμου καὶ τῶν ἀναλωμάτων τὸ πλῆθος καὶ τῶν ἀρίστων ἀνδρῶν τὴν σύνοδον οὐδενὸς ἕνεκα, ὦ νεανία, πεποιήμεθα, ἀλλ' ἢ τῆς ἀλκῆς ἧς ἔχεις καὶ ῥώμης ἐπίδειξιν βουλόμενοί σε ποιήσασθαι, ἵνα ἐπί σοι σεμνυνώμεθα αὐτοί τε οἱ τοῦ γένους καὶ ἡμεῖς οἱ ἡλικιῶται· σὺ δὲ μὴ ἐν φαύλῳ τὰ τῆς ἐπιδείξεως ποιήσῃ· 4. καὶ εἰ μὲν ἀθληταὶ ἦμεν, καὶ ἀγωνίζεσθαι Ὀλυμπίασιν ἔδει ἢ Πυθοῖ πρὸς ἄνδρας ἀθλητάς, ἐχρῆν καὶ βραβεῖον προκεῖσθαι καὶ κήρυκα παρεῖναι καὶ κριτήν τινα τῆς νίκης καὶ στάδιον ὑπάρχειν δημόσιον· ἐπεὶ δὲ τελετὴ γάμου τὰ δρώμενα, βραβευτὴς δὲ Ἔρως, κῆρυξ δὲ Ὑμέναιος, καὶ στάδιον ὑμῖν ὁ θάλαμος, φέρε μὴ τὰ τῶν φευγόντων ἐν τοῖς πολέμοις πάθῃς δεδοικὼς καὶ πρὸ τῆς συμβολῆς τὴν τροπήν, ἀλλὰ νόμισον ἔνθεν μὲν παρεστάναι σοι Πόθον, ἔνθεν δὲ Γάμον, Ἔρωτα δὲ συμβραβεύειν, Ὑμέναιον δ' ἐπιφωνεῖν, Ἴθι, τῶν πατέρων ἀξίως ἀγωνιούμενος. 5. καιρὸς δὲ τελετῆς ὃς καὶ φίλος ἐστὶ τῷ θεῷ τῶν γάμων· ἕσπερος μὲν γάρ ἐστιν ὕπαιθρος καὶ λαμπρός, ἅμαξα δὲ διαφανὴς ἤδη, καὶ ὁ τῆς Ἀφροδίτης ἀστὴρ καταυγάζει τὸ φαινόμενον, οὐρανὸς δὲ πεποίκιλται τοῖς χοροῖς τῶν ἄστρων.

6. Καί τινα τοιαῦτα διεξελθὼν ἁβρῶς περὶ τοῦ καιροῦ πάλιν ἐπιχειρήσεις ἀπὸ τῶν ἑστιωμένων, ἀπὸ

3. Here we must guard against seeming to say anything disgraceful, vulgar, or crude by stooping to shocking or petty things. We must talk of what is respectable, dignified, and urbane. You should begin along these lines. "Young man, we have made these wedding preparations, gone to enormous expense, and gathered the best men for one simple reason: we want you to display the valor and strength that you possess, so that the members of your family and we your age mates may be proud of you. Do not take your performance lightly. 4. If we were athletes and had to compete against other athletes at Olympia or at Pytho,[1] a prize would be offered, a herald would be on hand, along with someone to judge the victory, and there would be a public stadium. But since this performance is a marriage rite, the umpire is Eros, the herald is Hymenaeus, and the stadium is your wedding chamber. Do not behave like those cowards in battle by fearing a rout even before the engagement begins, but imagine that Desire (Pothos) stands by you on one side and Marriage (Gamos) on the other, that Eros acts as umpire and Hymenaeus is proclaiming, 'Go on! Compete as well as your fathers did.' 5. Now is the time beloved by the god of marriage for his ritual: the evening is clear and bright, the Wagon[2] is already visible; the star of Aphrodite is lighting up the heavens, and the sky is festooned with choruses of stars."

6. After reciting such charming details about the hour, you should take up the feasters and the others present.

[1] Delphi.
[2] Ursa Major.

τῶν παρόντων, ὅτι οἱ μὲν ἐπικροτοῦσιν, οἱ δέ σε νῦν
ἐπὶ στόματος καὶ γλώσσης ἔχουσι καὶ τὴν κόρην,
407 ὁπότερος ἄρ' ἰσχυρότερος πρὸς τὴν τελετὴν φανήσε-
ται· διηγεῖται δὲ ἴσως ἕκαστος αὐτῶν πρὸς τὸν πλησίον οἰκεῖα νεανιεύματα· εἰσὶ δὲ οἳ καὶ εὔχονται σφί-
σιν αὐτοῖς γενέσθαι παραπλησίαν πανήγυριν.

7. Προτρέψῃ δ' αὐτὸν καὶ ἀπὸ τοῦ κάλλους τοῦ
θαλάμου, ὃν αἱ Χάριτες κατεποίκιλαν, καὶ ἀπὸ τῆς
ὥρας τῆς κόρης καὶ ὁποῖοι περὶ ἐκείνην θεοὶ γαμή-
λιοι· Ἀφροδίτη καὶ Ἵμερος προδώσουσί σοι ταύτην
καὶ ἐγχειρίσουσιν, ἵνα δημιουργήσητε παῖδας ὁμοίους μὲν σοί, ὁμοίους δὲ ἐκείνῃ· ἐὰν δέ σε καὶ ἀπατᾶν
ἐπιχειρήσῃ αἱμύλα κωτίλλουσα, φύλαξαι τὴν ἀπά-
την· περίκειται γὰρ καὶ Ἀφροδίτης κεστόν, ἐν ᾧ διὰ
λόγων ἐστὶν ἀπάτη. 8. [προτρέψῃ δ' αὐτὸν καὶ ἀπὸ τῆς
ὥρας τῆς κόρης καὶ τῆς ἰδέας καὶ τοῦ κάλλους][2] καὶ
ἐπάξεις ὅτι ὀνειράτων ὄψεις ἡδίστας ὄψεσθε μαντευ-
ομένας ὑμῖν ἐπ' αἰσίοις τὰ μέλλοντα, παίδων γενέσεις, βίου παντὸς ὁμόνοιαν, οὐσίας αὔξησιν, οἰκονο-
μίαν τῶν ὄντων ἐπαινετήν.

9. Χρὴ δὲ παραγγέλλειν τῷ νυμφίῳ μέλλοντι ταῖς
πράξεσιν ἐπιχειρεῖν εὐχὰς ποιεῖσθαι τῷ Ἔρωτι, τῇ
Ἑστίᾳ, τοῖς γενεθλίοις, ἵνα συλλαμβάνωνται αὐτῷ
πρὸς τὸ ἐγχείρημα. εἶτα εὐχὴν ἐπάξεις αἰτῶν παρὰ
τῶν κρειττόνων αὐτοῖς εὐμένειάν τε καὶ ὁμόνοιαν,

[2] secl. Bursian, RW

"Some are applauding, others now have you and the bride on their lips and tongues, wondering which of you will prove stronger in the marriage rite. No doubt every man is telling his neighbor about his own youthful prowess, while others are praying to have a similar festival for themselves."

7. You may also exhort him by citing the beauty of the wedding chamber adorned by the Graces, the youthful beauty of the bride, and the gods of marriage attending her. "Aphrodite and Desire (Himeros) will deliver her into your hands, so that you may create children like yourselves. And if she tries to deceive you 'with wheedling words,'[3] beware of her deceit: she is wearing Aphrodite's girdle, in which there is deceit through words."[4] 8. You may add, "You two will see the sweetest visions in dreams, prophesying for you an auspicious future, the birth of children, lifelong concord, increase of wealth, and praiseworthy stewardship of your possessions."

9. You should advise the bridegroom, as he is about to engage in action, to offer prayers to Eros, Hestia, and the family gods, to aid him in his undertaking. Then you should add a prayer, asking the gods to grant the couple

---

3 Hes. *Op.* 374.

4 At Hom. *Il.* 14.214–21, Hera receives the desire-inducing girdle (κεστός) from Aphrodite to seduce Zeus. "Deceit through words" renders 216–17: ἐν δ᾽ ὀαριστὺς | πάρφασις, ἥ τ᾽ ἔκλεψε νόον ("in it is sweet-talking, persuasion that steals away the mind"). Bursian and RW bracket the following sentence: "You will exhort him as well by mentioning the girl's youth, appearance, and beauty."

συμπλοκῆς †ἐστίαν†,[3] κρᾶσιν ψυχῶν ὥσπερ καὶ τῶν
σωμάτων, ἵνα οἱ παῖδες ἀμφοτέροις ὅμοιοι γένωνται.

10. Οὕτω μὲν οὖν πως προάγειν τοὺς τοιούτους
λόγους διὰ συντόμων δυνήσῃ· κἂν μὲν ἀδελφὸς ἢ
συγγενὴς ᾖ ὁ συναπτόμενος, λέγε τὰ πρόσφορα πρὸς
συγγενεῖς, ὅτι ὁ προτρεπόμενός σοι οὐκ ἀλλότριος,
ἀλλὰ φίλος καὶ εὔνους, τῶν καὶ εἰς τὰ μάλιστά σοι
συνηδομένων, καὶ πείθεσθαί σε δεῖ. ἂν δὲ προειληφὼς
ᾖς τῷ γεγαμηκέναι αὐτός, λέγε ὅτι καὶ αὐτὸς ἔμπει-
ρός εἰμι τῶν τοιούτων ἀγώνων, καὶ οὐχ ἡρέθην οὐδ᾽
ἡττήθην, ἀλλ᾽ εἰ προὔκειτο στέφανος, ἐγὼ ἂν ἀπη-
νεγκάμην, ἄριστα διαθλήσας τότε. 11. ἂν δὲ ἀλλότριος τυγχάνῃ, πάλιν καὶ τοῦτο διαιρήσεις· ἐὰν μὲν
γὰρ νέος πρὸς νέον, ἐρεῖς τὸ Ὁμηρικὸν ἐκεῖνο

ἄλκιμος ἔσσ᾽ ἵνα τίς σε καὶ ὀψιγόνων εὖ εἴπῃ·

ἐὰν δὲ προεληλυθὼς τὴν ἡλικίαν, μὴ δοῦναι ὑπόνοιαν
τοῖς παροῦσι περὶ σαυτοῦ ὡς ἀσθενοῦς. προσθήσεις
δ᾽ ὡς ἵνα καὶ παῖδας φυτεύσητε τῇ πατρίδι λόγοις
ἐνακμάσοντας, φιλοτιμίαις, ἐπιδόσεσι.

12. Προσθήσεις δέ που καὶ ἀπὸ τοῦ καιροῦ τι· εἰ
μὲν γὰρ εἴη ἔαρ, ὅτι ἀηδόνες καὶ χελιδόνες ὑμᾶς
καταμουσίζουσαι καὶ κατακηλοῦσαι νῦν μὲν εἰς
ὕπνον καθέλκουσι, νῦν δὲ πάλιν ὑπὸ τὴν αὐγὴν τερε-
τίζουσαι ἀναστήσουσι μεμνημένους, καὶ ὅτι νῦν ἡ γῆ

408

---

[3] obel. RW: ἀστασίαν mW: εὐαρεστίαν tent. Bursian

goodwill and concord, . . .[5] of union, a blending of souls as of bodies, so that children may be born like both their parents.

10. In this way, you will be able to treat such passages concisely. If the groom is your brother or a relative, say what is appropriate for relatives. "The one exhorting you is no stranger, but a well-meaning friend, one of those who most rejoice with you in this endeavor, and whom you must obey." If you are already married yourself, say, "I am a veteran of such contests myself, and I was not defeated or worsted. If a crown had been the prize then, I would have won it with the best performance." 11. If he happens to be unrelated, then this further distinction is required. If, on the one hand, you are both young, you can cite this verse of Homer:[6]

Be brave, so that men of future generations may
    speak well of you.

If, on the other hand, he is older, say, "Do not give the impression to everyone here that you are weak," adding, "so that you two may bear children for the city, who will flourish in speaking, public service, and acts of charity."

12. You should also add something about the time of year. If it is spring: "Now the nightingales and swallows are summoning you two to sleep with their seductive songs and enchantments, but then soon at daybreak their twittering will arouse you from sleep, fully initiated." Alterna-

[5] No satisfactory emendation has been proposed for the manuscripts' ἑστίαν or ἀστασίαν.

[6] Spoken by Athena/Mentes to young Telemachus at *Od.* 1.302.

ἄνθεσι καλλωπίζεται καὶ ὡραΐζεται τοῖς βλαστήμα-
σιν, ὥσπερ καὶ ὑμεῖς ἐν ὥρᾳ καὶ ἀκμῇ τοῦ κάλλους
τυγχάνετε, καὶ δένδρα δένδρεσιν ἐπιμίγνυται, ἵνα
τοῦτο γένηται τελετὴ καὶ γάμος. 13. ἐὰν δὲ μετόπωρον, ὅτι καὶ νῦν οὐρανὸς γαμεῖ τὴν γῆν ὄμβροις
ἐπάρδων, ἵνα μετὰ μικρὸν ἐκφύσῃ καὶ κοσμήσῃ
αὐτὴν δένδροις τε καὶ βλαστήμασι. ἂν δὲ χειμών, ὅτι
συνάγει ἡμᾶς εἰς θαλάμους καὶ οἰκουρεῖν ἀναγκάζει,
καὶ ταῖς νύμφαις τοὺς νυμφίους συμπλέκεσθαι, καὶ
πάντα ἐν θαλάμοις εἶναι πείθει,[4] τὰς ἀνάγκας ἡμῖν
καὶ φόβους ἐκ τῆς σφοδρότητος τῶν ἀέρων ἐπάγων
καὶ ὥσπερ ἀναγκάζων γαμεῖν. 14. ἐὰν δὲ θέρος, ὅτι
νῦν μὲν τὰ λήια κομᾷ τοῖς ἀστάχυσι καὶ ἡμερίδες
τοῖς βότρυσι καὶ ⟨ἀκρόδρυα⟩[5] τοῖς ὡραίοις, καὶ κατά-
κομα τῶν δένδρων ἄλση καὶ γεωργία πᾶσα. εἶτα
προσθήσεις, οἵας μὲν εὐχὰς εὔξονται ὑπὲρ ὑμῶν οἱ
πατέρες, οἷα δὲ ηὔξαντο ταύτην ἐπιδεῖν τὴν ἡμέραν·
πληροῦτε οὖν αὐτῶν τὸν πόθον, πληροῦτε τοῦ γένους
τὰς ἐλπίδας.

15. Προσθήσεις δέ τι καὶ ἀπὸ ἱστορίας περὶ γάμου
καὶ συμπλοκῆς, εἰ ἔχοις τινὰς νεανίας εἰπεῖν ἢ καὶ
δένδρων ἔρωτας. ἐρεῖς τι καὶ περὶ Διονύσου, ὅτι καλὸς
409 πρὸς γάμους ὁ θεός, ἀλκῆς ἐμπιπλῶν, θάρσους πλη-
ρῶν, εὐτολμίαν διδούς· καὶ γὰρ αὐτὸς οὐκ ὀκνηρός,
ἀλλ' εὔτολμος περὶ γάμους ὁ θεός. οὕτω καὶ Αἰακὸς

_____

[4] πείθει Kroll, RW: ἐπεὶ καὶ τὰς p: ἐπείγει Bursian
[5] suppl. RW

tively, "Now the earth is festooned with flowers and adorned with plants, just as you two are in full bloom of beauty, and trees are mating with trees, so that this becomes their rite of marriage." 13. If it is fall: "Now the sky is marrying earth and watering her with rain, so that soon she may give birth and adorn herself with trees and plants." If it is winter: "It brings us together in our bedrooms. It forces us to stay at home and induces grooms to embrace their brides. It persuades everyone to stay indoors, as it forces us to fear the severity of the weather—as if compelling us to marry." 14. If it is summer: "Now the fields are covered with ears of grain and the grapevines with clusters, and trees with their seasonal fruits, and groves of trees and all the farmland are covered with green." Then you can add, "Oh, the prayers your parents will pray for you. Oh, how they have prayed to behold this day. Fulfill then their desires, fulfill the hopes of your family."

15. You should also add material from stories about marriage and intercourse, if you have any young men to mention, or any love stories about trees.[7] You should also say something about Dionysus. "That god is a fine one for marriages, instilling valor, filling one with confidence, providing boldness, for the god was no slacker himself, but bold when it comes to marriages. Thus it is that Aeacus

---

[7] The text is in doubt. Perhaps the well-known story of Apollo and Daphne is implied; cf. [DH] 1.6.

Αἴγιναν τὴν Ἀσώπου κατενύμφευσεν, οὕτω καὶ Πηλεὺς τὴν Θέτιν, καὶ ὁ Ζεὺς τὴν Λήδαν, οὕτω καὶ Τηλέμαχος Πολυκάστην τὴν Νέστορος, οὕτω καὶ τὴν Ἀφροδίτην Ἀγχίσης ὁ βασιλεὺς τῆς περὶ τὸ Ἴλιον χώρας.

16. Ἐρεῖς τι καὶ πρὸς τοὺς ἀκούοντας, ὅτι ἕως αὐτοὶ τελοῦσι τὰ ὄργια τοῦ γάμου καὶ τελοῦνται, ἡμεῖς ῥόδοις καὶ ἴοις στεφανωσάμενοι καὶ λαμπάδας ἀνάψαντες περὶ τὸν θάλαμον παίξωμεν καὶ χορείαν στησώμεθα, καὶ τὸν ὑμέναιον ἐπιβοώμεθα, τὸ δάπεδον πλήττοντες τοῖς ποσίν, ἐπικροτοῦντες τὼ χεῖρε, ἐστεφανωμένοι πάντες· καὶ ὅσα προσέοικε τῇ τοιαύτῃ ὕλῃ προσάψεις.

17. Εὕρηνται δ' ἀφορμαὶ πλείους ἢ πρὸς ἓν σύνταγμα, ἵνα ᾖ σοι διαφόρως χρήσασθαι ἐν πλείοσιν ὑποθέσεσιν· οὐ γὰρ ἅμα πάντα ἐρεῖς, ἀλλ' ἀρκέσει σοι ἓν καὶ δεύτερον τῶν εἰρημένων. ὁδοποιήσει δέ σοι καὶ τὰ λοιπὰ ἡ θεωρία καὶ ἀναστρέψεις τὰ πολλάκις ῥηθέντα, οἷον τὰ πρῶτα τελευταῖα ποιήσεις, καὶ τὰ τελευταῖα πρῶτα, καὶ ὅλως ἡ ἐξαλλαγὴ καὶ ἡ καινοτομία δόξαν παρέξει σοι τοῦ μὴ ταὐτὰ λέγειν· 18. ἔστι γὰρ οὐκ ἀποδεδειγμένη διαίρεσις περὶ τοῦ τοιούτου εἴδους τοῦ λόγου, ἡμεῖς δὲ τὴν εἰρημένην ἐπινενοήκαμεν, ἣν οὐ πάντως φυλάττειν ἀναγκαῖον, διὰ τὸ μηδένα ὁμότεχνον τὰ τοιαῦτα ὁρίζειν· ὡς ἐμὲ γοῦν εἰδέναι οὐδέπω μέχρι καὶ τήμερον διαίρεσις ἐπεδείχθη τοιούτου λόγου.

19. Εἴ τι δὲ δεῖ στοχασάμενον τοῦ πρέποντος καὶ

made Aegina, Asopus' daughter, his bride, as did Peleus Thetis and Zeus Leda, as did Telemachus Polycaste, Nestor's daughter. Thus too Anchises, king of the Trojan land, wedded Aphrodite."

16. You should also speak a word to the audience. "While they are celebrating the mysteries of marriage and being initiated, let us crown our heads with roses and violets, light torches and frolic around the bridal chamber, form choruses and shout the wedding song, as we stomp the floor and clap our hands, all of us with heads crowned." You may then add any particulars that suit such material.

17. I have mentioned more starting points (*aphormai*) than needed for one composition, so that you may use them in different ways on any number of occasions. You must not use them all at the same time; one or two of the aforementioned points will suffice. This overview (*theōria*) will guide you for the rest, and you can rearrange these oft-repeated topics, for example, by putting first ones last and last ones first. As a general rule, variation and novelty will make it seem that you are not repeating yourself.

18. Since no analysis (*diairesis*) of this genre of speech has been published, I have devised the one above (not, however, to be followed in every detail), because no fellow theorist has defined such matters. As far as I know, until today no analysis of such a speech has ever been put forth.[8]

19. If I may mention something intended to be appro-

---

[8] RW ad loc. doubt the veracity of this claim, but there is no actual evidence to dispute it.

ἐγγὺς γενόμενον τοῦ δοκοῦντος εὖ ἔχειν εἰπεῖν, καλῶς
ἂν ἔχοι προοιμιάζεσθαι μὲν οὐ μακρῷ προοιμίῳ, ἢ
ἀπὸ τῶν παρόντων ὡς οὐ καλῶς ἐπέχοιεν ἔτι τὸν
νεανίαν, ἢ ἀπὸ τοῦ νεανίσκου ὡς οὐκ ὀρθῶς ῥᾳθυμοῦν-
410 τος τῆς ἀγωνίας, ἢ ἀπ᾽ αὐτοῦ τοῦ λέγοντος, ὅτι συμ-
βουλήν τινα ἥκω φέρων τῷ νεανίᾳ εἰς μέσον πεφρον-
τικῶς ὑπὲρ αὐτοῦ καὶ σπουδάζων αὐτὸν καλὸν ἐν ὑμῖν
ὀφθῆναι. 20. ἔσται δ᾽ οὐκ ἐγκατάσκευον τὸ προοίμιον,
ἀλλ᾽ ἀφελὲς καὶ ἁπλοῦν. ἔστι δ᾽ ὅτε καὶ ἀπ᾽ αὐτοῦ τοῦ
πράγματος ληφθήσεται ἡ ἔννοια· τίνος ἕνεκεν ἡμῖν ἡ
σύνοδος γέγονεν αὕτη; γάμου τοῦ νεανίου δηλονότι
καὶ τελετῆς ἐρωτικῆς· τί οὖν οὐκ ἤδη τὸ πρᾶγμα τελεῖται, ἐφ᾽ ᾧ δὴ καὶ συνεληλύθαμεν, συνησθησόμενοι
τοῖς γινομένοις;

21. Εἶτα μετὰ τὸ προοίμιον ἥξεις ἐπὶ τὴν τοῦ νεανίσκου προτροπήν· ᾔδειν σε ἐν τῷ πρὸ τούτου χρόνῳ
οὐδενὸς δεύτερον, ᾔδειν τὰς ἀρετὰς ἐν κυνηγεσίοις, ἐν
παλαίστραις· ταύτην ἐπίδειξαί μοι τὴν ῥώμην καὶ τὴν
ἀλκὴν ἐπὶ τοῦ παρόντος, μηδένα τῶν παρόντων ὡς
ὀνειδίζειν μέλλοντα φυλασσόμενος· γάμου γὰρ παῖδες ἅπαντες, καὶ οἱ μὲν ἐτελέσθησαν, οἱ δὲ μέλλου-
σιν, οἱ δὲ εὔχονται. 22. εἶτα παρακαλέσεις καὶ τοὺς
ἀκροατὰς συμπροτρέψασθαι καὶ ἑκόντα καὶ ἄκοντα
παραπέμπειν ἐπὶ τὸν θάλαμον. μετὰ ταῦτα ἥξεις ἐπὶ
τὸν καιρὸν καὶ τὴν ἑσπέραν, ἐν ᾧ διασκευάσεις καὶ
διαγράψεις τὰ κάλλη τῆς νυκτός, τοὺς ἀστέρας, τὰ
φέγγη τούτων, τὸν Ὠρίωνα, καὶ προσθήσεις ὅτι,
ὥσπερ ἑκάστη τελετὴ καιρὸν οἰκεῖον καὶ ἐπιτήδειον

priate and likely to be successful, it would do well to open with a brief introduction, based either on the attendees ("They should not delay the groom any longer"), or on the groom ("He should not be holding back from his encounter"), or on the speaker himself ("I have come into your midst bearing advice for the groom, out of concern for him and eager to make him shine in your eyes"). 20. This introduction should not be elaborate,[9] but plain and simple. Sometimes the topic should be based on the event itself. "What is the purpose of this gathering of ours? Obviously the marriage of the groom and his initiation into love. Why then isn't this deed already being performed? The very reason for our gathering is to share in the joy of these proceedings."

21. After the introduction comes the exhortation to the groom. "Until now, I knew you to be second to none; I knew your abilities in hunting and in wrestling. Show me that power and valor on the present occasion. Do not be afraid that anyone here will criticize you, for we all are children of marriage: some have been initiated, some are soon to be, others are praying to be." 22. You should then encourage the audience to join in your exhortation and escort him—willing or not—to the bedroom. After that, turn to the season of the year and the evening hour. Here you can provide a detailed description of the beauties of the night—the stars, their luster, Orion—and add, "Just as every ritual has its fitting and proper time, so marriage has

[9] "Elaborate," here and in §26, refers to the use of arguments and style typical of more formal speech. Cf. 2.5.4.

ἔχει, οὕτω καὶ ὁ γάμος γέρας εἴληφε τὴν νύκτα παρὰ
τῶν θεῶν. Πύθια μὲν γὰρ καὶ Ὀλύμπια καθ' ἡμέραν
τελεῖται, ‹τὰ›[6] Βάκχου δὲ καὶ Ἀφροδίτης νυκτός·
Ἔρωτι γὰρ καὶ Γάμῳ καὶ Ὑμεναίῳ καθιέρωται νύξ.

23. Εἶτα ἀπὸ τοῦ παρελθόντος προτρέψῃ χρόνου
λέγων· ἀναμνήσθητι τῆς μνηστείας, ἐν ὅσῳ χρόνῳ
γέγονεν, ἐν ὅσοις ἔτεσι μόλις ὑμῖν[7] κατωρθώθη, καὶ
ὅτι ἐπένευσαν [ἡμῖν][8] οἱ πατέρες τῆς κόρης ὀψέ ποτε·
εἶτα ταύτην ἔχων παρὰ σαυτῷ ῥᾳθυμεῖς, ὥσπερ ἐπι-
λελησμένος; μετὰ ταῦτα καὶ ἀπὸ τῆς ὥρας τοῦ ἔτους
ἐπιχειρήσεις [ἔαρος, μετοπώρου, χειμῶνος, θέρους][9]
411 ὡς ἤδη προείρηται [ἀπὸ τῶν περὶ ἕκαστον καιρὸν
ἐξαιρέτων, ὡς ὑποδέδεικται ἤδη].[10]

24. Καιρὸν ἔχεις μετὰ ταῦτα[11] καὶ ἱστοριῶν μεμνῆσθαι, ἐν αἷς ἕτεροι φαίνονται συναφθέντες γάμοις
θεοὶ καὶ ἡμίθεοι καὶ στρατηγῶν οἱ ἄριστοι καὶ ἀρι-
στέων οἱ ἐπιφανέστατοι. ἐπὶ τούτοις μνημονεύσεις
καὶ τοῦ κάλλους τῆς κόρης καὶ τοῦ κάλλους τοῦ θαλάμου καὶ τῶν παστάδων. καὶ τῶν θεῶν δ' οὐκ ἀμελήσεις τῶν περὶ τὸν θάλαμον ὡς συνεργούντων καὶ
συλλαμβανομένων τῷ μέλλοντι νυμφεύειν· καὶ καθ'
ἡδονὴν δὲ θεοῖς ὁ γάμος. ἐν ᾧ καὶ θέσιν βραχεῖαν
ἐρεῖς, ὅτι βουληθέντες αὐξάνεσθαι τῶν ἀνθρώπων τὸ
γένος γάμον ἐπενόησαν καὶ μίξεις σώφρονας, καὶ
εἰκὸς παρεῖναι τοὺς αὐτὰ νομοθετήσαντας, Ἀφροδίτην, ἔρωτας, ὑμεναίους, γάμους.

25. Εἶτα ἀπὸ τῆς ἐκβάσεως ἐπιχειρήσεις· τί οὖν τὸ
ἀπὸ τοῦ γάμου κέρδος; ὁμόνοια οἴκου καὶ περιουσίας

nighttime as its privilege from the gods. The Pythian and Olympic festivals are celebrated during the day, but those of Bacchus and Aphrodite are at night, because the night is sacred to Eros, Gamos, and Hymenaeus."

23. Next you should exhort him by bringing up the past. "Remember how long your courtship took, how many years before you two barely managed to have your way." Then add, "The bride's parents finally gave their consent—and now, having her for yourself, you hold back, as if you have forgotten?" After that take up the season of the year, as was already indicated.[10]

24. After this you have an opportunity to recall stories, in which others can be seen to have joined in marriage—gods, demigods, the greatest generals, and the most illustrious champions. Next you should mention the beauty of the bride and the beauty of the wedding chamber and bridal bedroom. Do not fail to mention the gods who are about the chamber aiding and supporting the future husband and what pleasure the gods take in marriage. Here you may state a brief general thesis. "Because the gods wished to increase the human race, they devised marriage and chaste sexual unions. Thus it is natural that they who instituted these laws be present: Aphrodite, Eros, Hymenaeus, and Gamos."

25. Your next argument should be based on the outcome. "What then is the advantage of marriage? It is do-

---

10 Cf. §§12–14.

---

6 suppl. RW   7 ὑμῖν RW: ἡμῖν codd.   8 secl. RW
9 secl. Nitsche, RW   10 secl. Nitsche, RW
11 καιρὸν ἔχεις μετὰ ταῦτα p: ἤδη καιρὸν ἔχοις μετὰ ταῦτα P: εἰ δὲ καιρὸν ἔχοις coni. Bursian

σωτηρία καὶ αὔξησις, καὶ τὸ μέγιστον παίδων γένεσις διαδόχων τοῦ γένους, φιλοτιμησομένων πατρίδι,[12]
διαθησόντων ἀγῶνας. εἶτα εὐχὴν ἐπιθήσεις τοῖς εἰρημένοις, αὐτὸς αἰτῶν αὐτοῖς παρὰ τῶν κρειττόνων
συζυγίαν ἡδίστην, εὐδαιμονίαν, βίον ἐπέραστον, παίδων γενέσεις καὶ ὅσα προείρηται.

26. Πειράσεις δὲ καὶ συντόμως ἅπαντα προαγαγεῖν
ταῦτα πανταχοῦ τῆς χάριτος μόνον καὶ τῆς ὥρας
φροντίζων. παραγίνεται δὲ χάρις καὶ ὥρα τῷ λόγῳ
οὐκ ἐκ τῶν ἱστοριῶν μόνον καὶ ἐκ τοῦ διηγήματος,
ἀλλ᾽ ἐκ τῆς ἀφελείας καὶ ἁπλότητος τοῦ ἤθους τοῦ
λέγοντος. ἀκατάσκευον γὰρ τὸν λόγον εἶναι δεῖ καὶ
τὰ πολλὰ ἀσύνδετον, οὐ κώλοις οὐδὲ περιόδοις συγ-
κείμενον, ἀλλὰ συγγραφικώτερον, οἷόν ἐστι καὶ τὸ
τῆς λαλιᾶς εἶδος. 27. γένοιτο δ᾽ ἂν καὶ ἀπὸ λέξεως
ἐπιτετηδευμένης καὶ κεκαλλωπισμένης χάρις ἐν λόγῳ,
οἵα ἐστὶν ἡ Πλάτωνος καὶ Ξενοφῶντος καὶ τῶν νεωτέρων, Δίωνος καὶ Φιλοστράτου καὶ τῶν σοφιστῶν
ὅσοι καὶ συντιθέναι τὸ συγγραφικὸν εἶδος ἔδοξαν
χαριέντως.

---

[12] Finckh, RW: πατρίδα mW: πατράσι p

mestic concord, the preservation and increase of wealth, and, greatest of all, the birth of children to be heirs of the family, to be benefactors of their hometown, and to sponsor athletic festivals." After these remarks you should add a prayer of your own, asking the gods to give them the sweetest lovemaking, happiness, a life full of love, the birth of children, and all the blessings mentioned above.

26. Try to present all these things briefly, everywhere mindful only of grace and beauty. A speech acquires grace and beauty not only from stories and the way they are told, but also from the plainness and simplicity of the speaker's character. For the speech must lack elaboration, and on the whole be loosely connected, not composed of clauses and periods, but proceeding more casually, as in the genre of the talk (*lalia*). (27) A speech may also derive charm from carefully wrought and ornate language, like that of Plato and Xenophon, including the moderns, Dio Chrysostom and Philostratus, and those sophists recognized for composing the casual type with charm.

2.7. ΠΕΡΙ ΓΕΝΕΘΛΙΑΚΟΥ

1. Ὁ γενεθλιακὸς λόγος διαιρεῖται οὕτως. πρῶτον μὲν ἐρεῖς προοίμια, μετὰ τὰ προοίμια τὴν ἡμέραν ἐπαινέ-σεις καθ' ἣν ἐτέχθη ὁ ἐπαινούμενος, καὶ εἰ μὲν ἐν ἱερομηνίᾳ ἢ ἄλλῃ τινὶ πανηγύρει, ἐρεῖς ἐγκώμιον ἀπὸ τῶν τῆς ἡμέρας, ὅτι ἐν ἱερομηνίᾳ ἐτέχθη, ὅτι ἐν πανη-γύρει· εἰ δὲ μηδὲν ἔχοις εἰπεῖν τοιοῦτον, ἐπαινέσεις τὴν ἡμέραν ἀπὸ ⟨τοῦ⟩¹ καιροῦ, ὅτι θέρους ὄντος ἐτέ-χθη, ὅτι ἔαρος ἢ χειμῶνος ἢ μετοπώρου, εἰ οὕτω τύ-χοι, καὶ ἐρεῖς τοῦ καιροῦ τὰ ἐξαίρετα.

2. Μετὰ τὸν τῆς ἡμέρας ἔπαινον ἐπὶ τὸ ἐγκώμιον ἥξεις αὐτοῦ τοῦ γένους, εἶτα τῆς γενέσεως, εἶτα τῆς ἀνατροφῆς, εἶτα τῶν ἐπιτηδευμάτων, εἶτα τῶν πρά-ξεων. ἐρεῖς δὲ καθ' ἕκαστον τῶν κεφαλαίων, ὡς ἤδη φθάσαντες πολλάκις εἰρήκαμεν, σύγκρισιν, εἶτα μετὰ τὸ καθ' ἕκαστον τῶν κεφαλαίων ἰδίαν σύγκρισιν ἐρ-γάσασθαι ἐρεῖς τελευταῖον σύγκρισιν πρὸς ὅλην τὴν ὑπόθεσιν.

3. Μετὰ ταῦτα πάλιν ἐπαίνει τὴν ἡμέραν οὕτως· ὦ πανευδαίμονος ἡμέρας ἐκείνης καθ' ἣν ἐτίκτετο, ὦ μη-τρὸς ὠδῖνες εὐτυχῶς ἐπὶ τοῦτο λυθεῖσαι. πρότερον ταῦτα καὶ τὰ τοιαῦτα ἐρεῖς. ἐὰν δὲ κομιδῇ τινος νέου

---

¹ suppl. Bursian, RW

2.7. THE BIRTHDAY SPEECH

1. The birthday speech (*genethliakos logos*) is analyzed as follows.[1] After first delivering introductory material, you should praise the day on which the honorand was born. If he was born during a sacred month or during some other festival, you should derive your praise from the circumstances of that day, namely that he was born during a sacred month or during a festival. If you have nothing of this sort to say, you should praise the day on the basis of the season, namely that he was born in summer, spring, winter, or fall, as the case may be. You may then mention the special attractions of the season.

2. After praising the day, you will come to the praise of his family, followed by his birth, upbringing, activities, and deeds. In each of these sections, as I have said many times,[2] you should make comparisons. Then, after making specific comparisons in each section, you should pronounce a comprehensive comparison of the whole subject.

3. After this, praise the day again in this fashion: "O blessed day on which he was born! How fortunate his mother's labor pains that resulted in his birth." You should say such things beforehand.[3] If you are going to deliver a

[1] [DH] 3 provides different and more detailed instructions for a birthday speech.   [2] Cf. 2.1.18, 36; 2.2.32; and again at 2.9.11.

[3] Presumably before the rest of the speech. RW obelize πρότερον and suggest that the whole sentence be deleted, perhaps rightly.

γενεθλιακὸν μέλλῃς λέγειν, ἐρεῖς ὅτι τοῦτο αὐτὸ τοῦ
νέου τὸ μέγιστον, ὅτι τοὺς λόγους ἐφ' ἑαυτὸν ἤδη
κεκίνηκεν, εἶτα μετὰ τὰ προοίμια τὴν ἡμέραν ἐγκωμιάσεις, καθ' ἣν ἐτέχθη, τῇ μεταχειρίσει τῇ προειρη-
μένῃ χρώμενος.

4. Μετὰ ταῦτα τὸ γένος ἐρεῖς, εἶτα τὴν γένεσιν, εἶτα
τὴν φύσιν· ἐπεὶ δὲ οὐδὲν ἔχεις ἕτερον παρὰ ταῦτα
εἰπεῖν τοῦ νέου (νέος γὰρ ὢν οὐδέπω πράξεις ἐπεδεί-
ξατο), ἐρεῖς ἐκ μεθόδου ἐγκωμιάζων οὕτω· τοῦτο δὴ
413 τεκμαιρόμενος περὶ τῶν μελλόντων μαντεύομαι, ὅτι
παιδείας εἰς ἄκρον ἥξει καὶ ἀρετῆς, ὅτι φιλοτιμήσεται
πόλεσιν, ἀγῶνας διαθήσει, κοσμήσει πανηγύρεις, καὶ
τὰ τοιαῦτα.

birthday speech for a very young child, you should say, "The most important thing about this child is that he has already inspired speeches about himself." After this introduction, you should praise the day on which he was born, employing the treatment specified above.

4. Next, you should talk about his family, followed by his birth and nature. Since you have nothing more than this to say of a young child—because, being young, he has as yet no deeds to show—you should praise him by using the following technique.[4] "Weighing his future on the basis of this, I predict that he will attain the heights of education and virtue, he will lavish benefits on cities, he will arrange games, he will sponsor festivals," and so on.

[4] That is, that of predicting the future; cf. 2.2.8 and 10.

2.8. ΠΕΡΙ ΠΑΡΑΜΥΘΗΤΙΚΟΥ

1. Παραμυθητικὸν δὲ ὁ λέγων ὀδύρεται μὲν καὶ αὐτὸς
τὸν πεπτωκότα καὶ ἐπὶ μέγεθος ἐγείρει τὴν συμφοράν, αὔξων ὡς οἷόν τέ ἐστι τῷ λόγῳ τὸ πάθος ἐκ τῶν
ἀφορμῶν ὧν εἴπομεν περὶ μονῳδίας· χρὴ δὲ εἰδέναι
ὅτι συνίσταται ἡ μονῳδία ἐκ τῶν ἐγκωμιαστικῶν [γέ-
νους, φύσεως, ἀνατροφῆς, παιδείας, ἐπιτηδευμάτων,
πράξεων].[1] οὐ μὴν φυλάξει τὴν ἀκολουθίαν τῶν ἐγκωμίων διὰ τὸ μηδ' ἑαυτοῦ δοκεῖν εἶναι τὸν λέγοντα,
ἀλλ' ἐξεστηκέναι ὑπὸ τοῦ πάθους.

2. Τὰ δὲ ἐγκώμια διαιρήσεις κατὰ τοὺς τρεῖς χρόνους, ὡς προείρηται· ὁ μέντοι γε παραμυθούμενος
ἐπιχειρήσας ἐκ τούτων[2] ἐν τῷ πρώτῳ μέρει τοῦ λόγου,
οἷον ὅτι νέος ὢν (ἂν οὕτω τύχῃ) παρ' ἡλικίαν πέπτωκεν, οὐχ ὡς ἂν εὔξαιτό τις, καὶ γένος ἐστέρησεν τῆς

---

[1] secl. RW   [2] ἐκ τούτων codd.: ἐκ τῶν αὐτῶν coni. RW

---

[1] In an alternate ordering, the monody evidently preceded
this speech. In the present (traditional) order, it is located at 2.15.

[2] RW bracket the list as a gloss; Bursian brackets the entire
sentence.

[3] That is, past, present, and future as outlined in the treatment
of the monody at 2.15.5–8. RW provide a helpful account of the
apparent train of thought: "(a) the *paramuthētikos* uses the mate-

2.8. THE CONSOLATION SPEECH

1. The speaker of a consolation speech (*paramythētikos logos*) personally laments the fallen one and builds up the magnitude of the calamity by amplifying the suffering as much as he can in his speech, using the starting points we mentioned concerning the monody.[1] One should note that the monody is constructed of the encomiastic topics [of birth, nature, upbringing, education, activities, and deeds].[2] All the same, it will not preserve the regular order of encomia, because the speaker should not give the impression that he has self-control, but rather that he is overcome with emotion.

2. You should divide the encomia into three time periods, as was mentioned.[3] The one offering consolation, however, should argue on the basis of these topics[4] in the first part of the speech. For example, one might say (if such was the case), "He was young and fell before his time, a thing no one would pray for, and has robbed his family,

rial of monody; (b) monody is made up of encomiastic elements; (c) but it will not keep the usual order of encomia because of the intense emotion, but use instead the 'past, present, future' scheme."

[4] That is, topics of the monody. RW suggest the conjecture ἐκ τῶν αὐτῶν, "the same topics" as in the monody. Whereas the monody begins with praise and concludes with lament, the consolatory speech begins with lament and concludes with hope.

ἐλπίδος καὶ γονέας καὶ πατρίδα· οὐ γὰρ ἦν ὁ τυχών,
ἀλλὰ τοῖος καὶ τοῖος· διὸ οὐδὲ μέμφομαι ποθοῦντας
καὶ ζητοῦντας τοιοῦτον.

3. Καὶ τὸν ἐπ᾽ αὐτῷ θρῆνον αὐξήσας, ὡς ἐνδέχεται,
ἐπὶ δεύτερον ἥξεις[3] μέρος τοῦ λόγου τὸ παραμυθητι-
κόν, ἄρξεται δὲ οὕτω πως· θαυμάζω δὲ εἰ μὴ ἐπελή-
λυθεν ὑμῖν, ὦ παρόντες γονεῖς, ἐννοεῖν, ἅ φησιν ἄριστος ποιητὴς Εὐριπίδης, ἄξιος ὡς ἀληθῶς Μουσῶν
νομίζεσθαι τρόφιμος· χρὴ γὰρ

τὸν [μὲν][4] φύντα θρηνεῖν εἰς ὅσ᾽ ἔρχεται κακά·
τὸν δ᾽ αὖ θανόντα καὶ πόνων πεπαυμένον
χαίροντας, εὐφημοῦντας ἐκπέμπειν δόμων.

4. οὐ θήσεις δὲ ἐξ ἅπαντος τὰ ἰαμβεῖα διὰ τὸ εἶναι
αὐτὰ συνήθη τοῖς πολλοῖς καὶ γνώριμα, ἀλλὰ παρῳ-
δήσεις μᾶλλον· καὶ ὅσα Ἡροδότῳ περὶ Κλεόβιδος
καὶ Βίτωνος εἴρηται. καὶ φιλοσοφῆσαι δὲ ἐπὶ τούτοις
οὐκ ἀπειρόκαλον καθόλου περὶ φύσεως ἀνθρωπίνης,
ὅτι τὸ θεῖον κατέκρινε τῶν ἀνθρώπων τὸν θάνατον,
καὶ ὅτι πέρας ἐστὶν ἅπασιν ἀνθρώποις τοῦ βίου ὁ
θάνατος, καὶ ὅτι ἥρωες καὶ θεῶν παῖδες οὐ διέφυγον.
5. ἐν ᾧ καὶ καιρὸν ἔχεις θεῖναι καὶ διηγήματα, καὶ ὅτι
πόλεις ἀπόλλυνται, καὶ ἔθνη ἐστὶν ἃ παντάπασιν ἐξ-

---

3 ἥξεις codd.: ἥξει coni. Bursian, RW
4 secl. Walz, Bursian

5 Eur., Fr. 449 N².

his parents, and his hometown of their hopes, for he was not just anybody, but 'so-and-so.' Therefore I do not blame them for missing and yearning for such a person."

3. Once you have amplified the lament (*thrēnos*) over him as much as possible, you will come to the second portion of the speech, the consolatory part. It should begin along these lines. "I am surprised that it has not occurred to you parents here present to have in mind the words of that excellent poet Euripides, worthy to be considered a true disciple of the Muses: 'We should

> lament the baby born for all the ills that he goes forth
> to meet,
> but when a man has died and ceased from toils,
> we should with joyful praise escort him from his
> home.'"[5]

4. You should not, however, quote all the verses of the passage, because they are familiar and most people know them well. Instead, adapt them,[6] as well as what Herodotus says of Cleobis and Biton.[7] It is not in bad taste here to philosophize on the nature of man in general, telling how the gods condemned men to death, how the end of life for all men is death,[8] and how the heroes and sons of gods did not escape it. 5. Here you have an opportunity to include narratives, telling how cities have perished and

---

[6] RW ad loc. point out that such citations preserve "a part of the passage in the original form, but the rest in a prose version adapted to the syntax of the context."   [7] Hdt. 1.31. These Argive brothers died peacefully after performing a noble deed.

[8] This clause is a close adaptation of Dem. 18.97: πέρας μὲν γὰρ ἅπασιν ἀνθρώποις ἐστὶ τοῦ βίου θάνατος.

ἔλιπεν, καὶ ὅτι βελτίων ἐστὶ τάχα ἡ μετάστασις
τοῦ τῆδε βίου, ἀπαλλάττουσα πραγμάτων [ἀδίκων],[5]
πλεονεξίας, ἀδίκου τύχης· οἷον γὰρ τὸ πλεῖον τὸ πράγμασιν ἀνθρωπίνοις συμπλέκεσθαι, νόσοις, φρον-
τίσι.

6. Ἐρεῖς δὲ μετὰ ταῦτα ὅτι εἰ μὲν κέρδος τὸ βιοῦν,
ἱκανῶς ἀπολέλαυκε, καὶ λέξεις ἃ σύνοιδας περὶ αὐτοῦ·
ὤφθη μὲν ἐν λόγοις (εἰ οὕτω τύχοι), ἐν πολιτείαις· εἰ
δὲ ἀτύχημα, τύχης τὸ πίπτειν ἐνθάδε, ἐξέφυγεν ἀνι-
αρὰ τοῦ βίου· εἶτα ὅτι πείθομαι τὸν μεταστάντα τὸ
Ἠλύσιον πεδίον οἰκεῖν, ὅπου Ῥαδάμανθυς, ὅπου
Μενέλεως, ὅπου παῖς ὁ Πηλέως καὶ Θέτιδος, ὅπου
Μέμνων· καὶ τάχα που μᾶλλον μετὰ τῶν θεῶν διαι-
τᾶται νῦν, περιπολεῖ τὸν αἰθέρα καὶ ἐπισκοπεῖ τὰ
τῆδε· 7. καὶ τάχα που καὶ μέμφεται τοῖς θρηνοῦσι·
συγγενὴς γὰρ οὖσα τοῦ θείου ἡ ψυχὴ κἀκεῖθεν κατ-
ιοῦσα σπεύδει πάλιν ἄνω πρὸς τὸ συγγενές· οὕτω καὶ
τὴν Ἑλένην, οὕτω καὶ τοὺς Διοσκούρους καὶ τὸν
Ἡρακλέα λέγουσιν συμπολιτεύεσθαι μετὰ τῶν θεῶν·
ὑμνῶμεν οὖν αὐτὸν ὡς ἥρωα, μᾶλλον δὲ ὡς θεὸν
αὐτὸν μακαρίσωμεν, εἰκόνας γράψωμεν, ἱλασκώμεθα
ὡς δαίμονα.

8. Ἔστω δὲ σύμμετρον καὶ τούτου τοῦ λόγου τὸ
μῆκος. γνωστέον δὲ ὅτι καὶ συντόνῳ λόγῳ παραμυθεῖσθαι δυνατὸν καὶ συγγραφικῷ πάλιν, ὡς ἄν τις
βούληται.

5 secl. RW

266

nations have completely vanished, and how the transition from this life is perhaps for the best, in that it frees us from troubles, greed, and unjust fortune, because for the most part it is a terrible thing to be enmeshed in human cares, illnesses, and worries.

6. After this you should say that if life is a blessing, he has enjoyed it sufficiently, and add what you know about him, that he was in the public eye for his oratory (if such was the case) and for his public service. If, on the other hand, life is a misfortune and it is fortunate to perish here and now, say that he has escaped the pains of life. Then, "I am confident that our departed one dwells in the Elysian Fields, where reside Rhadamanthys, Menelaus, the son of Peleus and Thetis,[9] and Memnon.[10] Or perhaps it may be that now he spends his time with the gods, traveling through the ether and observing things here on earth. 7. And it may even be that he finds fault with those who mourn him, for the soul, being akin to the divine and having descended from on high, hastens to go back up to its kin. Thus they say that Helen, the Dioscuri, and Heracles live in company with the gods. Let us therefore hymn him as a hero, or rather bless him as a god; let us paint images of him and propitiate him as a divine being."

8. The length of this speech should be moderate. Also note that it is possible to offer consolation in a formal speech or in a casual one,[11] as one prefers.

[9] Achilles.

[10] The Ethiopian son of Dawn granted immortality by Zeus.

[11] For the characteristics of formal (*syntonos*) and casual (*syngraphikos*) styles, see 2.5.2–4.

2.9. ΠΕΡΙ ΠΡΟΣΦΩΝΗΤΙΚΟΥ

1. Ὁ προσφωνητικὸς λόγος ἐστὶν εὔφημος εἰς ἄρχοντας λεγόμενος ὑπό τινος, τῇ δὲ ἐργασίᾳ ἐγκώμιον, οὐ
μὴν τέλειον· οὐ γὰρ ἔχει πάντα τὰ τοῦ ἐγκωμίου,
ἀλλὰ κυρίως ὁ προσφωνητικὸς γίνεται, ὅταν ἐξ αὐτῶν
τῶν πραττομένων ὑπ᾽ αὐτοῦ πράξεων ὁ λόγος τὴν αὔξησιν λαμβάνῃ.

2. Διαιρεῖται δὲ οὕτως. μετὰ τὰ προοίμια ἥξεις ἐπὶ
τὸν τῶν βασιλέων ἔπαινον, καὶ τοῦτον ἐρεῖς διὰ πάνυ
βραχέων διαιρῶν αὐτὸν δίχα εἰς τὰ κατὰ πόλεμόν τε
καὶ εἰρήνην, οὐκ ἐνδιατρίψεις δὲ διότι οὐ τέλειόν ἐστι
βασιλέων ἐγκώμιον· αὐξήσεως γὰρ ἕνεκα παραλαμ-
βάνεται ἐν τῷ προσφωνητικῷ τῶν ἐπαίνων τοῦ ἄρχοντος.

3. Ἀπὸ δὲ τοῦ λόγου τοῦ κατὰ τοὺς βασιλέας ἥξεις
ἀκολούθως ἐπὶ τοῦ προσφωνουμένου ἔπαινον, λέγων
ὅτι τά τε ἄλλα θαυμάσιοι οἱ βασιλεῖς καὶ ἐν ταῖς τῶν
ἀρχόντων αἱρέσεσιν· οἷον γὰρ ἡμῖν νῦν τοῦτον τὸν
γεννάδαν κατέπεμψαν ἐπὶ σωτηρίᾳ τοῦ γένους. καὶ[1]
εὐθέως ἐπαινέσεις μάλιστα μέν, ὡς ἔφην, ἀπὸ τῶν
πράξεων, οὕτω γὰρ ἄμεινον. 4. εἰ δ᾽ ἄρα φιλότιμον καὶ
σφόδρα ἔνδοξον εἴη τὸ γένος, μνημονεύσεις διὰ βραχέων καὶ γένους, εἶθ᾽ οὕτω τῶν πράξεων, καὶ μάλιστα

[1] RW: ὃν codd.

2.9. THE ADDRESS

1. The address (*prosphōnētikos logos*) is a laudatory speech delivered by an individual to governors.[1] In practice, it is an encomium, but not a full-scale one, since it does not include all the elements of an encomium. It becomes an address in the strict sense, when it derives its amplification from the actual deeds performed by the governor.

2. It is divided in the following way. After the introduction, you should move on to praise the emperors. You should treat this very briefly, dividing it according to matters of war and peace. You must not dwell on it, because it is not a full-scale encomium of emperors, but is included in the address in order to augment the governor's praise.

3. After this portion on the emperors, praise of the addressee naturally follows. "The emperors are admirable in many other respects, but especially for their selection of governors.[2] How noble indeed is this one they have now sent us for the salvation of our people!" Immediately following this, you should praise him chiefly, as I said, for his deeds, for that is the best course. 4. If, however, his family happens to be public-spirited and very famous, you may briefly mention this before turning to his deeds, especially

[1] Cf. the instructions of [DH] 5 for an "address" to governors, which places greater emphasis on the situation of the speaker.

[2] For the same topic, cf. [DH] 5.2.

μὲν ἀπὸ τοῦ παρόντος χρόνου καὶ τῆς παρούσης ἀρχῆς τῶν ἐν χερσί· μνημονεύσεις δὲ καί, ἂν τύχῃ ἄρ-
ξας ἑτέραν ἀρχὴν καὶ ἐνδόξους ἔχῃ τὰς πράξεις, τῶν
τότε πράξεων.

5. Ὑπομεριεῖς δὲ τὸν ἐπὶ ταῖς πράξεσιν ἔπαινον εἰς
τέσσαρας ἀρετάς, φρόνησιν, δικαιοσύνην, σωφροσύνην, ἀνδρείαν· καὶ ἐν μὲν τῇ φρονήσει τὴν ἐμπειρίαν
τῶν νόμων, τὴν παίδευσιν ἐπαινέσεις, τὸ προορᾶσθαι
τὰ μέλλοντα, τὸ περὶ τῶν παρόντων ἀκριβῶς βουλεύ-
εσθαι δύνασθαι, τὸ βασιλεῦσιν ἀντιγράφειν περὶ ὧν
ἂν ἐπιστέλλωσιν οὕτως ὥστε ἐκείνους ἐπαινεῖν καὶ
θαυμάζειν, τὸ διελέγχειν τοὺς ῥήτορας, τὸ γινώσκειν
ἐκ προοιμίων τὴν ὅλην διάνοιαν τῆς ὑποθέσεως. ἐν ᾧ
416 καὶ καιρὸν ἕξεις Δημοσθένους μνήμην καὶ Νέστορος
καὶ νομοθετῶν ἀρίστων ποιεῖσθαι· τεχνικὸν γὰρ καθ᾽
ἕκαστον μέρος ἀρετῆς καὶ συγκρίσεις οἰκείας παραλαμβάνειν, ἵνα ὁ λόγος δι᾽ αὐτῶν πλείους τὰς αὐξήσεις λαμβάνῃ.

6. Ἐν δὲ τῇ δικαιοσύνῃ πάλιν ἐρεῖς τὴν πρὸς τοὺς
ὑπηκόους φιλανθρωπίαν, τὸ ἥμερον τοῦ τρόπου, τὸ
ὁμιλητικὸν πρὸς τοὺς προσιόντας, τὸ καθαρὸν ἐν ταῖς
δίκαις καὶ ἀδωροδόκητον, τὸ μὴ πρὸς χάριν μηδὲ
πρὸς ἀπέχθειαν κρίνειν τὰς δίκας, τὸ μὴ προτιμᾶν
τοὺς εὐπόρους τῶν ἀδυνάτων, τὸ πόλεις ἐγείρειν· ἐν ᾧ
μέρει καὶ Ἀριστείδης ἔστω καὶ Φωκίων καὶ εἴ τις Ῥωμαίων ἐξ ἱστορίας λαμπρὸς ἐκ δικαιοσύνης.

those undertaken at the present time and during his current period in office. But if he has held another office previously and has notable deeds to his credit, you should refer to these as well.

5. You should subdivide the praise of his deeds according to the four virtues: intelligence, justice, moderation, and courage. As to intelligence, praise his experience in the law and his education, as well as his ability to anticipate the future, to provide meticulous advice about current issues, to compose responses to emperors concerning their edicts so as to win their praise and admiration, to dispute with orators, and to grasp the entire point of a subject from its mere introduction. Here you will have an opportunity to call to mind Demosthenes, Nestor, and the greatest lawmakers, for it is correct procedure to make relevant comparisons in each of the portions on virtue. That way, the speech acquires more means of amplification.

6. As to justice, speak of his humanity toward his subjects, his gentle manner, his affability[3] toward people who approach him, his integrity and incorruptibility in law cases, his adjudications without favoritism or enmity, his refusal to favor the wealthy over the powerless, and his support for cities. In this portion belong Aristides, Phocion, and any Roman famous in history for justice.[4]

---

[3] Affability of governors is especially stressed in the "address" of [DH] at 5.1, where Isocrates' advice to Demonicus is quoted.

[4] The same two Greek exemplars of justice are cited in 2.2.10. Possible Roman examples are the two Catos, for, as RW point out, Plutarch pairs them with Aristides and Phocion in his *Parallel Lives*.

7. Οὐχ ἁπλῶς δὲ ἐρεῖς τὰς ἀρετάς, ὅτι δίκαιος, ἀλλὰ καὶ ἐκ τοῦ ἐναντίου ἐπιχειρήσεις πάλιν, ὅτι οὐκ ἄδικος, οὐκ ὀργίλος, οὐ δυσπρόσοδος, οὐ χάριτι κρίνων, οὐ δωροδέκτης· πέφυκε γὰρ ὁ λόγος αὔξησιν λαμβάνειν ὅταν καὶ τὰς κακίας ἐξαιρῇς καὶ τὰς ἀρετὰς αὔξειν ἐθέλῃς.

8. Μετὰ ταύτην ἥξεις ἐπὶ τὴν σωφροσύνην, ἐν δὲ ταύτῃ πάλιν ἐρεῖς τὴν περὶ τὰς ἡδονάς, τὴν περὶ γέλωτα ἐγκράτειαν. ἐνταῦθα Διομήδης ἔχει καιρὸν πρὸς τὴν σύγκρισιν ὁ τιτρώσκων τὴν Ἀφροδίτην διὰ σωφροσύνην· μόνος γὰρ ἀνάλωτος τῶν Ἀφροδίτης παθῶν. καὶ Ἱππόλυτος δ' ἔστω· καὶ γὰρ καὶ οὗτος σώφρων ὑπείληπται.

9. Τὴν δὲ ἀνδρείαν θαυμάσεις ἀπὸ τῆς πρὸς τοὺς βασιλέας παρρησίας, ἀπὸ τῆς ὑπὲρ τῶν ὑπηκόων πρὸς τὰ λυποῦντα μάχης, ἀπὸ τοῦ μὴ ὀκλάζειν μηδὲ ἐνδιδόναι πρὸς φόβους, ἐν ᾧ καὶ οἱ Αἴαντες καὶ Περικλῆς καὶ Ἀλκιβιάδης καὶ εἴ τις τοιοῦτος.

10. Οὐκ ἐνδιατρίψεις δὲ τούτοις οὐδὲ ἐπεξελεύσῃ ἀκριβῶς ἅπασι (τοῦτο γὰρ ἐγκωμίου τελείου), ἀλλὰ γέγραπται μὲν ἐνθάδε ὑφ' ἡμῶν καὶ εἴρηται, ἵνα μηδὲν παραλιπεῖν δοκῶμεν ἀλλ' ἔχῃς εὐπορίαν πανταχόθεν· χρήσῃ δὲ τοῖς κατεπείγουσιν· ἔστι γὰρ ὁ προσφωνητικὸς ἐγκωμίου εἰκών, ἀκροθιγῶς τῶν ἐγκωμιαστικῶν τόπων ἐφαπτόμενος, οὐκ ἐνδιατρίβων δ' ὡς <ἐν>² ἐγκωμίῳ τελείῳ, εἰ μή τις ἐθέλοι διὰ φιλοτι-

417

² suppl. RW

272

7. Do not simply name virtues and say, for example, "He is just," but also argue from the opposite point of view: "He is not unjust, nor irascible, nor unapproachable; he does not judge with favoritism; he does not take bribes." A speech naturally acquires amplification when you both negate bad traits and choose to amplify the virtuous ones.

8. After justice comes moderation. In this case you should speak of his moderation with regard to pleasures and excessive laughter.[5] Here Diomedes provides an opportunity for comparison. It was thanks to his self-control that he wounded Aphrodite, for he alone was unaffected by her passions.[6] Hippolytus belongs here as well, for he too is considered chaste.

9. You should commend his courage on the basis of his frankness with the emperors,[7] his fight on behalf of his subjects against any harm, and his refusal to cower or give in to fear. Here belong the two Ajaxes, Pericles, Alcibiades, and their like.

10. You should not dwell on these matters nor treat them all in great detail, for that belongs to a full-scale encomium. All the same, I have written them down here and discussed them, so that you may have abundant material from every source and I may not be thought to have omitted anything. You should, however, use only essential topics, for the address is the semblance of an encomium that touches lightly on encomiastic topics. It does not dwell on them as in a full-scale encomium—unless some-

---

[5] Arist. *Eth. Nic.* 4.8.10.28a33 defines the buffoon as one who cannot resist making a tasteless joke.   [6] Cf. Hom. *Il.* 5.330–51.

[7] For the association of frankness ($\pi\alpha\rho\rho\eta\sigma\acute{\iota}\alpha$) toward the emperor with courage, cf. 2.2.31.

μίαν ὥσπερ τελείαν ὑπόθεσιν τὸν προσφωνητικὸν ἀπεργάζεσθαι.

11. Ἥξεις μετὰ τὰς ἀρετὰς ἐπὶ σύγκρισιν· ἄλλο γάρ ἐστι τὸ συγκρίνειν ἀθρόως, καὶ ἄλλο τὸ κατὰ μέρος. κατὰ μέρος μὲν γάρ ἐστι συγκρίνειν, οἷον ὅταν δικαιοσύνην συγκρίνωμεν δικαιοσύνῃ, φρόνησιν φρονήσει, ἀθρόως δέ, ὅταν ἀρχὴν ὅλην πρὸς ὅλην ἀρχήν. ἐρεῖς δ᾽ ὡς Ὅμηρος

πρόσθε μὲν ἐσθλὸς ἔφευγε, δίωκε δέ μιν μέγ᾽
ἀμείνων.

12. οἷον πολλοὶ πολλάκις γεγόνασιν ἄρχοντες καλοὶ κἀγαθοί, οἱ μὲν ἐπὶ τῆς Ἀσίας, οἱ δὲ ἐπὶ τῆς Εὐρώπης, ἐπαινετοὶ μὲν κἀκεῖνοι καὶ οὐδενὸς τῶν εἰς ἀρετὴν ἐνδεεῖς, ἀλλὰ σοῦ βελτίων οὐδείς· ὑπερβέβηκας γὰρ ἀθρόως ἅπαντας. εἶτα ἐπίλογον ἐπὶ τούτοις ἐργάσῃ.

13. Πρὸ δὲ τοῦ ἐπιλόγου ἐὰν τὴν πόλιν, ἐν ᾗ καὶ ὁ λόγος, βουληθῇς ἐπαινέσαι—οὐ γὰρ ἀεὶ τοῦτο ποιήσεις, πλὴν εἰ βούλοιο—ἐρεῖς τι καὶ περὶ αὐτῆς ὧδέ πως, ὅτι λαμπρὰ μὲν ἡ πόλις ἡμῖν ἄνωθεν λιμένων κατασκευαῖς καὶ οἰκοδομημάτων κάλλεσι καὶ ἀέρων εὐκρασίαις καὶ τείχεσι, σὺ δ᾽ αὐτὴν περιβλεπτοτέραν ἀπειργάσω.

14. Οἱ δὲ ἐπίλογοι ἕξουσιν ἄλλα τοιαῦτα· ἀναθῶμεν τοῦτο τὸ ξίφος μὴ Ἄρεϊ μηδὲ Δειμῷ μηδὲ Φόβῳ, τοῖς Ἄρεος παισίν, ἀλλὰ Δίκῃ καὶ Θέμιδι ἀνάθημα καθα-

one aspires to work up an address as a complete subject in itself.

11. After the virtues comes a comparison. One type of comparison is comprehensive, another is partial. The partial comparison occurs, for example, when we compare justice with justice or intelligence with intelligence, but in a comprehensive one we compare an entire régime with another. You may speak as Homer does:

> In front a good man fled, but pursuing him was a
> much better one.[8]

12. For example, "There have often been many good and noble governors, some in Asia, others in Europe, and they are praiseworthy and in no way lacking in virtuous qualities, but none is better than you, for you have surpassed them, one and all." After this you should compose an epilogue.

13. If, however, before the epilogue you wish to praise the city where the speech is being delivered—and you need not always do this, but only if you wish—you may say something about it along these lines. "Our city has been illustrious from its beginning for the construction of its harbors and beauty of its buildings, its temperate climate, and its city walls; but you have made it even more admired."

14. The epilogue should contain other material of the following kind. "Let us dedicate this sword,[9] not to Ares nor to his sons Deimos and Phobos,[10] but to Justice and

[8] *Il.* 22.158.

[9] It is not clear whether this is an actual sword, or what it symbolizes.   [10] Terror and Fear.

275

ρὸν φόνων, καὶ εὐαγεῖς χοροὺς ἱστάτωσαν αἱ πόλεις,
ᾀδέτωσαν, εὐφημείτωσαν, ψηφίσματα γράφωμεν
πρὸς βασιλέας, ἐπαινοῦντες θαυμάζοντες αἰτοῦντες
χρόνους εἰς ἀρχὴν πλείονας, πέμπωμεν εἰκόνας εἰς
Δελφούς, εἰς Ὀλυμπίαν, Ἀθήναζε, πρῶτον πληρώσαν-
τες τὰς πόλεις τὰς ἡμετέρας· 15. γραφέσθω δὲ νῦν
418 περὶ αὐτὸν ἔχων κύκλῳ τὸ γένος τῶν ὑπηκόων, εὐφημοῦντας ἅπαντας, ἐπικροτοῦντας, προηγείσθωσαν
⟨ἐν⟩³ τῷ πίνακι καὶ πόλεις ἐν γυναικῶν σχήματι, φαι-
δραὶ καὶ γεγηθυῖαι. καὶ ὅσα ἐνδέχεται ἀπὸ τῶν πραγμάτων τούτοις προσθήσεις.

3 suppl. Nitsche, RW

276

Themis as a dedication unstained with blood. Let the cities institute sacred choruses, let them sing his praises and glorify him. Let us write decrees to the emperors, praising and admiring our governor, asking for his rule to continue for many more years. Let us send statues to Delphi, Olympia, and Athens, after filling our own cities with them. 15. Let him be depicted now, surrounded by the nation of his subjects, all praising him and applauding. Let the cities lead the procession in the picture, portrayed in the form of women beaming with joy." You may supplement this with whatever the circumstances allow.

2.10. ΠΕΡΙ ΕΠΙΤΑΦΙΟΥ

1. Λέγεται μὲν παρ' Ἀθηναίοις ἐπιτάφιος ὁ καθ' ἕκαστον ἐνιαυτὸν ἐπὶ τοῖς πεπτωκόσιν ἐν τοῖς πολέμοις λεγόμενος λόγος, εἴληφε δὲ τὴν προσηγορίαν οὐδαμόθεν ἄλλοθεν ἢ ἀπὸ τοῦ λέγεσθαι ἐπ' αὐτῷ τῷ σήματι, οἷοί εἰσιν οἱ τρεῖς Ἀριστείδου λόγοι· οἵους γὰρ ἂν εἶπεν ὁ πολέμαρχος, ἐπειδὴ καὶ τούτῳ τὸ τῆς τιμῆς ταύτης ἀποδέδοται παρ' Ἀθηναίοις, τοιούτους ὁ σοφιστὴς συνέταξεν. 2. ἐκενίκηκε δὲ διὰ τὸ χρόνον πολὺν παρεληλυθέναι ἐγκώμιον γενέσθαι· τίς γὰρ ἂν ἔτι θρηνήσειε παρ' Ἀθηναίοις τοὺς πρὸ πεντακοσίων ἐτῶν πεπτωκότας; Θουκυδίδης δὲ λέγων ἐπιτάφιον ἐπὶ τοῖς πεσοῦσιν ἐπὶ τοῖς Ῥειτοῖς κατ' ἀρχὰς τοῦ Πελοποννησιακοῦ πολέμου οὐχ ἁπλῶς ἐγκώμιον μόνον εἶπε τῶν ἀνδρῶν, ἀλλὰ καὶ ἐπεσημήνατο ὅτι πεσεῖν ἐδύναντο· ἀλλὰ καὶ τὸν ἀπὸ τοῦ θρήνου τόπον ἐφυλάξατο διὰ τοῦ πολέμου τὴν χρείαν, οὐ γὰρ ἦν ῥήτορος <ποιεῖν>[1] δακρύειν οὓς προετρέπετο πολεμεῖν· ἔθηκε δὲ τὸν ἀπὸ τῆς παραμυθίας τόπον.

---

[1] suppl. RW

---

[1] These speeches are not extant.

[2] The number is rough. RW point out that five hundred years would bring the date to circa 70 AD. That would be about a century earlier than Aristides and two centuries before M.

2.10. THE FUNERAL SPEECH

1. "Funeral speech" (*epitaphios logos*) is the name given in Athens to the speech delivered each year over those who have fallen in war. It is so named simply because it is spoken over the actual grave. Examples are the three speeches of Aristides,[1] for the sophist composed his speeches like ones that would have been delivered in Athens by the polemarch, to whom this honor is assigned. 2. But over the long course of time, it has evolved into an encomium, for who in Athens would still lament those who had fallen five hundred years before?[2] When Thucydides composed his Funeral Oration[3] over the fallen at Rheiti[4] at the beginning of the Peloponnesian War, he did not simply deliver an encomium of the men, but made the point that they had dared to fall in battle.[5] He also avoided the topic of lament because of the demands of the war, for it was not the task of an orator to bring to tears those whom he was exhorting to fight. He did, however, include the topic of consolation.[6]

[3] Thuc. 2.35–46 (delivered by Pericles). [4] A location in Attica where the Athenian cavalry was routed in 431 BC (Thuc. 2.19.2). [5] Cf. Thuc. 2.42.4: "but with life and limb [they] stood stoutly to their task, and in the brief instant ordained by fate, at the crowning moment not of fear but of glory, they passed away" (C. F. Smith, trans.).

[6] Cf. Thuc. 2.44.1: "I do not commiserate the parents of these men . . . but will try to comfort them" (C. F. Smith, trans.).

3. Οὕτω καὶ Ἀριστείδης, εἴ ποτε ἔλεγε τούτους τοὺς λόγους ἐπὶ τοῖς προσφάτως πεσοῦσιν, ἐχρήσατο ἂν τοῖς τοῦ ἐπιταφίου κεφαλαίοις, ὅσα ἐστὶν αὐτῷ οἰκεῖα· νῦν δὲ χρόνος πολὺς παρεληλυθὼς οὐκέτι δίδωσι χώραν οὔτε θρήνοις οὔτε παραμυθίαις· λήθη τε γὰρ ἐγγέγονε τῷ χρόνῳ τοῦ πάθους, καὶ ὃν παραμυθησόμεθα οὐκ ἔχομεν· οὔτε γὰρ πατέρες ἐκείνων οὔτε τὸ γένος γνώριμον. ἄτοπον δὲ ὅλως εἰ καὶ γνώριμον τυγχάνοι, καὶ προσέτι ἄκαιρον τὸ μετὰ πολὺν χρόνον ἐγείρειν εἰς θρῆνον ἐθέλειν κεκοιμισμένης ἤδη τῷ χρόνῳ τῆς λύπης.

4. Οὐκοῦν ὁ μετὰ χρόνον πολὺν λεγόμενος ἐπιτάφιος καθαρόν ἐστιν ἐγκώμιον, ὡς Ἰσοκράτους ὁ Εὐαγόρας. εἰ δὲ μὴ πάνυ μετὰ πολὺν λέγοιτο, ἀλλ᾽ ἑπτά που μηνῶν ἢ ὀκτὼ παρελθόντων, ἐγκώμιον μὲν λέγειν δεῖ, πρὸς δὲ τῷ τέλει χρῆσθαι τῷ παραμυθητικῷ κεφαλαίῳ οὐδὲν κωλύσει, πλὴν ἐὰν μὴ συγγενὴς ἐγγυτάτω τυγχάνῃ τοῦ τεθνεῶτος ὁ λέγων. τούτῳ γὰρ οὐδὲ μετ᾽ ἐνιαυτὸν δίδωσιν ἀνάπαυλαν τοῦ πάθους ἡ μνήμη· διόπερ οὗτος σώσει καὶ μετ᾽ ἐνιαυτὸν τοῦ παθητικοῦ λόγου τὸν χαρακτῆρα.

5. Διαιρεθήσεται δὲ ὁ ἐπιτάφιος λόγος, ὁ παθητικός, ὁ ἐπὶ προσφάτῳ τῷ τεθνεῶτι λεγόμενος, τοῖς ἐγκωμιαστικοῖς κεφαλαίοις, πανταχοῦ ἐφεξῆς ἑκάστῳ τῶν κεφαλαίων παραμιγνυμένου τοῦ πάθους ἐκ μεταχειρίσεως οὕτως· ὧ πῶς συνοδύρωμαι τῷ γένει τὸ πάθος, ὦ τὴν ἐπιβολὴν τοῦ θρήνου πόθεν ποιήσομαι; ἀπὸ τοῦ γένους εἰ βούλεσθε πρῶτον· τοῦτο γὰρ αὐτὸ

3. So, if Aristides had delivered those speeches over men who had recently fallen, he would have employed all the sections (*kephalaia*) germane to the funeral speech. In fact, however, the long lapse of time leaves no place for lament or consolation, because over time the sorrow is forgotten and we have no one to console, since neither their fathers nor their families are known. And even if the family were known, it would be wholly absurd and inappropriate to want to stir them to lament after so long, when their pain has long since been put to rest by time.

4. As a result, a funeral speech delivered after a long time is a pure encomium, like Isocrates' *Evagoras*. And even if it is not delivered long afterward—say after the passage of seven or eight months—one must still deliver an encomium, but nothing should prevent the use of a section of consolatory topics at the end. An exception with regard to time occurs if the speaker is a very close relative of the deceased, since not even after a year does memory relieve him of his sorrow. In that case, the speaker will preserve the characteristics of a sorrowful speech even after a year.

5. A sorrowful funeral speech that is spoken over one who has recently died should be divided according to the sections of encomiastic topics, but with sorrow consistently intermixed in each, in the following manner. "Oh, how shall I share the family's grief? Oh, where shall I begin my lament? With the family first, if you permit, for

κρηπὶς τῶν ὅλων. οὐκοῦν ὅτι λαμπρὸν τοῦτο ἐρεῖς, καὶ
τῶν ἐν τῇ πόλει μᾶλλον ἐνδοξότατον, ἀλλ᾽ ὥσπερ
λαμπάδα ἡμμένην ἐν τῷ γένει τὸν πεπτωκότα τοῦτον
δαίμων ἀπέσβεσε. χρὴ γὰρ τὰ κεφάλαια μὴ καθαρεύ-
ειν τῶν θρήνων, ἀλλὰ κἂν γένος λέγῃς, θρηνεῖν κατ᾽
ἀρχὰς τοῦ γένους τὸν πεπτωκότα καὶ μεσοῦντος τοῦ
γένους καὶ τελευτῶντος, κἂν ἕτερόν τι κεφάλαιον.

6. Εἶτα μετὰ τὸ γένος τὰ περὶ τὴν γένεσιν αὐτοῦ
ἐρεῖς· ὦ ματαίων μὲν ἐκείνων συμβόλων, ματαίων δὲ
ὀνειράτων ἐπ᾽ ἐκείνῳ φανέντων ὅτε ἐτίκτετο, ὦ δυστυ-
χοῦς μὲν τῆς ἐνεγκούσης, ὠδῖνος δὲ ἐπὶ τούτοις δυσ-
τυχεστέρας· εἶδε[2] γὰρ ἡ μήτηρ σύμβολα· ὁ δεῖνα δὲ
προεφήτευσεν αὐτῇ τὰ[3] κάλλιστα, τῶν δὲ οἰκείων καὶ
τῶν φίλων εὔελπις ἦν ἕκαστος, ἔθυον δὲ θεοῖς γενεθλίοις, βωμοὶ δὲ ἡμάττοντο, ἦγε δὲ πανήγυριν ὁ σύμ-
420 πας οἶκος· δαίμων δέ, ὡς ἔοικεν, ἐπετώθασε τοῖς γινομένοις. παρεδίδοτο δὲ τροφεῦσιν ὁ παῖς· κρείττους
εἶχον ἐν τούτῳ τὰς ἐλπίδας οἱ τρέφοντες. ἀλλ᾽ οἴμοι
τῶν κακῶν, καὶ γάρ τοι νῦν οὗτος ἀνήρπασται.

7. Ὁμοίως δὲ καὶ τοῖς λοιποῖς ἐπεξελεύσῃ κεφαλαίοις τοῖς ἐγκωμιαστικοῖς, αὔξων δὲ καὶ τὸν θρῆνον. δεῖ
δήπου καὶ ἡπλωμένην ⟨εἶναι τὴν⟩[4] ἀπαγγελίαν τῶν
θρήνων, ἵνα καὶ ἡ λαμπρότης τῶν προσώπων φαίνηται, ἐπιστρέφῃς δὲ τὸν ἀκροατὴν αὖθις ἐπὶ τὸν θρῆνον. καὶ ὕλη σοι γινέσθω τὰ ἐγκώμια τῶν θρήνων.

2 εἶδε coni. RW: ὤδινε codd.: obel. Bursian
3 αὐτῇ τὰ coni. RW praeeunte Bursian: αὐτὰ codd.: τὰ Soffel
4 suppl. Nitsche, RW

the family itself is the foundation of everything." Then you may say, "The family is illustrious, by far the most famous family in the city, but the deceased, like a torch ablaze in the family, has been snuffed out by a god." None of these sections should be devoid of lamentation, but whether you are treating the family or any other section, you must lament the deceased at the beginning, middle, and end.

6. After the family, discuss the circumstances of his birth. "Oh, those false portents and false dreams that appeared at his birth. Oh, unfortunate the mother who carried him! More unfortunate the pains of childbirth that followed! His mother saw portents, and someone predicted the happiest future for her; every relative and friend had high hopes; they sacrificed to the family gods; the altars ran with sacrificial blood; the entire household was celebrating—but a god, so it seems, made a mockery of it all! The child was handed over to his caretakers, and they had the highest hopes for him. But, alas for the misfortune! Now he has been snatched away!"

7. Proceed in a similar fashion in the remaining sections of praise, as you amplify the lament. Clearly the style of the laments must be simple,[7] so that the brilliance of the persons is apparent,[8] and so that you can direct the audience again to the lament. Let the encomia provide material for your laments.

---

[7] ἡπλωμένα (simple) describes a loose, nonperiodic style, as is evident in the short paratactic clauses in the example just given. The term also appears at 2.5.4.

[8] Praise of the persons in the encomiastic portions thus leads to the laments over their loss. This sentence is unclear; I follow the suggestions of RW.

8. Ἐγκωμιάσεις δὲ ἀπὸ πάντων τῶν τόπων τῶν ἐγκωμιαστικῶν, γένους, γενέσεως, φύσεως, ἀνατροφῆς, παιδείας, ἐπιτηδευμάτων, τεμεῖς δὲ τὴν φύσιν δίχα, εἴς τε τὸ τοῦ σώματος κάλλος, ὅπερ πρῶτον ἐρεῖς, εἴς τε τὴν τῆς ψυχῆς εὐφυΐαν. πιστώσῃ δὲ τοῦτο διὰ τριῶν κεφαλαίων τῶν ἑξῆς, λέγω δὲ διὰ τῆς ἀνατροφῆς καὶ τῆς παιδείας καὶ τῶν ἐπιτηδευμάτων· ἐργαζόμενος γὰρ αὐτοῦ τὸ ἐγκώμιον διὰ τούτων ἑκάστου ἐρεῖς μὲν τὴν ἀνατροφήν, ὅτι ἐνέφηνε διὰ τούτων τῆς ψυχῆς τὴν εὐφυΐαν εὐθὺς τρεφόμενος καὶ ὀξύτητα—δευτέραν τιθεὶς ταύτην, ‹πρώτην›[5] δὲ τὴν εὐφυΐαν—ἐρεῖς δὲ τὴν παιδείαν, ὅτι ἐδείκνυε καὶ ἐπὶ τούτῳ προσχεῖν τῶν ἡλίκων. διὰ δὲ τῶν ἐπιτηδευμάτων πιστώσῃ τὸ κεφάλαιον οὕτως, ὅτι δίκαιον παρεῖχεν ἑαυτόν, φιλάνθρωπον, ὁμιλητικόν, ἥμερον.

9. Τὸ δὲ μέγιστον κεφάλαιον τῶν ἐγκωμιαστικῶν εἰσιν αἱ πράξεις, ἅστινας θήσεις μετὰ τὰ ἐπιτηδεύματα· οὐκ ἀφέξῃ δὲ τοῦ καὶ ἐν ἑκάστῃ πράξει θρῆνον ἐπεμβαλεῖν. θήσεις δὲ μετὰ τὰς πράξεις καὶ τὸν ἀπὸ τῆς τύχης τόπον, λέγων ὅτι παρωμάρτησεν αὐτῷ καὶ δεξιά τις τύχη ζῶντι ἐφ᾽ ἅπασι, πλοῦτος, παίδων εὐτυχία, φίλων περὶ αὐτὸν ἔρωτες, τιμὴ παρὰ βασιλέων, τιμὴ παρὰ πόλεων.

10. Εἶτα τὰς συγκρίσεις μετὰ ταῦτα θήσεις πρὸς ὅλην τὴν ὑπόθεσιν, ὡς κεφάλαιον ἴδιον, οὐκ ἀπεχόμενος μὲν οὐδὲ ἐφ᾽ ἑκάστῳ κεφαλαίῳ συγκρίσεως ‹ἣν›[6] πρὸς ἐκεῖνο τὸ κεφάλαιον ὃ λέγεις παραλαμβάνειν δεῖ. καὶ ἐνταῦθα δὲ προδήλως πρὸς ὅλην τὴν ὑπόθε-

8. You should base your praise on all the encomiastic topics: family, birth, nature, upbringing, education, and activities. You should divide the part on nature into physical beauty, which you should mention first, and intellectual ability. You should offer proof of this in the three following sections, namely, upbringing, education, and activities. In composing his praise in each of these, you should say the following. As to his upbringing, "He revealed his intellectual ability in this way at the very beginning of his nurture, and his quickness too" (putting this second and his ability first). As to his education, "Here too he showed himself to surpass his age mates." As to activities, you should confirm this section in the following way. "He showed himself to be just, humane, affable, and gentle."

9. The most important section of praise is that of deeds, which you should place after activities. Do not fail, however, to insert a lament as you treat each deed. After deeds you should include the topic of fortune. "Good fortune followed him in everything while he was alive: wealth, the blessing of children, love from his friends, honor from emperors, and honor from cities."

10. After this, in a separate section, you should include comparisons of your entire subject. This does not preclude any comparison you must make in each section that is relevant to that section. Here, however, you will openly make a comparison that embraces the entire subject. For

---

⁵ suppl. RW
⁶ suppl. Bursian, RW

MENANDER RHETOR

σιν παραλήψη τὴν σύγκρισιν· οἷον ἄνωθεν ἐπιδραμὼν
τὰ κεφάλαια ἐρεῖς ὅτι ἐὰν τοίνυν ἐξετάσωμεν ταῦτα
σύμπαντα περί τινος τῶν ἡμιθέων ἢ τῶν νῦν ἐναρέ-
των, οὐδενὸς δεύτερος· τῷ δὲ ταῦτα ἄμεινα[7] ὑπῆρξεν·
11. δεῖ γὰρ καλοῦ καλλίονα ἀποδεικνύναι ἢ ὁτῳοῦν[8]
ἐνδόξῳ ἐφάμιλλον, οἷον ἢ τῷ Ἡρακλέους βίῳ τὸν
βίον αὐτοῦ ἢ τῷ Θησέως παραβάλλοντα. ἐπὶ τούτοις
πάλιν κεφάλαιον θήσεις τὸν θρῆνον, ὅτι διὰ ταῦτα
τοῦτον ὀδύρομαι, ἐργασίαν δοὺς ἰδιάζουσαν, καθα-
ρεύουσαν λοιπὸν ἐγκωμίων, οἶκτον κινῶν, εἰς δάκρυα
συγχέων τοὺς ἀκούοντας.

12. Μετὰ τοῦτο τὸ κεφάλαιον θήσεις κεφάλαιον
ἕτερον τὸ παραμυθητικὸν πρὸς ἅπαν τὸ γένος, ὅτι οὐ
δεῖ θρηνεῖν· πολιτεύεται γὰρ μετὰ τῶν θεῶν, ἢ τὸ
Ἠλύσιον ἔχει πεδίον. ἰδίᾳ δ' αὖ πάλιν τὰ νοήματα
μεριεῖς τῶν κεφαλαίων οὕτως· ἰδίᾳ μὲν πρὸς τοὺς παῖδας, ἰδίᾳ δὲ πρὸς τὴν γυναῖκα, ἐξάρας πρότερον τὸ
πρόσωπον τῆς γυναικός, ἵνα μὴ πρὸς φαῦλον καὶ
εὐτελὲς διαλέγεσθαι δοκῇς πρόσωπον· ἐπὶ γὰρ τῶν
ἀνδρῶν οὐ φέρει ψόγον ὁ λόγος ἄνευ τινὸς προκατα-
σκευῆς λεγόμενος, ἐπὶ δὲ γυναικὸς ἀναγκαίως προ-
καταλήψῃ τὸν ἀκροατὴν τῇ ἀρετῇ[9] τῆς γυναικός. 13.
ἐὰν δὲ νέαν ἄγωσι πάνυ τὴν ἡλικίαν οἱ παῖδες, συμβουλευτικὸν μᾶλλον θήσεις τὸν τόπον, οὐ παραμυθη-
τικόν· οὐ γὰρ αἰσθάνονται τοῦ πάθους· μᾶλλον δὲ
οὕτω προσθήσεις τινὰ τῷ παραμυθητικῷ συμβουλὴν
καὶ ὑποθήκην πρὸς τὴν γυναῖκα καὶ πρὸς τοὺς παῖ-

example, after a summary review of the previous sections, you could say, "If, then, we consider all these qualities as they pertain to some demigod or outstanding contemporary, he is second to none, for his qualities are superior." 11. Thus, you need to demonstrate that he is more noble than any noble man, or that he is a match for any famous man, by comparing, for example, his life to that of Heracles or Theseus. After this, include another section of lament. "These are the reasons I grieve for him." Give it its own treatment, now free of encomium, as you arouse pity and move the listeners to tears.

12. After this section, include a separate one of consolation for the whole family. "There is no need to mourn, for he is now a citizen living with the gods," or "He dwells in the Elysian Fields." Separate your considerations in these sections into ones addressed to the children and ones to the wife. You should first elevate the wife's character, to avoid giving the impression of addressing a lowly or common person. For in the case of men, no one criticizes an address made without some preliminary remarks, but in the case of a woman, you will need to convince the audience of her virtue in advance.[9] 13. If the children are very young, you should employ the topic of advice rather than consolation, for they do not feel the sorrow. Instead, you can add some advice and counsel when consoling the

---

[9] For using caution when praising women, cf. 2.5.20.

---

[7] δεύτερος· τῷ δὲ ταῦτα ἄμεινα Bursian: δευτέρῳ τῷδε ταῦτα ἄμεινον codd.: ἄμεινον obel. RW

[8] Bursian, RW: ὅταν codd.

[9] Kroll, RW: τῆς ἀρετῆς codd.: ταῖς ἀρεταῖς coni. Spengel

δας, εἰ ἄγαν νέοι τυγχάνοιεν ὄντες, τὴν μὲν ζηλοῦν τὰς ἀρχαίας καὶ ἀρίστας τῶν γυναικῶν καὶ ἡρώνας, τοὺς δὲ παῖδας ζηλοῦν τὰς τοῦ πατρὸς ἀρετάς. 14. εἶτα

422 ἐπαινέσεις τὸ γένος, ὅτι οὐκ ἠμέλησαν τῆς κηδεύσεως οὐδὲ τῆς κατασκευῆς τοῦ μνήματος. εἶτα εὐχὴν πρὸς τῷ τέλει τοῦ λόγου θήσεις εὐχόμενος αὐτοῖς παρὰ τῶν θεῶν ὑπάρξαι τὰ κάλλιστα.

wife and the children (if they are very young): she should emulate the most noble women and heroines of old, and they should emulate their father's virtues. 14. Next praise the family. "They have spared no expense on the funeral nor on the furnishing of the tomb." Finally, include a prayer at the end of the speech, asking the gods to grant them the finest blessings.

2.11. ΠΕΡΙ ΣΤΕΦΑΝΩΤΙΚΟΥ

1. Ἐν τῷ στεφανωτικῷ προοιμιάσῃ εὐθὺς ἀπὸ τοῦ στεφάνου καὶ τῆς δόξης τοῦ βασιλέως, καὶ ὅτι φθάνει μὲν τὸ κρεῖττον αὐτῇ τῇ βασιλείᾳ στεφάνῳ τιμῶν, καὶ ἡ σύμπασα οἰκουμένη τῷ μεγίστῳ στεφανοῦσα στεφάνῳ, ταῖς εὐφημίαις· ἥκει δὲ παρά σε καὶ ἡ πόλις ἡ ἡμετέρα, οὐδεμιᾶς τῶν σῶν ὑπηκόων οὔτε δόξαις οὔτε μεγέθεσιν οὔτε κάλλεσιν ἡττωμένη, λόγοις τε ἅμα στεφανοῦσα καὶ χρυσῷ τῷ στέμματι.

2. Ἐὰν μὲν σχῇ γένος εὐδόκιμον, μετὰ τὸ προοίμιον ποιήσῃ τοῦ βασιλέως τὸ ἐγκώμιον ἀπὸ τοῦ γένους· εἰ δὲ μή γε, εὐθὺς ἀπὸ τῆς τύχης ἀντὶ τοῦ γένους, ὅτι θεὸς κατοικτείρας ἄνωθεν τὸ ἀνθρώπινον γένος καὶ βουληθεὶς ταῖς εὐδαιμονίαις παραμυθήσασθαι τὴν σὴν παρήγαγε γένεσιν ἐπ' ἀγαθῇ μοίρᾳ τῆς οἰκουμένης.

3. Εἶτα ἐρεῖς ἐὰν ἔχῃς παιδείαν καὶ ἀνατροφὴν ἔνδοξον. εἶτα ἐφάψῃ τῶν ἀρετῶν ἐπὶ τούτοις, τῆς ἀνδρείας πρώτης· ὅτι <καὶ>[1] γάρ τοι διατελεῖς ἐν δουρὶ καὶ ἵππῳ καὶ ἀσπίδι ἄθλους μεγίστους ἀγωνιζόμενος ὑπὲρ τῆς ὑφ' ἥλιον, καθάπερ Ἡρακλέα φασὶ τὸν Διός· ἐν ᾧ μνημονεύσεις ὅτι βαρβάρων οἱ μὲν τελέως

[1] suppl. RW

2.11. THE CROWN SPEECH

1. In the crown speech (*stephanōtikos logos*), lead off your introduction with the crown and the emperor's glory. "Heaven was the first to honor you with the crown of the empire itself, and the whole world[1] crowns you with the greatest crown of all, words of praise. Our city too comes before you, one not inferior to any other city under your rule with respect to glory, size, or beauty, and she crowns you with words and with this wreath of gold."

2. Following the introduction, you should fashion an encomium of the emperor on the basis of his distinguished family, if indeed he has one. But if not, immediately take up the topic of good fortune instead. "Because a god on high took pity on the human race and wished to console it with prosperity, he brought about your birth for the good fortune of the world."

3. Next, speak of his glorious education and upbringing, if you can do so. After that, touch on his virtues, beginning with courage. "For you constantly engage in the mightiest battles with spear, horse, and shield on behalf of all the world under the sun, as they say Zeus' son Heracles did." Here you can mention, "Some barbarians have been

---

[1] That is, the "inhabited" world (ἡ οἰκουμένη).

ἀπολώλασιν, οἱ δὲ δυστυχοῦσιν, οἱ δ' αἰχμάλωτοι
παρ' ἡμᾶς ἤχθησαν, οἱ δὲ οὐδὲ ἀντέχειν δύνανται,
ὥσπερ οὐδὲ πρὸς τὰς ἡλίου βολὰς ἀτενίζειν τολμῶν-
τες.

4. Μετὰ τὴν ἀνδρείαν, ἐν ᾗ καὶ τὰ κατὰ τὸν πόλεμόν ἐστιν, ἐρεῖς λοιπὸν περὶ τῶν κατὰ εἰρήνην, καὶ
μετὰ ταῦτα ἐπάξεις ὅτι τοιγάρτοι διὰ τοῦτο στεφανοῖ
σε ἡ πόλις, ἅμα μὲν χάριτας ἐκτιννῦσα ὑπὲρ ὧν ὁση-
423 μέραι εὐεργετούμεθα, ἅμα δὲ καὶ δεομένη καὶ ἱκετεύ-
ουσα καὶ θαρροῦσα τῇ σῇ περὶ πάντα φιλανθρωπίᾳ,
ὅτι οὐδενὸς ἀποτεύξεται. εἶτα ἀξιώσεις ἀναγνωσθῆναι
τὸ ψήφισμα. ἔστω δέ σοι ὁ λόγος μὴ πλειόνων ἑκατὸν
πεντήκοντα ἢ καὶ διακοσίων ἐπῶν.

completely destroyed, some are in distress, some have been brought to us as slaves, and some are not even able to offer resistance, as if not daring to stare at the rays of the sun."

4. After courage, which comprises deeds of war, you should speak of deeds of peace, after which you can add, "So, for this reason our city crowns you, rendering thanks for the benefactions we receive every day, and at the same time she begs and pleads with you, confident in your humanity in all matters, that she will not fail in any request." Then ask for the decree[2] to be read. Your speech should not exceed one hundred fifty to two hundred lines.

[2] That is, the decree of the city, granting the crown to the emperor.

2.12. ΠΕΡΙ ΠΡΕΣΒΕΥΤΙΚΟΥ

1. Ἐὰν δὲ ὑπὲρ πόλεως καμνούσης δέῃ πρεσβεῦσαι, ἐρεῖς μὲν καὶ ταῦτα ἃ προείρηται ἐν τῷ στεφανωτικῷ, πανταχοῦ δὲ τὸ τῆς φιλανθρωπίας τοῦ βασιλέως αὐξήσεις, καὶ ὅτι φιλοικτίρμων καὶ ἐλεῶν τοὺς δεομένους, καὶ ὅτι διὰ τοῦτο ὁ θεὸς αὐτὸν κατέπεμψεν, ὅτι ᾔδει αὐτὸν ἐλεήμονα καὶ εὖ ποιοῦντα τοὺς ἀνθρώπους.

2. Καὶ ὅταν εἴπῃς τὰ ἀπὸ τῆς ἀνδρείας ἐν τοῖς πολέμοις καὶ τὰ ἀπὸ τῆς εἰρήνης ἀγαθά, ἥξεις ἐπὶ τὴν μνήμην τῆς πόλεως, ὑπὲρ ἧς πρεσβεύεις. ἐν δὲ ταύτῃ δύο τόπους ἐργάσῃ, ἕνα μὲν τὸν ἀπὸ τῆς τοῦ ἐναντίου αὐξήσεως, οἷον· ἦν ποτε τὸ Ἴλιον πόλις λαμπρὰ καὶ ὀνομαστοτάτη τῶν ὑφ' ἥλιον πασῶν, καὶ ἀντέσχεν πρὸς τοὺς ἀπὸ τῆς Εὐρώπης πολέμους τὸ παλαιόν· 3. εἶτα τὸν ἐκ διατυπώσεως, ἐν ᾧ καὶ διασκευάσεις τὴν παροῦσαν τύχην, ὅτι πέπτωκεν εἰς ἔδαφος, καὶ μάλιστα ἐκείνων μνημονεύσεις ἃ πρὸς τὴν χρείαν καὶ τὴν ζωὴν συμβάλλεσθαι πέφυκε, καὶ ὧν εἰώθασιν οἱ βασιλεῖς προνοεῖσθαι, οἷον ὅτι λουτρὰ συμπέπτωκεν, ὑδάτων ὀχετοὶ διεφθάρησαν, κό-

2.12. THE AMBASSADOR'S SPEECH
(*presbeutikos logos*)

1. If you are called upon to serve as an ambassador on behalf of a city in distress, include what was prescribed for the crown speech, but at every point amplify the emperor's humanity, saying how sympathetic and compassionate he is to those in need of help, and how the gods sent him down for that very reason, because they knew him to be merciful and benevolent to mankind.

2. After speaking of his courageous acts in wars and benefactions in peacetime, proceed to mention the city on whose behalf you are serving as ambassador. Here you should develop two topics. The first consists of amplifying the opposite case.[1] For example, "The city of Ilium was once illustrious and the most famous of all cities under the sun, and it held out long ago against attacks from Europe."[2] 3. The second consists of a vivid description, in which you elaborate the present misfortune, saying how the city has fallen to the ground. You should mention especially those things that naturally contribute to people's needs and livelihoods, things that emperors usually see to. For example, "The baths have collapsed, the aqueducts

[1] That is, stressing how blessed the city formerly was.
[2] The example again suggests that the treatise centers on Alexandria Troas. See Introduction.

σμος ὁ τῆς πόλεως συγκέχυται· 4. καὶ τὰ τοιαῦτα
ἐλεεινολογησάμενος ἐπάξεις ὅτι διὰ ταῦτα ἱκετεύομεν,
δεόμεθα, πρὸ τῶν γονάτων πίπτομεν, τὰς ἱκετηρίας
προτείνομεν· νόμιζε γὰρ τὴν τοῦ πρεσβευτοῦ φωνὴν
εἶναι πάσης τῆς πόλεως, δι᾽ ἧς νόμιζε καὶ παῖδας καὶ
γυναῖκας καὶ ἄνδρας καὶ πρεσβύτας δάκρυα προχέ-
424 ειν, παρακαλεῖν σε πρὸς ἔλεον. εἶτα ἀξιώσεις ἐπινεῦ-
σαι αὐτὸν δεχθῆναι τὸ ψήφισμα.

are in ruins, the beauty of the city has been destroyed."[3] 4. After such appeals to pity, you should add, "For these reasons we come before you as suppliants, we beg, we fall at your knees, we extend to you these olive branches of supplication. Imagine that the voice of this ambassador is that of the entire city, and through its voice imagine that the children, women, men, and elders are shedding tears and begging for your mercy." Then ask that he deign to accept the petition.

[3] Various disasters could occur throughout the empire; cf. Aristid. *Or.* 19, an appeal to Marcus Aurelius for aid after the 178 AD earthquake that devastated Smyrna.

2.13. ΠΕΡΙ ΚΛΗΤΙΚΟΥ

1. Ἐὰν ἄρχοντα καλῇς εἰς πανήγυριν, ὡς ἔθος, ἐρεῖς μὲν ἐν τοῖς προοιμίοις τὴν αἰτίαν τῆς ἀφίξεως καὶ τῆς κλήσεως, ὅτι πέπομφεν ἡ πόλις πάλαι μὲν καὶ ἄνευ προφάσεως ποθοῦσα καὶ βουλομένη τῶν σοι προσόντων ἐξαιρέτων μετέχειν ὁσημέραι· πολὺ δὲ πλεῖον ἐπὶ τοῦ παρόντος, ὅτι καὶ πανήγυριν ἄγει καὶ δεῖται μείζονος θεατοῦ πρὸς τὰ δρώμενα.

2. Εἶτα ἐρεῖς ἐγκώμιον τῆς πανηγύρεως, ἐφ᾽ ἣν ἡ κλῆσις, εἰπὼν ὧδέ πως· ἵνα δὲ γνῷς τὴν ὑπόθεσιν καὶ τὴν πανήγυριν ἐφ᾽ ἣν ἡ κλῆσις, μικρὸν ἄνωθεν ἄρξομαι. καὶ ἐρεῖς τῆς πανηγύρεως ἐγκώμιον [μετὰ δὲ τὴν πανήγυριν ἐπαινῶν καὶ]¹ λέγων ὅτι τίθεται θεῶν τινι ἢ ἡρώων.

3. Μετὰ δὲ τὸν τῆς πανηγύρεως ἔπαινον ἐρεῖς ἐγκώμιον τῆς πόλεως, εἴ τι ἀρχαῖον ἔχεις, εἶτα τοῦ ἄρχοντος ἀναγκαίως. δεῖ γὰρ πρότερον ἐγκωμιάσαι τὴν πανήγυριν (τοῦτο γὰρ ἐνταῦθα τὸ προηγούμενον καὶ ἀπὸ τῶν προηγουμένων ἄρχεσθαι μάλιστα δεῖ), εἶτα τὴν πόλιν, καὶ μετὰ ταῦτα τὸν ἄρχοντα. προσθήσεις δὲ πανταχοῦ τὸ τῆς πανηγύρεως· πλέον γάρ τι ἐχέτω καὶ οὗτος ὁ λόγος τὸ τῆς πανηγύρεως, διότι οὐχ

2.13. THE INVITATION SPEECH
(klētikos logos)

1. If you are inviting a governor to a festival, as customarily happens, you should state in the introduction the reason for your coming and for the invitation. "The city has sent me because of its longstanding yearning and desire— even without a pretext[1]—to enjoy your outstanding qualities each and every day, but much more so on the present occasion, for it is holding a festival and needs a spectator of greater importance to witness the events."

2. Next you should praise the festival to which he is being invited, saying something along these lines. "So that you may appreciate the circumstances and the festival to which you are being invited, I shall begin with a bit of background." You should praise the festival, telling how it is held for one of the gods or heroes.

3. After this encomium of the festival, you should praise the city—if, that is, you have some ancient legend to tell of—and then, by necessity, the governor himself. You must praise the festival first (for this is the principal subject in this case and one must above all begin with things of primary importance), next the city, and then the governor. At every point, bring up the topic of the festival, for this speech should devote a greater portion to it, as it

---

[1] secl. Bursian: τῆς . . . λέγων secl. RW

ἁπλῶς κλῆσίς ἐστιν, ἀλλὰ καὶ ἐπὶ πανήγυριν. ἔφαμεν
δὲ δεῖν πανταχοῦ τὸ ἐξαίρετον τῆς ὑποθέσεως πλεο-
νάζειν.

4. Λέγε δὲ τὰ κατὰ τὴν πανήγυριν μετὰ τὸν ἄρχοντα οὕτως, ὅτι σεμνὴ καὶ ὅτι θαύματος ἀξία πολλοῦ, καὶ ὅτι θεάσῃ δήμους, πόλεις συνεληλυθυίας,
ἀθλητὰς πανταχόθεν τοὺς ἀρίστους, κιθαριστάς, αὐ-
λητάς, οὐκ ὀλίγους τῶν τὴν μουσικὴν μετιόντων ἀν-
δρῶν· οἵ σε περιμένουσι καὶ οὐδὲ τούτων οὐδεμίαν
ἀπόλαυσιν ἕξειν ἡγούμενοι χωρὶς τῆς σῆς ἐπιδημίας
425 καλοῦσιν ἐπὶ τὴν πανήγυριν νῦν, ἵνα ὑπὸ σοὶ θεατῇ
ταύτην τελέσωσι. τίς δὲ οὐ θαυμάσει πεισθέντα σε;
τίς δ' οὐ θέαμα τῆς πανηγύρεως αὐτῆς τάχα σεμνό-
τερον ἴδοι σέ; 5. εἶτα ἐρεῖς· αἰδεῖσθαι δέ σε δεῖ καὶ τὸν
θεόν, ᾧ τελεῖται τὰ τῆς πανηγύρεως, καὶ χαρίζεσθαι
τούτῳ· καὶ γὰρ εὐσεβὴς ὁμοῦ καὶ πείθεσθαι δόξεις.
εἶτα ἐρεῖς· καὶ τὰ μὲν τῆς πανηγύρεως ἅπαντα παρ-
εσκεύασται, μόνος δὲ σὺ ταύτῃ λείπεις, ὥστε ἥκοις
ἄν.

6. Εἶτα συγκρινεῖς τὴν πανήγυριν ἑτέρᾳ πανηγύρει,
δεικνὺς οὐκ εἰς μικράν τινα καὶ εὐτελῆ καλῶν ἑορτήν.
προσθήσεις δὲ ὅτι εἰ μὲν πεισθείης, ἐνδοξότερος ἐγὼ
πείσας, ἐνδοξότερα δὲ τὰ δρώμενα, σεμνοτέρα δὲ ἡ
πόλις, ὁ δὲ θεὸς ἡσθήσεται· 7. εἰ δὲ ἀποτύχοιμι, ὅπερ
οὐκ οἴομαι μηδὲ εἴη, ἄλλην μὲν ὁδὸν ἐγὼ τραπήσο-
μαι. τίς γάρ μοι τῆς πατρίδος ἔτι πόθος ἀποτυχόντι

---

1 For the thought, cf. 2.2.25 and 2.15.2. M. frequently men-

is not just any invitation, but one to a festival. We have said that at every point one must stress what is distinctive about a subject.[1]

4. After praising the governor, speak of the festival along these lines. "It is dignified and worthy of great admiration. You will see townships (*demes*) and cities gathered together, the best athletes from everywhere, lyre players, flutists, and no dearth of accomplished musicians. They are waiting for you, and because they believe that they will derive no enjoyment from their performances without your presence, they are inviting you now to the festival, so that they can celebrate it with you looking on. Who will not marvel at your acceptance? Who would not see you as a spectacle perhaps more awe-inspiring than the festival itself?" 5. Then you should say, "You must also show respect for the god for whom the festival is celebrated, and do him this favor, for thus you will be seen as both reverent and obliging." Then add, "All the preparations for the festival have been made. All it lacks is you, so please do come."

6. Next, compare the festival with another, showing that you are not inviting him to some insignificant celebration. Then add, "If you accept, I will be more famous for gaining your acceptance, the events of the festival will be more famous, the city will gain more dignity, and the god will be pleased. 7. But if I should fail—which I neither expect nor hope will happen—I shall take some other road,[2] for how could I desire my homeland any longer, if

tions singling out special qualities ($\tau \grave{\alpha}$ $\dot{\epsilon} \xi \alpha \acute{\iota} \rho \epsilon \tau \alpha$) to praise; cf. 2.2.16; 2.3.24, 26; 2.6.23; and 2.7.1.

[2] That is, than one leading back home.

τῆς τοσαύτης πρεσβείας; ἡ δὲ πόλις ἀντὶ πανηγύρεως ἕξει συμφοράν, ὅπερ οὐδὲ λέγειν ἄξιον· οὐκοῦν
σπεῦδε θᾶττον ἐπ' αἰσίοις συμβόλοις πεισθεὶς τῇ πόλει παρακαλούσῃ, σπεῦδε εἰς τὴν πανήγυριν—ὁ γὰρ
τοῦ πρεσβευτοῦ λόγος φωνὴ τῆς πόλεως—ἵνα σου
μετὰ τῶν ἄλλων πράξεων καὶ τοῦτο καταλέγωμεν.

8. Ἐὰν δὲ μήτε πανήγυρις μήτε ἱερομηνία τυγχάνῃ,
δι' ἣν ἡ κλῆσις, ἀλλ' ἁπλῶς ἐπὶ πόλιν καλῇς, εὐθέως
ἐν προοιμίοις ἐρεῖς· φθάνεις μὲν ἴσως καὶ πρὸ τῶν
ἡμετέρων λόγων εὖ διακείμενος πρὸς τὴν πόλιν τὴν
ἡμετέραν καὶ πόθον ἔχων τῆς θέας· καὶ γὰρ τοῦτο
τεθρύληται· ὅμως δὲ κέρδος μέλλοντες κερδαίνειν
οὐχὶ σμικρὸν ἥκομεν τῆς προαιρέσεως χάριν ἐκτιννύντες διὰ τῆς εὐφημίας, καλοῦντες δὲ οὐδὲν ἧττον καὶ
παρακαλοῦντες ἐφ' ἣν σπεύδεις ἐλθεῖν.

9. Εἶτα ἐὰν ἀξίωμα ὁ καλῶν ἔχῃ λαμπρόν, ἐρεῖς τι
καὶ περὶ τούτου ἐν προοιμίῳ δευτέρῳ· πολλοὶ μὲν οὖν
την χειροτονίαν ταύτην ἐμνήστευον καὶ πρέσβεις
αἱρεθῆναι παρὰ τὴν σὴν μεγαλοπρέπειαν ἔσπευδον,
ἡ πόλις δὲ εἵλετο τάχα που τῶν μνηστευσάντων οὐ
τὸν χείρω, πάντως δὲ ἔξεστί σοι μαθεῖν τῶν Ἀθηναίων λόγων τὸν τρόφιμον. ἀτύφως δὲ ἐρεῖς τὸ προοίμιον ἐμφαίνων μὲν τὸ ἀξίωμα, μὴ παρεχόμενος δὲ
φορτικὸν τὸν λόγον.

10. Μετὰ δὲ τὰ προοίμια ἥξεις ἐπὶ τὰ ἐγκώμια τῆς
πόλεως, οὐ θέσιν μὲν ἐνταῦθα ἐκφράζων, οὐδὲ ἀέρων
φύσεις, ἐπὶ δὲ τὰς πράξεις καὶ τὴν ἀξίαν μᾶλλον τρέ-
ψεις τὸν λόγον οὕτω πως· πάλαι μὲν οὖν ἐσεμνύνετο

I fail on an embassy of such importance? Instead of a festival, the city will have a disaster about which nothing deserves to be said. Therefore, accept the city's invitation and with good omens make haste and come to the festival, for this ambassador's words are the voice of the city: let us include your attendance among all your other accomplishments."

8. If neither a festival nor the celebration of a holy month provides the reason for your invitation, but you are simply inviting him to your city, you can say right away in your introduction, "Perhaps even before we speak you hold our city in high regard and desire to see it, for that is widely reported. Nevertheless, expecting to gain no small benefit, we have come to repay with praise your decision to visit us, by inviting you all the same and summoning you to the city you are eager to visit."

9. Then, if the speaker issuing the invitation has an illustrious reputation, you may say a word about it in a second introduction. "Many were seeking this appointment and were eager to be chosen as ambassadors to your Excellence. The city, though, chose one who is perhaps not the worst of the candidates—at least, you can recognize a student of Athenian oratory." You must deliver this introduction without arrogance, by emphasizing your status, but without making your speech offensive.

10. After these introductions comes the praise of your city, but at this point do not describe its location or climate. Instead, direct your speech to its deeds and merits

παλαιοῖς διηγήμασιν ἡμῖν ἡ πόλις Ἀλεξάνδρου καὶ
τοῖς κάλλεσι τῶν οἰκοδομημάτων, νυνὶ δὲ ἁπάντων
ἀμελήσασα τῶν τοιούτων ἐπὶ σοὶ μόνῳ σεμνύνεται.

11. Εἶτα εὐθὺς ἐρεῖς, εἴ τι λέγειν ἀρχαῖον ἔχοις τῆς
πόλεως, καὶ μετὰ ταῦτα τὸν τοῦ ἄρχοντος ἔπαινον· τίς
δὲ οὐκ ἂν ἄνδρα ταῖς ἀρεταῖς ὑπερβάλλοντα θαυμά-
σειεν; εἶτα ἐρεῖς περὶ τῶν ἀρετῶν τῶν τοῦ ἄρχοντος
οἷός ἐστι· καὶ ἐὰν μὲν πρώτως ἐπιδημεῖν μέλλῃ, μετὰ
τὰ ἐγκώμια τοῦ ἄρχοντος ἐρεῖς ἔκφρασιν διὰ βραχέων τῆς χώρας, εἶτα τῆς πόλεως, ὥσπερ προείρηται,
λοιπὸν παρακαλέσεις ἐπὶ ταῦτα ἐλθεῖν· 12. ἴθι τοιγαροῦν ταῦτα ἐποψόμενος, ἴθι προσθήσων τοῖς κάλλεσιν, ἄλλος Ἀλέξανδρος ἡμῖν γενόμενος· εὑρήσεις[2]
πρὸς ὑποδοχὰς τῶν ἀρχόντων οὐδὲν λεῖπον,[3] οὐκ ἀέρων χάριν, οὐκ ἦθος ἀνδρῶν, οὔτε μετριότητα τρόπων, οὔτ' ἄλλην σεμνότητα· ἔστι γὰρ ἡμῖν ἡ πόλις
ὥσπερ τέμενος ἀρετῶν. Ἀθηναῖοι μὲν οὖν ἐπὶ παλαιοῖς σεμνύνονται διηγήμασι καὶ μουσείοις καὶ λόγοις,
ἡμῶν δὲ πολλοὶ τὰ τῶν Ἀθηνῶν ἠρανίσαντο,[4] μου-
σεῖον δὲ οὐδὲν ἧττον τὸ παρ' ἡμῖν τῶν παρ' ἐκείνοις·
καὶ γὰρ ἀρίστους ἐκπέμπομεν καὶ τελείαν τὴν ἀρετὴν
κτησαμένους παρ' ἐκείνων δεχόμεθα· οὗτοί σε δορυ-
φορήσουσιν, οὗτοί σε δεξιώσονται.

13. Εἶτα συγκρινεῖς τὴν πόλιν ἢ ταῖς Ἀθήναις ἢ τῇ
Ῥώμῃ ἢ ἄλλῃ τινὶ τῶν ἐνδόξων πόλεων· καὶ διὰ

---

[2] εὑρήσεις Kroll: εὐτυχήσεις Bursian: εὐτυχήσας P: εὐτυ-
χής p: obel. RW   [3] οὐδὲν λεῖπον m: οὐδέποτ' Pp: obel. RW

304

along these lines. "Our city of Alexander[3] had long prided itself on its ancient stories[4] and beautiful buildings, but now it pays no heed to all such things and prides itself on you alone."

11. Here you should immediately relate some ancient story you can tell about the city, and then turn to the praise of the governor. "Who would not admire a man of such surpassing virtues?" You should then discuss his virtues. If this will be the governor's first visit, you should follow up his praise by briefly describing your country and then your city, as was recommended.[5] Finally, you should invite him to come visit all this. 12. "So come and see them, come and add to their beauty, become our second Alexander. You will find nothing lacking for a governor's welcome, when it comes to a pleasant climate, the morals of our people, the moderation of their behavior, or any other aspect of dignified conduct, because our city is a veritable sanctuary of virtues. Yes, the Athenians pride themselves on their ancient stories, schools, and oratory, and many of us have taken our share of Athenian offerings, but our school is not at all inferior to theirs. We send off our best men and receive them back from Athens with their excellence perfected. These will escort you, these will welcome you."

13. Next, you should compare your city with Athens or Rome or some other famous city. "Since, for these reasons,

[3] That is, Alexandria Troas.
[4] That is, about Troy.   [5] Cf. §3.

---

[4] Nitsche, RW: ἠρήσαντο codd.

ταῦτα οὖν, ὅτι οὐδεμιᾶς τῶν μεγίστων λείπεται, προσήκει σοι ταύτην ἰδεῖν· ὥσπερ γὰρ ὁ πλούτῳ κομῶν
καὶ περιουσίαν ἔχων τοῖς ἐξαιρέτοις τῶν κτημάτων
ὡραΐζεται, οὕτω προσήκει καὶ τὸν ἄρχοντα ταύταις
ταῖς μεγίσταις τῶν πόλεων σεμνύνεσθαι καὶ παρὰ
ταύτας σπεύδειν, ὅσαι τὸ μεῖζον ἔχουσι πλεονέκτημα,
τοὺς λόγους, καὶ τὰ λοιπὰ πρὸς ἀρετὴν ἥκοντα.

14. Εἶτα διαγράψεις τῷ λόγῳ τὸν ὅλον τόπον ὡς
ἐπιλογικόν,[5] ὃν δὴ διϊὼν ὄψεται, καὶ ὅλην παραπέμ-
ψεις αὐτὸν τῷ λόγῳ τὴν ὁδὸν ἐκφράζων ἠπείρους,
ὄρη, πελάγη. εἶτα μετὰ ταῦτα ἐπιστήσας αὐτὸν τῇ
πόλει ἐρεῖς οἷα κάλλη διαδέξεται αὐτόν, καὶ οἷα προ-
απαντήσει αὐτῷ τῆς πόλεως θεάματα, ἄλση καὶ πο-
ταμοὶ καὶ ὅσα τοιαῦτα. 15. προσθήσεις δὲ τοῖς ἐπιλόγοις καὶ ὅτι ἔστηκεν ἡ πόλις ἤδη πρὸ τῶν πυλῶν σὺν
ὁλοκλήροις τοῖς γένεσι προαπαντῶσα, δεξιουμένη,
εὐχομένη τῷ κρείττονι οὐκ εἰς μακράν σε θεάσασθαι·
μὴ τοίνυν διαψεύσῃς αὐτὴν τῆς ἐλπίδος μηδὲ εἰς ἀηδίαν τὴν προσδοκίαν αὐτῆς μεταβάλῃς. ὥσπερ γὰρ
τὸν Ἀπόλλω πολλάκις ἐδέχετο τοῖς Σμινθίοις, ἡνίκα
ἐξῆν θεοὺς προφανῶς ἐπιδημεῖν εἰς ἀνθρώπους, οὕτω
καὶ σὲ ἡ πόλις προσδέχεται, καὶ ποιηταὶ μὲν εὐτρε-
πεῖς ἔχοντες ἤδη Μουσῶν ἔργα πεποιημένα, καὶ συγ-
γραφεῖς καὶ πάντες πρὸς ὕμνον σὸν καὶ εὐφημίαν
εὐτρεπεῖς· 16. καὶ νόμιζε τὴν πόλιν αὐτὴν παρεστῶ-
σαν παρακαλεῖν καὶ τῶν αὑτῆς ἀρχαίων ὑπομιμνή-
σκειν, ὡς οὐδεμιᾶς τῶν ὑπηκόων λείπεται, τάχα που
καὶ πολλῶν κρείττων· δίδου τι καὶ σεμνύνεσθαι τῷ

it is not inferior to the greatest cities, you must come see it. For just as someone who glories in his wealth and who has it in abundance takes pride in his exceptional possessions, so it befits a governor to be proud of his greatest cities and hasten to visit those offering the greater advantage, namely oratory and all else that leads to virtue."

14. Then, as an epilogue, you should describe in your speech all the territory he will in fact see as he passes through it, and you will escort him in your speech along his entire route, as you describe the continents, mountains, and seas. Then bring him to the city and tell what beautiful features will greet him, and what sights of the city will meet his eyes—the groves, rivers, and all such things. 15. You should add to this epilogue: "The city already stands before her gates, with whole generations to meet you, to greet you, praying to heaven not to wait long to see you. So do not dash her hopes nor sour her expectations, for just as she often used to welcome Apollo to his Sminthian festival, in those days when gods could openly visit humans, so now the city awaits you. Poets are on hand with works of the Muses already prepared, prose writers too, all ready to hymn and praise you. 16. Imagine that the city herself is standing at your side, inviting you and reminding you of her ancient traditions, and how she is not inferior to any of your subjects' cities—perhaps even superior to many. Give her ambassador something to be

---

⁵ ὡς ἐπιλογικόν obel. RW

πρεσβεύσαντι, καὶ γὰρ ἀκήκοας ὡς οὐ φαῦλος ἐν πρώτοις

428 τῶν μὴ σύ γε μῦθον ἐλέγξῃς
μηδὲ πόδας,

καθάπερ τις ἥρως πρεσβεύων παρ᾿ Ὁμήρῳ φησί. πεί-θομαι δὲ σὺν ἐμαυτῷ καὶ τὸν Ἀπόλλω παρεῖναι τὸν Σμίνθιον· τί γὰρ οὐκ ἔμελλεν ἀνδρὶ μουσικῷ καὶ λο-γίῳ σοὶ προσεῖναι;

17. Ἐὰν δὲ τύχῃ φθάσας τὴν θέαν τῆς πόλεως πρὸς ἣν ἡ κλῆσις αὐτῷ, αὐτὰ πάλιν ταῦτα τὰ τῆς πόλεως ὡς πρὸς εἰδότα ὑπομιμνήσκων λέγε, τὴν μὲν αὐτὴν ἀκολουθίαν τῶν κεφαλαίων σώζων ὡς διῃρήκαμεν, μεθοδεύων δὲ ἄλλως τὰ ἐγκώμια, οἷον τυγχάνεις μὲν θεασάμενος τὸ κάλλος τῆς πόλεως καὶ τὴν θέσιν, εἰ δέ σε ᾕρηκεν ὁ πόθος, ἴθι καὶ δεύτερον καὶ πολλάκις· οἱ γὰρ ἐρασταὶ τῶν ἐρωμένων εἰώθασιν ἐμπίπλασθαι μὲν πολλάκις, ἀποσχισθέντες δὲ καὶ εὐθὺς ἐρᾶν.

18. Καὶ τοιούτοις χρήσῃ νοήμασιν ἐν τοῖς κεφα-λαίοις. εἰ δὲ βούλει καὶ ἀπὸ προοιμίων ἀκούειν, λεγέ-σθω πάλιν διὰ βραχέων. οὐκοῦν ἐν μὲν τῷ προοιμίῳ εὐθὺς ἐρεῖς· ᾕρηκας τὴν πόλιν τὴν ἡμετέραν τῷ πόθῳ, ὦ πάντων ἀρχόντων ἄριστε, καὶ τοῦτό σοι τῶν ἐρώ-των σημεῖον ἔσται, πέπομφε πάλιν καλοῦσα καὶ δεύτερον, οὐδεμίαν ἡμέραν ἐνεγκεῖν δυνηθεῖσα, ἀλλ᾿ ὥσπερ οἱ

μανικῶν τόξοις πληγέντες ἐρώτων

proud of, and since you have heard that he is no mean figure among the leading men,

> do not disrespect the plea of these men,
>   nor their coming here,

as a hero[6] on an embassy in Homer says. I am confident that Sminthian Apollo too is here by my side, for how could he not be on hand for one as cultured and eloquent as you?"

17. If he has already seen the city to which he is being invited, then mention those same features of the city, but in the form of a reminder to one who is already familiar with them. Preserve the same order of sections as we laid out, but present the praise differently. For example, "You have seen the beauty of the city and its location. If longing for it has seized you, come back again and often, for lovers regularly grow tired of their beloved, but as soon as they are separated fall in love again."

18. Such are the thoughts you should employ in the main sections. If, however, you wish to hear the procedure from the introduction on, here is a brief account. In the introduction, say straightaway, "You have captivated our city with desire for you, O best of all governors, and this will be a sign to you of her love: she has sent another embassy to invite you a second time, unable to bear a single day without you. Just as those who are

> struck by the arrows of frenzied love[7]

---

[6] Phoenix in the embassy to Achilles (*Il.* 9.522–23).

[7] Part of an unknown hexameter.

οὐκ ἀνέχονται μὴ τοὺς ἐρωμένους ὁρᾶν, οὕτως ἐπὶ σοὶ
ἐκχυθεῖσα ἡ πόλις μικροῦ μὲν ἅπασα ἐκινδύνευεν
εἰσδραμεῖν· 19. πέπομφε δὲ ὃν ᾤετο μάλιστα πείσειν
σε τὸ δεύτερον· ηὔχετο μὲν οὖν τῷ θεῷ μηδὲ τὴν
ἀρχὴν ἀπολιπεῖν, μηδὲ ἄλλην προτιμοτέραν ἑαυτῆς
ἡγήσασθαι. ἐπεὶ δὲ νικᾷς ἐν πᾶσι καὶ ἔδει παραχω-
ρεῖν ἕως ἐξῆν, συγχωρήσασα πάλιν ἱκετεύει παρ'
αὑτὴν ἐλθεῖν σε καὶ δεύτερον.

20. Εἶτα ἐπιβαλεῖς τὰ ἐγκώμια τῆς πόλεως ἐκ μεταχειρίσεως λέγων· εἰ μὲν οὖν ἠγνόεις παρ' ἣν σπεύ-
429 δεις, ἔδει καὶ διδάσκειν τυχόν· εἰ δὲ τὴν Ἀλεξάνδρου
πόλιν τοῦ Διὸς οὐκ ἀγνοεῖς, οὐδὲ τῶν ἀρχαίων [οὐδὲ][6]
τῶν παρ' ἡμῖν οὐδὲν ἴσως ἀγνοοῦντι ⟨τί⟩[7] σοι ἐρῶ;
καὶ ἕξεις λοιπὸν τῆς μνήμης καιρὸν τῶν ἀρχαίων· 21.
διὰ γὰρ τούτων σε ἐλθεῖν παρ' ἑαυτὴν ἔπεισε καὶ
πρότερον, νῦν δὲ οὐκ ἀξιοῦσα πάλιν ὀφθῆναι μᾶλλον
ταύτην πεποίηται τὴν κλῆσιν, ἀλλὰ τοὐναντίον ἀξιοῦσα σὲ διὰ τὰς ἀρετὰς ἰδεῖν· οὐ γὰρ ἀγνοεῖ τὴν σὴν
δικαιοσύνην· οἷς καὶ συνάψεις αὐτοῦ τὰ ἐγκώμια πανταχοῦ προστιθεὶς ἐφ' ἑκάστου τῶν ἐπιχειρημάτων τὸ
ὅτι διὰ ταῦτά σε καλεῖ. δεῖ γὰρ ἐν τοῖς κλητικοῖς καὶ
τὰς αἰτίας τῆς κλήσεως προστιθέναι, ἵνα τὸ ἴδιον ἔχῃ
τοῦ κλητικοῦ, ὥσπερ καὶ ἐν ταῖς ἄλλαις ὑποθέσεσι τὰ
ἑκάστῃ οἰκεῖα.

22. Μετὰ δὲ τὰ ἐγκώμια τοῦ ἄρχοντος ἐκ μεθόδου
πάλιν ἐρεῖς πρότερον μὲν τὴν θέσιν τῆς χώρας καὶ
τῆς πόλεως, εἶτα τὸ κάλλος τῆς πόλεως· ὡραΐζεται

[6] secl. Nitsche, RW   [7] suppl. Walz, Bursian, RW

cannot bear not to see their beloved, so devoted is the city to you that she nearly came running to you en masse. 19. Instead, she has sent the one person she considered most likely to persuade you to visit her a second time. Indeed, she prayed to the gods that you not leave her in the first place, nor hold any other city in greater honor. But since you prevail in all matters, she was forced to yield until the possibility could arise. So, after acquiescing, she again begs you to return to her once more."

20. Next, you should include praise of the city in the following manner. "Now, if you were unfamiliar with the city to which you are headed, perhaps I would need to inform you, but since you are familiar with the city of Alexander, Zeus' son, and no doubt fully aware of our ancient legends, what can I tell you?" Here you will have the opportunity to mention those legends. 21. "These were the reasons the city persuaded you to visit her last time, but now she has issued this invitation not in order to be seen again, but, on the contrary, in order to see *you* because of your virtues, for she is well acquainted with your sense of justice." Here you should include praise of the governor, always appending to each argument, "This is why she is inviting you." In invitation speeches it is necessary to add the reasons for the invitation, so that it maintains what is essential to an invitation speech, just as in other subjects one must add what is distinctive to each.

22. After praising the governor, you should follow the prescribed order[8] and speak first of the location of the country and city, and then of the city's beauty. "The city

---

[8] Cf. §14.

μὲν γὰρ ἡ πόλις κάλλεσιν ἱερῶν καὶ στοῶν καὶ λουτρῶν μεγέθεσιν, ὡς αὐτὸς ἑώρακας, ἀλλὰ ταῦτα σύμπαντα μικρὰ πρὸς τὴν σὴν θέαν ὑπολαμβάνει· τί γὰρ
οὐκ ἐξαίρετον τῶν παρ᾽ ἡμῖν; τί δ᾽ οὐ κάλλιστον; οὐχ
ἵππων ἄμιλλαι; οὐ θεάτρων τέρψεις καὶ πανηγύρεων;
καὶ ὅσα τοιαῦτα προείρηται ἡμῖν ἐπὶ τοῦ ⟨μὴ⟩[8] φθά-
σαντος [κλητικοῦ][9] ἐρεῖς.

23. Εἰ δὲ παρὰ πόλιν καλοίης ἄρχοντα μὴ πάνυ τι
σεμνὸν μηδὲ ἀρχαῖον ἔχουσαν, ὅπερ οὐκ οἶμαι, τὴν
θέσιν ἐρεῖς μετὰ τὰ προοίμια τῆς χώρας, εἶτα τῆς
πόλεως, εἶτα τοῖς ὅλοις ἐφεξῆς χρήσῃ κεφαλαίοις·
ἀναπληρώσει γάρ σοι ἡ θέσις τὸν τῆς πόλεως ἔπαινον.

24. Ἔνιοι δὲ διαιροῦσι τὸν κλητικὸν μετὰ τὰ προοίμια ἑτέρως, κατὰ ἔνωσιν ὡς ἂν εἴποι τις τὸ τῆς
πόλεως ἐγκώμιον καὶ τὸ τοῦ ἄρχοντος προάγοντες,
τοῖς δὲ ἄλλοις οὕτως, ὡς ἤδη φθάσαντες εἴπομεν,
χρώμενοι· κατὰ ἔνωσιν δὲ ἔφην οὕτως, οἷον θαυμα-
στὸν μὲν ἡμεῖς αὐχοῦμεν οἰκιστήν, οὗτος δὲ γένος·
φιλάνθρωπος ἡ πόλις· καὶ τούτου τὸ πλεονέκτημα.
25. ἢ τοὐναντίον τὰ τοῦ ἄρχοντος προτάττουσιν, ὅπερ
ἄμεινον, τὰ δὲ τῆς πόλεως τοῖς ἐκείνου ὑποβάλλου-
σιν, οἷον γένος σοι λαμπρὸν καὶ ἡμῖν οἰκιστὴς θαυ-
μαστός· δίκαιος ⟨εἶ⟩,[10] οὐδὲ ἡ πόλις ἀμοιρεῖ τοῦ πλε-
ονεκτήματος· φιλανθρωπίαν τιμᾷς, καὶ ἡ πόλις ἡ
καλοῦσα φιλάνθρωπος. προάξεις δὲ καὶ τὸν κλητικόν,
ὡς ἂν αὐτὸς ἔχειν δοκιμάσῃς.

[8] suppl. RW   [9] secl. RW   [10] suppl. Bursian, RW

prides itself on its beautiful temples and colonnades and on the grandeur of its baths, as you have seen for yourself, but it considers all of them insignificant in comparison with seeing you. What is not exceptional in our city? What is not of utmost beauty? Are there not horse races, not the pleasures of theaters and festivals?" You should include here all such things that we mentioned in the case of someone who had not previously visited.[9]

23. If you are inviting a governor to a city which has nothing impressive or ancient to speak of (which I consider unlikely), after the introduction you should speak of the location of the country, then that of the city, and then employ all the sections that follow. In that way, the topic of location will fill in for praise of the city.

24. Some people divide up the invitation speech differently after the introduction. They treat as a unity, so to speak, praise of the city and that of the governor, while employing the other topics in the way we have described. By unity, I mean, for example, "We are proud of our marvelous founder, and the governor is proud of his race; our city is humane, and that is his outstanding quality."[10] 25. Or, as I prefer, they put the governor's praises first and subordinate the city's to his. For example, "Your race is illustrious and our founder is marvelous; you are just and the city is not devoid of this outstanding quality; you esteem humanity and the city inviting you is humane." Ultimately, you should handle the invitation speech as you yourself consider best.

[9] Cf. §4.

[10] For a similar technique of praising two entities by comparisons, cf. 2.5.18–19.

2.14. ΠΕΡΙ ΣΥΝΤΑΚΤΙΚΟΥ

1. Ὁ συνταττόμενος δῆλός ἐστιν ἀνιώμενος ἐπὶ τῷ χωρισμῷ, καὶ εἰ μὴ ὄντως ἀνιῷτο, προσποιήσεται πεπονθέναι πρὸς ἐκείνους ἐρωτικὸν οἷς συντάττεται. προὔλαβε μὲν οὖν ὁ θεῖος Ὅμηρος καὶ τοῦτο τὸ εἶδος· κινῶν γὰρ ἐκ τῆς Φαιακίας Ὀδυσσέα ποιεῖ συνταττόμενον αὐτὸν Ἀλκινόῳ καὶ Φαίαξι καὶ μικρὸν ὕστερον Ἀρήτῃ τῇ Ἀλκινόου, καὶ περιτέθεικεν αὐτῷ συνταττομένῳ τῇ γυναικὶ ταῦτα τὰ ἔπη·

χαῖρέ μοι, ὦ βασίλεια, διαμπερὲς εἰσόκε γῆρας
ἔλθοι καὶ θάνατος, τά τ᾽ ἐπ᾽ ἀνθρώποισι
   πέλονται,
αὐτὰρ ἐγὼ νέομαι, σὺ δὲ τέρπεο τῷδ᾽ ἐνὶ οἴκῳ
παισί τε καὶ λαοῖσι καὶ Ἀλκινόῳ βασιλῆϊ.

2. πρὸς δὲ τοὺς Φαίακας καὶ Ἀλκίνοον ἡνίκα συνετάττετο φησὶν αὐτὸν εἰρηκέναι ἐν τῇ ῥαψῳδίᾳ ταῦτα·

Ἀλκίνοε κρεῖον, πάντων ἀριδείκετε λαῶν,
πέμπετέ με σπείσαντες ἀπήμονα, χαίρετε δ᾽
   αὐτοί·

314

2.14. THE LEAVE-TAKING SPEECH
(*syntaktikos logos*)

1. Someone who is taking leave of others manifests his pain at parting. Even if he is not truly distraught, he must pretend to suffer pangs of love for those he is leaving behind. Divine Homer introduced this genre too, for when he sends Odysseus off from Phaeacia, he shows him taking leave of Alcinous, the Phaeacians, and soon thereafter Alcinous' wife Arete, and ascribes these verses to him as he says goodbye to the queen:[1]

> May you fare well, O Queen, for all your days until
>   old age
> and death come, as they do to all humans.
> I shall go. I bid you take delight in this home of
>   yours,
> in your children, your people, and Alcinous your king.

2. And when Odysseus was bidding farewell to the Phaeacians and Alcinous in the episode,[2] Homer has him say:

> Lord Alcinous, most distinguished of all the people,
> may you all pour libations and send me off safely, and
>   yourselves fare well,

[1] *Od.* 13.59–62.
[2] *Od.* 13.38–41. The term ῥαψῳδία could possibly refer to the entire book (as it does in Eustathius' commentary).

315

ἤδη γὰρ τετέλεσται ἅ μοι φίλος ἤθελε θυμός,
πομπὴ καὶ φίλα δῶρα,

καὶ τὰ ἑξῆς. ἐπειδὴ δὲ δεῖ τὸν ῥήτορα καὶ περιεργό-
τερον χρῆσθαι τῷ εἴδει καὶ ἐξεργασίᾳ πλείονι, φέρε
μὴ ἀφιστάμενοι τοῦ Ὁμηρικοῦ ἔθους διέλωμεν.

3. Χάριν ὁμολογήσει τῇ πόλει, ἐξ ἧς ἡ ἐπάνοδος,
431 ἐπαινέσει δὲ αὐτήν, ὁπόθεν ἂν ὁ καιρὸς αὐτῷ διδῷ τὰ
ἐγκώμια, οἷον ἀπὸ τῶν ἀρχαίων εἴ τι σεμνὸν ἔχοι,
ἀπὸ τῶν ἀέρων, ἀπὸ τοῦ εἴδους τοῦ κάλλους, οἷον ἀπὸ
στοῶν καὶ λιμένων καὶ ἀκροπόλεως καὶ ἱερῶν πολυ-
τελῶν καὶ ἀγαλμάτων. 4. ἐπαινέσει δὲ μετὰ ταῦτα καὶ
τὰς ἐν αὐτῇ πανηγύρεις καὶ ἱερομηνίας καὶ μουσεῖα
καὶ θέατρα καὶ ἀγώνων διαθέσεις, πανταχοῦ παρα-
πλέκων, ἵνα μὴ ἁπλοῦν γένηται ἐγκώμιον, τὸ ὅτι
ἀνιᾶται μέλλων τούτων χωρίζεσθαι ἐφ' ἑκάστῳ σχεδὸν εἰπεῖν τῶν νοημάτων, ἵνα συντακτικὸν εἶδος ὁ
λόγος λάβῃ. ἐπαινέσει δὲ καὶ τοὺς ἄνδρας, οἷον ἱε-
ρέας, εἰ τύχοι, δᾳδούχους τε καὶ ἱεροφάντας, καὶ τὰ
ἤθη τῶν ἀνδρῶν, ὅτι ἥμεροι καὶ φιλόξενοι· καὶ ἑταί-
ροις δὲ ὁμοίως συντάξεται, κἀνταῦθα ἐνδεικνύμενος
τὸ ἀλγεῖν καὶ δακρύειν ἐπὶ τῷ χωρισμῷ.

5. Μετὰ δὲ τὸ πρῶτον μέρος ἥξει πάλιν ἐφ' ἕτερον
μέρος, ἐν ᾧ μνησθήσεται καὶ τῶν τόπων εἰς οὓς ἐπε-

for already has been accomplished what my dear
    heart desired,
an escort and loving gifts,

and so forth. Since, however, an orator must employ this
genre more extensively and with greater elaboration, let
us provide an analysis, while not departing from the manner of Homer.

3. The speaker should express his gratitude to the city
he is leaving to return home, and praise it for whatever
attributes the particular situation warrants. Examples
include any distinguished ancient tradition it may have,
its climate, and its beautiful appearance, including, for
example, its colonnades, harbors, acropolis, magnificent
temples, and works of art. 4. Next, he should extol its
festivals, holy-month celebrations, schools, theaters, and
hosting of games. However, to keep the speech from becoming a mere encomium, he must continually weave in,
after practically every statement, how pained he is at being
separated from these attractions. This insures that it takes
on the form of a leave-taking speech. He should also praise
individuals, for example, priests, and, if it is the case,
torchbearers and hierophants,[3] as well as the gentle and
hospitable character of the people. He should likewise
take leave of his comrades, here too expressing pain and
tears at having to part.

5. After this first part, he should proceed to the second.
Here he should mention the places to which he will travel.

---

[3] Torchbearers led the nighttime processions of the Eleusinian mysteries at Athens; hierophants initiated the members; cf.
2.3.15.

λεύσεται. καὶ εἰ μὲν εἶεν ἄγνωστοι οἱ ἄνδρες παρ' οὓς καὶ σπεύδειν ἔκρινεν, ἐρεῖ· πῶς ἄρα ἡμᾶς ὑποδέξονται, τίνες ἄρα πάλιν συνήθεις; εἰ δὲ παρὰ τὴν αὑτοῦ πατρίδα σπεύδει, ἐρεῖ· τίς γὰρ οὐκ ἂν ποθήσειε τὴν οἰκείαν; ἴσως γὰρ ἀκούετε καὶ ὑμεῖς· ἔνδοξος γὰρ καὶ λαμπρὰ παρὰ πᾶσιν ἡμῶν ἡ πόλις.

6. Εἶτα συνεύξῃ που τούτοις παρὰ τῶν ποιητῶν ἐξελὼν τὰ κάλλιστα, καὶ ὅτι πολλῶν ἂν χρημάτων προτιμήσειας πυνθάνεσθαι δὴ περὶ αὐτῶν τὰ βελτίω, καὶ ὅτι ἐπιλήσῃ αὐτῶν οὐδέποτε, καὶ ὅτι διαδώσεις λόγον ἁπανταχοῦ θαυμάζων αὐτῶν τὰ ἐξαίρετα. συνεύξῃ δὲ ἑαυτῷ καὶ πλοῦν ἀγαθὸν καὶ ἐπάνοδον χρηστήν, καὶ ὅτι, ἂν οὕτω τύχῃ καὶ εἰ παῖδας ποιήσειας, ἀποστελεῖς αὐτοὺς ὀψομένους αὐτῶν πόλιν.

7. Ἐὰν δὲ τῇ πατρίδι συντάττεσθαι μέλλῃς, ἔστω μέν σοι ὁμοίως τὰ πρῶτα ἐρωτικά, καὶ ἐχέτω ἔνδειξιν τῆς λύπης ὁ λόγος, ἣν ἔχεις τῶν τοσούτων καλῶν κἀγαθῶν χωριζόμενος, τὰ δὲ δεύτερα τοῦ λόγου ἐχέτω ἔπαινον τῆς πόλεως ἐφ' ἣν σπεύδεις, οἷον τῆς δόξης, τῆς εὐκλείας, ὅτι πυνθάνομαι τὴν πόλιν εἶναι μεγάλην καὶ θαυμαστήν, ὅτι ἀκούω λόγων αὐτὴν εἶναι καὶ Μουσῶν ἐργαστήριον. 8. ἐνδιατρίψεις δὲ τῷ λόγῳ τῷ περὶ τῆς χρείας καὶ τῆς αἰτίας δι' ἣν ἐπείγῃ, ὅτι ἐκεῖ πυνθάνομαι Πιερίαν ὄντως, ἐκεῖ τὸν Ἑλικῶνα· καὶ ὅταν αὐξήσῃς τοῦτο τὸ μέρος, καὶ τὴν χρείαν ἐρεῖς δι' ἣν σπεύδεις· δεῖ γὰρ ταῖς ἀνάγκαις τοῦτο θεραπεύειν· ὁρῶμεν δὲ καὶ τὴν φύσιν τοῦ παντὸς πειθομένην ταῖς τῆς φύσεως ἀνάγκαις καὶ οἷς ὁ πατὴρ τῶν

If he is unacquainted with the people he has decided to visit, he should say, "How then will they receive us? Who will be our comrades then?" If, on the other hand, he is going to his own country, he should say, "Who would not long for his own country? Perhaps you have heard about it, for our city is famous and illustrious among all peoples."

6. Then, at some point, you should say a prayer for those you are leaving. Select the best examples from the poets, and say that you would give much wealth to hear good news about them, that you will never forget them, and that you will spread the word everywhere, expressing your admiration for their outstanding attributes. Say a prayer for yourself as well, for a good voyage and successful return home, and say that if you are fortunate to have children, you will send them to see their city.

7. If you are going to leave your own hometown, the first part of the speech should once again[4] contain expressions of love and exhibit the distress you feel at being separated from so many excellent things, while the second part should contain praise of the city to which you are heading, citing, for example, its fame and glory. "I understand that the city is great and marvelous," or "I hear that it is a workshop of oratory and of the Muses." 8. You should dwell on the portion that explains why you need to make such haste. "I am told that it is a veritable Pieria there, a Helicon."[5] Once you have amplified this portion, you should state the need that compels you to go, for you must attribute your departure to the power of necessity. "We see that the physical world obeys the demands of nature and the laws that the father of all has laid down. Therefore

---

[4] Cf. §1.   [5] Haunts of the Muses in Thessaly and Boeotia. That city is undoubtedly Athens; cf. §4 and 2.13.9, 12.

ὅλων ἐνομοθέτησε. διὸ καὶ πᾶσα ἀνάγκη τῷ νόμῳ
πείθεσθαι τῆς πατρίδος.

9. Τοῦτο δέ σοι ἁρμόσει λέγειν οὐχ ὅταν ἀπὸ τῆς
αὑτοῦ πατρίδος ἐφ' ἑτέραν σπεύδῃς γῆν, ἀλλ' ὅταν
ἀπ' ἄλλης εἰς τὴν σαυτοῦ πατρίδα καλῇ. ἐρεῖς δὲ ἐν
τούτῳ ὅτι λαμπρὰ καὶ μεγάλη ἡ πατρὶς καὶ ἀξία
ποθεῖσθαι, ἀλλ' ὅμως ὑμεῖς ἐμοὶ ποθεινότεροι. καλὸν
μὲν καὶ τὸ περιπτύξασθαι γονέας καὶ ἀδελφοὺς καὶ
γένος, ἀλλ' ὅμως οὐ μείονας ἔχω καὶ περὶ ὑμᾶς τοὺς
ἔρωτας· ἀλλὰ τί γὰρ δεῖ ποιεῖν· ἀνάγκη γὰρ ἐπείγει.
ταῦτα δὲ ἐρεῖς, ὅταν εἰς τὴν ἑαυτοῦ πατρίδα, ὡς ἔφαμεν, ἀπὸ τῆς ἀλλοδαπῆς ἀπαίρειν μέλλῃς. ἐρεῖς δὲ ἐν
ἀρχῇ τοῦ δευτέρου μέρους τῆς συντακτικῆς ταῦτα
εὐθὺς μετὰ τὰ ἐρωτικά, εἶτα δὲ ἄλλα τάξεις ἐφεξῆς,
ὡς ἔφαμεν.

10. Ἐπανέλθωμεν δὴ πάλιν εἰς τὸν προκείμενον
λόγον, ὅταν τις ἀπαίρειν ἀπὸ τῆς ἰδίας πατρίδος εἰς
ἄλλην πόλιν βούληται. οὐκοῦν ἐφεξῆς μετὰ τὰ προειρημένα περὶ τούτου, λέγω δὴ μετὰ τὸ εἰπεῖν ὅτι πυνθάνομαι τὴν Πιερίαν ὄντως ἐκεῖ τυγχάνειν καὶ τὸν
Ἑλικῶνα, ⟨ἐρεῖς⟩[1] ὡς ἐνδέχεται ἔτι τὰ τῆς ἡλικίας
433 λόγους πονεῖν. εἶτα ἐπάξεις πάλιν ὅτι ἐρανιοῦμαι καὶ
λόγους καὶ φιλοσοφίαν, μαθήσομαι δι' ὑμᾶς καὶ τὴν
κοινὴν πατρίδα, καὶ ὅταν αἴσθωμαι τελέως οἷός τε ὢν
τὴν ἐνεγκοῦσαν ὠφελεῖν, τότε πάλιν ποθήσω τὴν πόλιν καὶ τὸ γένος. 11. τίς γὰρ Σειρῆσι παρατυχὼν ἢ
παρὰ Λωτοφάγους ἀφικόμενος οὐκ ἂν ὑμᾶς προτιμή-
σειεν;

320

it is absolutely necessary to obey the law of one's home-town."

9. It will be appropriate for you to say this when you are being summoned from another land to your home-town, but not when you are going from your hometown to another land. In the former case, you may say, "My home-town is splendid, great, and deserving of my longing, but even so, to me you are more desirable. It is good to em-brace parents, brothers, and kin, but all the same my love for you is no less strong. But what can I do? Necessity compels me." You should say this when, as we said, you are going to leave a foreign city for your home. You should say it at the beginning of the second portion of a leave-taking talk[6] right after the expressions of love. You should then add the other topics afterward, as we prescribed.[7]

10. But let us return to the proposed speech, that is, when a speaker wishes to leave his own city for another. In that case, right after the statement, "I am told that it is a veritable Pieria and Helicon there," you should say: "It still admits people my age to study oratory." Then you should add, "I shall obtain my share of oratory and phi-losophy. I shall learn for your sakes and for the sake of the city we share, and when I feel fully able to benefit the town that gave me birth, then I shall again long for my city and my family. 11. For who encountering the Sirens or coming to the Lotus Eaters would not prefer you?

---

[6] For the distinction between a speech and a talk (*lalia*), cf. §15 below.

[7] In §§4–6.

---

[1] suppl. Bursian, RW

ὡς οὐδὲν γλύκιον ἧς πατρίδος οὐδὲ τοκήων,

ὡς Ὅμηρός πού φησι,

ἧς γαίης καὶ καπνὸν ἀποθρώσκοντα νοῆσαι.

12. Μετὰ δὲ ταῦτα συνεύξῃ τῇ τε πόλει τὰ κάλλιστα, καὶ σαυτῷ περὶ τῆς ὁδοῦ καὶ περὶ τοῦ τυχεῖν
τούτων ὧνπερ σπουδάζεις σὺν ἀγαθῇ καὶ λαμπρᾷ
τύχῃ, καὶ περὶ τῆς ἐπανόδου πάλιν· καλλωπίσεις δὲ
τὸν λόγον καὶ εἰκόσι καὶ ἱστορίαις καὶ παραβολαῖς
καὶ ταῖς ἄλλαις γλυκύτησι καὶ ἐκφράσεσί τισιν ἐν τῷ
ἐπαίνῳ τῆς πόλεως, στοῶν καὶ λιμένων καὶ ποταμῶν
καὶ πηγῶν καὶ ἀλσέων, καὶ ἦθος δὲ περιθήσεις τῷ
λόγῳ μέτριον καὶ ἁπλοῦν καὶ δεξιόν, τὴν ἐπιείκειαν
πανταχοῦ ἐμφανίζων μετὰ τοῦ μὴ καθαιρεῖν τὸ ἀξίωμα μηδὲ ὑποπεπτωκέναι.

13. Μεμνῆσθαι δέ σε χρὴ τοῦ θεωρήματος ὅτι
πᾶσα ἀνάγκη καὶ πρώτην ἐπαινεῖν καὶ πρώτην θαυμάζειν τὴν πόλιν πρὸς ἣν ἂν ὁ λόγος σοι γίγνηται,
ἀφορᾶν δὲ χρὴ καὶ πρὸς τὰς πόλεις εἰς ἃς σπεύδει
τις, καὶ εἰ μὲν ἐφάμιλλοί εἰσιν αἱ πόλεις ἢ ὀλίγῳ
βελτίους ἢ καὶ πολλῷ τῆς πόλεως πρὸς ἣν ἂν συν-
τάττηταί τις, ἐρεῖς ὅτι οὐ μείων ἐκείνης αὕτη· δεῖ γὰρ
μηδαμῶς καθαιρεῖν τὴν πόλιν ἣν ἐπαινεῖν προειλό-
μεθα καὶ πρὸς ἣν συνταττόμεθα. 14. εἰ δὲ πολλῷ ἐλάττους εἶεν αἱ πόλεις παρ' ἃς ἂν σπεύδῃ τις, τότε τὴν
χρείαν μᾶλλον αὐξήσεις δι' ἣν σπεύδεις, ὅτι κρείττων
μὲν ἡ ὑμετέρα πόλις πρὸς ἣν συντάττομαι, ἡ δὲ

for nothing is sweeter than one's homeland and
  parents,[8]

as Homer says,

and to see even the smoke rising from his own land."[9]

12. After that, you should pray for the finest blessings
for the city and for yourself—for your journey, for success
with splendid good fortune in your endeavors, and for
returning home again. Embellish your speech with images, stories, comparisons, and other pleasantries, and, in
praising the city, include some descriptions of its colonnades, harbors, rivers, springs, and groves. You should
endow your speech with a character that is moderate, sin-
cere (*haplous*), and courteous (*dexios*), and throughout
you should display evenhandedness, avoiding both deni-
gration and flattery.

13. You must keep in mind the rule that it is absolutely
necessary to praise and admire first and foremost the city
you are addressing. You must also take into account the
cities to which you are going. If they are comparable to,
slightly better than, or even far superior to the one you are
leaving, say, "This city is not inferior to that other one," for
we must in no way denigrate the city which we have undertaken to praise and to which we are bidding farewell.
14. But if the cities to which you are going happen to be
far inferior, then you should put greater stress on why you
must go. "Your city, to which I bid farewell, is superior, but

---

[8] Hom. *Od.* 9.34, also quoted at 2.3.13.

[9] *Od.* 1.58–59 (slightly adapted from ἱέμενος καὶ καπνὸν
ἀποθρῴσκοντα νοῆσαι | ἧς γαίης).

ἀναγκαία χρεία τοῦ κτήματος, ὃ βούλομαι ἐρανίσα-
σθαι, μόλις ἂν <εἰ μὴ>[2] δι' ἐκείνης γένοιτο.

434   15. Ἔστω δέ σοι τὸ μέτρον τοῦ λόγου ἡ χρεία. καὶ
εἰ μὲν ὡς ἐν λαλιᾷ, βραχὺς δὲ ὁ τῆς λαλιᾶς λόγος,
διὰ συντόμων ἐρεῖς, καὶ μάλιστα ὅταν πρὸς τῇ λαλιᾷ
ταύτῃ μέλλῃς ἕτερον εὐθὺς παρέχεσθαι λόγον· εἰ δὲ
συντάξασθαι μόνον προθυμηθείης, καὶ ταύτην ἐπίδειξιν μόνην κατ' ἐκείνην τὴν ἡμέραν ποιήσασθαι, προάξεις τὴν συντακτικὴν συγγραφικῶς καὶ ἄχρι διακοσίων στίχων ἢ τριακοσίων, εἰ βουληθείης, καὶ οὐδείς
σοι μέμψεται εὖ φρονῶν.

2 tent. RW

324

the urgent need for what I wish to obtain could scarcely be satisfied except in that city."

15. Let need determine the length of the speech. If it is in the form of a talk (*lalia*)—which is short—then you will speak succinctly, especially if you are going to make another speech immediately after this talk. But if you intend only to bid farewell and to make this the sole performance of the day, you should compose the leave-taking talk in casual prose[10] of up to two hundred or three hundred lines if you so wish, and no reasonable person will find fault with you.

[10] For casual, nonperiodic prose (*syngraphikōs*) opposed to formal (*syntonos*) style, see 2.5.2, 4; 2.6.26–27; and 2.8.8.

2.15. ΠΕΡΙ ΜΟΝΩΙΔΙΑΣ

1. Ὅμηρος ὁ θεῖος ποιητὴς τά τε ἄλλα ἡμᾶς ἐπαί-
δευσε καὶ τὸ τῆς μονῳδίας εἶδος οὐ παραλέλοιπε· καὶ
γὰρ Ἀνδρομάχῃ καὶ Πριάμῳ καὶ τῇ Ἑκάβῃ λόγους
μονῳδικοὺς περιτέθεικεν οἰκείους ἑκάστῳ προσώπῳ,
ὥσπερ ἐκδιδάξαι βουλόμενος ἡμᾶς μηδὲ τούτων ἀπείρως ἔχειν. χρὴ τοίνυν λαβόντας παρὰ τοῦ ποιητοῦ
τὰς ἀφορμὰς ἐπεξεργάζεσθαι ταύτας γνόντας τὸ θεώρημα ἐξ ὧν ὁ ποιητὴς παρέδωκεν. 2. τί τοίνυν ἡ
μονῳδία βούλεται; θρηνεῖν καὶ κατοικτίζεσθαι, κἂν
μὲν μὴ προσήκων ᾖ ὁ τεθνεώς, αὐτὸν μόνον θρηνεῖν
τὸν ἀπελθόντα, παραμιγνύντα τὰ ἐγκώμια τοῖς θρήνοις, καὶ συνεχῶς τὸν θρῆνον ἐμφανίζειν, ἵνα μὴ ἀπο-
λύτως ἐγκώμιον ᾖ, ἀλλ᾽ ἵνα πρόφασις τοῦ θρήνου ᾖ
τὸ ἐγκώμιον· ἂν δὲ προσήκων ᾖ, οὐδὲν ἧττον καὶ
αὐτὸς ὁ λέγων οἰκτίσεται ἢ ὅτι ὀρφανὸς καταλέλει-
πται ἢ ὅτι ἀρίστου πατρὸς ἐστέρηται καὶ τὴν ἐρημίαν
ὀδύρεται τὴν ἑαυτοῦ αὐτός.

3. Ἐὰν δὲ καὶ πόλεως τύχῃ προεστὼς ὁ μεταστάς,
ἐρεῖς τι καὶ περὶ αὐτῆς τῆς πόλεως, μεταχειριζόμενος
καὶ ταύτης τὰ ἐγκώμια πρὸς τὴν ὑπόθεσιν, ὅτι λαμπρὰ μὲν ἡ πόλις, ὁ δὲ ἐγείρας αὐτὴν ὁ πεπτωκώς

2.15. THE MONODY

1. The divine poet Homer, who taught us so much else, did not neglect the genre of the monody (*monōdia*). He attributed monodic speeches to Andromache,[1] Priam,[2] and Hecuba[3] that were appropriate for each of their characters, as if he intended to provide instructions and familiarize us with these types.[4] Therefore it behooves us to take our starting points from Homer and elaborate on them, discerning the scheme from the examples the poet has left us. 2. What then is the intention of the monody? To lament and express one's own grief. If the deceased is not a relative, the point is simply to lament the departed one, and, while mixing praise with the lamentations, to emphasize the lament throughout, so that it does not become a mere encomium, but rather the encomium becomes the motivation for the lament. But if it is a relative, the speaker should pity himself no less, either because he has been left an orphan, or because he has lost an excellent father and bewails the emptiness that is now his.

3. If the deceased is a leader in the city, you should say a word about the city itself, treating its praises with a view to the subject. "The city is illustrious, but the one who

---

[1] *Il*. 22.477–514 and 24.725–45. [2] *Il*. 22.416–28.
[3] *Il*. 22.431–36 and 24.748–59. [4] For Homeric models of other speeches, cf. 2.3.13 (talk), 2.13.16 (invitation), 2.14.1–2 (leave-taking), and 2.16.2 (Sminthian oration).

ἐστιν. ἢ οὕτω· τίς ἐπιμελήσεται, τίς διασώσει, καθά-
435 περ ἐκεῖνος; ἐὰν δὲ νέος τύχῃ ὁ τελευτήσας, ἀπὸ τῆς
ἡλικίας τὸν θρῆνον κινήσεις, ἀπὸ τῆς φύσεως ὅτι
εὐφυής, ὅτι μεγάλας παρέσχεν τὰς ἐλπίδας, καὶ ἀπὸ
τῶν συμβάντων, ὅτι †ἀνύοντι†[1] αὐτῷ ἔμελλε μετὰ μικρὸν ὁ θάλαμος, ἔμελλον αἱ παστάδες· ἀπὸ τῶν περὶ
τὴν πόλιν, ὅτι ἡ πόλις ἐπίδοξος ἦν ἕξειν τὸν προστη-
σόμενον, τὸν δημηγορήσοντα, τὸν ἀγῶνας διαθή-
σοντα.

4. Πανταχοῦ δὲ ἐκ μεταχειρίσεως αὐτὰ ταῦτα
ἀφορμὰς ποιεῖσθαι τῶν θρήνων δεῖ. χρὴ τοίνυν ἐν
τούτοις τοῖς λόγοις εὐθὺς μὲν σχετλιάζειν ἐν ἀρχῇ
πρὸς δαίμονας καὶ πρὸς μοῖραν ἄδικον, πρὸς πεπρω-
μένην νόμον ὁρίσασαν ἄδικον, εἶτα ἀπὸ τοῦ κατεπεί-
γοντος εὐθὺς λαμβάνειν· οἷον ἐξήρπασαν, οἷα κατὰ
τοῦ πεσόντος ἐκώμασαν. ἀλλ' ἵνα μὴ πολλάκις ταὐτὰ[2]
λέγωμεν, ἁπλῶς χρήσῃ ταύτῃ τῇ τέχνῃ, καὶ διαιρήσεις πρὸς τὰς τοιαύτας ὑποθέσεις τὸν λόγον.

5. Διαιρήσεις δὲ τὴν μονῳδίαν εἰς χρόνους τρεῖς,
τὸν παρόντα εὐθὺς καὶ πρῶτον· μᾶλλον γὰρ ὁ λόγος
κινητικώτερος εἰ ἀπὸ τῶν ἐπ' ὄψιν καὶ τῶν νῦν συμβάντων οἰκτίζοι τις, εἰ τὴν ἡλικίαν ἢ τὸν τρόπον τοῦ
θανάτου λέγοι τις, εἰ μακρᾷ νόσῳ περιπεπτωκὼς εἴη,
εἰ ὀξὺς ὁ θάνατος· <ἢ>[3] ἀπὸ τῆς συνόδου τῶν παρόν-

---

[1] obel. RW: ἀνύων ὅτι αὐτῷ P: ἀνύων τι αὐτῷ p: ὅτι ἀνύειν
τι Spengel: συμβάντων ἂν, οἷον ὅτι αὐτῷ Bursian: [ἀνύων] ὅτι
αὐτῷ Soffel

raised it up has fallen." Or, "Who will care for it? Who will preserve it as he did?" If the deceased is young, you should stir up lament because of his young age, because of his nature ("he was talented and inspired high hopes"), because of the consequences ("the wedding chamber and bridal bed were soon to be his"[5]), or because of the city ("it expected to have in him a future leader, statesman, and organizer of games").

4. At every turn, our procedure must be to make these considerations the starting points of the lament. Therefore, right at the beginning of these speeches you must complain about the gods, unjust fate, and the destiny that ordained an unjust law, and then immediately take up the matter at hand. "What a man they have snatched away! How they exulted over his death!" But to avoid my repeating the same things over and over, you should apply this technique overall[6] and divide the speech according to the following subjects.

5. Divide the monody into three time periods. First and foremost is the present, for the speech is more moving if a speaker expresses pity over what is in plain sight and what is now the situation. One might speak of his age or the manner of death (whether he succumbed to a long illness or died suddenly), or refer to the present gathering:

[5] The text is doubtful. RW obelize ἀνύοντι. I hesitatingly translate Soffel's suggestion.

[6] That is, the student should complain (σχετλιάζειν) in all the divisions and therefore needs no further examples.

---

[2] πολλάκις ταὐτὰ Bursian: πολλὰ τοιαῦτα codd.

[3] suppl. Bursian, RW

των, ὅτι συνεληλύθασιν οὐκ εἰς θέατρον εὔδαιμον, οὐκ εἰς θέαν εὐκταίαν.

6. Εἶτα ἀπὸ τοῦ παρεληλυθότος χρόνου, οἷος ἦν ἐν νέοις ὅτε ἦν νέος, οἷος ἐν ἀνδράσιν ἀνὴρ τυγχάνων, ὅπως ὁμιλητικός, ὅπως ἤπιος, ὅπως ἐπὶ λόγοις διαπρέπων, ὅπως ἐν νεανίσκοις καὶ ἡλικιώταις γαῦρος, οἷος ἐν κυνηγεσίοις, οἷος ἐν γυμνασίοις.

7. Ἀπὸ δὲ τοῦ μέλλοντος, οἵας εἶχεν ἐλπίδας ἐπ' αὐτῷ τὸ γένος, εἶτα ἀποστροφῇ χρήσῃ· ὦ γένος λαμπρὸν καὶ εὐδόκιμον ἄχρι τῆς παρούσης ἡμέρας, ἐκόμας μὲν ἐπὶ χρυσῷ καὶ ὄλβῳ καὶ εὐγενείᾳ τῇ θρυλουμένῃ, ἀλλ' ἅπαντα συνέχεεν καὶ ἀνεσκεύασεν ὁ πεσών. τί τοιοῦτον κειμήλιον κέκτησαι οἷον ἀποβέβληκας; συνοδύρου οὖν καὶ πατρὶ καὶ μητρί, καὶ αὐξήσεις τὸν οἶκτον οἵων ἐλπίδων ἐστέρηνται.

8. Καὶ ἀπὸ τῆς πόλεως ἐπιχειρήσεις λέγων πάλιν, οἷος ἂν περὶ αὐτὴν ἐγένετο, οἷον ἂν παρέσχεν ἑαυτὸν εἰς φιλοτιμίαν, καὶ οἷον παρεῖχεν. κἂν μὲν τῶν πολιτευομένων ᾖ, ἐρεῖς τούτων τὰ πολλὰ ἐν τῷ παρεληλυθότι χρόνῳ· εἰ δὲ τῶν μελλόντων προστατεῖν, ταῦτα ἐρεῖς ἐν τῷ μέλλοντι, καὶ ὅλως ἐφαρμόσεις τοῖς χρόνοις ἀεὶ τὰ ἀπὸ τῶν προσώπων.

9. Εἶτα μετὰ τοὺς τρεῖς χρόνους διαγράψεις τὴν ἐκφοράν, τὴν σύνοδον τῆς πόλεως· εἴθε μὲν οὖν προεπέμπετο εἰς θάλαμον, εἴθε μὲν οὖν εἰς ἀποδημίαν ἐξ ἧς ἔμελλεν ἐπανιέναι, εἴθε ἀκροασόμενοι λόγων αὐτοῦ συνεληλύθειμεν.

"They have come together not for a happy show nor for a spectacle they wished to see."

6. Then there is the time gone by, including what he was like when a boy among boys, and as a man among men—how affable, how gentle, how distinguished in speaking, how stately among young men and his age mates; what a hunter, what an athlete!

7. As to the future, tell what hopes his family had for him, at which point you should apostrophize them: "O you illustrious and famous family—until, that is, this very day. You took pride in your gold and wealth and acclaimed high birth, but the deceased has confounded and destroyed it all! What family heirloom do you possess like the one you have lost?" Then mourn with the father and mother and amplify the grief by mentioning what hopes they have been stripped of.

8. You should also argue from the city's perspective. "What a champion he would have been for it, what a benefactor he would have proven to be—and already was." If he is a politician, you should speak of this mostly in the past, but if he is one of the upcoming leaders, you should speak of the future. In general, match personal attributes with the time period.

9. After the three time periods, you should describe the funeral procession and the gathering of the city. "Would that he were being escorted to his wedding chamber or were going abroad whence he would return! If only we were gathered to hear *his* words!"

10. Εἶτα διατυπώσεις τὸ εἶδος τοῦ σώματος· οἶος ἦν, οἶον ἀποβέβληκε τὸ κάλλος, τὸ τῶν παρειῶν ἐρύθημα, οἶα γλῶττα συνέσταλται, οἶος ἴουλος φαίνεται μαρανθείς, οἶοι βόστρυχοι κόμης οὐκέτι λοιπὸν περίβλεπτοι, ὀφθαλμῶν δὲ βολαὶ καὶ γλῆναι κατακοιμηθεῖσαι, βλεφάρων δὲ ἕλικες οὐκέτι ἕλικες, ἀλλὰ συμπεπτωκότα πάντα.

11. Εὔδηλον δὲ ὡς αἱ μονῳδίαι εἰώθασιν ἐπὶ νεωτέροις λέγεσθαι, ἀλλ᾽ οὐκ ἐπὶ γεγηρακόσι· τοὺς γὰρ πρεσβύτας ὡς νέους ἐν μονῳδίᾳ θρηνεῖν πῶς οὐ περιττὸν ὄντως καὶ μάταιον; ῥηθείη δ᾽ ἂν μονῳδία καὶ ἀνδρὸς ἐπὶ τῇ αὐτοῦ γυναικὶ λέγοντος· ἐχέτω δὲ μνήμην καὶ ζώων ἀλόγων, οἶον οὐδὲ ἄλογα ζῷα, οἶον βοῦς ἢ ἵππος ἢ κύκνος ἢ χελιδών, ἀνέχεται χωριζόμενα ἀλλήλων, ἀλλ᾽ ἐπισημαίνει τῇ φωνῇ ὀδυρόμενα, οἶον ὁ κύκνος ἀνεὶς τὸ πτερὸν τῷ ζεφύρῳ δακρύει τὸν σύννομον καὶ ὀδύρεται, καὶ ἡ χελιδὼν[4] τὴν μουσικὴν εἰς θρῆνον μεταβάλλει πολλάκις καὶ ἐπὶ τῶν πετάλων τῶν δένδρων ἱζάνουσα κατοδύρεται.

437   12. Ἔστω δὲ μὴ πέρα τῶν ἑκατὸν πεντήκοντα ἐπῶν ὁ λόγος διὰ τὸ μὴ ἀνέχεσθαι τοὺς πενθοῦντας μακρᾶς σχολῆς μηδὲ λόγων μήκους ἐν συμφοραῖς καὶ ἀκαιρίαις. ἡ μονῳδία δὲ ἀεὶ ἄνετος.

---

4 ὀδύρεται, καὶ ἡ χελιδὼν Nitsche, Soffel, RW: καὶ χελιδὼν ὀδύρεται καὶ codd.

10. Next describe in vivid detail his physical appearance in life. "What beauty he has lost—the blush of his cheeks! What a tongue has been stilled! His youthful beard, how haggard it appears! The curls of his hair, now no longer to be admired! The lively glances of his eyes and his pupils have been put to sleep; his eyelids open no longer—all of it fallen into ruin!"

11. It is obvious that monodies are normally spoken over young people rather than old ones, for would it not be excessive and foolish to lament elders in a monody as one would young people? A monody may be spoken by a husband over his wife. It should make mention of animals. For example, "Not even dumb animals—cows, horses, swans, and swallows—can bear to be separated from each other, but give voice to their laments. The swan droops his wing to the west wind, weeping and bewailing his mate, and the swallow often changes her song to a lament and mourns as she sits on the branches of a tree."

12. The speech should not exceed 150 lines, because mourners cannot tolerate long delays or lengthy speeches in the midst of calamity and misfortune. The style of a monody is always loose (*anetos*).[7]

---

[7] That is, composed in a loosely structured, nonperiodic style. Cf. 2.10.7 for a "simple" style in the highly emotional funeral speech.

2.16. ΠΕΡΙ ΣΜΙΝΘΙΑΚΟΤ

1. Δεῖ μὲν ὁμολογεῖν σε εὐθὺς ἐν προοιμίῳ τῷ πρώτῳ ὅτι δεῖ τὸν λόγους κτησάμενον ἀποδοῦναι λογίῳ θεῷ τὰς χάριτας διὰ τῶν λόγων οὓς δι' αὐτὸν τὸν μουσηγέτην κεκτήμεθα, ἄλλως τε καὶ ὅτι προστάτης καὶ συνεργὸς τῆς ἡμετέρας πόλεως, οὐ μόνον νῦν ἀλλὰ καὶ ἀνέκαθεν, ὥστε διπλῆν τὴν χάριν ὀφείλεσθαι, ὑπέρ τε τῶν λόγων ὑπέρ τε τῶν εὐεργεσιῶν, καὶ τρίτον ὅτι καὶ ἄλλως ὁμολογούμενόν ἐστι δεῖν ἀνυμνεῖν τοὺς κρείττονας καὶ τῆς εἰς αὐτοὺς εὐφημίας μηδέποτε ῥᾳθυμεῖν.

2. Τὸ δεύτερον ἐργάσῃ λαβὼν τοιαύτην ἔννοιαν· Ὅμηρος μὲν οὖν πάλαι <καὶ ἐν>[1] ὕμνοις καὶ τῇ μεγάλῃ ποιήσει τοὺς πρὸς ἀξίαν ὕμνους εἴρηκε τοῦ θεοῦ καὶ παρέλιπε τοῖς μετ' αὐτὸν ὑπερβολὴν οὐδεμίαν· καὶ ὅτι αἱ Μοῦσαι καθ' Ἡσίοδον πρὸς τὴν ἀξίαν ὑμνοῦσιν ἀεὶ τὸν Ἀπόλλωνα· προὔλαβε δὲ καὶ Πίνδαρος ὕμνους γράφων εἰς τὸν θεὸν ἀξίους τῆς ἐκείνου λύρας· ὅμως δ' ἐπειδήπερ εἰώθασιν οἱ κρείττους καὶ τὰς σμικροτάτας τῶν θυσιῶν ἀποδέχεσθαι, ὅταν γίγνωνται εὐαγῶς, οὐκ ἀφέξομαι δὴ καὶ αὐτὸς κατὰ

[1] suppl. Bursian, RW

2.16. THE SMINTHIAN ORATION
(*sminthiakos logos*)

1. You should acknowledge right away in the first introduction: "One who possesses the faculty of speech must give thanks to the god of eloquence,[1] by using the speech that we have acquired from the Leader of the Muses himself, especially since he is the champion and helper of our city,[2] not only now but since its founding, so that double gratitude is due him—for the faculty of speech and for his benefactions—and thirdly, because in any case it is acknowledged that one must hymn the gods and never neglect their praise."

2. You should compose the second introduction by taking up a topic like the following. "Long ago, in both his *Hymns* and his major poetry, Homer gave voice to hymns worthy of the god that none of his successors could surpass. And, according to Hesiod,[3] the Muses forever sing hymns worthy of Apollo. Pindar, too, preceded us in writing hymns to the god worthy of the god's own lyre.[4] Nevertheless, since gods are wont to accept even the smallest sacrifices when piously offered, I for one shall not shrink

---

[1] That is, Apollo, immediately identified as Musegetes, Leader of the Muses.   [2] Alexandria Troas, identified here with ancient Troy. Cf. 2.13.10.

[3] Perhaps a vague reference to Hes. *Theog.* 9–21.

[4] Cf. especially *Pyth.* 1.1–12 and perhaps Pindar's *Paeans*.

δύναμιν ὕμνον ἀναθεῖναι τῷ Ἀπόλλωνι. εὔχομαι δὲ
αὐτῷ τῷ Σμινθίῳ Ἀπόλλωνι δύναμιν ἐμποιῆσαι τῷ
λόγῳ ἀρκοῦσαν πρὸς τὴν παροῦσαν ὑπόθεσιν.

3. Τρίτον· εἰ μὲν οὖν ἡρώων τινὸς ἔμελλον λέγειν
ἐγκώμιον, οὐκ ἂν διηπόρησα περὶ τῆς ἀρχῆς, οὐδ'
ὅθεν δεῖ πρῶτον τὴν ἀρχὴν τοῦ λόγου ποιήσασθαι.
ἐπεὶ δέ μοι καὶ ὁ λόγος τετόλμηκεν ⟨προσειπεῖν⟩[2] τὸν
μέγιστον τῶν θεῶν, ἐδεήθην μὲν χρησμῳδῆσαί μοι
τὴν Πυθίαν σεισθέντων τῶν τριπόδων, ὅθεν δεῖ κατα-
τολμῆσαι τοῦ πράγματος, ἐπεὶ δὲ κρύπτει τέως ἡμῖν
τὰ μαντεύματα, τοῦτο δόξαν ἴσως τοῖς κρείττοσιν, αἰ-
τήσω παρὰ τῶν Μουσῶν μανθάνειν, καθάπερ Πίνδαρος τῶν ὕμνων πυνθάνεται, "ἀναξιφόρμιγγες ὕμνοι,"
πόθεν με χρὴ τὴν ἀρχὴν ποιήσασθαι; δοκεῖ δ' οὖν μοι
πρῶτον ἀφεμένῳ τέως τοῦ γένους ὕμνον εἰς αὐτὸν
ἀναφθέγξασθαι.

4. Μετὰ τὰς ἐννοίας ταύτας τὰς προοιμιακὰς ἐρεῖς
εἰς αὐτὸν ὕμνον τὸν θεόν, ὅτι, ὦ Σμίνθιε Ἄπολλον,
τίνα σε χρὴ προσειπεῖν; πότερον ἥλιον τὸν τοῦ φωτὸς
ταμίαν καὶ πηγὴν τῆς οὐρανίου ταύτης αἴγλης, ἢ
νοῦν, ὡς ὁ τῶν θεολογούντων λόγος, διήκοντα μὲν διὰ
τῶν οὐρανίων, ἰόντα δὲ δι' αἰθέρος ἐπὶ τὰ τῇδε; ἢ
πότερον αὐτὸν τὸν τῶν ὅλων δημιουργόν, ἢ δευτερεύ-
ουσαν δύναμιν, δι' ὃν σελήνη μὲν κέκτηται σέλας, γῆ
δὲ τοὺς οἰκείους ἠγάπησεν ὅρους, θάλαττα δὲ οὐχ
ὑπερβαίνει τοὺς ἰδίους μυχούς. 5. φασὶ γὰρ τοῦ χάους

---

[2] coni. RW: εἰς codd.

from dedicating a hymn to Apollo to the best of my ability, and I pray to Sminthian Apollo himself to endow my speech with a capacity adequate to the subject at hand."

3. Thirdly: "If I were going to deliver an encomium of some hero, I would not have been in doubt about a starting point, or where I needed to begin my speech, but since my speech has dared to address[5] the greatest of the gods, I asked the Pythia to prophesy to me from her shaken tripods,[6] and tell from what point I ought to brave my daunting task. But since thus far she is keeping her oracles from me—apparently the gods deem that best—I shall ask for instructions from the Muses, just as Pindar asks of his hymns, 'Hymns that rule the lyre,'[7] where should I begin? Consequently, I think it best at the start to set aside his lineage for now and address my hymn to the god himself."

4. After these introductory considerations, you should hymn the god himself. "O Sminthian Apollo, what am I to call you? As the sun, the steward of light and source of that heavenly radiance? Or as mind, as the theologians claim, diffused through the heavens and traveling through the ether to the things here on earth? Or as the artificer of the universe, or as a secondary power through which the moon has acquired its gleam, the land has accepted its own boundaries, and the sea does not overflow its proper gulfs? 5. They say that when chaos held the universe in its grip

---

[5] Accepting the conjecture of RW for the nonsensical εἰς.

[6] The Pythia sat on (or near) the tripods, which shook when she received an oracle from Apollo. Cf. §8 below.

[7] *Ol.* 2.1.

κατειληφότος τὰ σύμπαντα καὶ πάντων συγκεχυμέ-
νων καὶ φερομένων τὴν ἄτακτον ἐκείνην καὶ ἀμειδῆ[3]
φοράν, σὲ ἐκ τῶν οὐρανίων ἁψίδων ἐκλάμψαντα σκε-
δάσαι μὲν τὸ χάος ἐκεῖνο, ἀπολέσαι δὲ τὸν ζόφον,
τάξιν δ' ἐπιθεῖναι τοῖς ἄπασιν. ἀλλὰ ταῦτα μὲν σοφῶν παισὶ φιλοσοφεῖν παραλείπω, ἣν δὲ ἀκήκοα
μυθολογούντων γένεσιν, ταύτην καὶ δὴ πειράσομαι
λέγειν· πάντως δὲ οὐδὲ οὗτος ἀπὸ τρόπου σοι ὁ λόγος, ὃς κεκρυμμένην εἶχεν ἐν ἑαυτῷ τὴν ἀληθεστέραν
γνῶσιν.

6. Εἶτα ἐρεῖς κεφάλαιον μετὰ τὸν ὕμνον δεύτερον
τὸ γένος, ἄρξῃ δὲ ἐκεῖθεν· Ζεὺς ἐπειδὴ κατέλυσε τοὺς
Τιτᾶνας ἀρχὴν ἄνομον καὶ ἀκόλαστον ἄρχοντας,
μᾶλλον δὲ ὥσπερ βίαιον τυραννίδα διέποντας, καὶ
439 Ταρτάρου μυχοῖς παραδέδωκεν, τότε γένεσιν παίδων
δημιουργεῖν ἐνενόησεν, μεθ' ὧν τὰ πάντα ἄριστα
καταστήσειν ἔμελλεν, καὶ μίαν τῶν Τιτανίδων νύμ-
φην ἐξελόμενος, ἐπειδὴ τοὺς πρὸς Ἥραν θεσμοὺς
ἑτέροις τόκοις ἐφύλαττεν, ἐδημιούργει μετ' ἐκείνης τὸν
τόκον· κάλλει μὲν γὰρ καὶ ὥρᾳ σώματος διέφερεν,
ἔπρεπε δὲ γενέσθαι μητέρα Ἀπόλλωνος καὶ Ἀρτέμιδος. 7. καταλαμβάνει δὲ τὴν Δῆλον μέλλουσα τίκτειν
ἡδέως, οἱ δέ φασι τὴν Λυκίαν. καὶ λέγουσι μὲν οἱ τὴν
Δῆλον εὐτυχῆσαι φάσκοντες τὴν ὑποδοχὴν ἀνασχεῖν

---

[3] ἀμειδῆ mWp: ἀμειγῆ P: obel. RW

and everything was jumbled together and being borne along in that random motion hidden in gloom, you shone forth from the vaults of heaven and dispersed that chaos, put an end to the darkness, and imposed order on everything. But I leave all that for philosophers to ponder,[8] and will attempt to relate your origin, as I heard it from mythographers.[9] And in no way will you find this account unsuitable, for it has the truer knowledge hidden within itself."[10]

6. Following this hymn, deliver the second section on birth, beginning from here: "After Zeus defeated the Titans, whose rule had been lawless, unrestrained, and exercised more like a violent tyranny, and had consigned them to the depths of Tartarus, he then decided to create the birth of children, with whose help he could arrange everything for the best. Since he was keeping his commitments to Hera for other offspring, he chose one of the Titans' daughters,[11] and created children with her, for she excelled in beauty and the loveliness of her body, and was suitable to become the mother of Apollo and Artemis. 7. When she was about to give birth, she gladly[12] came to Delos, although others say it was Lycia. Those who say that Delos had the good fortune to receive her, claim that the island had previously been hidden under the waves, but

[8] For the topics of philosophical hymns, cf. 1.5.

[9] For mythological hymns and their concern with genealogies, cf. 1.6.　　　[10] It is not apparent what truthful knowledge is hidden in the forthcoming account of Apollo's birth.

[11] Leto.　　　[12] *Hymn Hom. Ap.* 30–92 details Leto's travels to find a place to give birth, as she is rejected by all the places she visits, until she comes to Delos, who accepts her.

μὲν ἐκ θαλάττης πρὸ τοῦ κρυπτομένην καὶ οὖσαν
ὕφαλον, ὑποδέξασθαι <δὲ>[4] πλανωμένην τὴν θεὸν ἐκ
Σουνίου τῆς Ἀττικῆς ἐπιβᾶσαν τῇ νήσῳ· Ὅμηρος δὲ
οἶδε μὲν ἐν Λυκίᾳ γεννώμενον—λέγει γάρ που Λυκη-
γενεῖ κλυτοτόξῳ—καὶ τὸν τόπον ἐκεῖνον εὐτυχήσαντα
τοῦ θεοῦ τὴν γένεσιν. 8. φασὶ δ' οὖν ἐκφανέντα τῶν
ὠδίνων τὸν θεὸν λάμψαι μὲν τοσοῦτον, ὅσον ἐπισχεῖν
γῆν καὶ θάλατταν καὶ οὐράνιον κύκλον, Χάριτας δὲ
καὶ Ὥρας περιχορεῦσαι τὸν τόπον, καὶ τί γὰρ οὐ
σύμβολον αἴσιον ἐκ γῆς καὶ θαλάττης καὶ οὐρανοῦ
δειχθῆναι. ἐκ δὲ Λυκίας παρ' ἡμᾶς ἀφικέσθαι λέγουσι τὸν θεὸν καὶ καταλαμβάνοντα τὸ Σμίνθιον
μαντεῖον ἐγκαταστῆσαι τῷ τόπῳ καὶ κινῆσαι τρίποδας.

9. Ἐπειδὴ δὲ τὰ κατὰ τὸν τόπον τῆς γενέσεως τοῦ
θεοῦ ζητεῖται, τῶν μὲν λεγόντων ὅτι ἐν Δήλῳ, τῶν δὲ
ὅτι ἐν Λυκίᾳ, κατασκευάσεις ὅτι ἀξιόπιστος μάρτυς ὁ
ποιητὴς πρὸς τὸ σαυτῷ συμφέρον, ὅτι Λυκηγενῆ αὐτὸν εἴωθεν καλεῖν [ὁ ποιητής].[5] ἐπάξεις ἀκολούθως ὅτι
εἰκὸς ἐν Λυκίᾳ γεννηθέντα καὶ παρ' ἡμῖν πρῶτον
ὀφθῆναι. οὐ γὰρ ἂν μέλλων διαβαίνειν ἐπὶ τὰς νή-
σους καὶ Κασταλίαν καὶ Δελφοὺς τῶν μὲν παρ' ἡμῖν
440 ἠμέλησεν, παρὰ δὲ ἐκείνους ἔδραμεν, ἄλλως τε καὶ ὅτι
τιμῶν τοὺς ἡμετέρους πατέρας καὶ ῥυόμενος κινδύνων
φαίνεται· οὐκ ἂν δὲ τοῦτο ἐποίησε μὴ πάλαι καὶ πρότερον εὐμενῶς πρὸς τὴν χώραν διακείμενος. 10. Δελ-

[4] suppl. RW   [5] secl. Walz, RW

rose from the sea[13] and welcomed the goddess as she set foot on the island, when she wandered there from Sunium in Attica. Homer, however, knows that Apollo was born in Lycia, for he speaks of 'the Lycian-born famous bowman,'[14] and says that the god was born in that fortunate place. 8. In any case, they say that when the god emerged from the womb, he shone so brightly as to fill the earth and sea and dome of heaven, and that the Graces and Hours danced around the place. What auspicious portent was not shown forth from earth, sea, and sky? They say that it was from Lycia that the god came to us[15] and took over his Sminthian temple, established his oracle here, and made his tripods shake."

9. Since the location of the god's birthplace is at issue—with some saying that it was Delos, others Lycia—you should argue that Homer is a credible witness for your position, because he regularly calls him "Lycian-born." You should then draw the conclusion, "It is probable that being born in Lycia he would appear first among us. For if he was going to cross over to the islands[16] and Castalia[17] and Delphi, he would not have neglected our people and gone straight to those others, especially since he so clearly honored our forefathers and protected them from dangers.[18] He would not have done this unless he had been well-disposed to this land long before that. 10. As it is, the

---

[13] Before receiving Leto, the island was thought to wander or be underwater; cf. Pind., Frr. 33c–d.   [14] *Il.* 4.101, 119, spoken by Pandarus, the Lycian.   [15] In Alexandria Troas.

[16] The Aegean islands, primarily to Delos.

[17] The spring at Delphi.

[18] This presumably refers to Apollo's protection of Troy.

φοὶ μὲν οὖν μεγαλαυχούμενοι τὴν Πυθίαν προβάλλον-
ται καὶ Παρνασσὸν καὶ Κασταλίαν, καὶ τὸν θεὸν
μόνοι τῶν ἁπάντων αὐχοῦσιν ἔχειν, ἐγὼ δὲ εἰ δεῖ
τἀληθὲς εἰπεῖν συνήδομαι μὲν αὐτοῖς τῆς χάριτος, οὐ
μὴν κρίνω γε πράττειν αὐτοὺς τῶν παρ' ἡμῖν εὐχερέσ-
τερον· καὶ γὰρ ἡμεῖς μετέσχομεν τούτων πρῶτοι τῶν
μαντείων, καὶ δεξάμενοι τὸν θεὸν τοῖς ἄλλοις περι-
επέμψαμεν, καὶ τὴν παρ' ἡμῶν ἀπορροὴν ἐκεῖνοι ἀφ'
ἡμῶν κέκτηνται· ἐπίσης τε χαίρει ταῖς προσωνυμίαις
τῶν τόπων ὁ θεός, καὶ ὥσπερ ὁ Πύθιος, οὕτω καὶ ὁ
Σμίνθιος.

11. Μετὰ ταῦτα ἐρεῖς ἐγκώμιον τῆς χώρας, ὅτι
εἰκότως δὲ τὴν ἡμετέραν χώραν ἠγάπησεν ὁ θεός,
ἰδὼν αὐτὴν κάλλει διαφέρουσαν· ἐν ᾧ καὶ ἐκφράσεις
τὴν χώραν οἷα ἐστίν, οὐκ ἀκριβῶς μέν, ἐπεξιὼν [τῇ
χώρᾳ, γράφε]⁶ δὲ τῆς χώρας ἃ δυνατὸν κινῆσαι τὸν
ἀκροατήν, τὰ μᾶλλον ἐξαίρετα λέγων. εἶτα μετὰ τὴν
χώραν ἐπάξεις ἀκολούθως, ὅτι τοιγάρτοι καὶ τιμῶν
καὶ συμμαχῶν τοῖς ἡμετέροις διετέλεσεν, ἐν πολέμοις, ἐν χρησμῳδίαις διαφθείρων παντοδαπῶς τοὺς
πολεμίους.

12. Εἶτα μετὰ τοῦτο τὸ κεφάλαιον πάλιν διαιρήσεις
εἰς τέσσαρα μέρη τὴν δύναμιν τοῦ θεοῦ καὶ ἐρεῖς
οὕτως· ἀλλὰ γὰρ οὐκ οἶδα πῶς ἡ μνήμη τῆς χώρας
παρήνεγκεν ἡμᾶς τῆς συνεχοῦς μνήμης τοῦ θεοῦ, διόπερ ἐπανακτέον πάλιν. διὰ τοῦτο δὲ μετὰ τὴν γένεσιν εὐθὺς ἐμνημονεύσαμεν τῆς χώρας, ἵνα μήτε ἀπό-
λυτος ὕμνος γένηται [ὕμνους γὰρ καλοῦσι τὰ τῶν

342

proud Delphians cite in their favor the Pythian festival and Parnassus and Castalia, and boast that they alone of mankind possess the god, but for my part—if I may state the truth—I congratulate them for his favor toward them, but I really do not think that they fare any better than we do, for we were the first to make use of those oracles, and, after welcoming the god, we sent him around to others, and they acquired from us what was ours to begin with. The god delights equally in his various place-names: just as he is Pythian, so too is he Sminthian."

11. After this you should deliver an encomium of the land. "Naturally the god fell in love with our land after seeing how exceedingly beautiful it was." Here you may describe the land's qualities, not in detail, but by running through those attributes that can move the audience, mentioning its most attractive features. After treating the land, you should draw the conclusion, "As a result, he has continually honored and supported our people in wars and in oracles, vanquishing our enemies in every way."

12. After this section you should divide the god's powers into four parts, first saying, "But I have no idea how this mention of the land has diverted us from our continual attention to the god. We must therefore go back again." We had mentioned the land right after his birth, so it would not be a generic hymn nor one generally common

---

6 secl. RW

θεῶν ἐγκώμια],[7] μήτε κοινὸς ἁπλῶς πρὸς πᾶσαν θεῶν
ὑπόθεσιν, ἀλλ᾽ ἵνα ἔχῃ τὸ ἴδιον τοῦ Σμινθιακοῦ ἐκ τοῦ
441   τόπου. τίνες γοῦν εἰσιν αἱ δυνάμεις τοῦ θεοῦ; τοξική,
μαντική, ἰατρική, μουσική.

13. Μέλλων οὖν ἄρχεσθαι μιᾶς δυνάμεως προοιμιάσῃ πρῶτον (καλῶς δ᾽ ἂν ἔχοι τῆς τοξικῆς πρώτης,
ἐπειδὴ καὶ ταύτης πρώτης ἅψασθαι λέγεται μετὰ τὴν
γένεσιν)· βούλομαι δὲ τὰς ἀρετὰς μὴ πάσας ἅμα
μηδὲ συναθροίσας τῷ λόγῳ δοκεῖν συγχεῖν, ἀλλὰ
διελόμενος χωρὶς καθ᾽ ἑκάστην περὶ αὐτῶν διελθεῖν
ὅσον οἷόν τε μνησθῆναι· οὐ γὰρ εἰπεῖν ἅπαντα ῥᾴδιον. λέγεται τοίνυν, ἐπειδὴ πρῶτον ἀγωνισμάτων
εἴχετο τὰ τόξα μεταχειρισάμενος καὶ τὴν φαρέτραν
λαβών, τούτοις γὰρ αὐτὸν ὥπλισεν ὁ πατήρ, ἀμύνε-
σθαι τῆς τόλμης τὸν Τιτυόν, ἀνθ᾽ ὧν εἰς τὴν μητέρα
ἠσέβησε Διὸς κυδρὴν παράκοιτιν, Πυθωνά τε κατει-
ληφότα Δελφοὺς κτεῖναι τοῖς ἑαυτοῦ βέλεσιν. 14. ἵνα
δὲ Πύθων ὅστις ἦν εἴπω, μικρὸν ἀναλήψομαι. ἤνεγκεν
ἡ γῆ δράκοντος φύσιν οὔτε λόγῳ ῥητὴν οὔτε ἀκοῇ
πιστευθῆναι ῥᾳδίαν· οὗτος πᾶσαν λυμαινόμενος γῆν,
ὅση πρόσοικος Δελφοῖς καὶ Φωκίδι, καταλαμβάνει
τὴν Παρνασσόν, ὄρος τῶν ὑπὸ τὸν οὐρανὸν τὸ μέγιστον, οὐκ Ὀλύμπου χεῖρον οὐδ᾽ Ἴδης τῆς ἡμετέρας
λειπόμενον. τοῦτο τοίνυν ἐκάλυπτε μὲν ταῖς σπειραῖς
καὶ τοῖς ἑλιγμοῖς, καὶ ἦν τοῦ ὄρους γυμνὸν οὐδέν, τὴν

[7] secl. Bursian, RW

to any divine subject, but would preserve what is specific to the Sminthian Oration, namely its location.[19] What then are the god's powers? archery, prophecy, medicine, and music.

13. When about to begin with one of his powers, you should first provide a preface. It would be best to begin with archery, because it is the first thing he is said to have taken up after his birth. "I do not intend to lump together all his virtues in my speech and seem to confuse them, but to discuss each one separately and thus treat them all, insofar as it is possible to do so, for to discuss everything is no easy task. It is said, then, that when he first engaged in battle, he took his bow in hand and took up his quiver— for his father[20] had armed him with them—to avenge Tityus for his impudence and acts of impiety against Apollo's mother,[21] 'Zeus' glorious bedmate.'[22] After that he used those arrows of his to kill Pytho, who had taken possession of Delphi. 14. To explain who Pytho was, I shall provide a bit of background. The earth produced a snake whose nature cannot be described in words nor easily believed if heard. It was ravaging all the land around Delphi and Phocis and occupied Parnassus, the greatest mountain under heaven, no smaller than Olympus nor inferior to our own Ida. Moreover, it covered that mountain with its coils and spirals, and no place on it was left bare, as it held its

[19] This sentence explains why the digression on the land was necessary, in spite of the feigned claim of being carried away by its attractive features designed to move the audience.

[20] Zeus.   [21] For Tityus' attempted rape of Leto and his punishment in Hades, see Hom. *Od.* 11.576–81.

[22] Hom. *Od.* 11.580.

κεφαλὴν ὑπὲρ αὐτὴν τὴν ἄκραν ἔχων, ἄνω μετεωρί-
ζων πρὸς αὐτὸν τὸν αἰθέρα. 15. καὶ ἡνίκα μὲν πίνειν
ἔδει, ποταμοὺς ὁλοκλήρους ἐδέχετο, ἡνίκα δ᾽ ἐσθίειν,
πάσας ἀγέλας ἠφάνιζεν· οὗτος ἀβάτους μὲν ἐποίει
Δελφοὺς τοῖς ἅπασιν, ᾤκει δὲ τὸν τόπον οὐδείς, ἦν δὲ
τὸ Θέμιδος μαντεῖον ἔρημον. ἄτοπα δὲ καὶ ἀμήχανα
ὁ θεὸς τοὺς ἀνθρώπους πάσχειν ὑπολαβὼν καὶ βουλόμενος πανταχόθεν αὐτοῖς θεσπίζειν τὰ συμφέροντα
δι᾽ ὧν ὁ βίος εὐδαιμονεῖν ἔμελλε, κτείνει καὶ τοῦτον
442 μιᾷ τοξείᾳ ταῖς αὐταῖς ἀκίσι καὶ βέλεσι. 16. τὰ δὲ
παρ᾽ ἡμῖν ἀγωνίσματα τίς ἂν εἴποι τοῦ θεοῦ κατ᾽
ἀξίαν, τὰ κατὰ τῶν Ἀχαιῶν ἀσεβούντων εἰς τοὺς θεούς, τὰ κατὰ τοῦ Πηλέως μήνιδι τῶν περὶ Ἕκτορα
τολμηθέντων παρανόμων· καὶ ὅτι κυνηγέτης ὁ θεὸς
καὶ τοῖς τόξοις αἱρεῖν εἴωθε τὰ θηρία, καὶ ὅτι τοξικὴν
αὐτὸς εὗρε πρῶτος ἅμα τῇ ἀδελφῇ τῇ Ἀρτέμιδι.

17. Μέλλων δὲ ἐμβάλλειν εἰς ἕτερον κεφάλαιον
ὁμοίως ἐρεῖς τοῦ θεοῦ τὸ μέγιστον καὶ ἐξαίρετον, ὅτι
μάντις. ἐνταῦθα δὲ καὶ θέσιν διὰ βραχέων περανεῖς,
ὅτι ἀγαθὸν ἡ μαντική, καὶ διὰ ταύτης τὰ μέγιστα τῶν
ἀνθρωπίνων κατορθοῦσθαι πέφυκε, ταύτην δὲ μάλιστα Ἀπόλλων ἐτίμησε καὶ ἐθαύμασε· καὶ ὅτι ἐπὶ τῶν
τριπόδων θεσπίζων ᾤκισε τὴν ἤπειρον, ᾤκισε δὲ τὴν
θάλασσαν, νῦν μὲν εἰς Λιβύην ἐκπέμπων, νῦν δὲ οἰκί-

---

[23] The oracle at Delphi originally belonged to the ancient
goddess Themis.
[24] That is, speaking as ancient Trojans.

head above the mountain peak and lifted it up toward the very sky. 15. And when it needed to drink, it would consume entire rivers, and when it needed to eat, it would annihilate entire herds. It made Delphi inaccessible to everyone, and nobody inhabited the place. In addition, the oracle of Themis was deserted.[23] Because Apollo recognized that men were suffering outrageous things they could not help, and because he wished to prophesy useful things to them in every way that would make their lives happy, he killed that snake in one feat of archery with those very darts and arrows. 16. Who could worthily tell of the god's struggles here among us[24]—what he did to the Achaeans when they sinned against the gods,[25] and to Peleus' son in his wrath at the outrageous things that hero dared to do to Hector."[26] Also mention that the god is a hunter, wont to shoot animals with his bow, and that he invented archery together with his sister Artemis.

17. Similarly, when about to embark on the second section,[27] you should state that the god's most distinctive attribute is that he is a prophet. Here you should briefly advance the general thesis that prophecy is a good thing, and that because of it the greatest human endeavors have succeeded—and that Apollo especially honored and admired it. "By prophesying on his tripods, he colonized both the mainland and the sea, at one time sending settlers

[25] Apollo defended Troy and was offended at the Greeks' misbehavior during and after the sack.

[26] Apollo was particularly offended by Achilles' mistreatment of Hector's body; cf. Hom. *Il*. 24.32–54. In some versions Apollo subsequently killed Achilles; cf. Pind. *Pae*. 6.78–86.

[27] That is, of those concerning the god's four powers; cf. §12.

ζῶν τὸν Ἑλλήσποντον, τὴν Ἀσίαν, τὴν ἑῴαν πᾶσαν.
18. τοῦτο δὲ τὸ μέρος αὐξήσεις τῷ μεγέθει τῶν ἐγκωμίων ἐπεργαζόμενος, ὅτι ἐκινδύνευσε μὲν ἀοίκητος
εἶναι γῆ πᾶσα, εἰ μὴ τὰ μαντεῖα τοῦ θεοῦ πανταχοῦ
δὴ γῆς ἐπεφοίτησε παρ' ἡμῶν, ἐκ Δελφῶν, ἐκ Μιλή-
του· ἐν ᾧ μέρει, ἐάν τι μάθῃς ἐκ πατρίων ἐνεργή-
σαντα τὸν θεὸν ἀπὸ τῶν μαντευμάτων, πρόσθες.

19. Μετὰ τοῦτο τὸ κεφάλαιον ⟨ἐπ'⟩ ἄλλο ἥξεις,[8] ὅτι
μουσικὸς ὁ θεός. ἐνταῦθα καιρὸν ἕξεις, ὅπως μὲν κατ'
οὐρανὸν μέσος ἐν μέσοις θεοῖς πλήττει τὴν λύραν,
ὅπως δὲ μετὰ τῶν Μουσῶν ἐν Ἑλικῶνι καὶ ἐπὶ τῆς
Πιερίας. καὶ φιλοσοφήσεις μετρίως ἐνταῦθα· εἰ δὲ δεῖ
καὶ τὸν ἀπορρητότερον λόγον εἰπεῖν, ὃν φιλοσόφων
παῖδες πρεσβεύουσι, λέγουσιν αὐτὸν [μὲν][9] ὄντα τὸν
ἥλιον μουσικῇ μὲν αὐτὸν κινεῖσθαι, κατὰ μουσικὴν
δὲ περιδινεῖν περὶ αὐτὸν[10] τὸν πόλον, καὶ δι' ἁρμονίας
ἅπαντα τὸν κόσμον διοικεῖν. 20. οὐ μὴν ἀλλ' ἐπειδὴ
ταῦτα τοῖς θεολόγοις παρεῖναι δεῖ, λέγωμεν μᾶλλον
τὰ γνωριμώτατα· ὁ γὰρ Ὀρφεὺς ὁ δι' αὐτὸν εὐδόκιμος
εἰς τοσοῦτον εὐμουσίας προῆλθεν, ὥστε καὶ θηρία
συλλέγειν, εἰ πλήττοι τὴν λύραν, καὶ λίθους κινεῖν
καὶ πᾶν ὁτιοῦν καταθέλγειν πιπτούσης εἰς αἴσθησιν
αὐτῶν τῆς ἁρμονίας. Ἀμφίονος μνημονεύσεις, Ἀρίονος, ὅτι ὁ μὲν τὰς Θήβας ἐτείχισε τῇ λύρᾳ τὰς πέτρας
μετάγων, ὁ δὲ τὸ Τυρρηνικὸν ἔπλευσεν ἐπὶ δελφῖνος

443

---

8 ⟨ἐπ'⟩ ἄλλο ἥξεις coni. RW: ἄλλο ⟨τὸ⟩ τῶν πράξεων codd.
9 secl. Nitsche, RW   10 RW: αὐτὸν codd.

off to Libya,[28] at another colonizing the Hellespont, Asia, and the entire East." 18. You should amplify this portion by adding majestic praise: "The entire earth risked being uninhabited had the god's prophecies not spread throughout the world, from us, from Delphi, and from Miletus." In this section, add anything you know from local traditions that the god has accomplished through his prophecies.

19. After this section, move on to another, on his role as the god of music. Here you will have the opportunity to say how he plays his lyre in heaven surrounded by the gods, and how he does so with the Muses on Helicon and in Pieria. Here you should also include a bit of philosophy. "If I may bring up a rather esoteric doctrine that philosophers hold dear, they say that he is the sun, that it is by music that he moves, that through music he makes the heavens revolve around him, and that he directs the whole universe by means of harmony. 20. All the same, we should leave these matters to the theologians. Let us instead speak of what is well known. Orpheus, made famous by Apollo, attained such mastery of music that he gathered together even wild animals whenever he played his lyre, and moved rocks and enchanted everything upon whose senses his harmony fell." You should also mention Amphion and Arion, how the first gathered boulders with his lyre to build Thebes' walls,[29] and the other crossed the Etruscan Sea[30] riding on a dolphin. You should always

[28] For the founding of Cyrene by Battus, cf. Pind. *Pyth*. 5.54–62.

[29] Cf. Ap. Rhod. 1.735–41.

[30] Between Sicily and the Peloponnesus; cf. Hdt. 1.23–24.

ὀχούμενος. ἀνοίσεις δὲ τὰ ἐγκώμια ἐπὶ τὸν μουσηγέτην, ὡς παρ' ἐκείνου λαμβανόντων τὴν μουσικήν.

21. Μετὰ δὲ τὴν ἀρετὴν ταύτην τοῦ θεοῦ ἥξεις ἐπὶ
τὴν τετάρτην, ὅτι καὶ ἰατρός, ἀεὶ δὲ προοιμιάσῃ καθ'
ἑκάστην τῶν ἀρετῶν, ὡς μὴ δοκεῖν μικρὰ μηδὲ φαῦλα
τὰ ῥηθησόμενα· αἱ γὰρ διὰ μέσων τῶν λόγων ἔννοιαι
προοιμιακαί, προπαρασκευάζουσαι τὸν ἀκροατὴν καὶ
προσεχέστερον διατιθεῖσαι, ταῖς ὑποθέσεσιν αὐξήσεις ἐργάζονται. 22. οὐκοῦν ἐρεῖς ὅτι καὶ τὴν ἰατρικὴν
ταύτην ὁ θεὸς ἡμῖν ἐξεῦρεν· ἐν ᾧ καὶ θέσιν ἐρεῖς ὅτι
διαφθειρομένου τοῦ γένους ταῖς νόσοις καὶ τοῖς πό-
νοις κατοικτείρας ἡμᾶς τὴν ἰατρικὴν ἐξεῦρεν, ἧς τί ἂν
γένοιτο τοῖς ἀνθρώποις χρησιμώτερον; τίς μὲν γὰρ
ἂν εἰργάσατο γῆν, τίς ἂν ἔπλευσε θάλασσαν, τίς δ'
ἂν πόλεις ἔκτισε, τίς δ' ἂν νόμους ἡμῖν ἔθηκε μὴ τῆς
ἰατρικῆς παρελθούσης; ὅθεν καὶ παιᾶνα αὐτὸν καὶ
πέπονα καὶ ἀλαλκέα ὀδυνῶν καὶ σωτῆρα καλεῖν εἰώθασι καὶ ποιηταὶ καὶ ⟨συγγραφεῖς⟩[11] σύμπαντες.
23. θήσεις δὲ ἐπὶ τούτοις καὶ τὴν Ἀσκληπιοῦ γένεσιν·
βουλόμενος δὲ αὐξῆσαι τὴν τέχνην ὁ θεὸς καὶ μετα-
δοῦναι ταύτην τῷ τῶν ἀνθρώπων γένει τὴν Ἀσκληπιοῦ γένεσιν ἐδημιούργησεν, ἧς πῶς ἄν τις κατ'
ἀξίαν μνησθείη; ζητήσεις δὲ ἐφ' ἑκάστῳ τῶν κεφαλαίων τῶν πατρίων τινὰ καὶ τῶν μυθευομένων καὶ
προσθήσεις, ἵνα μᾶλλον οἰκεῖον γένηται.

24. Μετὰ ταῦτα κεφάλαιον θήσεις τοιοῦτον περὶ τῆς

[11] suppl. RW

bring your praise back to the Leader of the Muses, on the ground that these two acquired their music from him.

21. After treating this power of the god, you should proceed to the fourth one, namely that he is also a doctor. You should always provide a preface for each power, to avoid giving the impression that what you will say is insignificant or commonplace. For in the course of speeches, prefatory comments that prepare the listener and make him more attentive serve to amplify your subjects.[31] 22. You should say then that the god invented the art of medicine for our benefit. Here you may advance a general thesis. "When the human race was wasting away with diseases and pains, he took pity on us and invented medicine. What could be more beneficial to humans than that? Who would have worked the land, who would have sailed the sea, who would have founded cities, who would have made laws for us, without the presence of medicine? For this reason all the poets and prose writers customarily call him 'paean'[32] 'gentle,' 'protector from pain,' and 'savior.'" 23. Here is the place to add the birth of Asclepius. "Wishing to further his art and to pass it on to the human race, the god brought about the birth of Asclepius. How could anyone worthily commemorate that?" In each of these sections you should look for any local legends or mythological details, and add them, to make the material more relevant.

24. Next, you should add a section on the city like the

[31] Cf. 2.1.17.
[32] "healer."

MENANDER RHETOR

πόλεως, ὅτι τοιγαροῦν Ἀλέξανδρος τὴν Εὐρώπην χει-
ρωσάμενος καὶ διαβεβηκὼς ἐπὶ τὴν Ἀσίαν ἤδη,
ἐπειδὴ προσέβαλε τῷ ἱερῷ καὶ τοῖς τόποις, σύμβολα
μὲν ἐκίνησεν ἐπὶ τὴν κατασκευὴν τῆς πόλεως, τοῦ
θεοῦ ταῦτα καταπέμποντος, καὶ κατασκευάζει τὴν εὐ-
δαίμονα ταύτην πόλιν, καθιερώσας αὐτὴν Ἀπόλλωνι
τῷ Σμινθίῳ, δίκαιον αὐτοῦ προφαίνοντος κρίνας
αὐτοῦ δεῖν κατοικίζειν πόλιν, καὶ τὸν τόπον ⟨τὸν⟩[12]
πάλαι τῷ θεῷ καθιερωμένον μὴ περιϊδεῖν ἔρημον καὶ
ἀοίκητον τὴν χώραν. 25. τοιγάρτοι καὶ ἡμεῖς πειρώμε-
νοι ἀεὶ τῆς τοῦ θεοῦ προνοίας τε καὶ εὐμενείας οὐ
ῥαθυμοῦμεν τῆς περὶ αὐτὸν εὐσεβείας, καὶ ὁ μὲν δι-
ατελεῖ καρπῶν ἀφθόνων διδοὺς φορὰν καὶ ῥυόμενος
κινδύνων, ἡμεῖς δὲ ὕμνοις ἱλασκόμεθα·[13] τοιγάρτοι
κρείττονα ἀγῶνα τὸν ἱερὸν τοῦτον διὰ ταῦτα τίθεμεν
καὶ πανηγύρεις συγκροτοῦμεν καὶ θύομεν, χάριτας
ἐκτιννύντες ἀνθ᾽ ὧν εὖ πάσχομεν. 26. καὶ διαγράψεις
τὴν πανήγυριν, ὁποία καὶ ὅπως πλήθουσα ἀνθρώπων
συνιόντων, καὶ ὅτι οἱ μὲν ἐπιδείκνυνται τὰς αὐτῶν
ἀρετὰς ἢ διὰ λόγων ἢ διὰ σώματος εὐεξίας, καὶ τὰ
τοιαῦτα, οἱ δὲ θεαταί, οἱ δὲ ἀκροαταί· καὶ διὰ βραχέων ἐργάσῃ θέσιν, ὡς Ἰσοκράτης ἐν τῷ Πανηγυ-
ρικῷ, λέγων ὅσα ἐκ τῶν πανηγύρεων καὶ τούτων τῶν
συνόδων εἴωθεν ⟨ἀγαθὰ γίγνεσθαι⟩.[14]

27. Καθόλου δέ σοι ἔστω τὸ τοιοῦτο θεώρημα ἐν
τοῖς τοιούτοις, λέγω δὴ τοῖς ὁμολογουμένοις ἀγαθοῖς
ἤτοι ἐνδόξοις προτάττειν μὲν τὴν θέσιν, οἷον ὅτι

following. "And so, when Alexander, after subduing Europe and having just crossed over to Asia, came to the temple and its site, he solicited portents concerning the founding of the city, and when the god[33] sent them down, he built this blessed city and dedicated it to Sminthian Apollo. For since the god was ordaining it, he thought it only right to found the god's city, and not to leave the site—long since dedicated to the god—deserted and the land uninhabited. 25. Therefore we too, who have continually experienced the god's foresight and beneficence, are not remiss in revering him, and, for his part, he continually provides abundant harvests of crops and protects us from dangers, while we in turn propitiate him with hymns. So, for these reasons we hold this great holy contest, arrange civic festivals, perform sacrifices, and render thanks for all the blessings we enjoy." 26. You should describe what the festival is like—how full of attendees, how some exhibit their skills in oratory or in physical prowess, and so forth, while the others are spectators or listeners. You should briefly work up the general thesis, as Isocrates does in his *Panegyricus*,[34] by mentioning all ‹the good things› that customarily result from these civic festivals and gatherings.

27. In general, you should observe the following rule in treating subjects of this nature, namely, things acknowledged to be good or highly regarded. Open with a general

---

[33] Apollo.   [34] *Paneg.* 43–44.

---

[12] suppl. Bursian, RW   [13] ὕμνοις ἱλασκόμεθα RW ex
2.1.4: ὅμοια διδασκόμεθα codd.: εὐνοίᾳ ἱλασκόμεθα Bursian
[14] suppl. RW ex Isoc.

καλὸν ἡ μουσική, καλὸν ἡ τοξική, καλὸν ἡ πανήγυρις, ἐπάγειν δὲ τὰ καθ᾽ ἕκαστον· οὐ μὴν ἐνδιατρίψεις
ταῖς θέσεσι ταύταις, ἐπειδὴ δοκοῦσιν ἐν τῇ ὑποθέσει
ταύτῃ πλείους εὑρίσκεσθαι.

445   28. Μετὰ δὲ τὴν ἔκφρασιν τῆς πανηγύρεως ἐκφράσεις τὸν νεών· εἰ μὲν ὑψηλὸς εἴη οἷον ἀκροπόλει ἐξει-
καστέος, ὡς μεγέθει μὲν τοὺς τοιούτους καὶ ὑπερμε-
γέθεις ὑπερφέρων, ὕψει δὲ τὰ ὑψηλότατα τῶν ὀρῶν· εἰ
δὲ ἐναρμόνιος εἴη ἢ ἐκ λίθου[15] τοῦ [τῶν ὀρῶν][16] καλ-
λίστου, ἔτι τοίνυν τὴν τοῦ νεὼ στιλπνότητα καὶ τὴν
αὐγὴν τίς οὐκ ἂν ἐκπλαγείη; καὶ τὴν ἁρμονίαν τοῦ
λίθου εἴποις ἂν τῇ λύρᾳ τοῦ Ἀμφίονος συντεθεῖσθαι.
29. ποῖα μὲν οὕτω τείχη Βαβυλώνια κατεσκευάσθη
[καὶ λέγεται];[17] ποῖα δὲ τείχη Θηβαῖα; ποῖος νεὼς τῶν
παρ᾽ Ἀθηναίοις; τάχα που καὶ αὐτὴ τῇ λύρᾳ τοῦ θεοῦ
καὶ τῇ μουσικῇ συνετέθη· τὰ μὲν γὰρ Λαομέδοντος
τείχη Ἀπόλλων καὶ Ποσειδῶν κατασκευάσαι λέγον-
ται, τὸν δὲ παρ᾽ ἡμῖν νεών Ἀπόλλων σὺν Ἀθηνᾷ καὶ
Ἡφαίστῳ μᾶλλον δεδημιούργηκεν.

30. Ἐπὶ τούτοις ἐκφράσεις τὸ ἄγαλμα τοῦ θεοῦ
παραβάλλων τῷ Ὀλυμπίῳ Διί, καὶ Ἀθηνᾷ τῇ ἐν
ἀκροπόλει τῶν Ἀθηναίων. εἶτα ἐπάξεις, ποῖος Φειδίας,
τίς Δαίδαλος τοσοῦτον ἐδημιούργησε ξόανον; τάχα
που ἐξ οὐρανοῦ τὸ ἄγαλμα τοῦτ᾽ ἐρρύη. καὶ ὅτι ἐστε-
φάνωται δάφναις, φυτῷ προσήκοντι τῷ θεῷ κατὰ
Δελφούς. καὶ τὸ ἄλσος ἐκφράσεις καὶ ποταμοὺς τοὺς
ἐγγὺς καὶ τὰς πηγάς· καὶ ὅτι οὐ πολὺ τὸ διάστημα,

thesis to the effect that music is a good thing, archery is good, and festivals are good, and then supply details. But you should not dwell on these generalizations, since it appears that numerous ones can be found in this subject matter.

28. After the description of the festival, you should describe the temple. If it is lofty, compare it to an acropolis, on the grounds that it surpasses similar massive temples in size, and in height surpasses the highest mountains. And if it has harmonious proportions or is made of very beautiful stone, say, "Moreover, who would not be astonished at the temple's luster and brilliance? You might say that its harmonious stonework was fashioned by Amphion's lyre. 29. What walls at Babylon were constructed like this? what walls at Thebes? what temple in Athens? Perhaps it was built by the music of the god's own lyre. For Apollo and Poseidon are said to have built Laomedon's walls, but Apollo constructed our temple with the help of Athena and Hephaestus."

30. After this, describe the statue of the god and compare it with that of Zeus at Olympia or Athena on the acropolis at Athens. Then add, "What Phidias, what Daedalus constructed so great a statue? Perhaps it fell from heaven." And further, "It is crowned with laurel, the plant belonging to the god according to the Delphians." You should also describe the temple precinct and nearby rivers and springs, saying that the distance between them is not

---

15 ἐκ λίθου RW: λίθος ἐκ codd.
16 secl. Bursian, RW
17 om. mW: secl. RW

καὶ ὅτι πᾶσα ἡ ἄνοδος ἡ ἐπὶ τὸ ἱερὸν ἱερὰ καὶ ἀνα-
κειμένη Ἀπόλλωνι.

31. Μέλλων δὲ πληροῦν τὴν ὑπόθεσιν χρήσῃ ἀνα-
κλητικοῖς ὀνόμασι τοῦ θεοῦ οὕτως· ἀλλ᾽ ὦ Σμίνθιε καὶ
Πύθιε, ἀπὸ σοῦ γὰρ ἀρξάμενος ὁ λόγος εἰς σὲ καὶ
τελευτήσει, ποίαις σὲ προσηγορίαις προσφθέγξομαι;
οἱ μὲν σὲ Λύκειον λέγουσιν, οἱ δὲ Δήλιον, οἱ δὲ
Ἀσκραῖον, ἄλλοι δὲ Ἄκτιον, Λακεδαιμόνιοι δὲ Ἀμυ-
κλαῖον, Ἀθηναῖοι πατρῷον, Βραγχιάτην Μιλήσιοι·
πᾶσαν πόλιν καὶ πᾶσαν χώραν καὶ πᾶν ἔθνος διέπεις
446 καὶ καθάπερ τὸν οὐρανὸν περιχορεύεις ἔχων περὶ σεαυτὸν τοὺς χοροὺς τῶν ἀστέρων, οὕτω καὶ τὴν οἰκου-
μένην πᾶσαν διέπεις· 32. Μίθραν σε Πέρσαι λέγουσιν, Ὧρον Αἰγύπτιοι (σὺ γὰρ εἰς κύκλον τὰς ὥρας
ἄγεις), Διόνυσον Θηβαῖοι, Δελφοὶ δὲ διπλῇ προση-
γορίᾳ τιμῶσιν, Ἀπόλλωνα καὶ Διόνυσον λέγοντες·
περὶ σὲ †θοῦραι†,[18] περὶ σὲ Θυάδες, παρὰ σοῦ καὶ
σελήνη τὴν ἀκτῖνα λαμβάνει, Χαλδαῖοι δὲ ἄστρων
ἡγεμόνα λέγουσιν· εἴτε οὖν ταύταις χαίρεις ταῖς
προσηγορίαις, εἴτε τούτων ἀμείνοσι, σὺ μὲν ἀκμάζειν
ἀεὶ ταῖς εὐδαιμονίαις τὴν πόλιν τήνδε δίδου, ἐσαεὶ δὲ
τήνδε συγκροτεῖσθαί σοι τὴν πανήγυριν· νεῦσον δὲ
καὶ χάριν τοῖς λόγοις· παρὰ σοῦ γὰρ καὶ οἱ λόγοι καὶ
ἡ πόλις.

[18] obel. RW: Μοῦσαι coni. Spengel: alia alii

great, and that the entire approach to the temple is sacred and dedicated to Apollo.

31. When you are about to conclude your subject, employ epithets of the god in the following way. "O Sminthian and Pythian, since my speech began with you and with you it will end, with what names shall I address you? Some call you Lycian, others Delian, others Ascraean,[35] others Actian.[36] The Lacedaemonians call you Amyclaean, the Athenians Patroös, the Milesians Branchiate. You rule over every city, every land, and every nation, and you govern the whole inhabited world, as you dance across the sky surrounded by choruses of stars. 32. The Persians call you Mithras, the Egyptians Horus (for you bring round the seasons),[37] the Thebans call you Dionysus; the Delphians honor you with two names, calling you Apollo and Dionysus, for around you are frenzied women,[38] around you are Bacchants. From you the moon derives its splendor, while the Chaldeans call you the leader of the stars. So, whether you delight in these appellations, or in some more favored than these, grant that this city may forever flourish in prosperity and that it may forever hold this festival in your honor. And grant grace to these words, for both these words and the city are gifts from you."

---

[35] The hometown of Hesiod in Boeotia.   [36] Actian Apollo was thought to have favored Octavian when he defeated Antony at Actium in 31 BC.   [37] There is a play on the names Hōrus and Hōrai (Seasons).   [38] Manuscript p reads θοῦραι (frenzied women). Spengel's conjecture of Μοῦσαι makes good sense (cf. §19), but it is difficult to imagine how such an obvious reading would be corrupted to θοῦραι. With the manuscript reading, both groups of women indicate Apollo's Dionysiac aspect.

[DIONYSIUS OF
HALICARNASSUS]
ARS RHETORICA

INTRODUCTION

The same tenth-century manuscript (Parisinus Graecus 1741) that contains the two treatises of Menander Rhetor includes eleven chapters (incorrectly) attributed to Dionysius of Halicarnassus, the early first-century AD author of *Roman Antiquities* and various literary studies.[1] Of these eleven chapters, the first seven are addressed to one Echecrates and provide instructions on composing selected epideictic speeches to be delivered on specific occasions: 1. panegyrics praising a public festival, 2. wedding speeches, 3. birthday speeches, 4. epithalamia, 5. addresses to arriving governors, 6. funeral speeches, and 7. exhortations to athletes. Five of these chapters treat similar occasions as those in M.'s second treatise: wedding speeches (M. 2.6), epithalamia (M. 2.5), birthday speeches (M. 2.7), addresses to arriving magistrates (M. 2.2), and funeral speeches (M. 2.8, 2.10, and 2.15). Only panegyrics (1) and exhortations to athletes (7) are unique to the *Ars*.

These seven chapters are in all likelihood of the same period as Menander's treatises. First of all, the mention of

[1] The attribution to Dionysius of Halicarnassus goes back to a scholion at the beginning of chapter 10, which conjectures, on the basis of a reference to a work on *Mimesis*, that the author is Dionysius. This attribution was subsequently applied to the entire treatise in the earliest editions.

emperors in the panegyric speech (1.7) and addresses to arriving magistrates (5.1–2) point to a period much later than that of Dionysius of Halicarnassus and are consistent with M.'s repeated references to emperors and the governors they send to the provinces. A secure *terminus post quem* is provided by a reference at 2.9 to Nicostratus (a second-century sophist, also mentioned by M. at 2.3.5). In addition, his frequent citation of Plato is consistent with M.'s practice in Treatise I. Consequently, a date of mid-to-late third century AD is likely.

THE UNITY OF *ARS RHETORICA*, CHAPTERS 1–7

These chapters are unified by a consistent style, repeated addresses to one Echecrates (apparently a former student), and by similar instructions on composing the speeches, laying out topics and usually ending with observations on the appropriate style. The four chapters that follow in the manuscript (8–11) are undoubtedly from a separate treatise and very probably by a different author, and are therefore excluded from this edition.[2] Chapters 8 and 9 treat figured speech in which covert meanings are concealed in the discourse, while chapters 10 and 11 treat mistakes in declamations.

The order of the seven chapters is of particular interest. The author explicitly remarks at 4.1 that birthday speeches (3) should have followed epithalamia (4), but

[2] Heath provides an excellent survey of these four chapters and argues that they may date from the second century AD. See also Russell 1979b and Kennedy, 299–300.

adds cryptically, it "nearly slipped my mind because of the noise and confusion surrounding my departure." At the beginning of exhortations to athletes (7), he states that it naturally follows the preceding instructions on panegyrics (1), which indeed form a logical pair.[3]

THE IDENTITY OF ECHECRATES

Whereas M. never names the second-person singular "you" in his two treatises, only once referring to "my dearest companion" ($\hat{\omega}$ γλυκύτατε τῶν ἑταίρων), at 2.2.34, without naming him, Echecrates is addressed by name three times, at the beginning of 1, 5, and 7. The name is rare in the second and third centuries, and given the well-known Echecrates of Plato's *Phaedo*, the name is likely a literary pseudonym. This probability is reinforced by the strong influence of Plato throughout the treatise, beginning with the quotation from Plato's *Laws* in the very first sentence at 1.1.[4] Plato is named at 3.1, 5.1, and 6.2, 3, and 6. In addition, the funeral speech (6) draws heavily (without acknowledgment) on Plato's *Phaedo* for consolatory topics.[5]

Not only is he named, but Echecrates is given a personality within the treatise as a student and close friend of the author. In 1.1 the author tells Echecrates that he will guide him "down a path untrodden by many" by imparting

---

[3] For a detailed overview of the treatise, see Korenjak. His arguments for an overarching structure if one moves chapter 7 after 1 are (to me) unconvincing.

[4] The reference at the end of the chapter to "the leader and head of our chorus" (1.8) undoubtedly refers to Plato.

[5] See the note on 6.6.

the rhetorical wisdom he has inherited from the poetic tradition going back as far as Hesiod and the Muses. At 2.1 he warmly addresses "my dear friend" (μετὰ σοῦ τῆς φίλης ἐμοὶ κεφαλῆς) as a fellow rhetor and stresses the strong bond of affection between them in spite of being separated at the moment. He goes on to say that Echecrates had studied with him as a young man and composed rhetorical exercises. It is implied at 2.8 that Echecrates himself may be the groom delivering the speech and that these instructions constitute a wedding gift. At 5.1 he says that he and Echecrates share Isocrates as a "companion" (ὁ σὸς ἑταῖρος καὶ ἐμός). All these remarks imply that Echecrates is a budding rhetor who may be called upon to deliver a variety of speeches, ranging from intimate wedding, birthday, and funeral speeches to public addresses given to governors and large audiences at public festivals and athletic games.

MANUSCRIPTS

The principal manuscripts that serve as the basis of modern editions are:

P Parisinus graecus 1741   mid 10th c.
G Codex Guelferbytanus 14   15th c.   a copy of P

EDITIONS AND TRANSLATIONS

Aldus Manutius. 1508. *Rhetores Graeci*. Vol. 1, 225–80, *editio princeps*. Venice: Aldus.

Sylburg, F. 1586. Διονυσίου Ἁλικαρνάσεως τὰ εὑρισκόμενα. Francofurdi: Andraea Wecheli. This edition offers a number of emendations.

Reiske, J. J. 1775. *Dionysii Halicarnassensis Opera Omnia Graece et Latine*. Vol. 5, 225–80. Leipzig: Weidmann. A complete text with Latin translation and some notes.

Schott, H. A. 1804. TEXNH PHTOPIKH *Quae Vulgo Integra Dionysio Halicarnassensi Tribuitur, Emendata, Nova Versione Latina et Commentario Illustrata*. Leipzig: E. B. Suicquerti. It contains a text, Latin translation, and extensive notes.

Usener, H., and L. Radermacher. 1904. *Dionysii Halicarnasei Opuscula*. Vol. 2. Leipzig: Teubner. *Ars Rhetorica*, 253–92 (= *Dionysii Halicarnasei Quae Exstant*, vol. 6; *Opuscula*, vol. 2, 1929). The standard text, often reprinted.

Russell, D. A., and N. Wilson. 1981. *Menander Rhetor*. Oxford: Oxford University Press. *Appendix*, Pseudo-Dionysius, *On Epideictic Speeches*, 362–81. It provides a complete English translation (the first in a modern language) with brief notes on the Greek text and some explanatory notes.

Manieri, A. 2005. *Pseudo-Dionigi di Alicarnasso, I discorsi per le feste e per i giochi (Ars. Rhet. I e VII Us.-Rad.). Edizione, traduzione e commento*. Rome: Ateneo. A valuable edition with a conservative text, translation, and full-scale commentary on panegyrics (1) and exhortations to athletes (7).

REFERENCES

Heath, M. 2003. "Pseudo-Dionysius *Art of Rhetoric* 8–11: Figured Speech, Declamation, and Criticism." *AJP* 124: 81–105.

Kennedy, G. A. 2003. "Some Recent Controversies in the Study of Later Greek Rhetoric." *AJP* 124: 295–301.

Korenjak, M. 2010. "Ps-Dionysius 'Ars Rhetorica' I–VII: One Complete Treatise." *HSCP* 105: 239–54.

Russell, D. A. 1979a. "Rhetors at the Wedding." *PCPS* 25: 104–17.

———. 1979b. "Classicizing Rhetoric and Criticism: The Pseudo-Dionysian *Exetasis* and *Mistakes in Declamation*." In *Le classicisme à Rome aux 1ers siècles avant et après J.-C.*, edited by H. Flashar, *Entretiens Fondation Hardt* 25, 113–34. Geneva.

CONTENTS

Following are the seven chapters in this edition with references to Radermacher's pagination and lineation. R.'s pages are indicated in the margin of the Greek text.

1. ΤΕΧΝΗ ΠΕΡΙ ΤΩΝ
ΠΑΝΗΓΥΡΙΚΩΝ

255 1. Πανηγύρεις εὕρημα μὲν καὶ δῶρον θεῶν εἰς ἀνά-
παυσιν τῶν περὶ τὸν βίον αἰεὶ πόνων παραδιδόμεναι,
ὥς που ὁ Πλάτων φησίν, οἰκτειράντων τῶν θεῶν τὸ
ἀνθρώπειον ἐπίπονον γένος· συνήχθησαν δὲ ὑπὸ ἀνθρώπων σοφῶν, κατεστάθησαν δὲ ὑπὸ πόλεων κοινῇ
κοινῷ δόγματι εἰς τέρψιν καὶ ψυχαγωγίαν τῶν παρόντων. συντέλεια δὲ ἡ εἰς τὰς πανηγύρεις ἄλλη ἄλλων·
παρὰ μὲν τῶν πλουσίων δαπάναι χρημάτων, παρὰ δὲ
τῶν ἀρχόντων κόσμος περὶ τὴν πανήγυριν καὶ τῶν
ἐπιτηδείων εὐπορία· οἱ δὲ ἀθληταὶ τῇ ῥώμῃ τῶν σωμάτων κοσμοῦσι τὴν πανήγυριν, καὶ ὅσοι γε δὴ Μου-
256 σῶν καὶ Ἀπόλλωνος ὀπαδοί, τῇ μουσικῇ τῇ παρ' ἑαυτῶν. ἀνδρὶ δὲ περὶ λόγους ἐσπουδακότι καὶ σύμπαντα

---

1 An adaptation of Leg. 2.653d: θεοὶ δὲ οἰκτείραντες τὸ τῶν
ἀνθρώπων ἐπίπονον πεφυκὸς γένος ἀναπαύλας τε αὐτοῖς τῶν

THE *ARS RHETORICA*
ATTRIBUTED TO DIONYSIUS
OF HALICARNASSUS [DH]

1. THE ARTFUL COMPOSITION
OF PANEGYRICS

1. Panegyric festivals are an invention and gift of the gods passed on to us to provide a respite from the continuous labors of life, as Plato says, because the gods took pity on the toiling human race.[1] Festivals were convened by wise men and established in cities by common consent with a public decree to provide enjoyment and entertainment for those who attend. Contributions to panegyric festivals by individuals vary. Rich people contribute expenditures of money, while magistrates see to the splendor of the festival and provide an abundance of necessary provisions. The athletes grace the festival with their physical strength, as do those who are servants of the Muses and Apollo with their musical performances. And, in my opinion, it is proper for a man who has studied oratory and devoted his

πόνων ἐτάξαντο τὰς τῶν ἑορτῶν ἀμοιβάς ("The gods, in pity for the human race thus born to misery, have ordained the feasts of thanksgiving as periods of respite from their troubles" (R. G. Bury, trans.).

369

τὸν ἑαυτοῦ βίον ἀνατεθεικότι τούτοις πρέποι ἂν οἶμαι
τοῖς τοιούτοις [λόγοις]¹ κοσμεῖν τὴν πανήγυριν, τέχνῃ
μετιόντι τὸν λόγον, ὡς μὴ κατὰ τοὺς πολλοὺς εἴη
αὐτῷ γινόμενος.

Φέρε οὖν εἰς τοῦτο, ὦ Ἐχέκρατες, λέγωμέν σοι,
ὥσπερ ὁδοῦ τινος ἀστιβοῦς τοῖς πολλοῖς ἡγεμόνες
γιγνόμενοι, ἃ πάλαι παρὰ τῶν πατέρων τῆς ἡμεδα-
πῆς σοφίας παραλαβόντες ἔχομεν, ἐκεῖνοι δὲ καὶ οἱ
ἔτι τούτων ἀνωτέρω παρ' Ἑρμοῦ τε καὶ Μουσῶν λαβεῖν ἔφασαν οὐ μεῖον' ἢ ὁ Ἀσκραῖος ποιμὴν [ποίη-
σιν]² παρὰ τῶν αὐτῶν τούτων ἐν τῷ Ἑλικῶνι. ἴθι οὖν
σὺν τέχνῃ οὑτωσὶ μετίωμεν τοὺς λόγους.

2. Θεὸς μέν γέ που πάντως πάσης ἡστινοσοῦν
πανηγύρεως ἡγεμὼν καὶ ἐπώνυμος, οἷον Ὀλυμπίων
μὲν Ὀλύμπιος Ζεύς, τῆς³ δὲ ἐν Πυθοῖ Ἀπόλλων. ἀρχὴ
μὲν δὴ τοῦ λόγου τοῦδε τοῦ θεοῦ, ὅστίς ποτ' ἂν ᾖ,
ἔπαινος ἡμῖν γιγνέσθω, ὥσπερ πρόσωπόν τι τηλαυ-
γὲς προκείμενος τοῦ λόγου. ἐπαινέσεις δὲ ἀπὸ τῶν
προσόντων τῷ θεῷ· εἰ μὲν Ζεύς, ὅτι βασιλεὺς θεῶν,
ὅτι τῶν ὅλων δημιουργός· εἰ δὲ Ἀπόλλων, ὅτι μουσι-
κῆς εὑρετής, ὅτι ὁ αὐτὸς Ἡλίῳ, Ἥλιος δὲ πάντων
257   πᾶσιν ἀγαθῶν αἴτιος· εἰ δὲ Ἡρακλῆς, ὅτι Διός, καὶ ἃ

---

¹ secl. Hermann, RW
² secl. Radermacher
³ RW: τοῦ codd.

---

² He cannot be identified. The best known Echecrates is the
interlocutor in Plato's *Phaedo*. In view of the previous citation of

370

entire life to it to grace the festival by such means, composing his speech with artfulness so that it may avoid being merely ordinary.

To achieve this, Echecrates,[2] let me tell you—like a guide down a path untrodden by many—what I have inherited from the fathers of my wisdom, which they themselves and their predecessors claimed to have received from Hermes and the Muses, no less than what Hesiod the Ascraean shepherd had acquired from those same Muses on Mt. Helicon.[3] Let us then compose our speeches with artfulness in the following way.

2. Now, a god always presides at any festival and gives his name to it, as Olympian Zeus with the Olympic games and Apollo at the festival at Pytho.[4] The speech should begin with praise of this god, whoever he may be, placed like "a far-shining façade"[5] at the front of the speech. You should praise the god through his attributes. If it is Zeus, say that he is king of the gods and the creator of the universe; if Apollo, that he invented music, that he is the same as the Sun,[6] who is the source of all good things for everyone; if Heracles, say that he is the son of Zeus and tell what

Plato (and the admiration for Plato in [DH]), the name may be both fictional and allusive. He is also named at the beginning of essays 5 and 7 (and alluded to at 2.1).

[3] Cf. Hes. *Theog.* 22–34, although no specific instructions are given there.

[4] That is, Delphi, where Pythian Apollo presides.

[5] That is, of a building; cf. Pind. *Ol.* 6.3–4 (πρόσωπον . . . τηλαυγές).

[6] Cf. M. 1.5.2 and 2.16.4.

παρέσχεν τῷ βίῳ. καὶ σχεδὸν ὁ τόπος συμπληρωθή-
σεται ἐξ ὧν ἕκαστος ἢ εὗρεν ἢ παρέσχεν τοῖς ἀνθρώποις. ἐν βραχεῖ δὲ ταῦτα, ὡς μὴ τοῦ ἐπιόντος ὁ λόγος
ὁ προάγων μείζων γίγνοιτο.

3. Ἐφεξῆς ἐπιέναι χρὴ τὸν ἔπαινον τῆς πόλεως, ἐν
ᾗ ἡ πανήγυρις· περὶ θέσεως αὐτῆς, περὶ γενέσεως· ἐν
ᾧ τίς ὁ κτίστης θεὸς ἢ ἥρως, καὶ εἴ τι ἔχεις περὶ
αὐτοῦ εἰπεῖν· εἴ τι πέπρακται τῇ πόλει ἢ ἐν πολέμοις
ἢ ἐπ᾽ εἰρήνης. ἁρμόσει δὲ καὶ περὶ μεγέθους λέγειν,
εἰ μεγάλη, ἢ <εἰ>[4] σμικρά, ὅτι κάλλει διαφέρουσα, ὅτι
εἰ καὶ σμικρά, ἀλλὰ δυνάμει ἰσοῦται ταῖς μεγάλαις.
ὅσα περὶ κόσμου, οἷον ἱερῶν ἢ τῶν ἐν τούτοις ἀναθη-
μάτων, δημοσίων οἰκοδομημάτων, ἰδιωτικῶν, ὥς που
καὶ Ἡρόδοτος πεντώροφα καὶ ἐξώροφα φησὶν εἶναι
ἐν Βαβυλῶνι· ἂν ποταμὸς ᾖ μέγας ἢ καθαρὸς ἢ συμ-
βαλλόμενος τοῖς ἐνοικοῦσι τὴν χώραν· εἰ δὲ δὴ καὶ
μῦθος εἴη λεγόμενός τις περὶ τῆς πόλεως, οὕτω μὲν
ἂν καὶ πολλὴν γλυκύτητα ἔχοι ὁ λόγος.

4. Λεκτέον δὲ ἐπὶ τούτοις καὶ περὶ αὐτοῦ τοῦ ἀγῶνος, τίς ἀρχὴ καὶ κατάστασις αὐτοῦ ἢ ἐφ᾽ οἷστισιν
ἐτέθη, εἴτε μῦθός τις εἴη εἴτε ἄλλό τι ἀρχαῖον. ἐν
τούτῳ δὲ γενόμενος μὴ ἁπλῶς παρέλθῃς τὸν τόπον,
258 ἀλλὰ παραβαλεῖν χρὴ πρὸς τοὺς ἄλλους ἀγῶνας.
τοῦτο δ᾽ εὐπορήσεις τῷ λόγῳ, οἷον ἀπὸ καιροῦ παρα-
βάλλων· εἰ μὲν πρὸς ἔαρ ἄγοιτο, ὅτι ἐν τῷ συμμετρο-
τάτῳ πρὸς ἑκάτερα. εἰ δὲ ἐν χειμῶνι, ὅτι ἐν τῷ ἐρρω-

4 suppl. Radermacher

he contributed to human life.[7] In sum, this topic will be full of the blessings that each god invented or provided for human beings. These should be brief, however, lest the introduction be longer than what follows.

3. Next you should take up praise of the city where the festival is being held, including its location, its origin, and its founding god or hero, along with anything you can say about him and anything the city has accomplished in war or peace. It is also appropriate to mention its size if it is great, or, if it is small, that it is distinguished by its beauty, and that even though small, it is as influential as big cities. Tell too of its adornments such as temples or the dedications in them, public buildings, and private ones like those in Babylon of five or six stories that Herodotus referred to,[8] and mention if there is a river that is big or clear, or supplies the inhabitants of the region. Finally, if there is any legend told about the city, the speech would gain much sweetness by its inclusion.

4. After this, you should speak about the games themselves,[9] telling of their origin and establishment, or why they were instituted, whether in myth or some other ancient legend. At this point, do not simply pass over this topic, but compare the games with others. You will have plenty of material for this in your speech, for example by comparing the seasons. If they are held in the spring, say that it is the most balanced season with respect to heat or

---

[7] That is, by ridding the world of vicious beings. Cf. M. 2.3.4: "bring up Heracles and tell how he always obeyed Zeus' commands, how he labored on behalf of human life."   [8] Hdt. 1.180, where, however, he cites buildings of three or four stories.

[9] Cf. M.'s treatment of panegyric festivals at 1.16.28–33.

μενεστάτῳ καὶ ἀνδρειοτάτῳ, ὡς ἂν εἴποι τις, καιρῷ· εἰ
δ' ἐν θέρει, ὅτι πρὸς ἄσκησιν καὶ ἡ θεωρία⁵ τῶν θεω-
μένων κατεστάθη, καὶ ὅτι ἔλεγχος τῆς προαιρέσεως,
[ὡς]⁶ καὶ μὴ ὄντων ἀθλητῶν τοὺς θεωμένους ἀγωνίζεσθαι. ἔχοις δ' ἂν καὶ τὸ φθινόπωρον ἐπαινεῖν καὶ
[ὅτι]⁷ ἀπὸ συγκομιδῆς τῶν καρπῶν καὶ ἀπὸ τοῦ ἤδη
παύεσθαι τοὺς ἀνθρώπους τῶν πόνων.

5. Σκοπεῖσθαι δὲ καὶ τὸν τρόπον τῆς διαθέσεως τοῦ
ἀγῶνος δεῖ. εἰ μὲν μουσικὸς καὶ γυμνικὸς εἴη, ὅτι τε-
λεώτατος ὁ ἀγὼν καὶ ἀνενδεῶς κεκραμένος καὶ ῥώμῃ
σωμάτων καὶ καλλιφωνίᾳ καὶ τοῖς λοιποῖς μέρεσι τῆς
μουσικῆς· εἰ δὲ γυμνικός, ὅτι τὴν μουσικὴν ὡς ἐκθη-
λύνουσαν τὴν ψυχὴν παρῃτήσατο, τὴν δὲ ῥώμην τῶν
σωμάτων παρέλαβεν, καὶ ὅτι ὁ τρόπος τῆς ἀγωνίας
χρήσιμος πρὸς τὴν ἀνδρείαν τὴν ἐν τοῖς πολέμοις.

6. Μὴ παρέργως δὲ μηδὲ αὐτὸν τὸν στέφανον παρέλθῃς, ὅστις ἐπῇ (οὐδὲ γὰρ ἐν τούτῳ γενόμενος ἀπορήσεις ἐπαίνου)· τὴν μὲν δρῦν, ὅτι ἱερὰ Διός, καὶ ὅτι
ἡ πρώτη καὶ πρεσβυτάτη τροφὴ τῶν ἀνθρώπων, καὶ
ὅτι οὐκ ἄφωνος, ἀλλὰ καὶ ἐφθέγξατό ποτε ἐν Δωδώνῃ.
259 εἰ δὲ ἐλαία, ὅτι ἱερὰ τῆς Ἀθηνᾶς, καὶ ὅτι ἄκος πόνων,
καὶ ὅτι τὰ τρόπαια ἀπὸ τούτου τοῦ φυτοῦ ἀνέθεσαν

---

⁵ ἡ θεωρία Nissen: θεωρίαν P   ⁶ om. G
⁷ secl. Sylburg

---

10 Cf. M. 1.11.5: "We should consider those cities to be most
temperate that remain in each state [i.e., heat and cold] for a
satisfactory length of time."

cold;[10] if in winter, that it is the most powerful and, so to speak, manliest season; if in summer, that the spectacle was set up to give the spectators exercise,[11] that it tests their determination and makes them struggle, even without reference to any athletes. You can also praise autumn both for its harvest of crops and because at that time men have respite from their labors.

5. You must also consider what kind of competition has been arranged. If it is both musical and athletic, say that it is the most perfect kind and is a complete mixture of physical strength, beautiful singing, and other aspects of music. If it is only athletic, say that it has rejected music as making the soul effeminate and has chosen physical strength, adding that this type of competition is useful for developing courage in war.

6. Do not pass lightly over the crown itself, whatever sort it is, because you will not lack for praise on this point either. If the crown is of oak, say that it is sacred to Zeus, that it was the first and most ancient food for men,[12] and that it is not voiceless, for it actually spoke in the past at Dodona.[13] If it is of olive, say that it is sacred to Athena, that it is a salve for pains,[14] that ancients erected trophies

---

[11] Hot summers were arduous times for sports. Pind. *Ol.* 3.11–24 tells of Heracles bringing wild olive trees from the far north to provide shade at Olympia, where the festival was held in August. [12] Primitive man supposedly fed on acorns; cf. Ap. Rhod. 4.264–65. [13] Cf. Aesch. *PV* 832: "and the astonishing marvel of the talking oaks" (τέρας τ᾽ ἄπιστον, αἱ προσήγοροι δρύες). Cf. also Hom. *Od.* 14.327–28 and Ap. Rhod. 1.524–27.

[14] Pl. *Menex.* 238a calls olive oil a "balm for pains" (πόνων ἀρωγήν). Cf. also Pl. *Prt.* 334b.

οἱ παλαιοί, καὶ ὅτι τῆς νίκης τοῦτο σύμβολον τὸ
φυτόν, καὶ ὅτι ἡ Ἀθηνᾶ τούτῳ πρώτη ἐστέψατο νική-
σασα τὸν Ποσειδῶνα, καὶ ὅτι οἰκειότατον τοῖς ἀγωνιζομένοις (τὰ γὰρ γυμνάσια διὰ τοῦ ἐλαίου διαπο-
νεῖται), καὶ ὅτι συναγωνίζεται πρὸς τὸν λόγον δι' οὗ
πανηγύρεις κοσμοῦνται. καὶ τὴν δάφνην δὲ ἐρεῖς ὅτι
καὶ ἱερὰ τοῦ Ἀπόλλωνος καὶ μαντικὸν τὸ φυτόν· εἰ
δὲ βούλει καὶ τοῦ μύθου ἐφάπτεσθαι τοῦ περὶ τῆς
Δάφνης, οὐδὲ τοῦτό σοι ἀπὸ[8] τρόπου εἴη ἂν εἰρημένον.
ὁμοίως δὲ καὶ ἕτερον εἰ ἐπείη, οἰονεὶ καρποὶ Δημητρια-
κοὶ ἢ πίτυς, εὐπορήσεις που καὶ περὶ τούτων ἑκάστου. οὐκ ἔξω δὲ φιλοτιμίας οὐδὲ τὸ παραβαλεῖν τὸν
στέφανον πρὸς τοὺς παρ' ἄλλοις.

7. Ὁ δέ σοι τοῦ παντὸς λόγου οἰονεὶ κολοφὼν ἐπ-
ήχθω τοῦ βασιλέως ἔπαινος, καὶ ὅτι τῷ ὄντι ἀγωνοθέτης πάντων ἀγώνων ὁ τὴν εἰρήνην πρυτανεύων, δι'
ἣν καὶ τοὺς ἀγῶνας ἐπιτελεῖν οἷόν τε. ἤδη δέ τινες καὶ
τοὺς διατιθέντας τοὺς ἀγῶνας ἐπήνεσαν, εἰ ἄρα ἔνδο-
ξοί τινες οὗτοι, ὅτι καὶ ἐν ἄλλοις πρότερον γενόμενοι
χρήσιμοι, καὶ ἐν τούτοις ὅτι φιλοτιμότατοι. εἰ δὲ μὴ

---

[8] corr. Aldus hic et 3.4, 7.2: ἄπο P

---

[15] A close imitation of Aristid. *Panath.* 41: Ἀθηνᾶ . . . κατα-
δείκνυσι τὸν θάλλον νίκης εἶναι σύμβολον ("Athena designates
the branch to be the symbol of victory").

[16] In the contest over patronage of Athens; cf. M. 1.16.12.

[17] Athletes anointed their bodies with olive oil for protection
from the sun, dryness, and dirt.

made of this tree, that the plant is a symbol of victory,[15] that Athena was the first to crown herself with it when she prevailed over Poseidon,[16] that it is especially appropriate for those who compete because exercise is performed with the aid of olive oil,[17] and that olive oil assists in preparing the speech[18] that graces panegyric festivals. If it is of laurel, say that it is sacred to Apollo and is a prophetic tree.[19] If you wish to include a story about Daphne,[20] this would not be inappropriate. Likewise, if another plant is awarded, like Demeter's grain or pine,[21] you will have plenty to say about each of these as well. It would also confer distinction to compare this crown with those in other contests.

7. You should make praise of the emperor the finishing touch,[22] so to speak, of the entire speech, and say that the true organizer of all games is the one presiding over the peace that makes it possible to hold the games. Some have praised the actual organizers of the games, if in fact they are distinguished, by noting that though they were previously benefactors in other ways, in this case they are especially munificent. But if you do not have any former deeds

---

[18] That is, it provides fuel for the lamp (the midnight oil) for composing the speech.

[19] Fumes from burning laurel supposedly inspired the Pythia at Delphi to prophesy.

[20] For Apollo's falling in love with Daphne (Laurel), cf., for example, Ov. *Met.* 1.452–567.

[21] Crowns of barley (Demeter's grain) were awarded at the Eleusinia (cf. schol. Pind. *Ol.* 9.150b and *Isthm.* 1.81a), those of pine at the Isthmia.

[22] κολοφών (summit, crown, apex).

ἄλλα ἔχεις πρεσβύτερα, ὅτι ἀρχὴ τῆς φιλοτιμίας τῆς
περὶ τὴν πατρίδα μεγίστη καὶ Ἑλληνικωτάτη.

260   8. Ἡ δὲ λέξις ἄλλη μὲν κατὰ τὴν ἑκάστων φύσιν
ἢ βούλησιν. εἰ δὲ δὴ κρατεῖν χρὴ τὴν ἐμὴν γνώμην,
οὐ μονότροπον ταύτην συμβουλεύσαιμ᾽ ἂν εἶναι ἀλλὰ
ποικίλην καὶ μεμιγμένην, καὶ τὰ μὲν <ἐν>[9] τῇ ἀφελείᾳ
προάγοντα, τὰ δὲ ἐν ἀντιθέτοις τε καὶ παρισώσεσιν
Ἰσοκράτους, τὰ δὲ διῃρημένως. ταύτην γὰρ τὴν ὁδὸν
καὶ τὸν τοῦ ἡμεδαποῦ χοροῦ ἡγεμόνα τε καὶ κορυ-
φαῖον οἶδα μετιόντα <πάντῃ>[10] ὡς ἔπος εἰπεῖν ἢ ἐν
τοῖς πλείστοις, εἰ μή τι πρὸς εἶδος γράφειν τι
προὔθετο· ἑκάστης δὲ ἰδέας ἔδωκεν ἡ ὕλη τὴν ἀφορ-
μήν. δεῖ δὲ τοῖς νοήμασιν ἐπακολουθοῦσαν καὶ τὴν
ἑρμηνείαν ἐπάγειν, οἷον τὰ μὲν ἀφηγηματικὰ καὶ μύθου τινὸς ἐχόμενα ἀφελῶς προάγοντα· ὅσα δὲ περὶ
βασιλέων ἢ θεῶν, σεμνῶς· ὅσα δὲ περὶ παραβολῶν
καὶ συγκρίσεων, πολιτικῶς· εἰ μὴ ἄρα τις πρὸς τὸ
ἀξίωμα <μίαν>[11] τινὰ ἰδέαν λόγου διὰ πάντων παρ-
έχοιτο· ἐπιδεικτικώτερον δὲ τὸ προειρημένον καὶ δη-
μοτερπέστερον.

[9] suppl. Radermacher
[10] suppl. Radermacher
[11] πρὸς τὸ ἀξίωμα <μίαν> Radermacher: πρὸστὸ ἀξίαν
τινὰ PG

[23] RW (followed by Manieri) interpret this sentence to mean:
"If you have nothing more important to put forward, make the

to mention, say that this first act of generosity to the city is the greatest and one most characteristically Greek.[23]

8. The style should vary according to each person's talents or purpose. If my own opinion is to prevail, I would advise against a uniform style in favor of one that is varied and mixed, treating some subjects with simplicity,[24] some with Isocratean antithesis and balancing of clauses, and others in an elevated style.[25] That is the procedure I know was followed by the leader and head of our chorus[26] nearly everywhere, or at least in most instances, unless, that is, he had determined to write in one particular manner. The subject matter gave him the impetus for each type of style. You must adopt a style that accords with the thoughts expressed. For example, you should treat narratives and mythical subjects simply; emperors or gods solemnly; comparisons and contrasts in the style of public oratory[27]—unless, that is, one employs a single style throughout the speech for the sake of dignity. What was said before,[28] however, is more appropriate for an epideictic performance and provides more pleasure to a general audience.

point that this is the greatest and most truly Hellenic foundation of patriotic ambition."

[24] For characteristics of a plainer style (ἀφελής, ἁπλοῦς, ἐρριμμένος, ἀκατασκεύαστος, συγγραφικός, ἄνετος), cf. M. 2.3.5, 22; 2.5.13; 2.6.26; and 2.14.15.

[25] For characteristics of an elevated style (σύντονος, διηρμένος), cf. M. 2.5.2–4, 2.8.8, and [DH] 5.7 and 6.6.

[26] Presumably Plato, quoted in §1.

[27] That is, in a mixed or periodic style.

[28] That is, before an exception was made for a single style.

2. ΜΕΘΟΔΟΣ ΓΑΜΗΛΙΩΝ

1. Ἐμοὶ μὲν ἦν τερπνὸν αὐτὸν παρόντα καὶ συγχορεύοντα καὶ ἀναβακχεύοντα μετὰ σοῦ τῆς φίλης ἐμοὶ κεφαλῆς ὑμνεῖν τε καὶ ἀνυμνεῖν τὸν μικρὸν ὕστερον ἐπιτελεσθησόμενον γάμον καὶ ᾄδειν γε τὸν ὑμέναιον τὸν ἐπὶ τοῖς γάμοις πρέπουτα λέγεσθαι. ἐπεὶ δὲ ἔοικεν δεσμός τις οὗτος ὁ πρὸς τοῖς λόγοις καὶ τῇ παιδεύσει τῇ παρούσῃ διαιρεῖν ἡμᾶς τοῖς σώμασιν καὶ τοῖς τόποις ἀπ' ἀλλήλων (μὴ γὰρ δὴ ταῖς ψυχαῖς τε καὶ διαθέσεσιν καὶ εὐνοίαις ταῖς ἐπ' αὐταῖς χωρισθείημέν ποτε), ἀλλ' οὖν ἔστω σοι ὥσπέρ τι δῶρον παρ' ἐμοῦ εἰς συντέλειάν τε καὶ κόσμον τῶν γάμων τὸ μηδὲ τῶν περὶ τούτων εἰωθότων λέγεσθαι μηδὲ αὐτὸν ἀπείρως ἔχειν, εἴτ' οὖν αὐτὸς καὶ παρὰ σεαυτῷ φυλάττειν βούλοιο εἴτε καὶ ἑτέρῳ τινὶ τοῦτον οἷον ἔρανόν τινα εἰς χάριν συνεισφέρειν.

Τάχα μὲν οὖν καὶ αὐτὸς ἤδη ποτὲ καὶ ἄλλοτε προανεκρούσω ἐν τοῖς τοιούτοις τῶν λόγων, ὁπηνίκα κομιδῇ νέος ὢν παρ' ἐμοὶ τὴν πρώτην ὁδὸν τῶν ῥητορικῶν μετῄεις, τά τε ἄλλα γράφων καὶ συγγράφων γυμνάσματά τε καὶ ἀσκήματα τῆς ῥητορικῆς, καὶ δὴ καὶ τὰς θέσεις οὕτω λεγομένας, καὶ τούτων τὰ εἰς τὸν περὶ αὐτοῦ τοῦ γάμου λόγον συντείνοντα καὶ τὴν

2. HOW TO COMPOSE
MARRIAGE SPEECHES

1. I would have enjoyed being with you, my dear friend, to dance and revel with you and to sing the praises of the marriage that is shortly to take place, and indeed to sing the hymeneal song that is duly intoned at weddings. But since our bondage (so to speak) to oratory and to our current teaching seems to separate us from each other physically and spatially—may we never be separated, however, in our souls and dispositions, and in the affection that results from these—please accept this gift from me for the purpose of celebrating and gracing weddings, so that you yourself may not be unfamiliar with the things that are usually said on these occasions, whether you wish to keep this information for yourself or to share it with someone else as a favor.

No doubt you yourself have on earlier occasions already made initial attempts at speeches such as these, when as a youngster you took your first steps on the path of rhetoric with me, by writing and composing rhetorical exercises and practice pieces—especially the ones called theses,[1] among which are arguments for marriage itself

[1] That is, general topics proposed for compositions.

προτροπὴν τὴν εἰς αὐτόν. 2. προκεχείρισται γὰρ ἐν
τοῖς μάλιστα καὶ τοῦτο πρὸ πάντων τοῖς νεωτέροις εἰς
γραφήν, εἰ γαμητέον. οὐ πόρρω δὲ οὐδ᾽ ὁ νῦν ὑφ᾽
ἡμῶν προχειριζόμενος λόγος τῆς περὶ τὰς τοιαύτας
ἰδέας τῶν λόγων θήρας. ἀμέλει γε τοιοῖσδε τόποις,
οἷς πέρ που καὶ ἐν ταῖς θέσεσιν ‹καὶ ἐνταῦθα χρησό-
262 μεθα. καὶ ἀρξόμεθα μὲν›[1] ἀπὸ θεῶν, καὶ ὅτι οὗτοι οἱ
εὑρόντες καὶ δείξαντες τοὺς γάμους τοῖς ἀνθρώποις·
Ζεὺς γὰρ καὶ Ἥρα, πρῶτοι ζευγνύντες τε καὶ συν-
δυάζοντες· οὕτω τοι ὁ μὲν καὶ πατὴρ καλεῖται πάντων,
ἡ δὲ Ζυγία ἀπὸ τοῦ ζευγνύναι τὸ θῆλυ τῷ ἄρρενι, καὶ
ἀπὸ τούτων τῶν θεῶν καὶ ὁ τῶν λοιπῶν θεῶν χορὸς
παρῆλθεν εἰς τὸν βίον τῶν ἐπιφημισθέντων τοῖς γάμοις, γαμηλίων τε καὶ γενεθλίων οὕτως ὀνομαζομέ-
νων· καὶ ὅτι ὁ γάμος αἴτιος τοῦ τε ὀνομασθῆναι τούτους τοὺς θεοὺς καὶ τιμᾶσθαι· ἄνευ γὰρ τῶν γάμων
οὐδ᾽ ἂν αἱ τιμαὶ τούτων παρῆλθον εἰς ἀνθρώπους.

3. Ἐφεξῆς ἐπάγειν χρὴ τὸν περὶ τῆς φύσεως λόγον,
καὶ ὅτι τοῦτο αὐτῆς ἔργον, τὸ γεννᾶν τε καὶ κυΐσκειν·
καὶ ὅτι διῆλθεν διὰ πάντων τὸ ἔργον αὐτῆς καὶ ζώων
καὶ φυτῶν. εἶτα τὴν διαφορὰν ἐπάξομεν τῆς ἐν τοῖς
ἀνθρώποις μίξεως καὶ κοινωνίας, ὅτι τὰ μὲν ἁπλῶς
καὶ ὡς ἔτυχεν μίγνυται, ὁ δὲ ἄνθρωπος τάξιν τινὰ καὶ
νόμον ἐξεῦρεν τοῦ γάμου, οὐκ ἀγεληδὸν δίκην θηρίων
ἐπιτρέπων μίγνυσθαι, ἀλλὰ σύμμιξιν καὶ κοινωνίαν
δυοῖν τὴν προσφορωτάτην εἰς ἅπαντα τὸν βίον με-

---

[1] lacunam stat. Radermacher et sugg. exempli causa

and exhortation to it.[2] 2. That is because more often than not one of the first assignments for young students is the composition, "should a person get married?" Nor is the speech I now propose far removed from the pursuit of that sort of composition. Indeed, ⟨we shall use here⟩[3] the same kind of topics as in those theses, ⟨and will begin⟩ with the gods, saying that they invented marriage and revealed it to humans, for Zeus and Hera were the first to join together and have intercourse, and that is why Zeus is called the father of all,[4] and Hera is called the Joiner (Zygia) because she joins female with male. And it was from these two gods that the chorus of the other gods hailed at weddings came into being, the ones called the gods of marriage (gamēlioi) and of birth (genethlioi). And marriage is the reason these gods are so named and honored, for without marriages they would never have found honor among men.

3. Next introduce the argument based on nature, namely that begetting and conception are nature's work, which pervades all beings, both animals and plants. Then we should introduce the singular quality of human intercourse and companionship, noting that animals and plants simply couple at random, whereas humans have invented order and regulation in marriage and do not sanction mating in herds like wild animals, but have devised the intercourse and companionship of two people as being of great-

[2] On this topic, cf. M. 2.5.6–12.

[3] These are Radermacher's suggested additions to fill the lacuna.

[4] Cf., for example, Hom. *Il.* 1.544: "father of men and gods."

μηχανημένος. ἐν ᾧ, ὅτι τοῦ μὲν θηριώδους καὶ πεπλα-
νημένου βίου ἀπηλλάγησαν, βίον δὲ ἥμερον καὶ τε-
ταγμένον ἔσχον διὰ τοῦ γάμου. καὶ ὅτι θνητὸν ὄν γε
τὸ ἀνθρώπειον ἐκ τῆς μίξεως καὶ κοινωνίας τοῦ γάμου
ἀθάνατον γέγονεν, ἐκ τῆς διαδοχῆς τῶν ἐπιγινομένων
263 ὥσπερ φῶς ἀναπτόμενον καὶ διαδιδόμενον ἀεὶ τοῖς
ἐπιγιγνομένοις τῇ γεννήσει τοῦ ἀνθρώπου καὶ μήποτε
ἀποσβεννύμενον. καὶ τοῦτον ἄν τις εἴποι δικαίως ἔρανον κάλλιστον οὐ χρημάτων οὐδὲ κτημάτων τινῶν,
ἀλλ᾽ αὐτῆς τῆς φύσεως καὶ τοῦ γένους.

4. Εἶτα ἐξετάσεις ἐπὶ τούτοις, ὅσα προσγίνεται τοῖς
γεγαμηκόσι. πρῶτον μὲν πρὸς δόξαν, ὅτι ἐνδοξότεροι
τὸ κάλλιστον μέρος τῆς ἀρετῆς εὐθὺς ἀπὸ τῶν γάμων
ἀρχόμενοι καρποῦσθαι, τὴν σωφροσύνην· ὁ γὰρ γάμος εὐθὺς καὶ σωφροσύνης δόξαν περιτίθησι τοῖς
ἀνθρώποις, καὶ οἱ τοιοῦτοι δοκοῦσιν τῆς μὲν ἀτάκτου
μίξεως ἀπηλλάχθαι, πρὸς δὲ μίαν ἀφορὰν μόνην τὴν
ἑαυτοῦ ἕκαστος γυναῖκα. ἐκ δὲ τούτου καὶ ἐντιμοτέ-
ρους ἀνάγκη γίγνεσθαι τοὺς ἀνθρώπους καὶ πιστοτέ-
ρους δοκεῖν καὶ εὐνουστέρους περὶ τὰς αὑτῶν πατρίδας ἐν παντὶ διὰ τὸ ὥσπερ ὅμηρα δεδωκέναι ταῖς
πατρίσι τοὺς ἑαυτῶν παῖδας, δι᾽ οὓς ἀναγκαῖον καὶ
μᾶλλον εἰς τὰς συμβουλίας παραλαμβάνεσθαι.

5. Καὶ πρὸς λύπας δὲ καὶ τὰ δυσχερῆ τὰ ἐν τῷ βίῳ
γάμος χρησιμώτατος, κουφότερα ταῦτα παρασκευά-
ζων ὥσπερ φορτία, μεταδιδόντων ἡμῶν ταῖς ἑαυτῶν
γυναιξὶν τῶν δυσχερῶν καὶ τῇ κοινωνίᾳ παρηγορου-
μένων. ἐν δὲ τούτῳ καὶ τὰ ἡδέα ἀνάγκη τερπνότερα

est advantage for their entire lives. Here, tell how humans freed themselves from the roaming life of animals and adopted an ordered and structured life thanks to marriage. Also, that through the intercourse and companionship of marriage, the human race, though mortal, has become immortal by passing on life to the next generations, like a lit torch never to be extinguished, continually handed on to successors by engendering human life. One might truly call this our greatest bequest—not one of money or possessions of any sort, but of nature herself and of the race.

4. Next you should examine all the advantages that married people gain. First comes reputation: they are held in greater esteem because with marriage they at once begin to enjoy the finest aspect of virtue, namely moderation (*sōphrosynē*). This is because marriage immediately gives people a reputation for moderation, since they are seen to have renounced promiscuous sex, as each man looks only to his own wife. And for this reason men necessarily become more respected and are considered more trustworthy and well-disposed toward their countries in every respect, because they have given their countries hostages, as it were, in the form of their own children, owing to whom they are bound to be more readily included in policymaking.

5. Marriage is also very helpful in facing the pains and hardships of life; it lightens these burdens, so to speak, when we share our troubles with our wives and are comforted by their companionship. Then too, pleasures are

φαίνεσθαι, μὴ αὐτῶν ἐφ' ἑαυτῶν εὐφραινομένων,
ἀλλὰ ἐχόντων καὶ τοὺς συμπανηγυρίζοντας καὶ τοὺς
264 συνευφραινομένους παῖδάς τε καὶ γυναῖκας καὶ τοὺς
ἄλλους συγγενεῖς· καὶ ἑορταὶ δὲ καὶ πανηγύρεις διὰ
τοῦτο τερπναί, ὅτι ἐν πολλοῖς γίγνονται. ἀνάγκη δὲ
ἐκ τούτου καὶ τὰς συγγενείας αὐξάνεσθαι· καὶ ὅτι ἐκ
τούτου πρῶτον μὲν συνοικίαι ἐγένοντο, εἶτα καὶ κῶ-
μαι, εἶτα καὶ πόλεις. ἐκ δὲ τῶν ἐπιγαμιῶν καὶ ἡ γνῶσις πλείων καὶ ἡ συγγένεια ὑπερορίοις. ἤδη παραθε-
τέον καὶ μνηστέον καὶ ἐνδόξων γάμων ἢ ἀρχαίων, καὶ
ὅσα ἀπὸ τούτων ἀγαθὰ ἐγένετο τοῖς ἀνθρώποις, καὶ
ὅση ἀποτροπὴ τῶν δυσχερῶν διὰ γάμον, οἷον ὅτι Μενέλεως ἀθάνατος ἐγένετο διὰ τὸν γάμον τῆς Ἑλένης
καὶ ὁ Πηλεὺς διὰ τὸν τῆς Θέτιδος, καὶ ὁ Ἄδμητος διὰ
τὴν Ἄλκηστιν τὸν ἐκ τῆς εἱμαρμένης θάνατον διέφυ-
γεν.

6. Ἐπειδὰν δὲ ἱκανῶς περὶ τούτων διέλθῃς, εὐχῇ
χρηστέον ἀγαθῶν μὲν αἴτησιν ἐχούσῃ περὶ τὸν γάμον καὶ τὰς παιδοποιίας, ἀποτροπὴν δὲ τῶν κακῶν.
εἶτα διατυπωτέον λόγῳ οἷον προαναφωνοῦντα, ὁποῖος
ἂν ὁ βίος ὁ μετὰ τῶν παίδων γένοιτο, ὅτι τερπνότατος
χορὸς παίδων εἰ[2] γένοιτο γέροντι, καὶ ὅτι τρόπον τινὰ
ἐξ ἀρχῆς ἀνανεάζεσθαι αὐτὸν <ποιεῖ>[3] καὶ ἀνηβά-
σκειν σὺν τοῖς αὐτοῦ παισίν. ἐν τούτῳ δὲ ἀνάγκη καὶ
ἀναμιμνήσκειν, ὧν ποτε καὶ αὐτὸς ἐν νεότητι ἐποίη-

2 εἰ P, RW: οἱ Radermacher
3 suppl. Sylburg, RW

bound to seem more gratifying when we do not enjoy them all by ourselves, but have children, wives, and relatives to celebrate and be joyful with us. Feasts and festivals are enjoyable because they include many people. Family connections also increase through marriage. From marriage, communities of families first developed, then villages, and then cities. From intermarriages came greater acquaintance and kinship with foreigners. Here you should adduce famous or legendary marriages, and mention all the good that has come to men from them and how much hardship is avoided through marriage, for example how Menelaus became immortal because of his marriage to Helen,[5] as did Peleus by his marriage to Thetis,[6] and how Admetus escaped his fated death through Alcestis.[7]

6. Once you have sufficiently treated this, you should offer a prayer asking for good fortune in the marriage and the birth of children, as well as avoidance of misfortune.[8] Then you should describe in detail—through prophecy, as it were—what life will be like with children: how completely delightful for an old man is a chorus of children, should they come along, and how in a certain way he is rejuvenated and becomes young again in the presence of his children. At this point you should remind him of the things he himself did in his youth, for sweet is the memory

[5] Cf. Hom. *Od*. 4.563–65, where Menelaus ends up on the Elysian Plain in the company of Rhadamanthys.

[6] According to Pindar at *Ol*. 2.68–78, Peleus ended up on the Isle of the Blessed (also with Rhadamanthys).

[7] Cf. Eur. *Alc.* and Pl. *Symp*. 179bc.

[8] For precatory and deprecatory prayers, see M. 1.9.1–3.

σεν· ἡδεῖα δὲ καὶ ἡ μνήμη τῶν ἐν παισὶν ἡμῖν πε-
πραγμένων. καὶ ὅτι οὐδὲν ἕτερόν ἐστι τὸ ποιοῦν ἐξ
ἀρχῆς πάλιν βεβιωκέναι. εἰ δὲ εἰκόνα τις ὁρῶν ἑαυτοῦ
265 ἄψυχον ἥδεται, ⟨πόσῳ μᾶλλον ἡσθήσεται⟩,[4] ὅταν καὶ
μὴ ἄψυχον ταύτην ὁρᾷ ἀλλὰ καὶ ἔμψυχον, μηδὲ μίαν
ἀλλὰ πολλάς, ἂν οὕτω τύχῃ; ἐπακτέον δὲ πάλιν καὶ
ἐνταῦθα ἱστοριῶν τινων μνημονεύοντα, ὅσοι ἀπὸ παίδων εὐτύχησαν, ὅσοι κακῶν ἀποτροπὰς εὕραντο, οἷον
τῷ Ἀγχίσῃ παρὰ τοῦ Αἰνείου.

Δεῖ δὲ μηδὲ τὰ πρόσωπα τῶν γαμούντων τε καὶ
γαμουμένων παρεῖναι, ἀλλὰ καὶ τούτων ἐπαίνους λέγειν. ποτὲ μὲν οὖν ἐν ἀρχῇ χρηστέον τῷ τόπῳ τούτῳ,
ποτὲ δὲ καὶ ἐπὶ τέλει· ἐὰν μὲν οὖν πάνυ ἔνδοξα ᾖ, ἐν
ἀρχῇ· ἐὰν δὲ ἥττονα, ὑπερβαλόντα καὶ ἐπὶ πᾶσι λέγοντα. 7. ὁ δὲ ἔπαινος ἅπερ ἐν τοῖς ἐγκωμίοις ἕξει, καὶ
τόποι οἱ αὐτοὶ καὶ ⟨ἐκεῖ, ὁ⟩[5] ἀπὸ τῆς πατρίδος, ὁ ἀπὸ
τοῦ γένους, ὁ ἀπὸ τῆς φύσεως, ὁ ἀπὸ τῆς ἀγωγῆς, καὶ
ὅτι ἴσοι καὶ ὅμοιοι καὶ βέβαιοι ἀμφότεροι, καὶ ἐκ
τοιούτων πατέρων καὶ προπατόρων· καὶ εἰ μὲν ἐκ τῆς
αὐτῆς πατρίδος, ὅτι ἐκ πολλοῦ προσῳκειωμένοι ὑπὸ
τοῦ τόπου· εἰ δὲ ἐκ διαφόρων, ὅτι καὶ ὑπὸ θεῶν συνήχθησαν εἰς τὴν κοινωνίαν. εἰ δὲ δὴ ἐκ τοῦ αὐτοῦ
γένους εἰσίν, ὅτι αὔξησις καὶ οἰκειότης συγγενείας
ἄλλη ἐπ᾽ ἄλλῃ γέγονεν, καὶ δεσμὸς βεβαιότερος καὶ
ἰσχυρότερος· ὅταν δὲ ἀπὸ διαφόρων ἐπιτηδευμάτων, ὁ

[4] suppl. Radermacher, RW
[5] suppl. Radermacher: αὐτοὶ καὶ ἀπὸ P

of our childhood activities. Add that nothing else enables us to relive our lives from the beginning. If a person takes delight in seeing a lifeless image of himself, how much more will he enjoy seeing not a lifeless but a living image—and not just one but many, if it should turn out that way. Here too you should mention some stories of those who were blessed with children and those who found in them deliverance from evils, as did Anchises in Aeneas.[9]

You must not omit the persons who are getting married, but must praise them too. Sometimes this topic should come at the beginning, sometimes at the end: if they are very famous, at the beginning; if less so, save it for the end. 7. This praise will contain what is said in encomia and will use the same topics, namely homeland, family, nature, and upbringing, telling how equal, similar, and constant they both are and how they come from similar fathers and forefathers. If they are from the same city, say that they have long associated with each other because of their proximity; if from different places, say that the gods brought them together as a couple. If they are from the same family, say that the closeness of their kinship has increased over what existed before and their bond is stronger and more secure. When they come from different oc-

[9] For Aeneas' devotion to his father, Anchises, cf. Verg. *Aen*. 3.

266 μὲν ἀπὸ στρατείας, ὁ δὲ ἀπὸ παιδείας, ὅτι ἁρμονία αὕτη ἀρίστη, τὸ εἰς ταὐτὸν σοφίαν τε καὶ ἀνδρείαν τελεῖν, καὶ οἵους εἰκὸς τοὺς ἀπὸ τούτων γενέσθαι.

8. Εἰ δὲ δὴ αὐτὸς εἴη ὁ γαμῶν ὁ τὸν λόγον διαθέμενος, περὶ αὐτοῦ τούτου προοιμιαστέον χαριέντως, ὥσπερ οὖν καὶ σοὶ ποιητέον, ὅτι εἰ καὶ οἱ ἐρασταὶ τὰ αὑτῶν παιδικὰ ἐπαινοῦσι, πολὺ δή που μᾶλλον αὐτῷ πρέπον τὸν γάμον ἐπαινεῖν [ἢ τὰ ἑαυτοῦ παιδικά].[6] καὶ ὅτι τῷ λόγῳ καὶ τῇ παιδείᾳ καὶ ἐπὶ τούτου χρηστέον. . . .[7] ὥσπερ ἤδη προοιμιαζόμενον καὶ προκαταμαντευόμενον περὶ τῶν παίδων, ὅτι καὶ αὐτοὺς εἰκὸς διαφέροντας περὶ παιδείαν γενέσθαι.

9. Λέξει δὲ χρηστέον ἀφελεῖ μᾶλλον ἐγγὺς Ξενοφῶντός τε καὶ Νικοστράτου βαίνοντα, ὀλιγαχοῦ δὲ ἐξαίροντα τὸν λόγον εἰς σεμνότητα, εἴ που τὰ ἐννοήματα ἀναγκάζοι.

---

[6] secl. Radermacher ut glossema
[7] lacunam indic. Radermacher

cupations, one from the military, the other from education, say that this makes the best harmony, one that combines wisdom and courage—and what children they are likely to have!

8. If the groom himself is composing the speech, he should make a charming introduction based on this very fact—as you too must do. Say that if lovers praise their beloved, then certainly it is much more fitting for one to praise marriage and use his oratory and education for that purpose . . . making a prelude, as it were, and predicting that their children are likely to become distinguished in education.[10]

9. You should employ a simple style like that of Xenophon and Nicostratus,[11] and only occasionally elevate the speech to achieve solemnity if the sentiments require it.

[10] This sentence fragment is out of place. RW propose that it belongs in the previous section.

[11] Nicostratus of Macedonia, second-century AD sophist, mentioned by M. at 2.3.5 (along with Xenophon) for his simple style. No writings of his are extant.

3. ΜΕΘΟΔΟΣ ΓΕΝΕΘΛΙΑΚΩΝ

1. Ἐχόμενος δέ σοι τούτου ὁ ἐπὶ ταῖς γενέσεσι τῶν παίδων λεγόμενος λόγος (γάμῳ γάρ που γένεσιν ἀνάγκη ἀκολουθεῖν)· ὃν καὶ αὐτὸν τελεῖν χρὴ τοῦτον τὸν τρόπον. ἐπεὶ γὰρ ἀρχὴ τῆς γενέσεως τῆς ἑκάστου ἡ ἡμέρα, ἐφ᾽ ἧς ἐγένετο, ἀναγκαῖόν που ὀλίγα ἄττα καὶ περὶ τῆς ἡμέρας εἰπεῖν οἷον ἐγκωμιάζοντα τὸ προσόν, εἰ ἄρα ἴδιόν τι ἔχει παρὰ τὰς ἄλλας ἡμέρας,

267 ἐπισημαινόμενον· εἰ μὲν τῇ νουμηνίᾳ, ὅτι ἀρχὴ τοῦ μηνός, ἀρχὴ δὲ κράτιστον καὶ ἐξ ἀρχῆς τὰ πάντα· καὶ ὅτι ἥμισυ τοῦ παντὸς ἢ τὸ πᾶν κατὰ τὸν Πλάτωνα. εἰ δὲ ἑβδόμη ἢ ἕκτη, ὅτι ἱεραὶ τοῖν θεοῖν, καὶ ὅτι κοινωνία πρὸς τὸ κρεῖττον κατὰ τὸ τῆς γενέσεως. ἔχοις δ᾽ ἂν καὶ περὶ τῆς ἐνάτης λέγειν, ὅτι ἱερὰ τοῦ Ἡλίου, καὶ ὅτι εἰκὸς ἐπίσημον τὸν τοιοῦτον γενέσθαι, τάχα δὲ καὶ εὐεργετικὸν κατὰ τὴν τοῦ Ἡλίου φύσιν. εἰ δὲ πεντεκαιδεκάτη εἴη, ὅτι καὶ αὐτὴ τῆς Ἀθηνᾶς, καὶ ὅτι τέλειος ἐν τούτῳ ὁ κύκλος, καὶ εἰκὸς ἀνενδεῆ τὴν τοιαύτην εἶναι γένεσιν τοῦ ἀνδρός. ὁμοίως δὲ καὶ εἰ ἄλλη τις ἡμέρα, ἢ τῇ ἀρχῇ ἢ τῷ τέλει προσβιβάζον-

---

1 Cf. M. 2.7.

2 At *Leg.* 6.753e, after citing "well begun is half done," the

3. HOW TO COMPOSE
BIRTHDAY SPEECHES[1]

1. The speech that comes next for you (since birth must follow marriage) is one spoken on the occasion of the birth of children. You should compose it in the following way. Since the day on which he was born marks the beginning of each person's life, you must say a few words about it as a sort of encomium of its attributes, noting if it has any special characteristic that other days lack. Thus, if it occurs at the new moon, say that it begins the month and that "the beginning is paramount" and "all things come from a beginning," and that "well begun is half done" or (according to Plato) "the beginning is everything."[2] If it is the sixth or seventh day, say that these days are sacred to the two gods[3] and that with this birth comes fellowship with divinity. If it is the ninth day, you could say that it is sacred to Helios, and that it is natural that such a person should be illustrious and probably beneficent as well, that being Helios' nature. If it is the fifteenth day, say that this is Athena's day, that the moon is full then, and that such a birth is likely to lack nothing that a man needs. So with other days, we must try to formulate our praise by relating them to

Athenian stranger actually says that a good beginning is "more than half" ($\pi\lambda\acute{\epsilon}o\nu\ \mathring{\eta}\ \tau\grave{o}\ \mathring{\eta}\mu\iota\sigma\upsilon$).

3 Possibly Artemis and Apollo, whose birthdays were celebrated on days six and seven of Thargelion.

τας καὶ τὸ προσὸν θεωροῦντας οὕτω πειρᾶσθαι τὸν
ἔπαινον ποιεῖσθαι.

2. Ἐπὶ δὲ τῇ ἡμέρᾳ τὸν καιρὸν ἐπιθεωρεῖν ἀναγκαῖον, ὁποῖός τις οὗτος· καὶ τοῦ καιροῦ τὸ μὲν κατὰ
τὴν ὥραν, οἷον ἐν χειμῶνι ἢ ἐν ἦρι ἢ ἐν τοῖς ἑτέροις
μέρεσι τοῦ ἔτους, ὥσπερ ἐν τοῖς περὶ τοῦ ἀγῶνος
ἐπαίνοις ἐπεσημαινόμεθα¹ τὰς ἰδιότητας τῶν καιρῶν,
τῷ μὲν τὸ ἀνδρεῖον, τῷ δὲ τὸ φαιδρὸν ἀπονέμοντες,
καὶ τῷ θέρει τὸ πεπληρῶσθαι τὴν γῆν ἐν τούτῳ τῶν
ἀγαθῶν, καὶ τῷ λοιπῷ δὲ τὸ ἐν ἀνέσει καὶ ἀναπαύλῃ
τῶν ἔργων γενέσθαι. ἐπισημαίνεσθαι δὲ καὶ τὰ
συμβεβηκότα ἐνίοτε τοῖς καιροῖς· οἷον εἰ ἐν ἑορτῇ τις
268   γέγονεν, οἱονεὶ ἐν Διονυσίοις ἢ ἐν μυστηρίοις ἢ
ἐν πανηγύρεσίν τισιν· ἅπαντα γὰρ ταῦτα ἀφορμὰς
παρέξει σοι εἰς τὸν ἔπαινον.

3. Ἀπὸ δὲ τούτου ἰτέον καὶ ἐπὶ τοὺς τόπους, ἐν οἷς
τις γέγονεν· πρῶτον μὲν ἐπὶ τὸ περιέχον τὸ ἔθνος,²
[Ἀσίαν, Εὐρώπην]³ καὶ τοῦτο αὖ πάλιν Ἑλληνικὸν ἢ
βάρβαρον, ἢ σοφίαν ἢ ἀνδρείαν τοῦ ἔθνους ἤ τι
τοιοῦτον ἐπισημαινόμενον. εἶτα ἐπὶ τὸ περιεχόμενον·
τίς ἡ πόλις καὶ ἡ μητρόπολις αὐτῷ· ἐχομένη ἡ πόλις
μητροπόλεως τῇ τιμῇ, μεγάλη, πολυάνθρωπος, εὔφορος πρὸς ἀνδρῶν ἀρετήν, ἢ ἄν τι ἕτερον ἀνδραγά-

¹ ἐπισημαινόμεθα Schott, Radermacher
² τὸ ἔθνος post Εὐρώπην transp. RW
³ seclusi

the beginning or the end of the month and by taking into consideration their attributes.

2. After the day, we must consider what the time of year is like, which includes the seasons such as winter, spring, or the other portions[4] of the year—just as in our praise of games we pointed out[5] the special characteristics of seasons, attributing manliness to one,[6] joyfulness to another;[7] to summer the abundance of the earth's good things at that time, and to the last one[8] rest and relaxation from labors. Also mention events that sometimes occur at the particular time of the year, for example, if someone is born during a festival, the Dionysia, the Eleusinian mysteries, or some panegyric celebration. All these will offer you starting points for praise.

3. After this, proceed to the place where he was born, first turning broadly to his race,[9] and in turn whether it is Greek or barbarian and whether it exhibits wisdom, courage, or some similar quality.[10] Then proceed specifically to his city and its metropolis: "His city matches its metropolis in honor; it is large, populous, and fosters manly virtue"—or any other human excellence the city may possess.

---

4 That is, summer and autumn.

5 Cf. 1.4. Shott's change of the verb to the present tense (followed by RW) makes this a general statement. On either reading, the sentence presents numerous difficulties.

6 That is, winter.

7 That is, spring.   8 That is, autumn.

9 I have deleted "Asia or Europe" as an interpolation.

10 For qualities associated with various barbarian races and with the three Greek races, cf. M. 1.15.5.

θημα τῆς πόλεως. ἔπειτα τὰ μὲν περιεχόμενα ἐν τῇ
πόλει· ποίας τινὸς οἰκίας, ὅτι οὐ φαύλης, ὅτι οὐκ
ἀδόξου, γένους ⟨ὅτι⟩[4] ἐνδόξου, ποίων τινῶν προγόνων
καὶ πατέρων, καὶ ἔπαινον ἐν βραχεῖ τούτων ἀπὸ τῶν
προσόντων.

4. Μετὰ ταῦτα δὲ καὶ ἐπ' αὐτὸν ἤδη τὸν ἔπαινον
ἰέναι τοῦ ἐγκωμιαζομένου καὶ οὗ ἡ γενέθλιος· ποίας
τινὸς φύσεως κατὰ σῶμα, κατὰ ἰσχύν. εἰ μέγας ἐστί,
κατὰ τὸν Αἴαντα· εἰ καλὸς καὶ ἀνδρεῖος, κατὰ τὸν
Ἀχιλλέα· καὶ εἰ ⟨εὔγλωσσος ἢ⟩[5] εὔβουλος ἢ δίκαιος
ἢ σώφρων εἴη, τὰ ἁρμόζοντα πρόσωπα, τὸν Νέστορα,
τὸν Θεμιστοκλέα, τὸν Ἀριστείδην, τὸν Φωκίωνα· εἰ
χρηστός· ὅτι θυμοειδὴς μετὰ τοῦ πράου, ὅτι ὀξὺς ἐνθυμηθῆναι. κἂν εἰ μικρός, ὅτι μείζων τὴν τῆς ψυχῆς
ἀρετήν, κατὰ τὸν Τυδέα, κατὰ τὸν Κόνωνα. 5. οἷός τις
τὰ περὶ τὸν βίον, εἰ φιλόκαλος, εἰ μεγαλοπρεπής· οἷος
πρὸς τοὺς ἰδιώτας, πρὸς τὴν πόλιν, καὶ τὰς φιλοτιμίας τὰς πρὸς τὴν πόλιν. κἂν εἰ ἐπιστήμης τινὸς ἐπή-
βολος εἴη, οἷον ἰατρικῆς ἢ ῥητορικῆς ἢ φιλοσοφίας,
θετικῶς ἐπάγοντα τὸν ἐν τούτοις ἔπαινον, εἰς ὅσα
τούτων ἕκαστον χρήσιμον· οὕτω γὰρ ἂν ἀμφιλαφὴς ὁ
λόγος γένοιτο. ποῖος ἤδη γέγονεν, ποῖός ἐστιν ἐν τῷ
παρόντι, καὶ ποῖον εἰκὸς ἔσεσθαι εἰς τὸν μέλλοντα

---

[4] suppl. Radermacher
[5] suppl. Radermacher

Then come specifics within the city, namely what his family is like (not lowly or undistinguished), his lineage (famous), what his forebears and parents were like—include brief praise of these with reference to their attributes.

4. After this, proceed finally to the praise of the honorand whose birthday it is. What are his natural qualities, his build, his strength? If he is big, he is like Ajax; if handsome and brave, like Achilles. If he is eloquent, prudent, just, or moderate, compare him with the appropriate persons: Nestor,[11] Themistocles,[12] Aristides,[13] or Phocion.[14] If he is a good man, say that he combines spirit with gentleness and is quick to understand. If he is small, say that he is of greater stature in the virtue of his soul, like Tydeus[15] or Conon.[16] 5. What is he like in his mode of life? refined? magnificent? What is his attitude toward individuals, toward the city, and what about civic benefactions? If he possesses some skill like medicine, rhetoric, or philosophy, introduce praise of these subjects in terms of a thesis,[17] detailing the ways in which each of these skills is useful, for this can give the speech amplitude. Tell what

[11] Cf. Hom. *Il.* 1.247–49: "sweet-speaking Nestor . . . whose speech flowed from his tongue sweeter than honey."

[12] Cf. Thuc. 1.138.3.

[13] Early fifth-century BC Athenian statesman known as "The Just." Aristides and Phocion are also paired at M. 2.2.10 and 2.9.6.

[14] Fourth-century BC Athenian general, known as "The Good," for being incorruptible. [15] Cf. Hom. *Il.* 5.801: "Tydeus was small in stature, but a fighter." [16] "We have been unable to find other evidence for this fact" (RW).

[17] That is, a general proposition on the usefulness of these skills. Cf. 2.1–2 for theses on marriage.

χρόνον. ἐν τούτῳ δὲ γενόμενοι οὐκ ἀπὸ τρόπου ἂν ποιοῖμεν καὶ εὐχόμενοι τοῖς τε ἄλλοις καὶ τοῖς γενεθλίοις θεοῖς περὶ τοῦ μέλλοντος βίου καὶ τοῦ ἀμείνω τοῦ παρεληλυθότος γενέσθαι τοῦτον, καὶ πολλὰς περιόδους χρόνων τελέσαντα εἰς λιπαρὸν καὶ εὔδαιμον γῆρας παρελθεῖν.

he was like in the past, what he is like now, and what he is likely to become in the future. At this point, it would be entirely appropriate for us to pray to the gods, including the gods of birth, that his future life may be even better than it has been, and that he may complete many more years and come to a splendid and happy old age.[18]

---

[18] For the phrase "splendid old age," cf. Hom. *Od*. 19.368 and Pind. *Nem*. 7.99. It appears again at 6.5.

4. ΜΕΘΟΔΟΣ ΕΠΙΘΑΛΑΜΙΟΥ

1. Πρὸ δὲ τοῦ περὶ τῆς γενέσεως λόγου (μικροῦ γάρ με παρῆλθεν ὑπὸ τοῦ θορύβου καὶ τῆς ταραχῆς τῆς περὶ τὴν ἔξοδον) ὁ ἐπὶ τῷ θαλάμῳ λεγόμενος λόγος· ἐχόμενος δ᾽ ὅ τι μάλιστα καὶ ἀκόλουθος <ἂν>[1] εἴη τοῖς γαμικοῖς τῶν λόγων, σχεδὸν εἷς καὶ ὁ αὐτὸς ὢν τῷ γαμικῷ, πλὴν τῷ χρόνῳ διαφέρων, ἐπὶ τετελεσμένοις τοῖς γάμοις λεγόμενος οὗτος· οὐ μὴν τοῖς γε ἄλλοις ἀπᾴδων τοῦ προειρημένου, καὶ ὥσπερ ἀντὶ ὑμεναίων ἐπᾳδόμενος τοῖς γάμοις. τινὰ μὲν οὖν καὶ παρὰ Σαπφοῖ τῆς ἰδέας ταύτης παραδείγματα, ἐπιθαλάμιοι οὕτως ἐπιγραφόμεναι ᾠδαί· ἀλλ᾽ ἐπειδὴ οὐχ ἡ αὐτὴ μεταχείρισις ποιήσεώς τε καὶ πεζοῦ λόγου, ἀλλ᾽ ὥσπερ τοῖς μέτροις, οὑτωσὶ δὲ καὶ τοῖς ἐννοήμασι διενήνοχεν ταῦτα, τοῦτον ἄν μοι δοκεῖς τὸν τρόπον καὶ τοῦτον τὸν λόγον προσφόρως μεταχειρίσασθαι, εἰ ἐν μὲν τῷ προοιμίῳ εὐθὺς αὐτὸ τοῦτο ἐπισημαίνοιο,

270

---

[1] suppl. Schaefer

---

[1] Compare M.'s instructions for an epithalamium at 2.5 and for a bedtime speech at 2.6 (which urges the couple to go to bed and have intercourse).

4. HOW TO COMPOSE AN EPITHALAMIUM[1]

1. Before the birthday speech[2] comes the speech delivered at the bedroom (which nearly slipped my mind because of the noise and confusion surrounding my departure).[3] It naturally follows wedding speeches, and indeed is almost identical to one except for its timing, being delivered after the wedding has concluded. In other respects it differs little from the wedding speech that was just treated and is sung at weddings, in place, so to speak, of the hymeneal song.[4] There are some examples of this type in Sappho, expressly labeled epithalamic songs.[5] But since the treatment in poetry is not the same as that in prose, differing in ideas as much as it does in meter, I think that you will treat this type of speech correctly if you state right at the

[2] Just treated in the previous section. [3] RW ad loc. interpret this cryptic statement as follows: "A curious touch of realism; the author is so disturbed not now by academic duties as at [2.1] but by some domestic move, that he forgets to write out the ἐπιθαλάμιος before the γενεθλιακός." Such an interpretation may be possible, but it is highly speculative.

[4] Traditionally, a song or a poem chanted at the conclusion of a wedding, conducting the bride or the couple to the bedchamber. Prominent examples include Ar. *Pax* 1329–59, Theoc. *Id.* 18, and Catull. 61.

[5] Frr. 104–17 PLF are thought to come from her epithalamia, although none is so labeled.

ὅτι οἱ μὲν ἄλλοι τὸν ὑμέναιον ᾄδουσιν, ἡμεῖς δὲ ἀντὶ
τοῦ ὑμεναίου τὸν λόγον, οὐχ ὑπ᾽ αὐλοῖς ἢ πηκτίσιν ἢ
νὴ Δία καλλιφωνίᾳ τινὶ τοιαύτῃ, ἀλλὰ ἐπαίνοις καὶ
ὕμνοις τῶν γεγαμηκότων.

2. Εἶτα ἐπὶ τούτοις ἐπάγειν, ὅτι ἀναγκαῖος ὁ γάμος
ἀνθρώποις γε οὖσι· σωτηρία γὰρ τοῦ γένους· καὶ ὅσα
ἀγαθὰ ἐκ τοῦ γάμου. εἶτα μεταβήσῃ ἐπὶ τὰ πρόσωπα
τῶν συνιόντων εἰς τὸν γάμον, ὁποῖοί τινες οὗτοι· ἐν ᾧ
περὶ γένους ἐρεῖς αὐτῶν καὶ τροφῆς, καὶ περὶ κάλλους
σωμάτων καὶ ἡλικίας· ὅσα ἐκ τύχης αὐτοῖς πρόσεστι,
271 καὶ περὶ ἐπιτηδευμάτων· ὅτι σπουδὴν ἔσχον περὶ τὸν
γάμον καὶ τὴν σύζευξιν αὐτοί· ὅπως διάκεινται ἐπὶ τῷ
γάμῳ οἱ οἰκεῖοι, οἱ ἀλλότριοι, ἡ πόλις αὐτὴ δημοσίᾳ·
ὅτι πᾶσι διὰ σπουδῆς ὁ γάμος ἐστίν, καὶ ὁ γάμος
ἔοικεν πανηγύρει τινὶ καὶ νεομηνίᾳ καὶ δημοτελεῖ
ἑορτῇ τῆς πόλεως. ὥσπερ δὲ ἐν τοῖς γαμικοῖς ἠξιοῦ-
μεν πρὸς τοῖς ἄλλοις ἐπισκοπεῖν, οἷον εἰ ἐκ τῆς αὐτῆς
πατρίδος, εἰ ἐκ τοῦ αὐτοῦ γένους, οὑτωσὶ δὲ μηδὲ ἐν
τούτῳ παρὰ φαῦλον ποιεῖσθαι τὸ μέρος τοῦ λόγου
τοῦτο.

3. Ἐπὶ δὲ τοῖς ἐπαίνοις καὶ τοῖς ἐγκωμίοις καὶ
προτροπή τις ἔστω τοῖς γαμοῦσιν πρὸς τὸ σπουδάζειν περὶ ἀλλήλους καὶ ὁμονοεῖν ὅ τι μάλιστα· καὶ
ὅσα ἀγαθὰ ἐκ τῆς τοιαύτης ὁμονοίας καὶ φιλίας
ἀνάγκη συμβαίνειν, ἀπὸ τοῦ καθόλου ἐπὶ τὸ ἴδιον
ἄγοντα τὸν λόγον· ὅτι ὁμόνοια πᾶσι μὲν ἀνθρώποις
ἡγεῖται τῶν ἀγαθῶν, μάλιστα δὲ τοῖς γεγαμηκόσιν·

opening, "Others sing the hymeneal song, but we offer instead a speech accompanied not by pipes or lyres, or indeed by any such lovely sounds, but by hymns in praise of the married couple."

2. Next introduce the argument that marriage is essential in order for human beings to exist because it preserves the race. Mention too all the good things that come of marriage. Then pass on to the characteristics of the persons who are coming together in marriage, among which you will speak of their family and upbringing; their physical beauty and age; the gifts that fortune has provided them; and their pursuits (*epitēdeumata*). Say how eager they themselves were to join together in marriage and mention how keen their relatives, strangers, and the city at large are, and how eagerly they all await the wedding, as if it were some panegyric celebration, or new-moon festival, or feast sponsored by the city. And just as in wedding speeches we thought fit to consider, among other things, whether the two parties were from the same homeland or family,[6] so in this case do not deem it unimportant to include this portion of the speech.

3. After these praises and encomia should come an exhortation to the couple to show concern for each other and to live in concord as much as possible. Tell of all the good that is bound to come from such concord and affection, steering the speech from general to specific instances. Say that while concord leads to good things for all people, this is especially true for wedded couples. To sup-

[6] Cf. 2.7.

καὶ εἰς τοῦτο καὶ τὸ τοῦ Ὁμήρου παραληπτέον ἐνδόξῳ κρίσει χρώμενον, ὅτι οὐδὲν μεῖζον ἀγαθὸν

> ἢ ὅτε ὁμοφρονέοντε νοήμασιν οἶκον ἔχητον
> ἀνὴρ ἠδὲ γυνή·

τίνα μὲν ἐκ τούτου τοῖς ἐχθροῖς ἀνιαρά, τίνα δὲ ἡδέα
τοῖς φίλοις. ἐπὶ τέλει δὲ καὶ εὐχῇ χρῆσθαι, ὅπως ὅ τι
τάχιστα παῖδες γένοιντο, ὡς καὶ τούτων ἐπιδεῖν γάμους καὶ ᾆσαι τὸν ὑμέναιον καὶ ὑπόθεσιν ἔχειν αὖθις
τοιούτων λόγων.

port this you should include a quote from Homer, citing his authoritative judgment,[7] to the effect that there is no greater good

> than when a man and a woman with like-minded
>   thoughts
> keep house.[8]

What pain this brings to their enemies and what pleasure to their friends! At the end pray that they may have children as soon as possible, and that you may attend their children's weddings, sing their hymeneal song, and have an occasion, once again, for speeches such as these.

---

[7] For the argument from authoritative judgment (ἀπὸ κρίσεως ἐνδόξου), see M. 1.16.26.

[8] *Od.* 6.183–84. The preceding and following verses (182, 184–85) are paraphrased.

5. ΜΕΘΟΔΟΣ ΠΡΟΣΦΩΝΗΜΑΤΙΚΩΝ

272   1. Ἰσοκράτης μὲν ὁ σὸς ἑταῖρος καὶ ἐμός, ὦ Ἐχέκρατες, εἴ περ ἄλλό τι, φησὶ χρῆναι προσεῖναι τοῖς σπουδαίοις ἀνθρώποις, ἐν τῇ παραινέσει τῇ πρὸς τὸν Ἱππόνικου, καὶ τὴν φιλοπροσηγορίαν· ὅ πέρ ἐστι τὸ προσφωνεῖν τοὺς ἀπαντῶντας, ὡς αὐτός φησιν. εἰ δὲ καὶ ἰδίᾳ χρῆν πρὸς ἕκαστον τοῦτο ποιεῖν, ὅπως καὶ τοὺς ἰδιώτας ὡς ὅ τι μάλιστα οἰκειοτέρως καὶ εὐμενεστέρως ἔχειν πρὸς ἡμᾶς παρασκευάζωμεν ἐκ τῆς τοιαύτης φιλοπροσηγορίας, πολλῷ δή που ἀναγκαιότερον τὸ πρᾶγμα καὶ ὁ τοιοῦτος τρόπος τῆς προσφωνήσεως, εἰ πρὸς τοὺς ἐν τέλει καὶ ἐν ἀρχαῖς γεγονότας ὑφ᾿ ἡμῶν γίγνοιτο καὶ μάλιστά γε δὴ τοὺς ἑκάστοτε ἐκ βασιλέων εἰς τὰ ἔθνη καὶ τὰς πόλεις τὰς ἡμετέρας παραγιγνομένους, ὅπως καὶ αὐτοὺς διὰ τοιούτου τρόπου καὶ πρὸς ἡμᾶς καὶ πρὸς τὰς αὐτῶν πατρίδας οἰκειοτέρως διακεῖσθαι παρασκευάσαιμεν. ἀμέλει γέ τοι καὶ τὸ πρᾶγμα ἤδη ἐπιχωριάζει ἐπὶ πᾶσι, καὶ καθάπερ τις οὗτος νόμος καὶ θεσμὸς διελήλυθεν διὰ πάντων, ὡς εὐθὺς ἅμα τε τῇ πρώτῃ τῶν

273 πυλῶν, ὡς ἂν εἴποι τις, εἰσόδῳ προσφωνεῖν τούτους

5. HOW TO COMPOSE ADDRESSES[1]

1. Isocrates, that companion of yours and mine,[2] Echecrates, says in his advice to the son of Hipponicus[3] that a quality serious men need to possess, as much as any, is affability (*philoprosēgoria*),[4] which involves, as he himself says, "greeting those whom you meet."[5] If we ought to do this to individuals in private life, in order to make ordinary people friendlier and better disposed to us as much as possible by such affability, then certainly the practice of this type of address is all the more important if we direct it to those who are in power and hold office, especially those sent periodically from emperors to our nations and cities, so that by such means we may make them more friendly to us and our countries. Of course the practice is already customary everywhere, having extended like a law or ordinance among all peoples, that cities publicly address those who arrive as soon as they set foot, so to speak,

[1] As in M. (2.9) these are addresses to welcome arriving governors.

[2] Isocrates was a very influential forerunner of epideictic prose. [DH] also mentions him at 1.8 and 6.1, and M. quotes him three times and alludes to several of his speeches (see citations).

[3] That is, Demonicus.   [4] This noun occurs only three times in extant Greek, at *ad Dem.* 20 and twice in this section.

[5] *ad Dem.* 20: ἔστι δὲ φιλοπροσηγορίας μὲν τὸ προσφωνεῖν τοὺς ἀπαντῶντας ("affability consists in greeting those whom you meet"). M. also stresses affability in his "address" at 2.9.6.

δημοσίᾳ τὰς πόλεις ὑφ᾽ ἑνὸς ὅτου οὖν τῶν ἀρίστων
κατὰ τὴν παιδείαν ὥσπερ δημοσίᾳ τινὶ φωνῇ καὶ
κοινῷ προσαγορεύματι προσαγορεύοντος. φέρε οὖν
εἴπωμέν τι καὶ περὶ τούτων τῶν λόγων, ὅπως ἂν καὶ
τούτους ἄριστα καὶ ῥᾷστα μεταχειριζοίμεθα.

2. Καθόλου μὲν ὁ τρόπος αὐτῶν τοιοῦτος, ὡς
σύστασίν τινα ἔχειν τῆς αὐτῶν πατρίδος πρὸς τοὺς
ἄρχειν μέλλοντας. δεῖ δὲ οὐκ αὐτὸ τοῦτο μόνον πρα-
γματεύεσθαι ἐν τῷ λόγῳ, ἀλλὰ μηδὲ ἑαυτῶν ἐν τῷ
τοιῷδε ὀλιγώρως ἔχειν. ἀρχὴ οὖν ἐμοὶ δοκεῖ ἀναγκαι-
οτάτη ἂν αὕτη γενέσθαι περὶ αὐτοῦ τε εἰπεῖν καὶ τῆς
ἑαυτοῦ προαιρέσεως, καὶ δι᾽ ὅ τι προκεχείρισται ἐκ
πάντων ἐπὶ τὸν λόγον, καὶ ὅτι ἀναγκαία αὐτῷ ἡ ὑπόθεσις τοῦ λόγου. ἐχέτω δὲ ἐν τούτῳ καὶ θεραπείαν
τινὰ τοῦ ἄρχοντος, ὡς ἀποδεχομένου τοὺς τοιούτους
ἅπαντας καὶ οἷον αὐτοῦ χεῖρα ὀρέγοντος, δι᾽ ὅπερ καὶ
ἑτοιμότερον ὑπήκουσεν· καὶ ὅτι ἦν μὲν καὶ ἀκούειν
τοῦτο εὐθὺς περὶ αὐτοῦ, πολὺ δὲ ἔτι ἐναργέστερον τῇ
ὄψει αὐτῇ πέφηνεν, ἀτεχνῶς οἷον ἐκ τοῦ προσώπου
[καὶ]¹ τῆς φαιδρότητος ὥσπερ ἐν κατόπτρῳ τοῦ ἤθους
καὶ τῆς πρὸς ταῦτα δεξιότητος φανερῶν γιγνομένων.
οὕτω δὲ προκαταστησάμενον τὸν λόγον ἑξῆς ἰτέον ἐπὶ
τὸ ἐγκώμιον τοῦ βασιλέως, ἐν βραχεῖ τοῦτο ποιησά-
μενον καὶ αὐτὸ τοῦτο ἐπισημηνάμενον, ὅτι οὐδ᾽ ἂν ὁ
σύμπας χρόνος ἐξαρκέσαι πρὸς τοῦτο, καὶ ὅτι ἑτέρου
καιροῦ, οὐ τοῦ παρόντος. κατακλείσεις δὲ τὸ ἐγκώμιον εἰς τοῦτο, ὅτι ἕν τι τῶν καλῶν τῶν βασιλέως καὶ
τοῦτο, τὸ τοιοῦτον ἄνδρα ἐπιλεξάμενον καταπέμψαι

274

within the city's gates, when one of the best educated citizens, speaking, as it were, as the voice of the city, offers a greeting on behalf of all. Let me then say some things about these speeches, so that we may treat them in the best and most expeditious way.

2. In general, the point of these speeches is to make a kind of recommendation of one's own country to the officials who are coming to govern it. This must not be the only thing accomplished in the speech; on such an occasion one should not neglect one's own interests either. Consequently, I think that the most compelling opening would be to speak of oneself and one's purpose, explaining why one has been chosen from all others to deliver this speech, and what makes its subject personally compelling. Here offer some compliments to the governor, by claiming that he welcomes all such orators and, as it were, holds out his hand to them. "That is why I agreed all the more readily. One can learn this about him just from hearsay, but it has become much more obvious at the actual sight of him. This is apparent from the brightness of his face, like a reflection of his character, and from his courtesy in this matter." Once you have set up the speech in this way, proceed to an encomium of the emperor, keeping it brief and making a point of the fact that all of time would not suffice to complete it, and that it remains for an occasion other than the present one. You should conclude this encomium by saying, "One of the emperor's finest achievements is hav-

---

[1] secl. Radermacher

ἐπὶ τὸ αὑτοῦ ἔθνος οὐ πόρρω βαίνοντα τῆς αὑτοῦ
προαιρέσεως.

3. Καὶ ἐντεῦθεν ἀρχέσθω σοι τὸ ἐγκώμιον τοῦ
ἡγουμένου. χρηστέον δὲ καὶ ἐνταῦθα τοῖς ἐγκωμιαστικοῖς τόποις, ἀπὸ γένους, ἀπὸ φύσεως, ἀπὸ ἀνατρο-
φῆς· εἰ μὲν φανερὰ εἴη, καθ' ἕκαστον ἀκριβῶς διεξι-
όντα· εἰ δὲ ἄδηλα, κατὰ τὸ πιθανὸν προάγοντα, ὅτι
ἀνάγκη τὸν τηλικούτων καὶ τοιούτων κατηξιωμένον
οὔτε γένει οὔτε φύσει οὔτε ἀνατροφῇ λείπεσθαί τινων,
ἀλλὰ διὰ ταῦτα προκεκρίσθαι· τά γε μὴν φανερὰ
ἀκριβέστερον ἐπισημαινόμενον, οἷον ‹εἰ›[2] ἐν νέᾳ ἡλικίᾳ τοιοῦτος, τί χρὴ προσδοκᾶν εἰς τὸν μέλλοντα
χρόνον; καὶ ὅτι νέος μὲν τὴν ἡλικίαν, πρεσβύτερος δὲ
τὴν φρόνησιν. εἰ δὲ πρεσβύτης, ὅτι ἐν πολλοῖς δοὺς
πεῖραν ἑαυτοῦ τῆς ἀρετῆς, εἰκότως καὶ τὴν ἀρχὴν
ταύτην ἐπιστεύθη· καὶ ὅτι καὶ τοῦτο τῆς εὐμοιρίας
τῆς περὶ αὐτὸν τὸ ἐν τῷ γήρᾳ ἀκμάζειν. εἰ δὲ δὴ καὶ
σεμνότης τις προσείη τῷ προσώπῳ, μηδὲ τοῦτο παρέργως παρατρέχειν. εἰ φιλόλογος εἴη, ἐγκώμιον παιδείας, καὶ ὅτι οἱ πεπαιδευμένοι μάλιστα ἄξιοι ἀρχῆς
καὶ τοιαύτης ἡγεμονίας. καὶ εἴτε τὴν Ῥωμαϊκὴν διά-
λεκτον εἴη πεπαιδευμένος, τοῖς ἀρίστοις τῶν Ῥωμαίων παραβάλλειν· εἴτε τὴν Ἑλληνικήν, τοῖς τῶν
Ἑλλήνων· διὰ τοῦτο δὲ καὶ δίκαιος καὶ σώφρων καὶ
περὶ τὰς δίκας ἀκριβής· παραδείγμασι δὲ καὶ ἐπὶ
τούτῳ χρηστέον προσώποις, τῷ Ἀριστείδῃ, τῷ Θεμι-
στοκλεῖ, ἐφαρμόζοντα καὶ παραβάλλοντα καὶ τούτων
ἀμείνω ἀποφαίνοντα.

ing chosen a man like this to send to this nation, a man after his own heart."

3. At this point you should begin praise of the governor. Here too employ the encomiastic topics of birth, nature, and upbringing. If these are illustrious, treat each one in detail. If they are undistinguished, make a plausible argument by claiming that a man deemed worthy of such great honors must not be inferior to anyone in birth, nature, or upbringing but rather has found preferment precisely because of them. Treat illustrious features in greater detail by saying, for example, that if he is like this at a young age, what must we expect to see in time to come? Or else that although young, he is wise beyond his years. If he is old, say that after proving his excellence in many situations, he has rightly been entrusted with this office, and that one aspect of his good fortune is his being at full bloom in old age. If he has a dignified demeanor, do not skim over this rapidly. If he is a lover of literature, praise his education by saying that well-educated people are especially deserving of command and of an office such as this. If he is educated in Latin, compare him to the best of the Romans; if in Greek, to the best of the Greeks, and state that for this reason he is just, moderate, and a meticulous judge of lawsuits. Here you should cite exemplary figures—Aristides, Themistocles—adapting and comparing them, and showing that he surpasses them.

---

[2] suppl. Radermacher

4. Ἐὰν δὲ ἔχωμεν καὶ πράξεις τινὰς αὐτοῦ προγε
γενημένας καὶ ἀρχὰς προηνυσμένας λέγειν ἢ ἐν
στρατείαις ἢ ἐν διοικήσεσιν, καὶ ταύτας παρατιθέναι.
ἐὰν δὲ καὶ ⟨τινας⟩[3] τιμὰς ἔχωμεν αὐτῷ ⟨τῶν⟩[4] πατέ
ρων γενομένας λέγειν, καὶ τούτων χρὴ μνημονεύειν.
καὶ ἐντεῦθεν προτροπὴ καὶ παράκλησις πρὸς εὔνοιαν
τῆς πόλεως, ἐπισημηνάμενον, ὅτι χρηστὴν ἐλπίδα
περὶ τούτου ἔχουσι. φανερὸν γάρ τοι ἀπὸ τοῦ οὕτως
ἀποδέξασθαι τὴν πόλιν, ἀπὸ τοῦ φιλανθρώπως καὶ
εὐπροσηγόρως ἅπασι προσενεχθῆναι καὶ ὁμιλῆσαι·
⟨καὶ⟩[5] ὅτι εἰκότως τοῦτο ἐποίησεν· τοιαύτη γὰρ ἡ πό
λις οἷα ἀμείβεσθαι τοὺς εὖ χρησαμένους ἑαυτῇ.

5. Καὶ ἐντεῦθεν ὁ ἔπαινος ὁ περὶ τῆς πόλεως, ἐὰν
θέλῃς· περὶ γένους αὐτῆς, περὶ δυνάμεως τῆς ἐν ταῖς
προσόδοις, περὶ παιδείας τῶν ἐνοικούντων, περὶ χώ
ρας τῆς ὑποτελοῦς, ἀφ᾽ ἧς ἡ πρόσοδος· εἰ μὲν πολλὴ
εἴη, εἰς ἰσχὺν τῆς πόλεως ἀναφέροντα· εἰ δὲ ὀλίγη, ὅτι
ἀρκεῖται καὶ ταύτῃ. ἔτι οὗπερ ἂν ᾖ κτίστου, ἀναγ
καῖον εἰπεῖν, ἐάν τε θεὸς ἐάν τε ἥρως ᾖ, εἴτ᾽ οὖν τῶν
276 ἀρχαίων τις εἴτ᾽ οὖν τῶν ἔναγχος γεγενημένων βασι
λέων. οἷον κἂν μύθους τινὰς ἔχωμεν προσόντας τῇ
πόλει, μηδὲ τούτους παραλιπεῖν. μετὰ ταῦτα περὶ με
γέθους τῆς πόλεως, περὶ κάλλους, περὶ θέσεως, εἴτε
ἠπειρωτικὴ εἴη, εἴτε ἐπιθαλαττίδιος ἢ νησιῶτις. κἂν
εἴ τινας τιμὰς ἔχοιμεν παρὰ βασιλέων, μηδὲ ταύτας
παραλιπεῖν, κἂν εἰ πράξεις τινὰς προγεγενημένας ἢ
παλαιὰς ἢ νέας, ἢ εἰ τιμὰς προϋπάρξας παρ᾽ ἡμῶν
πρὸς τοὺς ἄρχοντας τοὺς προγεγενημένους.

4. If we can speak of any previous achievements of his or offices that he has held, whether in war or in governance, we should add them. If we can speak of any honors conferred upon his forefathers, we should mention them as well. At this point should come an exhortation and appeal for his goodwill toward the city, explaining that the citizens have high hopes of him, since "This is certainly clear from the way he has embraced the city and conducted himself toward everyone in a humane and affable manner," adding, "It is natural that he has done so, because this is a city that shows gratitude to those who treat it well."

5. At this point comes praise of the city, if you so wish, including its origin, the strength of its revenues, the education of its citizens, and the territory subject to taxes from which its revenue accrues. If the revenue is large, say that it strengthens the city; if small, that even this is sufficient for it. In addition, you should speak of its founder, whoever that may be, whether god or hero, or else one of the ancient or recent emperors. If we can tell any stories about the city, we should not omit them. After this speak of the city's size, its beauty, and its location (whether inland, coastal, or insular). We should also not omit any honors bestowed by emperors, any previous accomplishments, ancient or recent, and any previous honors bestowed by us on past governors.[6]

---

[6] For such honors, cf. M. 2.9.14–15 (the crown speech).

---

[3] suppl. Nissen
[4] suppl. Radermacher
[5] suppl. Radermacher

6. Ἐν ἄπασι δὲ τούτοις μεμίχθω ἡ προτροπὴ καὶ παράκλησις πρὸς εὔνοιαν τῆς πόλεως· δεῖν γὰρ τοὺς ἀγαθοὺς ἄρχοντας ταῖς τοιαύταις πόλεσιν τὰς παρ' ἑαυτῶν εὐνοίας προσνέμειν. ἐπὶ δὲ τῷ τέλει εὐχῇ χρησόμεθα ὑπὲρ τοῦ βασιλέως καὶ ὑπὲρ αὐτοῦ τοῦ ἄρχοντος. καὶ ὑπὲρ ἡμῶν δὲ αὐτῶν πάλιν μνησθησόμεθα, εἰ μὲν τῶν ἀρχομένων εἴημεν, ὅτι ἀπὸ τοῦ τοιούτου ἡμεῖς τιμῆς καὶ δόξης τευξόμεθα· εἰ δὲ τῶν ἤδη προευδοκιμηκότων καὶ προειρηκότων, ἀνεπαχθῶς περὶ αὐτῶν εἰπόντες εἰς τοῦτο καταλύσομεν τὸν λόγον, ὡς ἐλπίδος τι καὶ αὐτοὶ ἔχοντες τοῦ μὴ φυλαχθήσεσθαι μόνον ἐπὶ τούτων τὴν δόξαν ἑαυτοῖς, ἀλλὰ καὶ πολλῷ ἀμείνω πρὸς τὸ λοιπὸν ἔσεσθαι.

7. Ἀπαγγελία δὲ πρέποι ἂν μάλιστα μεμιγμένη τῷ τοιούτῳ λόγῳ, ἐνιαχοῦ μὲν συνεστραμμένη, ἐνιαχοῦ δὲ διῃρημένη, ἐν τοῖς μύθοις ἀφελεστέρα. τὸ δὲ σαφὲς τῆς ἑρμηνείας δι' ὅλου τοῦ λόγου μάλιστα ἐν σπουδῇ ἔστω τῷ λέγοντι. [Καθόλου ὁ περὶ τῶν πανηγυρικῶν λόγος ὧδέ πως περαίνοιτο ἄν.][6]

---

[6] secl. ut interpolata Thiel

6. All of these topics should be combined with an exhortation and appeal for goodwill toward the city, on the grounds that good governors are bound to bestow their benevolence on cities such as ours. At the end we should say a prayer for the emperor and the governor himself. We should also speak again about ourselves. If we are at the beginning of our career, we should say that we will win fame and honor from such an occasion as this. If we are already well regarded and have spoken previously, we should acknowledge that fact in an inoffensive manner and then conclude the speech by saying that we have some hope that our reputation will not only be preserved on this occasion but be greatly enhanced in time to come.

7. A mixed style is most appropriate for this kind of speech, being sometimes compressed (*synestrammenē*),[7] sometimes elevated (*diērmenē*),[8] and simpler (*aphelestera*) in narrations. Clarity of style throughout the speech must be a particular concern for the speaker. [In general, the panegyric speech is composed along these lines.][9]

[7] That is, periodic; cf. 6.6.

[8] Cf. 1.8 and 6.6 (also part of a varied style).

[9] This concluding statement is obviously out of place here.

6. ΜΕΘΟΔΟΣ ΕΠΙΤΑΦΙΩΝ

1. Οὐ μὲν δὴ οὐδὲ τούτων ἀπείρως ἔχειν τόν γε δὴ ὁδῷ
τινι καὶ ἐπιστήμῃ μετιόντα λόγους χρή. ἀπευκτὰ μὲν
γὰρ τὰ τοιαῦτα, ἀναγκαῖα δὲ ἀνθρώποις γε οὖσι καὶ
παρελθοῦσιν εἰς τὸν ἀνθρώπινον βίον. ἀνθρώπῳ γὰρ
γενομένῳ κατὰ τὸν τοῦ Καλλαίσχρου τὸν τῶν τριά-
κοντα βέβαιον μὲν οὐδέν, ὅτι μὴ κατθανεῖν γενομένῳ,
καὶ ζῶντι εἶναι μὴ οἷόν τε ἐκτὸς ἄτης βαίνειν. ἐπειδὴ
τοίνυν ἀμφὶ ταφὴν δύο λόγοι μεμηχάνηνται, ὁ μὲν
κοινὸς πρὸς πόλιν ἅπασαν καὶ δῆμον [ὁ μὲν][1] τοῖς ἐν
πολέμῳ πεσοῦσιν, ἰδίᾳ δὲ καὶ καθ᾽ ἕκαστον ἅτερος
αὐτοῖν, οἷα δὴ τὰ πολλὰ ἐν εἰρήνῃ συμπίπτειν ἀνάγκη,
ἐν διαφόροις ἡλικίαις ἑκάστῳ τῆς τελευτῆς συμπε-
σούσης· ὄνομά γε μὴν ἀμφοῖν ἓν καὶ τὸ αὐτό, ἐπιτάφιος οὕτως ὀνομαζόμενος. παραδείγματα δὲ αὐτῶν
ἔστί που καὶ παρὰ τοῖς ἀρχαίοις, τοῦ μὲν κοινοῦ καὶ
πολιτικοῦ παρά γε τῷ τοῦ Ὀλόρου καὶ παρὰ τῷ τοῦ
Ἀρίστωνος, Λυσίας τε καὶ Ὑπερείδης καὶ ὁ Παιανιεὺς
καὶ ὁ τοῦ Ἰσοκράτους ἑταῖρος Ναυκράτης πολλὰς

278

[1] secl. Brinkmann

---

[1] Critias, a sophist and leader of the "Thirty" tyrants in Athens, was killed in 403 BC. This passage is cited only here (cf. 88
B49 DK).

6. HOW TO COMPOSE
FUNERAL SPEECHES

1. Anyone pursuing rhetoric systematically and expertly must be familiar with funeral speeches. Although we do not wish for such occasions, they are inevitable for beings who have entered into human life. For once a human is born, according to the son of Callaeschrus,[1] one of the Thirty, nothing for him is certain except that, having been born, he will die, and while alive he cannot avoid adversity. Now two speeches concerning burial have been devised. One is public, intended for the entire city and its populace, delivered over those who have fallen in war. The other is spoken privately on an individual basis, as most often happens during peacetime when death befalls individuals at different times of life. All the same, both share one name, *epitaphios*. There are examples of these in ancient writers. There are civic and public speeches in Olorus' son[2] and Ariston's son,[3] while Lysias,[4] Hyperides,[5] the Paeanian,[6] and Isocrates' student Naucrates[7] have fur-

[2] Thucydides' famous *epitaphios* (2.35–46), delivered by Pericles over the war dead in 431 BC.

[3] Plato's *Menexenus* contains a fictive *epitaphios* over the Athenian war dead in 390 BC.

[4] *Or.* 2.   [5] *Epitaphios*, delivered in 322 BC over the Athenian dead in the Lamian war.

[6] Dem. *Or.* 60.   [7] He composed a funeral speech for Mausolus (d. 353 BC) that is not extant.

417

ἡμῖν τοιαύτας ἰδέας παρέσχοντο. οὐκ ἀπορήσομεν δὲ
οὐδὲ τῶν πρὸς ἕκαστον· ἐπεί τοι καὶ τὰ ποιήματα με-
στὰ τούτων, οἱ ἐπικήδειοι οὕτως ὀνομαζόμενοι θρῆνοί
τε· ὡς αὕτως πλοῦτος πολὺς τῶν καταλογάδην ἐστὶ
τοιούτων λόγων ἔν τε τοῖς πάλαι καὶ τοῖς ὀλίγον τι
πρὸ ἡμῶν γενομένοις· ⟨οὐ⟩² λήξομεν δὲ οὐδὲ νῦν, ἔστ᾽
ἂν γένος ἀνθρώπων καὶ τὸ χρεὼν ἐπικρατοῦν ᾖ. μέτιμεν οὖν αὐτοῖν ἑκάτερον τὸν τρόπον τοῦτον.

2. Συνελόντι μὲν οὖν ὁ ἐπιτάφιος ἔπαινός ἐστι τῶν
κατοιχομένων. εἰ δὲ τοῦτο, δῆλόν που, ὡς καὶ ἀπὸ τῶν
αὐτῶν τόπων ληπτέον, ἀφ᾽ ὧν περ καὶ τὰ ἐγκώμια·
πατρίδος, γένους, φύσεως, ἀγωγῆς, πράξεων.³ ἄχρι
μὲν οὖν τινὸς τὴν αὐτὴν ἰτέον, οἷον περὶ πατρίδος
λέγοντα, ὅτι μεγάλη καὶ ἔνδοξος καὶ ἀρχαία, καὶ εἰ
τύχοι αὐτὴ πρώτη παρελθοῦσα εἰς ἀνθρώπους, οἷα
καὶ Πλάτων περὶ τῆς Ἀττικῆς διέξεισιν· εἰ δὲ μικρά,
ὅτι διὰ τούτους ἤδη καὶ τὴν ἀρετὴν τὴν τούτων καὶ
δόξαν ἔνδοξος καὶ αὐτὴ ἐγένετο, οἷον ἡ Σαλαμὶς διὰ
τὸν Αἴαντα ἢ τὴν ἀρετὴν τῶν ναυμαχησάντων, καὶ ἡ
279 Αἴγινα διὰ τὸν Αἰακόν. ἢ εἴ τι βέλτιον περὶ αὐτῆς
ἔχοιμεν λέγειν εἰρημένον, ὥσπερ ʻθείανʼ τὴν Σαλαμῖνα
εἶπεν ὁ Πύθιος· ὅτι ἐκ θεοῦ ἐκτίσθη, ὥσπερ Ἰωνία,
Βυζάντιον ἢ εἰ δή τις ἑτέρα πόλις. καὶ ἐπὶ μὲν τῶν ἐν

---

² suppl. Nissen
³ πράξεων RW: πράξεως codd.

nished many such types for us. Nor shall we lack speeches for individuals. Indeed, poetry is full of them, so-called dirges (*epikēdeioi*) and laments (*thrēnoi*), while there is an abundance of such speeches in prose in both our ancient and our recent predecessors. Nor shall we stop even now, so long as the human race continues and necessity rules. Therefore we shall treat each type as follows.

2. In a word, the funeral speech is an encomium of the departed. Consequently, it is obvious that we must adopt the same topics as those in encomia, namely native land, birth, nature, upbringing, and deeds. We must follow this, however, only to a certain extent. For example, in speaking of the native land, say that it is great, famous, and ancient, or perhaps that it happens to be the first land to bring forth humans, as Plato says of Attica.[8] If it is small, say that because of these men and their virtue and glory, it has gained its own fame, as did Salamis thanks to Ajax or to the valor of its sailors in battle,[9] and Aegina thanks to Aeacus.[10] Or else, we may cite some compliment paid it, such as "divine," which Pythian Apollo called Salamis.[11] We may mention that it was founded by a god, like Ionia,[12] Byzantium,[13] or other cities.[14] When speaking of those

---

[8] *Menex.* 237d: "our land . . . out of all living creatures chose to give birth to man." [9] That is, at the Battle of Salamis in 480 BC. [10] The son of Zeus and Aegina, who became a judge in the underworld; cf. M. 2.2.6, etc. [11] Cf. Hdt. 7.142: ὦ θείη Σαλαμίς, spoken by the Pythia at Delphi.

[12] There is no basis for this claim. RW suspect corruption.

[13] The legendary founder of Byzantium was Byzas of Megara, not any god. [14] M. 1.15.2 cites Hermopolis and Heliopolis as cities founded by gods.

πολέμοις πεσόντων κἂν ἐπιδαψιλεύσαιτό τις ἐν τούτοις. ἐπὶ δὲ τῶν καθ' ἕκαστον οὐ πάνυ τι ἀναγκαῖος
ὁ πολὺς περὶ τῆς πατρίδος λόγος.

Ἰτέον οὖν ἐπὶ τοὺς προγόνους, εἰ οἱ πρόγονοι μὴ
ἐπήλυδες, ἀλλ' αὐτόχθονες· καὶ εἰ ἐπήλυδες, ἀλλὰ κρίσει τὴν ἀρίστην γῆν λαβόντες, οὐ τύχῃ· καὶ ὅτι ἢ ἐκ
τοῦ Δωρικοῦ γένους, ὅ περ ἀνδρειότατον· ἢ ἐκ τοῦ
Ἰωνικοῦ, ὅ περ σοφώτατον, καὶ ὅτι Ἕλληνες. εἰ δὲ ἐπὶ
τινὸς εὐκλείας λόγος γίγνοιτο, ὅτι πατρὸς ἀγαθοῦ καὶ
προγόνων, καὶ ἐν βραχεῖ περὶ αὐτῶν εἰπεῖν τὸν ἔπαινον, ὁποῖοι δημοσίᾳ, ὁποῖοι ἰδίᾳ, ὁποῖοι ἐν λόγοις,
ὁποῖοι ἐν βίῳ, καὶ εἴ τι ἐν ἔργοις ἢ ἐν πράξεσιν· ἢ εἴ
τινα τοιαῦτα ἡ ποιότης τοῦ προσώπου παρέχοι ἐκ τῆς
φύσεως, ὅτι εὐφυὴς εἰς πάντα· κοινὸς δὲ ὁ τόπος
οὗτος.[4]

3. Ἐν δὲ τῇ ἀγωγῇ γενόμενοι ἐπὶ μὲν τῶν κοινῶν
τὴν πολιτείαν ληψόμεθα, ὅτι ἢ δημοκρατία ἢ ἀριστο-
κρατία· ἐν δὲ τοῖς ἰδίοις τὴν ἀνατροφὴν καὶ τὴν παιδείαν καὶ τὰ ἐπιτηδεύματα. ἐν δὲ ταῖς [κοιναῖς][5] πράξεσιν ὁ μὲν κοινὸς ἕξει τὰ κατὰ πολέμους ἔργα καὶ
280 ὅπως ἐτελεύτησαν, ὥσπερ ἀμέλει καὶ Πλάτωνί γε καὶ
Θουκυδίδῃ καὶ τοῖς ἄλλοις εἴρηται. ὁπόταν δὲ περὶ
ἑνός τινος λέγωμεν, περὶ τῆς ἀρετῆς ποιησόμεθα τὸν
λόγον, οἷον περὶ ἀνδρείας, περὶ δικαιοσύνης, περὶ σο-

---

[4] ὁ τόπος οὗτος Sauppe, RW: ὁ τοιοῦτος codd.
[5] secl. Schott

fallen in war, we may be lavish with these praises, but for individuals there is no need at all for a long treatment of the homeland.

So, passing on to the ancestors, say that they did not immigrate but rather were autochthonous,[15] or, if they were immigrants, that they chose the best land deliberately, not by chance. Also say that they were either of the Dorian race (the bravest) or of the Ionian (the wisest),[16] and state that they were Greeks. If there is a story about someone's high repute—how his father and forefathers were noble—praise them briefly, telling how they conducted themselves in public, in private, in speaking, in life, and anything they did or accomplished. Or else, if the person's natural qualities provide any similar grounds for praise, say that he was naturally equipped for everything. This is a commonplace.

3. When treating upbringing in public speeches, we should discuss the form of government, as being either a democracy or an aristocracy, whereas in private ones we should discuss rearing, education, and activities. On the subject of deeds, the public speech will include military actions and how the men died, as was done by Plato,[17] Thucydides,[18] and the others.[19] When speaking of an individual, we should mention virtues such as courage, justice, and wisdom, and tell how he demonstrated these with

---

[15] Cf. Pl. *Menex.* 237b for the contrast between immigrant (ἔπηλυς) stock and people of the soil (αὐτόχθονας).

[16] For qualities of the Hellenic races, cf. M. 1.15.5, where the Ionians are called the most highly regarded.

[17] Cf. *Menexenus*, passim.   [18] Cf. 2.42–43.

[19] Cf. Lys. 2.69–70, 79; Hyp. *Epitaphios* 16; Dem. 60.1.

φίας· ὁποῖος περὶ τὴν πόλιν ἐν τούτοις, ὁποῖος ἰδίᾳ
περὶ ἕκαστα· ὁποῖος περὶ φίλους, ὁποῖος περὶ ἐχθρούς·
καὶ ἔτι προστεθήτω, οἷος περὶ γονέας, οἷος ἐν ἀρχαῖς,
εἴ τινα ἦρξεν.

4. Μετὰ ταῦτα δὲ ἐν μὲν τοῖς κοινοῖς ἐπὶ τὸ προτρεπτικὸν μεταβησόμεθα, προτρέποντες ἐπὶ τὰ ὅμοια
τοὺς ὑπολειπομένους. καὶ πολὺς ὁ τόπος οὗτος. εἶτα
οὕτως ἐπὶ τὸ παραμυθητικὸν τῶν πατέρων, ὅσοι τε ἔτι
παιδοποιεῖσθαι ἱκανοί, ὅσοι τε ἔξω τῆς ὥρας ταύτης·
καὶ εἴρηται ταῦτα καὶ παρὰ τῷ Θουκυδίδῃ. ἐν δὲ τοῖς
ἰδίοις τὸ μὲν προτρεπτικὸν ἐνίοτε μὲν οὐδὲ ὅλως
παραλαμβάνομεν διὰ τὸ τάχα ἂν εἰ τύχοι παῖδας εἶναι τοὺς κατοιχομένους· ἐνίοτε δὲ ἐπὶ βραχύ, πλὴν ἐπὶ
τοῖς πάνυ ἐνδόξοις. ἐνταῦθα γὰρ οὐδὲν κωλύει καὶ ἐπὶ
πλεῖον χρῆσθαι τῷ εἴδει, οἷον ⟨εἰ⟩[6] ἐπὶ ἄρχοντός τινος
καὶ τοιούτου προσώπου ὁ ἐπιτάφιος γίνοιτο, ἀναγκαῖον παρακελεύεσθαι μιμεῖσθαι τοῖς παισὶν τοὺς
ἑαυτῶν τοκέας, καὶ ἐπὶ τὰ ὅμοια σπεύδειν.

281   Ἀναγκαιότερος δὲ ὁ παραμυθητικὸς παραμυθουμέ-
νων ἡμῶν τοὺς προσήκοντας. δεῖ δὲ εἰδέναι καὶ τὴν
μέθοδον τοῦ παραμυθητικοῦ· οὐ γὰρ θρηνεῖν ⟨δεῖ⟩[7]
οὐδὲ ἀπολοφύρεσθαι τοὺς ἀποθανόντας. οὐ γὰρ ἂν
παραμυθοίμεθα τοὺς ὑπολειπομένους, ἀλλὰ μεῖζον τὸ
πένθος παρασκευάζοιμεν· καὶ οὐ δόξει εἶναι τῶν κατοιχομένων ἔπαινος, ἀλλὰ ὀλοφυρμὸς ὡς τὰ δεινότατα
παθόντων. πειρᾶσθαι δὲ ἐν τῷ παραμυθεῖσθαι καὶ
ἐνδιδόναι τοῦ πάθους τοῖς ὑπολειπομένοις, καὶ μὴ
ἀντιτείνειν εὐθύς· ῥᾷον γὰρ ἐπαξόμεθα. ἅμα δὲ καὶ

regard to the city and privately in particular matters, including how he treated his friends and enemies. Add too how he behaved toward his parents and how he performed in any offices that he held.

4. After this, in public speeches, we should turn to exhortation, urging the survivors to perform similar deeds. This is a large topic. Next we should turn to consolation of the parents, both those still able to produce children and those beyond this age. This is treated in Thucydides.[20] In private speeches, on the other hand, we shall sometimes not even include the exhortation if the deceased happen to be children, while at other times we shall keep it brief, unless they are very famous, in which case nothing prevents a more extensive development of this topic. If, for example, the funeral speech is for a governor or some such person, we should urge the children to follow their parents' example and aim for similar accomplishments.

The consolatory portion is all the more important because we are comforting the relatives. You need to know the procedure for this consolation. The point is not to lament or bewail the deceased, because then we would not be comforting the survivors but instead adding to their grief, and it will not come across as praise of the departed but rather lamentation for their terrible suffering. In offering consolation, we must try to grant the survivors their pain and not hold back entirely, for that way we will win them over more readily. At the same time the speech will

---

[20] Cf. 2.44.3–4.

---

[6] suppl. Sylburg   [7] suppl. RW

ἔπαινον ἕξει ὁ λόγος, εἰ λέγοιμεν, ὅτι οὐ ῥᾴδιον ἐπὶ
τοῖς τοιούτοις ῥᾷον[8] φέρειν. ἐπειδὴ δὲ οἱ ἐν πολέμῳ
τελευτήσαντες ὅμοιοι ταῖς ἡλικίαις, οὐδὲν ἀπὸ τούτων
ἕξομεν εἰς παραμυθίαν ἐπιχειρεῖν, πλὴν ὅτι ἐνδόξως
ἀπέθανον ὑπὲρ τῆς πατρίδος καὶ οὗτοι, καὶ ὅτι ταχὺς
καὶ ἀναίσθητος ὁ τοιοῦτος θάνατος, καὶ ἐκτὸς βασά-
νων καὶ τῶν κακῶν τῶν ἐκ τῆς νόσου· ὅτι δημοσίας
ταφῆς ἔλαχον (ζηλωτὸν δὲ τοῦτο καὶ τοῖς μετὰ ταῦτα)
καὶ ἀθάνατος αὐτῶν ἡ δόξα.

5. Ἐπὶ δὲ τοῖς καθ᾽ ἕκαστον ⟨ἀπὸ τῶν περιστά-
σεων⟩[9] καὶ ἀπὸ τῶν ἡλικιῶν πολλὰς ἀφορμὰς παρέξει
ὁ λόγος εἰς παραμυθίαν· εἰ μέν τις ἄφνω τελευτήσειεν
καὶ ἀλύπως, ὅτι μακαρίως αὐτῷ ἡ τελευτὴ συνηνέ-
χθη· εἰ δέ τις νόσῳ καὶ πολὺν χρόνον νοσήσας, ὅτι
γενναίως ἐνεκαρτέρησεν τῇ νόσῳ· ἢ εἴ τις ἐν πολέμῳ,
ὅτι ὑπὲρ πατρίδος ἀγωνιζόμενος· ἢ εἴ τις ἐν πρεσβείᾳ,
ὅτι ὑπὲρ τῆς πόλεως· κἂν εἰ ἐν ἀποδημίᾳ, ὅτι οὐδὲν
διενήνοχεν· 'μία γὰρ καὶ ἡ αὐτὴ οἶμος' κατὰ τὸν Αἰ-
σχύλον 'εἰς Ἅιδου φέρουσα'· εἰ δέ τις ἐν τῇ πατρίδι,
ὅτι ἐν τῇ φιλτάτῃ καὶ τῇ γειναμένῃ καὶ τοῖς οἰκειοτά-
τοις πᾶσιν. ἀπὸ ἡλικίας· εἰ μὲν νέος ὢν τοῦτο πάθοι,
ὅτι θεοφιλής· τοὺς γὰρ τοιούτους φιλοῦσιν οἱ θεοί· καὶ
ὅτι καὶ τῶν παλαιῶν πολλοὺς ἀνήρπασαν, οἶον τὸν
Γανυμήδην, τὸν Τιθωνόν, τὸν Ἀχιλλέα, μὴ βουλόμε-
νοι αὐτοὺς ἐν τοῖς κακοῖς τοῖς ἐν τῇ γῇ καλινδεῖσθαι

282

8 ῥᾷον P: πράως Brinkmann, RW
9 suppl. Radermacher, RW

contain an element of praise if we say how difficult it is in such circumstances to bear up calmly. Since those who die in war are about the same age, we cannot use anything on that score for consolation except to say that they died gloriously for their fatherland; that such a death is swift and imperceptible[21] and thus avoids anguish and the woes of disease; and that they have been awarded a public burial—an enviable lot even to future generations—and their fame is immortal.

5. In the case of individuals, the speech will have many starting points for consolation based on circumstances and on age. If a man has died suddenly and painlessly, say that a blessed end came to him; if he died of a long illness, say that he bore it with nobility. If he died in war, say that he died fighting for his country. If he died on an embassy, say that died for his city. And if he died on a journey, say that it makes no difference because, as Aeschylus puts it, "one and the same is the way that leads to Hades."[22] If he died at home, say that he died in the beloved land of his birth among all his nearest and dearest. With regard to age, if he passed away at a young age, say that he was beloved of the gods, for the gods love the young,[23] and mention how they snatched up many youths of old such as Ganymede, Tithonus, and Achilles, not wishing them to wallow in earthly evils, nor to have their souls buried for years in

---

[21] Cf. Thuc. 2.43.6: ἀναίσθητος θάνατος (unfelt death).

[22] Cf. Pl. *Phd.* 107e–8a: "Telephus . . . says that a simple path leads to Hades." = Aesch., Fr. 239N².

[23] Men., Fr. 111 (Körte): ὃν γὰρ θεοὶ φιλοῦσιν ἀποθνήσκει νέος ("he whom the gods love dies young"). Plutarch cites this line in his *Consolation for Apollonius* (119E).

ἢ πολὺν χρόνον ἐγκατορωρύχθαι τὴν ψυχὴν ἐν τῷ
σώματι ὥσπερ ἐν τάφῳ ἢ ἐν δεσμωτηρίῳ μηδὲ δουλεύειν δεσπόταις κακοῖς, ἀλλὰ ἐλευθεροῦν· καὶ μακά-
ριοι φυγόντες τὰ ἀλγεινὰ τοῦ βίου καὶ τὰ πάθη τὰ
συμπίπτοντα τοῖς ἀνθρώποις, μυρία ταῦτα ὄντα καὶ
ἄπειρα, ὀφθαλμῶν πηρώσεις, ποδῶν, ἑτέρου τινὸς μέρους τοῦ σώματος, καὶ ὅτι τῷ ὄντι ἡ νόσος ἀλγεινο-
τάτη. εἰ δὲ μέσος τὴν ἡλικίαν, ὅτι ἐνακμάσας τῷ βίῳ
καὶ νῷ δεῖγμα τῆς ἀρετῆς τῆς ἑαυτοῦ παρέσχεν· καὶ
ὅτι ποθούμενος, οὐκ ἀηδὴς ἤδη διὰ τὸ γῆρας γενόμενος ἀπῆλθε τοῦ βίου, ἀλλ᾽ ἐν ἡλικίᾳ. εἰ δὲ δὴ ἐν γήρᾳ
τις τελευτήσειεν, ὅτι εἰς πᾶσαν ἀπόλαυσιν τῶν ἐν τῷ
283 βίῳ καλῶν συνεμετρήθη αὐτῷ ὁ χρόνος. ἐν τούτῳ
παρατιθέναι ἀναγκαῖον, ὁπόσα ἐν πανηγύρεσιν τερ-
πνά, ὅσα ἐν γάμοις, παιδοποιίαις, τιμαῖς ⟨ταῖς⟩[10]
παρὰ τῆς πατρίδος· ταῦτα γὰρ ἡ πλείων περίοδος τοῦ
χρόνου παρέχειν εἴωθεν· καὶ ὅτι ‘λιπαρὸν γῆρας’ κατὰ
τὸν Νέστορα ἐβίωσεν· ὅτι τούτου ἕνεκα ἐνδιέτριψεν,
ἵνα παράδειγμα γένηται τοῖς ἄλλοις, καὶ μάλιστα εἰ
ἔνδοξον εἴη τὸ πρόσωπον. ἐπὶ τέλει δὲ περὶ ψυχῆς
ἀναγκαῖον εἰπεῖν, ὅτι ἀθάνατος, καὶ ὅτι τοὺς τοιούτους ἐν θεοῖς ὄντας ἄμεινον ⟨ἔχειν⟩[11] εἰκὸς ἀπολαβεῖν.
ἀρχὰς δὲ ἐνίοτε αὐτὸ παρέξει τὸ πρόσωπον ἰδίας καὶ
μὴ κοινάς· οἷον εἰ ἀπὸ λόγων εἴη, ὅτι ἀκόλουθον τοῖς
λόγοις εὐφημεῖν αὐτόν· ἢ εἴπερ ἐπὶ ἑτέροις αὐτός τι
τοιοῦτον εἰρηκὼς εἴη, ὅτι τὸν αὐτὸν ἔρανον καὶ τούτῳ
ἀποδοτέον· ἢ ὅ τί ποτ᾽ ἂν ἡ ἰδιότης τοῦ προσώπου
παρέχῃ.

their bodies as in a tomb or prison, nor to be slaves to evil despots, but wishing rather to set them free. "They are blessed for having escaped the pains of life and the countless and unbounded sufferings that befall human beings," including the failure of eyes, feet, and other parts of the body, for illness is in truth excruciating. If he is middle-aged, say that at the peak of his life and intellect he gave proof of his excellence and is missed not as one who left life already made unsightly by old age, but in his prime. If, however, he died in old age, say that he was granted time to enjoy life's blessings to the full. Here one should include all the joys of festivals, marriages, childbirths, and honors bestowed by his country, for these are what a full cycle of time usually provides. Say that he lived to a "splendid old age"[24] like Nestor, and that he lived so long in order to serve as a model for others, especially if he was a well-known figure. At the end you must mention that the soul is immortal and that it is reasonable to assume that men like him are better off in the company of the gods. His personal qualities will occasionally provide openings specific to him and not to others. For example, if he is an orator, say that is fitting to laud him with oratory; or if he had delivered any similar speech on behalf of others, say that the same offering is owed him—or whatever his personal attributes provide.

[24] The phrase occurs at Hom. *Od.* 11.136, 19.368, and 23.283 (although not used of Nestor); it is also cited at 3.5.

---

[10] suppl. Radermacher
[11] suppl RW

6. Ἡ δὲ ἀπαγγελία ποικίλη, ἐν μὲν τοῖς ἀγωνιστι-
κοῖς συνεστραμμένη· ἐν δὲ τοῖς ἐνδόξοις καὶ μέγεθος
ἔχουσιν, οἷον ὅσα περὶ ψυχῆς, διῃρμένη καὶ μέγεθος
ἔχουσα καὶ ἐγγὺς βαίνουσα τῆς τοῦ Πλάτωνος.

6. The style should be varied: compressed (*synestram-menē*)[25] in argumentative passages; elevated (*diērmenē*) and with grandeur close to that of Plato in passages possessing splendor and grandeur, such as those on the soul.[26]

[25] That is, periodic; cf. 5.7, where the two styles are also paired.

[26] Many consolatory topics in these instructions can be found in Plato's *Phaedo*, such as the immortal soul being imprisoned or entombed in the body and having to endure servitude to masters on earth, and death as a setting free of the soul to be with the gods.

7. ΠΡΟΤΡΕΠΤΙΚΟΣ ΑΘΛΗΤΑΙΣ

1. Ἀκόλουθος ἂν εἴη καί, ὡς <ἂν>[1] εἴποι τις, συναφής,
ὦ Ἐχέκρατες, καὶ ὁ ἐν ταύταις ταῖς πανηγύρεσι λε-
284 γόμενος λόγος, οὐκ εἰς αὐτὴν μέντοι τὴν πανήγυριν,
ἀλλ' εἰς τοὺς ἀνταγωνιστὰς τοὺς ἐν τῇ πανηγύρει καὶ
τοῖς ἀγωνισταῖς ἀθληταῖς δή που, ὁ προτρεπτικὸς
οὕτως λεγόμενος. σκεπτέον οὖν πρῶτον εὐθύς, ὅς τίς
ποτε ὁ λέγων· νῦν μὲν γὰρ ἴσως πολίτης, νῦν δὲ καὶ
αὐτῶν τῶν περὶ τὸν ἀγῶνά τις, ἐγὼ δὲ ἤδη καὶ τὸν
ἀγωνοθέτην εἶδον ἀγωνιστὴν τούτου τοῦ λόγου γεγε-
νημένον, ὡς ἔγωγε οἶδα καὶ Ὀλυμπίασιν καὶ ἐπ' ἐμοῦ
τοῦτο γενόμενον καὶ Πυθοῖ καὶ ἄλλοθι πολλαχοῦ τισίν.[2]

2. Τὰς γὰρ ἀρχὰς ἴσως που καὶ ἐντεῦθέν τις οὐκ
ἀπὸ καιροῦ ποιήσεται. εἰ μὲν πολίτης εἴη, ὅτι καὶ
αὐτὸς πεισθεὶς τοῖς ἀγωνοθέταις καὶ τῷ τῆς πόλεως
νόμῳ εἰς τὸν ἀγῶνα καθῆκεν ἑαυτὸν καὶ παρεβάλετο
κινδύνῳ οὐχ ἧττον ὄντι ἐργώδει· ἐκεῖνος μὲν γὰρ σώματος, ὅδε δὲ ψυχῆς. χαλεπώτεροι δὲ οἱ ἀγῶνες οἱ τῆς
ψυχῆς ἢ <οἱ>[3] τοῦ σώματος. ἐπὶ μὲν γὰρ τῆς ἀγωνίας
τῶν σωμάτων καὶ φανερὰ ἡ νίκη καὶ ὑπὸ τοῖς ὀφθαλ-

---

[1] suppl. Sauppe   [2] ὡς ... τισίν huc transp. RW: post ὁ
λέγων codd.   [3] suppl. Radermacher

7. EXHORTATION TO ATHLETES

1. Following this speech,[1] and so to speak conjoined with it, Echecrates, is one which, though delivered at these panegyric festivals, focuses not on the festival itself but rather on the competitors in the festival, being addressed to them as an exhortation. First of all, we must take into account the speaker's identity. Sometimes it may be a private citizen, sometimes a person connected with the games; indeed I have even seen the organizer (*agōnothetēs*) of the games perform this speech, as I know has happened at Olympia in my time, and at Pytho,[2] and in many other places to various people.

2. It may well be appropriate to begin with this topic. If the speaker is a private citizen: "In obedience to the organizers and the law of the city, he has entered into competition and exposed himself to hazards no less arduous,[3] for that endeavor involves the body, this one the intellect, and contests of the intellect are more difficult than those of the body. In physical competition the victory is clear and witnessed by the sharpest of our senses, our eyes;

---

[1] That is, the panegyric speech (1), which this section apparently followed. For similar dislocations in M., see "The Condition of the Two Treatises" in the Introduction.

[2] That is, Delphi.

[3] That is, than the risk for athletic competitors.

μοῖς, ἥ περ ἐναργεστάτη τῶν αἰσθήσεων· ἔτι δὲ καὶ
βραβευτὴς ἐφέστηκεν ἐπ' αὐτῷ τούτῳ κρείττων τοῦ
παρὰ τῶν ἄλλων φθόνου. ἤδε <δὲ ἡ>⁴ κρίσις οὐκ ἐφ'
ἑνί, ἀλλ' ἐπὶ πολλοῖς· καὶ οὐκ ὀφθαλμοῖς κρίνουσιν,
ἀλλὰ γνώμῃ, ἐν ᾗ πολλὰ τὰ ἀντιστατοῦντα· ἄγνοια
καὶ φιλοτιμία καὶ φθόνος, ἐφ' ἅπασι δὲ τὸ μὴ βούλεσθαι τοὺς ἀκούοντας μείζονα εἶναι τὰ ἐπαινούμενα τῷ
περὶ αὐτῶν λόγῳ.

285   Τούτοις δὲ ὑποβάλλειν κἀκεῖνο ἀναγκαῖον, τὸ ἀνε-
λεῖν ὡς ἀντικείμενον ἐκ τῆς τοῦ προσώπου ποιότητος,
ὅτι μὴ καταφρονητέον λόγων τοῖς ἀθληταῖς ἅτε ἐν
ἔργοις ἀσκοῦσι. λόγος γὰρ εἰς πάντα ἐπιτήδειος καὶ
πρὸς πᾶν ἐπιρρώννυσιν· οὕτως καὶ ἐπὶ πολέμου καὶ
ἐπὶ παρατάξεως δέονται στρατιῶται τοῦ παρὰ τῶν
στρατηγῶν λόγου καὶ τῆς προτροπῆς, καὶ αὐτοὶ αὑτῶν ἐρρωμενέστεροι ἐγένοντο. μάλιστα δὲ οἱ ἀθληταὶ
δέοιντο ἂν τῆς ἀπὸ τοῦ λόγου προτροπῆς καὶ ἐπικε-
λεύσεως, ὄντες μὲν καὶ αὐτοὶ Ἑρμοῦ τε καὶ Ἡρακλέους μαθηταί τε καὶ ζηλωταί (ὧν ὁ μὲν εὑρετὴς τοῦ
λόγου ἢ αὐτὸ χρῆμα λόγος· ὁ δὲ σὺν τῇ Ἀθηνᾷ πάντα
κατώρθωσεν τὰ ἐπιταχθέντα· ἡ δὲ τί ἂν ἄλλο εἴη ἢ
νοῦς τε καὶ λόγος;), καὶ ὁσημέραι δὲ ἐπὶ ταῖς γυμνα-
σίαις ἑκάστοτε τοιούτους τοὺς ἐπικελευομένους ἔχοντες αὐτοῖς.

3. Εἶτα διαφορὰν ἐρεῖς, ὅσῳ κρείττων οὗτος τοῦ
ἐκείνων ἔπαινος· διὰ ταῦτα, ὅτι ὁ μὲν ἐκ τῶν ἐπιτυχόν-

⁴ suppl. Sauppe

in addition, an umpire presides over it, who is above the ill will felt by others. The decision in this case, however, rests not with one judge but with many, and they do not decide with their eyes, but with their opinions, which are subject to many conflicting factors: ignorance, rivalry, envy, and above all the unwillingness of an audience to accept that things that are praised are rendered greater by discourse about them."[4]

To this must be added a passage countering any prejudice arising from personal bias, namely that athletes should not look down on words just because they train for deeds. "For words are suitable for all purposes and add strength to any endeavor. Thus, soldiers in battle formation need a speech of exhortation from their generals, through which they surpass themselves in strength and vigor. Athletes in particular require exhortation and encouragement through speech. They are, after all, themselves students and followers of Hermes and Heracles, and while the former is the inventor (or the very embodiment) of speech,[5] the latter accomplished everything he was ordered to do[6] with the help of Athena—and what is she if not intellect and speech? So, day in and day out, athletes have people like these encouraging them every time they are training."

3. Next, draw a distinction, explaining that this praise is much more important than that which comes from

[4] For some of these difficulties a speaker faces in his audience, see Thuc. 2.35.2–3.

[5] That is, as the messenger god. He was also the patron of gymnasia.

[6] That is, by Eurystheus, who ordered Heracles' labors.

των, οὗτος δὲ ἀπὸ τῶν δεδοκιμασμένων καὶ βίῳ καὶ
λόγῳ καὶ δόξῃ· καὶ ἐκεῖνος μὲν ἔθει τινί, οὗτος δὲ
νόμῳ πόλεως καὶ δόγματι ἀρχόντων· κἀκεῖνος οἷον
ἐπιβόησίς τις, μηδὲν τῶν ἤχων διαφέρων, οὗτος δὲ
μετὰ ἐπαίνων καὶ ἀποδείξεων παράκλησις. εἶτ᾽ ἀκόλουθον τοῖς περὶ τὸ τοῦ σώματος καλὸν σπουδάσα-
σιν καὶ περὶ τὸ καλὸν τὸ ἐπὶ τῇ ψυχῇ σπουδάσαι καὶ
286 μᾶλλον, ὅσῳ τιμιώτερον ψυχὴ σώματος, εἰ μὴ καὶ
αὐτοὺς ἀσκοῦντας, ἀλλὰ τοῖς ἀσκήσασι πειθομένους·
ὅπερ οὐδὲ δυσχέρειάν τινα ἔχει οὐδὲ πόνον, ἄλλως τε
καὶ ἐπὶ συμφέροντι τῶν πεισθέντων τῆς πειθοῦς γι-
νομένης· ὥσπερ γὰρ καὶ ἐν στρατοπέδῳ οἱ γνησιώτα-
τοι παρὰ τῶν στρατηγῶν λόγους ἀκούσαντες μάλιστα φιλοτιμοῦνται περὶ τὴν νίκην, οὕτως καὶ οἱ ἐν
τοῖς ἀγῶσι προτρεπτικοὺς λόγους οἰκείως ἀναδεξάμε-
νοι· μάλιστα γὰρ ἂν ὀρέγοιντο τοῦ περιγενέσθαι. [καὶ
ὅτι τοῖς ἐπαγγελλομένοις τὴν σωτηρίαν τὴν τοῦ σώματος προσήκει καὶ ἀψευδεῖν.]⁵ ἐν τούτῳ· εἰ δήπου τις,
καίτοι τῆς ἀπὸ τούτων δόξης ἀδήλου τυγχανούσης,
ὅμως ἐφίεται τούτου ἄλλως μηδὲ ἀνάγκης οὔσης,
πόσῳ μᾶλλον <εἰκὸς>⁶ τοὺς ἐπ᾽ αὐτὸ τοῦτο παρόντας
καὶ παραδεδωκότας ἑαυτοὺς καὶ τούτου ἕνεκα ἐπὶ τοσοῦτον τοῖς γυμνασίοις χρησαμένους καὶ ὑπευθύνους
ἑαυτοὺς καταστήσαντας πειθομένους φαίνεσθαι τῷ
ἐπὶ τοῦτο ὑπὸ τῆς πόλεως καὶ τῶν ἀγωνοθετῶν καὶ
τοῦ νόμου προκεχειρισμένῳ;

⁵ secl. RW praeeunte Radermacher   ⁶ suppl. Radermacher

434

others,[7] for the following reasons. "Their praise comes from people who just happen to be in attendance, this praise from people well tested in life, speech, and reputation; theirs is prompted by mere habit, this by a law of the city and decree of its magistrates; theirs consists of mere shouting indistinguishable from noise, this consists of encouragement through praise and reasoned argument. Then too, it follows that those concerned with the beauty of the body should also be concerned with the beauty of the mind—even more so, indeed, to the degree that the mind is more esteemed than the body—not necessarily by practicing oratory themselves, but by heeding those who do. This involves neither difficulty nor hard work, especially since persuasion benefits those who heed it. Just as in an army the truest soldiers are those who, having listened to the words of their generals, are the most eager for victory, so too are those competitors in the games who take to heart speeches of exhortation, for they will be the most eager to win."[8] On this subject add, "If indeed, despite the fact that the fame deriving from it is uncertain, a person still desires to win, without purpose or compulsion, is it not much more likely that those who are here for that very purpose, who have devoted themselves to it and for its sake have engaged in such extensive physical training and subjected themselves to such scrutiny, should be seen to heed the speaker who has been appointed to this task by the city, the organizers of the games, and by the law?"

[7] That is, from cheering spectators.　　[8] RW bracket the following sentence (noted by Radermacher as out of place here): "And say that those who promise physical safety should not lie."

Εἰ δὲ δὴ καὶ ἀγωνοθέτης εἴη ὁ λέγων, πρὸς τούτοις
ἢ πρὸ ἁπάντων τούτων ἁρμόσει εἰπεῖν, ὅτι ‹εἰ ὁ›[7]
διατιθεὶς τὸν ἀγῶνα οὐκ ὤκνησεν ἀγωνιστὴν καὶ ἑαυτὸν καταστῆσαι καὶ ὑποβαλεῖν τῇ τῶν ἀκουόντων
κρίσει ἕνεκα τοῦ ἀγῶνος καὶ τοῦ ἔνδοξον καὶ μέγαν
287 καὶ περισπούδαστον τοῦτον γενέσθαι, πολλῷ δήπου
ἀναγκαιότερον αὐτοῖς ‹τοῖς›[8] ἀγωνιζομένοις καὶ κλη-
ρονομεῖν μέλλουσι τῆς τοῦ ἀγῶνος δόξης.

Τῷ δὲ ξένῳ καὶ τοῦτο ἂν ἁρμόζοι λέγειν, ὅτι προσήκων αὐτῷ ὁ λόγος διὰ τὴν ἐπιδημίαν καὶ τὴν μετου-
σίαν τῆς θέας· οἱ γὰρ τῆς θέας μεταδόντες καὶ τοῦ
λόγου τοῦ περὶ αὐτῆς μετέδοσαν ἄλλως τε καὶ ἐπὶ τῷ
ἐνδοξοτέραν τὴν πανήγυριν γενέσθαι. καὶ ὅτι γνήσιος πολίτης οὐχ ὁ ἐγγεγραμμένος μόνον, ἀλλὰ
πολλῷ μᾶλλον ὁ εὔνους τῇ πόλει καὶ περὶ τὰ καλὰ
μόνον τὰ τῆς πόλεως σπουδάζων. εἰ δὲ δὴ καὶ μὴ
πολίτης ὢν ἐπείσθη τοῖς ἐπιτάξασι καθεῖναι ἑαυτὸν
εἰς τὸν ἀγῶνα, πολλῷ δήπου μᾶλλον τοῖς ἀθληταῖς
σπουδαστέον περὶ αὐτὸν τοῖς ὡς ἂν εἴποι τις πολίταις
τοῦ ἀγῶνος οὖσι.

4. Τούτων δὲ τῶν ἀφορμῶν τάχα ἄν τινες καὶ εἰς
τὸν πανηγυρικὸν λόγον ἁρμόζοιεν, τοιούτων προσώπων πανηγυριζόντων καὶ τοιούτων ποιοτήτων ἐμπερι-
ειλημμένων. τοιαύτης δὲ τῆς προκαταστάσεως γενο-
μένης ὑποβλητέον καὶ τὸν περὶ τῶν πανηγύρεων
καθόλου λόγον ἔπαινον ἔχοντα τῶν προκαταστησα-

[7] suppl. Radermacher   [8] suppl. Sauppe

7. EXHORTATION TO ATHLETES

If the speaker is an organizer of the games, it is fitting for him to say, either in addition to all this or before it, that if the one organizing the games did not shrink from becoming a competitor and subjecting himself to the judgment of his audience for the sake of the games' prestige, greatness, and popularity, then surely this is much more necessary for the competitors themselves, who stand to inherit the renown of these games.

A foreign speaker might aptly say that speaking is appropriate for him because of his presence on the scene and his participation in the spectacle, since those who gave him a part in it also allowed him to speak about it, above all in order to enhance the festival's prestige. He may add, "The true citizen is not just the one who is registered as such, but much more so the man who is well-disposed toward the city and who, in matters of beauty, is devoted exclusively to the beauties of this city. And if indeed a noncitizen has obeyed the command to participate in the games, then surely the athletes are bound to show much more enthusiasm for this, since one might call them 'citizens' of the games."

4. Some of these starting points may also suit the panegyric speech, if similar persons are participating in the festival and if similar qualities are involved. After such preliminaries,[9] you should include a passage on panegyric festivals in general, with praise of those who instituted

[9] That is, those remarks in the previous three sections addressing the status of the speaker and encouragement of athletes.

μένων, ὅτι τῶν πολέμων καὶ τῶν πρὸς ἀλλήλους δια-
φορῶν καταπαύσαντες τὰς πόλεις συνήγαγον ὥσπερ
εἰς μίαν πόλιν τὴν πατρίδα πάντων, ὡς κοινῇ συνελ-
θόντας θύειν καὶ ἑορτάζειν λήθην ἁπάντων τῶν πρότερον ποιησαμένους· καὶ οὐ ταῦτα ἀπέχρησε μόνον,
ἀλλὰ καὶ θεάματα καὶ ἀκροάματα μυρία ἐπὶ μυρίοις
προέθεσαν, οὐκ εἰς ψυχαγωγίαν μόνον, ἀλλὰ καὶ
πρὸς ὠφέλειαν· διὰ μὲν τῶν μουσικῶν ἀκροαμάτων
παιδεύοντες ἡμᾶς, διὰ δὲ τῶν γυμνικῶν συνασκοῦντες
εἰς τοὺς πολέμους. καλὸν μὲν οὖν καὶ τοῖς ἐπιδημοῦσι
σπουδάζειν περὶ τὴν θέαν, πολὺ δὲ κάλλιον τοῖς ἀγωνιζομένοις αὐτοῖς. τοῖς μὲν γὰρ πρόσκαιρος ἡ τέρψις,
τοῖς δὲ ἀθάνατος ἡ δόξα· καὶ παραχρῆμα μὲν γίνεται
ἑκάστῳ τούτων εὐφημεῖσθαι καὶ δακτυλοδεικτεῖσθαι
ἐπὶ τοῖς καλλίστοις, νικᾶν, στεφανοῦσθαι, ἀναγορεύ-
εσθαι, διὰ μιᾶς πράξεως καὶ νίκης οὐ μιᾶς πόλεως
γενόμενον ἀλλὰ σχεδὸν ἁπάσης τῆς οἰκουμένης· ἕκαστος γὰρ τῶν παρόντων τῆς ἀρετῆς ἀποδεχόμενος τῇ
εὐνοίᾳ ὡς πολίτην αὐτοῦ προσοικειοῦται, τὸ τοῦ Ὁμήρου δὴ τοῦτο· 'ἐρχόμενον δὲ ἀνὰ τὴν πανήγυριν 'θεὸν
ὡς εἰσορόωσιν', οὐ μόνον γε ἀλλὰ καὶ μετὰ τὴν πανήγυριν, ὁπόταν αὐτὸν ἴδωσι μόνον. καὶ ἀγωνιζομένῳ
ταῦτα καθ' ἕκαστον ἀγῶνα· παυσαμένῳ δὲ παραμέ-
νουσιν τὸν βίον σύμπαντα οἱ καρποὶ ⟨οἱ⟩[9] ἀπὸ τῆς
νίκης, τὴν περιουσίαν τοῦ βίου ἄφθονον παρέχοντες·
μετὰ δὲ τὴν τελευτὴν ἡ μνήμη ⟨ἡ⟩[10] ἀπὸ τῶν ἀνδριάν-

288

[9] suppl. Radermacher   [10] suppl. Radermacher

them. "By putting a stop to the wars and disagreements among cities, the founders brought them together in a single city, so to speak, to serve as the homeland of all, so that they came together and held sacrifices and feasts in common, having put from their minds everything that came before. But that alone was not sufficient, so they instituted countless spectacles and performances, not only for the sake of amusement, but also for utility, for they educate us through musical performances and train us for war through athletic competitions. It is a fine thing for visitors to be enthusiastic about the spectacle, but it is much better for the competitors themselves, because the visitors enjoy a temporary pleasure, whereas the contestants gain immortal fame. Each contestant is applauded on the spot and pointed out for the noblest reasons: to win, to be crowned, to be proclaimed, to become through a single exploit and victory a citizen not of a single city but more or less of the entire world, for everyone present receives him with goodwill for his excellence (*aretē*) and treats him like a fellow citizen; as Homer says, 'They gaze upon him like a god as he goes through the festival'[10]—not only then, but after the festival as well, whenever they merely catch sight of him. This holds true at every competition for one who takes part in it, and once he has finished, the fruits of his victory remain for his entire life and provide abundant resources for living.[11] After he dies,

[10] *Od.* 8.173, spoken by Odysseus of a man gifted in speaking. [DH] substitutes "festival" for Homer's "town" (ἄστυ).

[11] For example, at Athens, free meals in the prytaneum; cf. Pl. *Ap.* 36de.

των καὶ τῶν εἰκόνων εἰς τὸ ἀνάγραπτον ἔχειν τὴν δόξαν οὐκ ἐν ταῖς μνήμαις σῳζομένην μόνον, ἀλλὰ καὶ
289 διὰ τῶν συγγραμμάτων συμπαραμένουσαν ἅπαντι τῷ
χρόνῳ.

5. Εἶτα ἐπὶ τούτοις προσάξεις καὶ τὸν περὶ τῆς
πόλεως λόγον, ὅτι καὶ διὰ τὴν πόλιν αὐτὴν σπουδαστέον περὶ τὸν ἀγῶνα. σύμμετρος δὲ γινέσθω ὁ ἔπαινος, ἐπειδὴ οὐ περὶ αὐτοῦ νῦν πρόκειται. ἀφορμαὶ δὲ
εἰς τοῦτο ἔσονται δήπου ἱκαναὶ αἱ προειρημέναι ἐν
ταῖς περὶ τοῦ πανηγυρικοῦ λόγου μεθόδοις. ὁμοίως δὲ
καὶ περὶ αὐτῆς τῆς πανηγύρεως ἐρεῖς ἐφεξῆς, καὶ πόθεν ἤρξατο, καὶ τίς ὁ καταστήσας, καὶ τίνων θεῶν
ἐπάγεται, καὶ τίς ὁ ἐπώνυμος αὐτῆς· καὶ ἔπαινος διὰ
βραχέων ἀπὸ τῶν αὐτῶν ἀφορμῶν τῶν ἐκεῖ παραδε-
δομένων. ἀναγκαῖον δὲ ἐνταῦθα γενόμενον καὶ σύγκρισιν ποιήσασθαι πρὸς τοὺς ἄλλους ἀγῶνας. ἡ δὲ
σύγκρισις ἔσται καὶ ἀπὸ τόπου τοῦ ἀγῶνος, οἷον ‹ὅτι
ἐνδοξότατος, καὶ›[11] ἀπὸ χρόνου, ὅτι ἀρχαιότατος· ἢ εἰ
νέος, ὅτι ὅσον τῷ χρόνῳ ὑποδεῖ, τοσοῦτον τῇ δόξῃ
προέχει· καὶ ὅτι εἰ νῦν περισπούδαστός ἐστι, πολλῷ
περισπουδαστότερος ἔσται λαβὼν τὸν χρόνον. εἰ θεὸς
εἴη ὁ ἐπώνυμος, τὰ προσόντα τῷ θεῷ· εἰ τῶν ἡρώων
τις, ὁμοίως τὰς πράξεις· εἰ ἐπιτάφιος, ὅτι καὶ αὐτὸς
διὰ τὴν ἀρετὴν τοῦ ἀγῶνος καὶ τῆς τούτου θέσεως
ἠξιώθη. ἔτι καὶ τὴν πόλιν παραβαλεῖς πρὸς τὰς ἄλλας, ἀπὸ μεγέθους, ἀπὸ κάλλους, ἀπὸ οἰκιστοῦ, ἀπὸ

11 suppl. Thiel ex Men. Rhet. 1.11.14

moreover, his memory lives on in statues and paintings to provide a record of his fame that is not only preserved in these memorials but also survives for all time in written forms."[12]

5. After this, proceed to speak of the city, saying that the city itself also provides a reason for the games' appeal. This praise should be brief, since at this point it is not the main topic. For this section you will find sufficient starting points previously mentioned in the instructions for composing a panegyric speech.[13] As in such a speech, you should deal next with the festival itself, telling how it began, who founded it, which gods it celebrates, and for whom it is named. This brief praise comes from the same starting points as those provided there.[14] At this point you must compare it with other games. This comparison will be based on the site of the games (e.g., it is very prestigious) and on its age (e.g., it is very ancient). Or else, if it is recent, say that what it lacks in age it makes up in reputation, and if it is now very popular, that it will become much more so in the course of time. If it was named for a god, cite the attributes of the god; if for a hero, cite his deeds; if it commemorates someone's death,[15] say that because of his excellence he deserved the founding of the games. In addition, you should compare the city with others on the basis of its size, beauty, founder, and singular

---

[12] Cf. M. 2.2.13: "Soon we shall erect statues, soon poets, historians, and orators will sing of your virtues and pass them on to all mankind."

[13] Cf. 1.3.   [14] Cf. 1.4.

[15] Examples include the Isthmian games for Palaemon and the Nemean for Archemorus, cited at M. 1.16.30.

290 οἰκειώματος· εἴρηται δὲ καὶ ταῦτα ἤδη. τούτων δὲ ῥη-
θέντων οἰκειότατα ἂν ἐπαχθείη ὁ πρὸς τοὺς ἀθλητὰς
λόγος κατὰ τὸν Θουκυδίδην· Περὶ τοιαύτης οὖν πόλεως καὶ τοιούτου ἀγῶνος πολλοὶ μὲν καὶ ἄλλοι καὶ
πάλαι ἐφιλοτιμήσαντο καὶ ἐσπούδασαν νικηφόροι
γενέσθαι.

6. Ἐπειδὴ δὲ διάφορα τὰ πρόσωπα, τὰ μὲν ἔνδοξα,
τὰ δὲ ἧττον, καὶ τὰ μὲν ἀπὸ στεφάνων πολλῶν, τὰ δὲ
νῦν πρῶτον ἀρχόμενα, πειρασόμεθα ἕκαστον ἀπὸ τῶν
οἰκείων καὶ προσφόρων προτρέψασθαι· οἷον τοὺς μὲν
πολλοὺς ἔχοντας στεφάνους, ὅτι καλόν, μὴ ὅπως καταισχῦναι τούτους, ἀλλὰ καὶ προσθεῖναι καὶ πλείους
ἀποφῆναι· συναύξεται γὰρ τοῖς στεφάνοις καὶ ἡ δόξα.
τοὺς δὲ ὀλίγους, ὅτι δεῖ μὴ τούτοις ἀρκεῖσθαι, ἀλλὰ
καὶ βεβαιώσασθαι τούτους ὅτι καὶ μετὰ τῆς ἀληθείας
καὶ προῖκα, τῷ ἐπαγωνίσασθαι καὶ προσλαβεῖν ἑτέρους. τοὺς δὲ νῦν πρῶτον ἀρξομένους· 'ἀρχὴ δέ τοι
ἥμισυ παντός'. καὶ τοῖς ἡττημένοις πρότερον καλὸν
ἀναμάχεσθαι, ἵνα μὴ καὶ ψυχῇ καὶ σώματι, ἀλλὰ
τύχῃ μᾶλλον δοκῶσιν τῇ ἥττῃ κεχρῆσθαι.

Εἶτα συμπροτρέψεις τοὺς μὲν κατὰ τὸ αἰσχρόν,
τοὺς δὲ κατὰ τὸ καλόν, ὅτι τοῖς μὲν πολλοὺς ἔχουσι
καὶ προνενικηκόσιν αἰσχρὸν τὸ ἡττηθῆναι τῶν μήπω
νενικηκότων, τοῖς δὲ ἄλλοις ἔντιμον καὶ οὐδὲ ὑπερβολὴν εἰς δόξης λόγον ἔχον ⟨τὸ⟩[12] τοὺς νενικηκότας

12 suppl. Radermacher

characteristics (these too have already been discussed).[16]
After these remarks, it would be especially fitting to open
your address to the athletes in the words of Thucydides:
"'For the sake of such a city, then,'[17] and for the sake of
such games, many others have long since sought honor
and striven to become victors."

6. Since contestants differ from one another—some
being famous, others less so, some with many crowns to
their credit, some just beginning their careers—we must
endeavor to exhort each one in terms that suit the individual. For example, to those who have many crowns, we
should say that it is noble not only to avoid tarnishing
them, but also to enhance their glory by displaying others
in addition. To those with few crowns, say that they should
not be satisfied with them, but rather should confirm that
they won them fairly and honestly by continuing to compete and adding others. To those just beginning, say "well
begun is half done,"[18] while to those who have previously
lost, say that it is noble to keep fighting, thus showing that
they owed their defeat not to a failure of mind or body but
rather to bad luck.

Next, you should exhort some by appealing to shame,
others to honor. To those with many crowns and previous
victories, say that it is shameful to be beaten by those who
have never won before. To the others, say that it is an
honor and glory beyond words to defeat victors and to

16 Cf. 1.3.

17 2.41.5. The context (Pericles' Funeral Oration) involves
soldiers' deaths, not athletes' victories.

18 Also quoted at 3.1.

κρατῆσαι καὶ δι' ἑνὸς στεφάνου προσλαβεῖν τὴν τούτων δόξαν.

291   Εἶτα πειρασόμεθα ἀναιρεῖν, δι' ἃ ἐπὶ τὸ διαφθεί-
ρεσθαί τινες τρέπονται, τῷ αἰσχρῷ καὶ ἀδόξῳ, ὅτι
αἰσχρὸν χρημάτων προέσθαι τὴν νίκην, κατὰ ἀμφότερα τὰ πρόσωπα τὸ αἰσχρὸν προσάπτοντες, καὶ
κατὰ τὸ τῶν διδόντων καὶ κατὰ <τὸ>[13] τῶν λαμβανόντων, ὅτι οἱ μὲν χρήματα ἀντὶ δόξης ἀνταλλάσσονται·
ἐν ᾧ οἷα μὲν τὰ χρήματα, οἷα δὲ ἡ δόξα· τὰ μὲν πρόσ-
καιρα, ἡ δὲ ἀθάνατος· καὶ τὰ μὲν τύχῃ καὶ χρόνος καὶ
πόλεμος ἀφεῖλεν, ἡ δὲ ἀναφαίρετος ὑπὸ τούτων· καὶ
τὰ μὲν ζῶντας εὐφραίνει, ἡ δὲ μετὰ τὴν τελευτὴν ζη-
λωτοὺς ἀποφαίνει· καὶ τὰ μὲν καὶ ἀπὸ κακίας περιγί-
νεται, ἡ δὲ ἀπὸ ἀρετῆς καὶ ἀνδραγαθίας. καὶ ὅτι χείρους τῶν προδοτῶν· ἐκεῖνοι μὲν γὰρ τοὺς ἄλλους
πωλοῦσιν, οὗτοι δὲ καὶ ἑαυτούς. καὶ ὅμοιοι τοῖς πόρ-
νοις εἰσὶν ἐπὶ τοῖς σώμασιν τοῖς ἑαυτῶν λαμβάνον-
τες· κἀκεῖνοι μὲν ἴσως καὶ δι' ἡλικίαν ἐξαπατηθέντες,
οὗτοι δὲ δι' αἰσχροκέρδειαν ἑαυτοὺς ἐκδόντες.[14] ἔπειτα
καὶ οἱ δόντες τῷ μὲν δοκεῖν νενικήκασιν, τῇ δ' ἀληθείᾳ ἐώνηνται τὴν νίκην· καὶ ὅτι οὐ δόξαν κτῶνται,
ἀλλ' αἰσχύνην, τὸ γὰρ μὴ μετὰ ἀληθείας κρατῆσαι
πρὸς αἰσχύνην μᾶλλον τῷ κρατήσαντι ἢ δόξαν· καὶ
ὅτι εἰ καὶ λανθάνοιεν τοὺς ἄλλους, ἀλλ' ἑαυτοῖς συν-
ίσασιν, καὶ παρὰ τοῖς ἄλλοις μὲν δοκοῦσι κρατεῖν,

---

[13] suppl. Sylburg   [14] καὶ ὅτι χείρους . . . ἑαυτοὺς
ἐκδόντες huc transp. RW: infra post τῆς ἐπονειδίστου νίκης P

acquire the fame that was theirs by means of a single crown.

Next, we should attempt to repudiate the reasons why some athletes turn to corruption,[19] by referring to the concepts of shame and dishonor. We should say that it is shameful to throw away victory for money and should place blame on both parties, those who offer it and those who accept it, because they are exchanging glory for money. Here you should point out how these two things differ: money is temporary, fame immortal; money can be lost through chance, time, and war, fame is impervious to them; money gives pleasure while we live, fame makes us admired after we die; money can result even from wrongdoing, fame comes from excellence and mettle. Those who accept bribes are worse than traitors, for traitors sell out others, whereas they sell themselves.[20] They are like prostitutes in taking money for their bodies; but whereas prostitutes are perhaps tricked into it on account of their young age, these men sell themselves for base gain. On the other hand, the ones who pay may seem to have won, but in reality they have purchased their victory; they have acquired not fame but shame, for shame rather than fame is what a dishonest victory brings the winner. In addition, though they may have fooled others, they themselves know what they have done; in the eyes of others they may seem to be victors, but in their own eyes they have been

[19] The issue involves one athlete (or his representatives) bribing a competitor to throw the match.

[20] RW convincingly move this sentence here from below, after "their disgraceful success remains with them forever."

παρὰ δὲ ἑαυτοῖς ἥττηνται· καὶ ὅτι οὐδὲ ἡδονὴ ἐπὶ τῆς
τοιαύτης νίκης· καὶ ὅτι ὁ τῆς αἰσχύνης ἔλεγχος ἀεὶ
292   συμπάρεστιν αὐτοῖς τῆς ἐπονειδίστου νίκης. εἶτα ὅτι
οὐδὲ λανθάνουσιν· ῥᾳδίως γὰρ ὁρῶνται καὶ ἐκ τῶν
σωμάτων καὶ ἐκ τῶν γυμνασιῶν καὶ ἐκ τῶν προγεγε-
νημένων ἀγώνων. ἐν ᾧ· τίνα τὰ ἐπὶ τούτοις; μάστιγες,
ὕβρεις, αἰκίαι σωμάτων, ἃ δούλων καὶ οὐκ ἐλευθέρων·
τὸ παρὰ τοῖς θεαταῖς βλασφημεῖσθαι ἀντὶ τοῦ ἐπαι-
νεῖσθαι κροτεῖσθαι στεφανοῦσθαι· ἐνίοτε δὲ [καὶ]¹⁵
ζημία καὶ τὸ ἐκβάλλεσθαι καὶ ἐκ τῶν σταδίων καὶ
ἀγώνων, μέγιστον δὲ ἐπ᾽ ἐλευθερίᾳ φρονοῦντας εἰς
τὰς τῶν δούλων τιμωρίας περιορᾶν αὐτοὺς ἐμπίπτον-
τας. καὶ ἂν μὲν δοῦλον αἰσθάνωνταί τινα τῶν ἀγωνι-
ζομένων εἶναι, κατηγορεῖν αὐτοῦ καὶ ὡς ἀνάξιον τοῦ
ἀγῶνος ἐκκρίνειν· αὐτοὺς δὲ τὰς παρὰ τῶν ἀθλοθετῶν
ψήφους τῆς ἐλευθερίας λαμβάνοντας τὴν τῆς δου-
λείας καθ᾽ ἑαυτῶν φέρειν.

7. Ἐν δὲ τούτῳ τῷ τόπῳ γενομένους ἀναγκαῖον καὶ
τῶν ἀρχαίων μνημονεύειν καὶ παραδείγματα φέρειν,
ὅσοι ἔνδοξοι· οἱ μὲν ὅτι ἀήττητοι, οἱ δὲ ὅτι πλείστας
νίκας ἤραντο, οἱ δὲ ὅτι εἰ καὶ ὀλίγας, ἀλλὰ τὰς ἐν-
δοξοτάτας, καὶ ὅτι πάσας προῖκα, καὶ ὅτι ἀπὸ σωφροσύνης, ἀπὸ ἐγκρατείας, ἀπὸ τῆς ἀσκήσεως τοιοῦτοι ἐγένοντο· καὶ ὅ τι αὐτοῖς τοιοῦτον συνέβη· ὅτι
πολλοὶ καὶ ἰσόθεοι ἐνομίσθησαν, οἱ δὲ καὶ ὡς θεοὶ
τιμῶνται τῶν πάλαι.

¹⁵ secl. Radermacher

446

defeated. There is not even any pleasure in such a victory, and the shameful proof of their disgraceful success remains with them forever. Then too, they don't even go undetected, for they are easily identified through their physical appearance, conditioning, and former competitions. Here you may add, "And what do they gain for it? whippings, insults, and physical abuse of a type appropriate to slaves not freeborn men; cursing from the spectators instead of praise, applause, and crowns; sometimes punishment and expulsion from the racecourses and the competitions; and worst of all seeing themselves as proud free men subjected to the punishments of slaves. If they become aware that a slave is one of the competitors, they accuse him and exclude him from the games for being ineligible, yet while receiving a verdict of freedom from the judges they bring a verdict of slavery against themselves."

7. At this point it is necessary to recall ancient stories and cite examples of famous athletes, some for being undefeated, others for winning the most victories, and others for winning few but the most glorious ones. Add that all of these victories were won fairly and honestly, that the victors became such by dint of their discipline, endurance, and training, and that their fate was of this sort—many were deemed godlike, while some victors of long ago are even honored as gods.[21]

[21] Prominent examples of divinized athletes are Heracles and Castor and Polydeuces.

APPENDIX I

CITATIONS IN MENANDER RHETOR

PASSAGES QUOTED OR ADAPTED

Homer, *Il.* 1.37–38 (1.3.4), 2.412–13 (1.9.1), 4.101 = 119 (2.16.7, 9),
    9.522–23 (2.13.16), 10.278–79 (1.9.1), 21.214 (2.1.25), 21.217–19
    (2.1.25), 22.158 (2.9.13); *Od.* 1.58–59 (2.14.11), 1.302 (2.6.11),
    5.463 + 13.251 (2.3.13), 9.34 (2.14.11), 9.34–35 (2.3.13, 2.14.11),
    11.580 (2.16.13), 13.38–41 (2.14.2), 13.59–62 (2.14.1), 13.89 (2.4.17)
Hesiod, *Op.* 374 (2.6.7)
Pindar, *Ol.* 2.1 (2.16.3)
Euripides, Fr. 449N² (2.8.3)
Thucydides 2.29.3 (1.6.7)
Isocrates, *Evag.* 23 (2.1.16); *Paneg.* 28 (1.6.7), 43 (1.16.30)
Plato, *Leg.* 2.672b (1.6.8); *Phdr.* 237a (1.3.3)
Demosthenes, *Or.* 18.1 (1.9.3), 18.141 (1.9.3)

ALLUSIONS TO KNOWN PASSAGES

Homer, *Il.* 14.216–17 (2.6.7), 14.231 (1.8.2), 15.119 (1.8.2), 18.491–95
    and 593–606 (2.5.24), 22.416–28 (2.15.1), 22.431–36 and 24.748–
    59 (2.15.1), 22.477–514 and 24.725–45 (2.15.1)
Plato, *Leg.* 4.712ce (1.16.3); *Menex.* 238c (1.16.3); *Phdr.* 237a (1.2.8),
    242d (1.8.1), 252bc (1.5.2), 279bc (1.2.8); *Symp.* 178a–80b (1.2.7),
    178b (1.8.1), 186be (1.8.1), 189c–93d (1.2.7), 189d–91d (1.8.1),
    194c–97e (1.2.7), 203b–4a (1.2.7)
Herodotus 1.31 (2.8.4)
Thucydides 2.35–46 (2.10.2)
Isocrates, *Helen* 23–31 (2.2.32); *Nic.*, *passim* (1.16.3); *Panath.* 114–50
    (1.16.3–4); *Paneg.* 43–44 (2.16.26), 187 (2.3.9)

APPENDIX I

Demosthenes, *Or*. 18.97 (2.8.4)
Dio Chrysostom, *Or*. 33.48, "To Tarsus" (1.16.9)
Aristides, *Or*. 17.2–4, "Smyrnaean Oration I" (1.15.10); *Or*. 26.90,
  "On Rome" (1.16.3); *Panath.* 9 (1.11.13), 10 (1.12.2), 16 (1.11.9),
  22 (1.11.10), 49–50 (2.1.16), 34 and 336 (2.2.24), 383–86 (1.16.4)

APPENDIX II

CITATIONS IN
[DIONYSIUS OF HALICARNASSUS]

PASSAGES QUOTED OR ADAPTED

Homer, *Od.* 6.182–85 (4.3), 8.173 (7.4), 11.136, etc. (6.5)
Aeschylus, Fr. 239N² (cf. Plato, *Phd.* 107e–8a) (6.5)
Pindar, *Ol.* 6.3–4 (1.2)
Thucydides 2.41.5 (7.5)
Plato, *Leg.* 2.653d (1.1), 6.753e (3.1); *Menex.* 237b (6.2), 237d (6.2), 238a (1.6)
Isocrates, *ad Dem.* 20 (5.1)
Aristides, *Panath.* 41 (1.6)

ALLUSIONS TO KNOWN PASSAGES

Homer, *Il.* 5.801 (3.5); *Od.* 4.563–65 (2.5), 11.136 etc. (6.5; cf. 3.5)
Hesiod, *Theog.* 22–34 (1.1)
Herodotus 1.180 (1.3), 7.142 (6.2)
Thucydides 2.42–43 (6.3), 2.43.6 (6.4), 2.44.3–4 (6.4)
Critias, Fr. 88 B 49 DK (6.1)
Plato, *Menex.*, *passim* (6.3)
Menander, Fr. 111 (Körte) (cf. Plutarch, *Consol. ad Apoll.* 119E) (6.5)

INDEX OF PROPER NAMES IN
MENANDER RHETOR

INDEX OF PROPER NAMES IN
[DIONYSIUS OF
HALICARNASSUS]

INDEX

MAPS

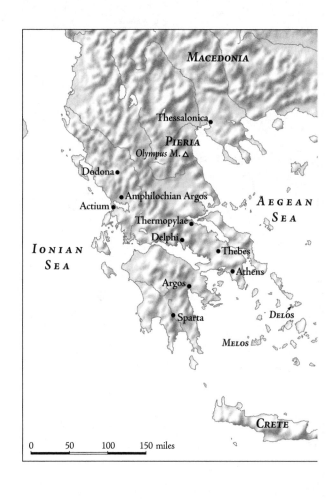

PONTUS EUXINUS
(BLACK SEA)

THRACE

Heraclea

PROPONTIS

Tenedos
Ilium/Troia
Alexandria Troas
△Mt. Ida

Cyzicus

PHRYGIA

Mytilene

LYDIA

Smyrna

Ephesus

Laodicea

Miletus

CARIA

Cnidus

LYCIA

RHODES

CYPRUS

LUTHERAN THEOLOGICAL SOUTHERN SEMINARY

3 5898 00173 4538

LINEBERGER MEMORIAL LIBRARY
LUTHERAN THEOLOGICAL SOUTHERN SEMINARY
CENTER FOR GRADUATE STUDIES OF COLUMBIA
LENOIR-RHYNE UNIVERSITY
COLUMBIA SC 29203